BETWEEN
MONTMARTRE
AND THE
MUDD CLUB

BETWEEN
MONTMARTRE
AND THE
MUDD CLUB

POPULAR MUSIC AND THE **AVANT-GARDE**

BERNARD GENDRON

THE UNIVERSITY OF CHICAGO PRESS   CHICAGO AND LONDON

Bernard Gendron teaches philosophy at the University of Wisconsin—
Milwaukee. He is the author of *Technology and the Human Condition*.

The University of Chicago Press, Chicago 60637
The University of Chicago Press, Ltd., London
© 2002 by The University of Chicago
All rights reserved. Published 2002
Printed in the United States of America

11 10 09 08 07 06 05 04 03 02   1 2 3 4 5

ISBN: 0-226-28735-1 (cloth)
ISBN: 0-226-28737-8 (paper)

Library of Congress Cataloging-in-Publication Data

Gendron, Bernard.
    Between Montmartre and the Mudd Club : popular music and the avant-garde / Bernard Gendron.
        p.   cm.
    Includes bibliographical references (p.   ) and index.
    ISBN 0-226-28735-1 (cloth : alk. paper) — ISBN 0-226-28737-8 (pbk. : alk. paper)
    1. Popular music—History and criticism.   2. Avant-garde (Aesthetics).   I. Title.
    ML3470.G48   2002
    781.64'09'04—dc21

                                                                        2001042791

∞ The paper used in this publication meets the minimum requirements of the
American National Standard for Information Sciences—Permanence of Paper for
Printed Library Materials, ANSI Z39.48-1992.

For my mother, Monique

CONTENTS

ACKNOWLEDGMENTS

MANY THANKS TO THE FRIENDS, COLLEAGUES, AND REVIEWERS who read chapters of the manuscript at various stages and who provided indispensable suggestions and encouragement: Connie Balides, Herbert Blau, David Brackett, Michael Coyle, Scott DeVeaux, Krin Gabbard, Andreas Huyssen, Loren Kruger, Susan McClary, Katharine Streip, Susan Suleiman, Carol Tennessen, Andrea Van Dyke, Bill Wainwright, Rob Walser, Lindsay Waters, Peter Winkler, Kathleen Woodward, and Carolyn Woollen-Tucker.

Thanks also to Kristie Hamilton, Alice Gillam, and Myrna Payne for their sustained friendship through the ups and downs of this project; to my children, Sarah and Tim, for helping me in more ways than they may know; and to my colleagues in the Philosophy Department at the University of Wisconsin–Milwaukee for their continued support of my research and teaching in popular music.

I am especially indebted to my research assistants, who helped organize and tame the mass of intractable archival materials of relevance to the manuscript: Sarah Gendron, Brooke Groskopf, Celi Jeske, Kerry Korinek, Renee Kuban, and Terri Williams.

I also owe much to the cooperative staffs at various research libraries for guiding me through the intricacies of their archival collections: first and foremost the Institute of Jazz Studies at Rutgers in Newark (Dan Morgenstern and Esther Smith in particular), but also the Bibliothèque Historique de la Ville de Paris, the Music Library at Bowling Green University, the Chicago Public Library, the New York Public Libraries (especially the Schomberg and Lincoln Center branches), and Widener Library (Harvard).

I want to acknowledge the kindness and patience of the staffs in the coffeehouses where virtually the whole book was written, especially the Coffee Connection (Cambridge, Massachusetts), the Coffee Pot (New York City), Scenes (Chicago), and in Milwaukee: the Comet, Starbucks on Downer, Schwartz Books, and Webster's.

ACKNOWLEDGMENTS

And finally a special note of appreciation to my editors at the University of Chicago, Doug Mitchell and Robert Devens, for so adroitly guiding the manuscript through the various production stages, and to the copy editor, Erin DeWitt, whose discerning suggestions and queries have greatly improved the text.

Earlier versions of chapters 4 and 6 were previously published in *Discourse* 12, no. 1 (fall–winter, 1989–90) and 15, no. 3 (spring 1993); chapter 5 in *Cultural Studies* 4, no. 2 (May 1990); and chapter 7 in the *Library Chronicle* 24, nos. 1/2 (January 1994).

CHAPTER 1
INTRODUCTION

I   In October 1967 the young literary theorist Richard Poirier caused a stir in intellectual circles with a scholarly article reverentially analyzing the words and music of the Beatles. Especially striking was the fact that this article, "Learning from the Beatles," was published by the dauntlessly modernist journal *Partisan Review,* which for decades had been in the forefront of attacks on mass culture. But Poirier was only one of a number of highbrows, among them musicologists and composers, who were jostling to pen the definitive effusive appraisal of the Beatles. Meanwhile, the middlebrow press, from *Time* to *New Yorker,* was only too eager to spread the news of highbrow approval to a wider and less sophisticated readership. This was a stunning turn of events, given that only three years before, the general adult consensus had been that the Beatles were charming but talentless musicians, successful only because of an uncanny ability to tap into the wellsprings of pubescent hysteria. The Beatles' music had changed, of course, during the intervening period, but so it appears had the public's aesthetic attitude.

Meanwhile, the Beatles themselves were leading a rock 'n' roll raid across the cultural borders, scavenging brazenly from the storehouse of avant-garde devices, such as collage, *musique concrète,* and irony. Accompanying them were Frank Zappa with his diverting parodies, the Beach Boys with their giddy electronic sounds, Eric Clapton and his improvisatory indulgences, and Jim Morrison, altogether infatuated with Baudelaire and Rimbaud. In three short years, rock 'n' roll had gone from being cast as vulgar entertainment not even suitable for adults to being hailed as the most important musical breakthrough of the decade.

In this period of revolutionary hubris and generational self-absorption, it seemed as if the whole cultural world was being turned on its head. To many, such transgressions across the barriers of high and low culture—evoked so powerfully by rock music but spreading to the other media—constituted a historically unprecedented set of events transformative enough to usher in a new cultural age. The opposition between art and entertainment, between elite and mass culture, which hitherto, it was thought, had been rigorously enforced and institutionalized, no longer seemed viable. The barriers between these two domains appeared to be on the verge of complete collapse. Various labels were introduced to baptize this new era—the "new sensibility" (Sontag), the age of "cool media" (McCluhan)—but "postmodernism" is the term that stuck. Leslie Fiedler gets credit for having married the idea of postmodernism to the imperative to "cross the border" and "close the gap" between elite and mass culture.[1] In contrast, the modernist era was cast as a period in which high culture was unremittingly hostile toward mass culture, a period happily and irreversibly left behind.

Today these claims seem overwrought, if not wrongheaded. In retrospect, the crossing of the great divide between rock music and high culture in the late 1960s may not appear as radical a cultural transformation as was imputed at the time. First, the ramparts between high and low culture did not topple nor were they as extensively dismantled as anticipated. Indeed, within a few months after bursting forth with accolades, the highbrows drew back from their preoccupation with rock, while the Beatles, with the White Album, led a swift retreat among rock musicians from avant-garde experimentalism back to rock 'n' roll roots. Since then rock has gained only a marginal foothold in conservatories, music departments, concert halls, and avant-garde spaces. It has not become part of high culture, nor is it constitutive of any synthesis of "high" and "low" that has obliterated the differences. This has been resisted by the rock community as well as by the powers of high culture. Rock critics in particular have looked askance at attempts to infuse rock with the aura of "art" or to saddle it with the apparatuses of the avant-garde. This is not to say that rock music has not been seriously complicit with high culture and its ideas since the late 1960s or that its cultural status has not been irreversibly transformed as a consequence of those original encounters. Far from it. We need only point, for example, to the very intimate alliance in the late 1970s between "new wave" rock and the New York art world, which, though short-lived, left an indelible mark on rock's future practices. But these alliances and complicities are more constrained and convoluted than the simplistic and totalistic idea of breakdown of the barriers conveys.

Second, the "postmodern" 1960s were by no means the first period in which the boundaries between popular music and high culture had been seriously challenged. Rock was not the first popular music to cross the divide between high and low. We need only recall the Jazz Age of the 1920s when the avant-gardes of Paris and Berlin were enthusiastically consuming jazz and attempting to assimilate its aesthetic into their own practices. Two decades later, with the bebop revolution, the jazz world returned the compliment by absorbing avant-garde devices and postures into its practices. Indeed, it seems that from the very beginnings of European modernism, there have been recurrent and highly amicable encounters between popular music and the avant-garde. The impressionists, of course, are known for their painterly preoccupations with cut-rate sites of popular entertainment, the Montmartre dance halls and the *cafés-concerts,* those garish venues of "vulgar" popular song along the boulevards. The fin de siècle artistic cabarets of Montmartre, by adjoining popular song with poetry readings in makeshift gallery spaces, were perhaps the first sites to operate squarely on the high/low dividing line. The growing realization of this has led to a spate of studies that detail European modernism's recurrently friendly encounters with the popular, thus collectively demolishing the once dominant view of modernism as inveterately hostile to mass culture.[2]

Thus, the original postmodern theory of high/low is altogether in tatters. The total breakdown of the barriers between high and low has not taken place, nor were the recurrent but restricted breachings of these barriers initiated by postmodernism. The discourses of aesthetic postmodernism have nonetheless survived and even thrived only because other concepts for distinguishing it from modernism have gradually emerged—irony, pastiche, heterogeneity, play, decenteredness, intertextuality—now familiar enough to be clichés. In addition, much of the theorizing around postmodernism has left the field of aesthetics for the domains of epistemology, gender studies, and politics, as in the work of Lyotard and Rorty.[3] Still, the incantations continue about postmodernism's unique disregard for the divisions between art and entertainment.[4] Could this be the expression of a residual insight that has yet to find its proper formulation? Perhaps postmodernism has introduced new dimensions to the century-old series of engagements between art and entertainment, or perhaps it has intensified engagements that in modernism had only occurred sporadically.[5]

II   In the case of popular music, the history of engagements with the avant-garde presents an especially daunting challenge to theory. Perhaps in no medium have such engagements been as frequent and richly endowed as in music, both in the modernist and postmodernist eras, and nowhere else have they had such a long-term impact on the practices of popular culture or its place in the cultural hierarchy. In the past few decades, a number of scholars have provided us with wonderfully detailed case studies of such musical border crossings, but few have tried to theorize beyond these historical instances.[6] Thus, a number of important questions have not been given even schematic or provisional answers. For example, are we to assume that the recurrence of these friendly intercalations between popular music and high culture is always simply a repetition of the same? Was highbrow fascination with rock music in the late 1960s just a replay of highbrow fascination with jazz in the 1920s? Were New York new wave musicians and their young artist colleagues in the 1970s simply reenacting the collaboratory practices between artists and cabaret songsters in late-nineteenth-century Montmartre? Or were these "postmodernists" from the high and low sectors interchanging in a quite novel way, clearly distinct from the way modernists negotiated these exchanges? In general, the question is whether in the past century there have been significant shifts and developments in the way these encounters are negotiated, and whether a meaningful historical trajectory can be discerned in this multiplicity. Further, we may wonder whether in the past few decades there has been such a radical break in the nature of these negotiations that it would legitimate referring to all those that came after as "postmodern." And finally we can ask if these historical shifts and breaks in the high/low encounters involving popular music really have made a difference. That is, what cumulative effect has this long historical process had on popular music's position in the cultural hierarchy? Is the "low" no longer as low as it once was, and the "high" not quite as high? There are no consensual answers to these questions at this time, nor even any clearly defined contending positions.

In this book I develop a theoretical account that hopefully goes a long way toward answering these questions. This account grows out of the study of five historical moments in which the encounter between popular music and the avant-garde was especially dramatic and portentous: the brief life of the artistic cabarets in late-nineteenth-century Montmartre, the Jazz Age in Paris after World War I, the rise of jazz modernism after World War II, the cultural accreditation of the Beatles in the late 1960s, and the New York new wave of the late 1970s. My approach is neither pure theory nor pure history, but theory through history, somewhat in the tradition of Michel Foucault. Throughout I view the various high/low interactions from the point of view of popular music and its interests (though I don't necessarily endorse those interests). My overarching concern is to determine what effects if any these boundary crossings have had on the cultural empowerment of popular music and how such empowerment, when it did occur, found expression in new aesthetic and entertainment practices.

From the outset then, I want to distinguish what this book is about, its subject matter, from the objective it means to achieve through examining this subject matter. The subject matter—the history of those high/low interactions that involve popular music—is a means to the further end, which is to sketch out a genealogy of the cultural empowerment of popular music. Pierre Bourdieu has taught us to think of cultural power in ways analogous to economic power.[7] Thus, there is cultural capital, which is expressed by one's position in cultural institutions, one's aesthetic authority and education, the extent to which one's works are sanctioned by cultural authorities, one's place in the cultural hierarchy, and so on. We can all agree that certain kinds of popular musics, rock and jazz in particular, have since their inception dramatically risen in the cultural hierarchy. This is easily demonstrated by the cultural capital now accruing to the various successful practitioners of the rock and jazz fields, critics as well as musicians, whose contributions are now heartily endorsed in university classrooms and the academic press.

That popular musicians, critics, and other professionals in the music industry have an abiding interest in enhancing their cultural prestige can hardly be denied. Critical approval, respect, canonization—all these are desirable goods even for those primarily preoccupied with commercial success. Early careers are kept alive by critical acclaim before the economic returns can set in, and the prospects for career longevity are certainly enhanced by canonization. Moving up in the cultural hierarchy means the conquest of new media and new markets, whose smallness is compensated for by affluence and influence. Conversely, musicians who maintain economic success over a long period of time, unbuffeted by the whims of the market, will tend to acquire cultural respectability in virtue of this alone—Sinatra and the Beatles are cases in point. In addition, we should not underestimate the importance of cultural recognition as an end in itself for many professionals of the popular music industry. For their part, avant-garde artists, even if consumed by the drive for cultural recognition, are not at all resistant to economic success. Indeed, in the history of the avant-garde, finding a public that pays has been a constant in the struggle for cultural recognition and influence, a fact amply documented in this book.

Thus, though the connections may be loose, the "markets" for economic capital and cultural capital in the popular and high arts are consistently enmeshed.[8] Allowing for this complicity between the two markets is not to deny the inherent tension between them, namely, that the full pursuit of economic capital is usually incompatible with the full pursuit of cultural capital. The inevitable entanglements between two opposite types of capital go a long way toward explaining the recurrently friendly engagements between popular music and the avant-garde in this century, against a background of mutual hostility and institutional segregation. A key working assumption for this book is that these crossings of the great cultural divide played an indispensable role, were a condition sine qua non, for the dramatic growth in the cultural capital of popular music in this century. Another working assumption is that popular music has reached such a critical mass in its own cultural empowerment that it no longer needs alliances with high culture to further its interests. In the cultural competition between popular music and high art, popular music has won, not by rising "higher" than high-cultural music—it is still ranked "lower"—but by making the latter less culturally relevant where it matters.[9]

Thus, the primary purpose of this genealogical inquiry is to highlight how dramatic shifts in the negotiations between popular music and the avant-garde have both affected and reflected the growing cultural power of popular music. A subsidiary but equally pervasive objective is to determine how these shifts have transformed the practices of popular music and the discourses that impinge on them. For example, rock and jazz have become thoroughly "aestheticized," altogether saturated with aesthetic discourses, something that was not the case when they were at the low end of the cultural hierarchy and viewed as mere "vulgar" entertainments. The emergence and development of jazz and rock aesthetics will be shown to have been catalyzed in the hothouse atmosphere of such historic collisions between high and low. This study is thus as much a genealogy of the aesthetics of popular music as it is of cultural empowerment—the one cannot go without the other.

My use of the term "genealogy" is derived from Foucault's work.[10] A genealogy does not seek to provide a continuous history, a seamless narrative, but rather focuses on certain eruptions, breaks, and displacements of the cultural field. It stresses heterogeneities and specificities. Genealogies focus on struggle and competition. It will be clear that many of the forays across the great cultural divide are part of a struggle for cultural capital, on the part of both high- and low-culture groups. This is why these overtly friendly encounters also exude a certain amount of mutual hostility, a mutual attraction unmistakably laced with distrust. Finally, genealogies are interested less in the narrative of events than in patterns and structures. In this case, I am interested in elaborating the patterns of aesthetic notions and tensions that underlie the practices operating at the interstices of avant-garde culture and popular music.

Such an approach, which ties the emergence of high/low interactions to the pursuit of cultural capital, may well reopen a space for theorizing about a postmodernist breakdown of barriers between high and low that can be contrasted with a modernist maintenance of such barriers. Though not construable in formal, stylistic, or institutional terms, where important separations still exist, this breakdown may well be expressible in terms of the cultural empowerment of the popular and the concomitant growth of a popular aesthetics. Is there a historical fault line when the engagements between popular music and the avant-garde signal or express a major shift in the cultural-power differential between them, when popular music abruptly becomes a cultural (and not merely economic) threat to the privileged position of high culture? Such an event might signal the birth of a postmodern era when high culture's monopoly over cultural capital, characteristic of modernism, can no longer be maintained. We can imagine that modernism, in its friendliest interchanges, was quarantining itself from the invasive power of popular music by absorbing its dynamism and co-opting its innovations. Popular music was the colonized and the avant-garde the colonizer. The postmodern moment would then arise when such an asymmetrical relation could no longer be maintained, when popular music and its industry finally became initiators and aggressors in high/low interchanges, reversing the net flow of cultural capital. Today art music may still have the edge in snob appeal, but arguably some pop musics (world music, jazz, alternative rock, electronic music) have collectively closed the gap in cultural capital. Such a thesis about modernism/postmodernism is the fulcrum on which the narrative of this book rests.

III   The idea for this book was occasioned by research on the New York punk and new wave rock movements in the late 1970s and their multifarious entanglements with the New York art scene. Operating out of the bohemia of the East Village, the bands—the Talking Heads, Television, Devo, the B-52s, even the Ramones—took on a distinctly postmodern art posture, displaying irony, pastiche, eclecticism, and a fascination with the kitsch and garish mass culture of the past. Rock musicians played in art venues and artists performed or displayed their wares in rock venues. Visual artists formed rock bands, while rock artists exhibited in art shows and did poetry readings. Punk and new wave rock were followed by punk and new wave art. These symmetrical crossings peaked at the Mudd Club, a nightclub that combined punk/new wave music with "art after midnight."[11]

It struck me at the time that there might be something quite unprecedented in this particular high/low encounter, a level of intensity and equality never before achieved. What became clear, with the rise of the new wave, was that rock had decisively won over one of the key demographic constituents of highbrow culture, the young avant-garde painters and filmmakers making their way in New York. Whereas in the 1950s and early 1960s, young artists such as Robert Rauschenberg and the fluxus group gave their support to the music of John Cage and Lamonte Young, in the late 1970s artists like Robert Longo turned to the music of the Talking Heads and the B-52s. Of course, recurrently in this century, many literary figures and visual artists have expressed an attraction to jazz, cabaret, and other popular musics. But this was usually a matter more of private consumer interest, public slumming, or momentary alliances than of aesthetic identification. Cocteau and Picasso may have made a public scene of liking jazz, but ultimately their aesthetic identification and collaborative efforts were with Stravinsky and Satie, whereas the primary aesthetic identification for young artists of the 1970s— Basquiat, Longo, Jarmusch—was with punk and new wave, and only secondarily with the highbrow minimalism of Philip Glass, Terry Riley, and Steve Reich. And in this new identity of aesthetic perspectives, it is New York new wave music that took the lead and the New York art world that proved more parasitic.

This first impression of a major aesthetic breakthrough for popular music in the 1970s led me back to other comparable historical moments, first to the Beatles and the cultural accreditation of rock in the late 1960s, then to the great historical encounters between jazz and the avant-garde, and finally to what seemed the beginning of it all, the artistic cabaret. What especially drew my attention as altogether crucial were the contrasting ways in which jazz and rock historically negotiated the high/low issues. There are probably no other two musical traditions that seem so similar and yet are so tantalizingly different. Both jazz and rock have strong roots in the blues and were originally vilified by official culture for their alleged vulgarity and sexuality. From the beginning, both were driven by negotiations and tensions across the racial divide. Both went through a later cultural transformation from pure entertainment music to recognized art forms—the rise of "modern jazz" in the 1940s and the transition from "rock 'n' roll" to "rock" in the mid-1960s. Both resisted assimilation to high culture and its standards, maintaining their own aesthetic specificity within the middle range of the cultural hierarchy. Yet jazz and rock have quite distinct constituencies with little overlap, quite often hostile to, or puzzled by, each other. As one rock fan once put it to me, rock and jazz seem as different as English and Chinese. As an enthusiast of both musical traditions, I have been at a loss to articulate the apparently deep differences, as well as similarities, between them. The usual shibboleths—jazz is an improvisatory, rock a riff-based, music—don't do justice to the complex aesthetic and cultural differences between the two musical traditions and their communities.

One useful side effect of my project is that it provides a partial solution to this quandary. For a study of how jazz and rock have historically negotiated with avant-garde culture reveals much about the "deep" differences between them. The outcomes of the transition from pure entertainment to art in each case contrasted so starkly as to suggest that altogether different aesthetic strategies were at stake. Jazz, in this transition, lost its mass audience and was left with a shrinking base of intellectuals, hipsters, college students, and middlebrows. Rock, on the other hand, expanded its base beyond teens to include young adults and cultural elites. Why rock held on to its "pop" moorings while becoming "art," whereas jazz did not, constitutes a central problematic of this book.

Racial matters were inevitably enmeshed in jazz's and rock's transitions from "entertainment" to "art," but here the contrasts are more shaded. In both cases, white males dominated the emerging institutions of criticism so crucial to the acquisition of cultural legitimacy, with discursive results that were at best racially skewed. The "modernist" jazz critics of the bebop era made it a point to champion the contributions of African Americans (e.g., Parker, Gillespie), but always while accentuating the European art component of the new music at the expense of the African American practices in which it was also embedded. The early rock critics of *Crawdaddy!* and *Rolling Stone* were more blatant, in that they gave very little attention to current black music in their initial attempts at legitimation. The tendency was discursively to relegate soul music to the domain of dance and amusement (and thus "entertainment") while reserving the good white "rock" music (the Beatles, Dylan, the Who) for careful listening and "meaning" (and thus "art").[12] Black musicians of previous decades (Chuck Berry, Robert Johnson) were, of course, accorded the honorific status of pioneers and "fathers." In general, it is impossible to deal with the negotiations between high and low culture in this century without consistently encountering the issues of race.

Unlike rock, which is altogether a postmodern phenomenon in its relation with the avant-garde, jazz historically has one foot in the modern era and one in postmodernism, one foot in Europe and one in America. The one major disanalogy between rock and jazz history is that jazz, in its infancy, in its very beginnings as a "vulgar" entertainment, was lionized by the European avant-garde, especially in Paris, which thereby became the capital of the Jazz Age of the 1920s. On the other hand, rock in its infancy was vilified or contemptuously ignored by middlebrows and highbrows alike. In its first encounter with high culture, jazz was only the latest genre of unadulterated pop music to have been adopted by the French avant-garde, having been preceded by cabaret song, the cancan, and music hall reviews. What was distinctive about this latest appropriation was its connection with a fad for all things "Negro," from African masks and myths, to the Brazilian samba and Josephine Baker.

So, in the history of high/low engagements, jazz is the music in between, the music of passage, the link between the earliest (cabaret music) and the latest (rock).

This linkage is not merely temporal—otherwise it would hardly be interesting—but conceptual, and a matter of aesthetic posture and practice. For the earlier encounter of "vulgar" jazz with the avant-garde in Paris could not be more different than modern jazz's later embroilment with high culture in New York. In the early 1920s it was the avant-garde that took the initiative in this alliance, using it to absorb new aesthetic stimulants and to broaden its public. Jazz was the passive recipient, unwitting and oftentimes unknowing. The cultural capital that it gained was adventitious, and only partly permanent. It did not take long for the avant-garde, looking for new thrills or simply growing more conservative, to abandon its protégé. In this respect, jazz suffered the same fate as its predecessors, such as cabaret music. Being cast in a passive role had been a mark of popular music's friendly associations with high culture since the rise of French modernism in the mid-nineteenth century.

But the rise of modern jazz in the mid-1940s altogether reversed this situation. In the transition from entertainment to art, it was the jazz world that took the initiative, with the art world looking on passively. Jazz musicians actively appropriated high-cultural forms, postures, and bohemian practices. Jazz critics scavenged from the storehouse of high-cultural discourses, resituating them in a distinctive way. This was an unprecedented event in the history of popular music, and indeed of popular culture, permanently shifting the terms of cultural power between high and the formerly low. Because jazz had already cleared the way, rock was able to negotiate the transition from pure entertainment to art in a much shorter time. Thus, if anything can count as the major historical break in the history of popular music's recurrent entanglements with high culture, it is the emergence of modern jazz and the dramatic rise in popular music's cultural empowerment that thereby ensued.

This major break can usefully be construed as a transition from modernism to postmodernism. There is no paradox in claiming that the rise of *modern* jazz is a *postmodern* event. It is generally understood to be a mark of postmodernism that mass media and popular arts, such as advertisements and MTV, scavenge unrestrainedly from the storehouse of modernist devices, such as collage. Modernism is not absent from postmodernism—it is simply broken up and resituated. But modern jazz's appropriations of modernism is part of a larger set of postmodern practices, at the center of which is a new and growing cultural activism on the part of popular music and the industry. With the advent of jazz modernism, popular music aggressively entered the struggle for cultural capital. Modern jazz did not necessarily want to join high culture, to become America's "classical music," but to contest high culture's monopoly over cultural capital. Modern jazz musicians and jazz critics were intensively engaged in a struggle to raise jazz from the lowly musical status to which it had been consigned. Thus, more than anything else, it is by overturning the traditionally passive role of popular music in high/low interactions, and thereby contesting high culture's monopoly over cultural respect, that modern jazz deserves the special distinction of having ushered in the postmodern age in high/low engagements. The formal appropriation of modernist devices is itself only a symptom of this larger transformation.

I want to make it clear that I am not introducing a new idiosyncratic conception of the postmodern in a field already saturated with other conceptions doing battle with each other. Rather, I am rehabilitating one of the earliest insights of aesthetic postmodern theory—that of Fiedler, Jencks, and Venturi—which looks to the field of engagements between high and low as the primary site of the postmodern. I simply shift the focus away from high culture's breachings of the divide, which are not particularly new, to those of mass culture. Furthermore, it must be emphasized that the different conceptions of the postmodern are not necessarily adversarial to one another, since they oftentimes operate in different fields, in the political and epistemological as well as aesthetic. Like Fredric Jameson, I view the postmodern as a cultural dominant constituted by many parameters, only one of which is the changing dynamic between high and low. I also believe that many of these parameters are functionally interconnected, though no integrated theory of the postmodern has yet appeared to show convincingly how this is so.

To some the mid-1940s may seem early for postmodernism to begin. But there really is no agreement on the periodization of postmodernism. Indeed, it would be a surprise if all the various postmodernisms—literary, architectural, epistemological, political, postcolonial, and so on—shared the same starting date. Rather, we should expect uneven development in the heterogeneous array of postmodernisms that have so far been identified or postulated. Even within aesthetic postmodernism, the different fields do not move in lockstep. Andreas Huyssen locates the rise of postmodern painting in the early 1960s with pop art; Ihab Hassan locates the first postmodern literary work, Joyce's *Finnegan's Wake,* in the late 1930s.[13] So, what I am saying is that in the arena of high/low interactions involving popular music, the decisive postmodern break came quite early.

To summarize: Postmodernism has not led to any massive breakdown of the institutional barriers separating popular music from high culture, though it has opened them up somewhat. Neither has there been any stylistic or aesthetic merger between the two domains, although they have at various times appropriated each other's formal devices and postures. Nor has popular music moved to the highest reaches of the cultural hierarchy, though jazz and certain members of the rock family are now firmly ensconced in the middlebrow sectors. The key mark of the postmodern in the high/low arena is the emergence of popular music as a major player in the struggle for cultural capital. Modern jazz began this process, but it is the rock family of musics, with its army of supporters in the press and the academy, that has driven popular music's accumulation of cultural capital to the point where it compares favorably with that of high culture. Nothing perhaps illustrates this better than the fact that classical music and contemporary art music have lost a large part of their audiences to rock, jazz, and related musics, or must share their audience with the latter. Highbrow consumers, once known for their exclusionariness and gatekeeping proclivities, have become omnivorous in their musical tastes, which include, in addition to jazz and rock, world pop music, folk music, and even trash lounge. As we move up the income, education, and social pedigree scales, we find more tolerance for different musical genres. Exclusiveness is now associated more with lowbrowness.[14] Such eclectivity is generally accepted as a mark of the postmodern. What is not always appreciated is that this eclectivity did not simply come out of the blue, but was due in large part to the aggressive struggles on the part of popular culture for cultural empowerment. The second part of this book, which deals with the postmodern turn, will focus on this struggle.

IV   The shift from modernist to postmodernist patterns in high/low musical engagements also has a geographical dimension. The avant-gardes of Western Europe, and especially Paris, took the lead during the modernist era in initiating such encounters, whereas it was in North America, and particularly New York, that the postmodern turn first manifested itself and was carried through most thoroughly. As the center for art and entertainment in turn-of-the-century Europe, Paris was naturally the primary modernist site for vigorous crossovers between art and entertainment. The Parisian avant-gardes set the pace in fostering and institutionalizing these border crossings, and pursued them more enthusiastically and extensively than anyone else in other modernist centers.

In the United States during the same period, high culture was more hostile to mass culture and sought clearly to distinguish itself from the latter, for reasons that are not difficult to decipher. American high culture did not have the support from state institutions and private sources typical of the Euro-

pean art and literary worlds, which otherwise would have put them on a better footing to protect themselves from, and to compete with, the incursions
of mass culture. American mass culture, in turn, was a much more economically potent force than its European counterparts. In addition, the European
avant-gardes added insult to injury by displaying much more interest in
American mass culture—Charlie Chaplin and Louis Armstrong—than in
American high culture, thus frustrating the efforts of the latter to achieve the
international prestige so far denied it. So, for the modernist period, this book
situates itself primarily in Paris, the site of the nineteenth-century artistic
cabaret and the avant-garde appropriation of jazz in the period following
World War I.

Correspondingly, I turn to the United States for examplars of specifically
postmodern engagements between high culture and popular music. New York
plays an important role here, but not the overwhelmingly central role previously played by Paris with respect to the rest of France. By the end of World
War II, the United States had clearly assumed international leadership in the
entertainment industry and New York was on its way to replacing Paris as the
international art center. Furthermore, American popular music took the lead
in crossings of the great cultural divide initiated from below. But even when
such musical leadership came from elsewhere, as in the case of the Beatles,
the public impact of these high/low border crossings, and the concomitant
gains in cultural capital for popular music, was especially dramatic in the
United States, if only because the division of high and low had been more
strongly policed by American high culture. For example, there was no modernist journal in Western Europe with the same local influence and prestige
that the *Partisan Review* enjoyed in America, with an agenda as overdetermi-
nately committed to the quarantining of high culture from popular culture.
And we cannot overlook the powerful influence of the Frankfurt School, ex-
iled in America, on the postwar American debates on mass culture. It was in
Europe, and not America, that Hollywood film "auteurs" (e.g., Hitchcock) and
genres (e.g., film noir) first received cultural accreditation, at a time (the
1950s) when American intellectuals were preoccupied with European commercial "art" film. Finally, it was in America that postmodernism, and its discourse about barrier breaking, first made a decisive appearance.

Thus, in the postmodern sections of this book, I focus as much on the special intensity of American culture's reaction to the aggressive crossover practices of popular music, wherever that music comes from, as on American
popular music's own involvements in these tactics. Accordingly, the chapter
on the Beatles pays special attention to the way their music got constructed
in American cultural discourse, which is quite distinct from the equivalent

British cultural discourses. Already a national treasure and economic re-source, the Beatles got a favorable reading from high culture in England years before they did in America and with considerably less fanfare. The matter-of-fact declaration in 1963 by *London Times* critic William Mann that "the outstanding English composers" of that year were "John Lennon and Paul McCartney, the talented young musicians from Liverpool," preceded by four years Richard Poirier's breathless encomium on "learning from the Beatles" in the *Partisan Review*.[15] Though I center on the responses of the American cultural press (rock critics, highbrow journals) to the Beatles and the punk movement, at crucial junctures I compare these to their British counterparts.

Among the many instances of engagement in the postmodern North American era between high culture and popular music, I have chosen to investigate those which were most unprecedented and transformative and which most dramatically exhibited the postmodern character of those transactions, such as the bebop revolution, the cultural accreditation of the Beatles, and the ir-ruption of the New York punk/new wave movement. I do not address beat po-etry and pop art, which, whatever their other innovations, continued in the modernist tradition of high/low interactions initiated from the top with at best only passive acquiescence from popular music. Jazz musicians, for ex-ample, hardly indicated any interest in alliances with beat culture and seemed contemptuous of most attempts to combine live music with poetic declamation. On the other hand, the 1960s free jazz movement, though push-ing to the extreme the avant-gardist proclivities of modern jazz and thus con-stituting a dramatic crossing of the barriers from below, did not really change the terms of engagement between jazz and high culture initiated by bebop, which remained still in discourse and at the level of musical appropriation. The next innovative step was taken by the New York new wave in rock music, which expanded the field of high/low interactions to institutional settings (the Mudd Club) and subcultural formations (the art-punk bohemias of the East Village).

V   So far I have referred rather loosely to "interactions," "engage-ments," and "alliances" between the "avant-garde" and "popular music," of "border crossings" and the "breaching of barriers" between these two do-mains. Let me now clarify some of these terms, starting first with the distinction between "high" and "low," or better still, between "art" and "en-tertainment." Bourdieu's "dual market" theory, to which I have already al-luded, is useful for explicating this distinction.[16] We can distinguish between a cultural market for material goods, that is, one driven primarily by the desire for income and wealth, and one for symbolic goods, where the rewards are prestige, canonization, accreditation. Bourdieu refers to the former as the "large scale" market, and the second as the "restricted" market. Production in the large-scale market is directed at a "general public," at anyone who will buy, and thus seeks to give this public what it supposedly wants. Production in the restricted market is aimed by cultural producers at other cultural producers—artists, critics, impresarios, gallery owners, the academy, and so on—who have or will have the power to accredit, canonize, or promote, and at certain prestigious consumers whose recognized "good taste" confers "symbolic" power upon the producer while providing material support. In the restricted market, agents compete to produce objects of the greatest symbolic value, objects deemed by peers to be "great works of art," and to receive accreditation from their peers. This distinction between the large-scale market and the restricted market in the sphere of culture coincides roughly with that between "entertainment" and "art," between "popular culture" and "high culture."

Typically, a restricted market of cultural goods requires a certain literacy on the part of the producers and consumers—in music, for example, the ability to decipher scores, some music theory, a certain aesthetic "sensitivity"— and is thereby somewhat inaccessible to the "public at large." Put in Bourdieu's language, a certain amount of cultural capital is both a requisite and a reward for successful participation in the restricted market, just as a certain amount of economic capital is both a requisite and reward for successful participation in the unrestricted market. The latter market thrives on, and promotes, innovations in the mass media, whereas the former is more associated with "live" or other intimate settings of consumption. Finally, unlike the large-scale market, the restricted market relies importantly on patronage and state subvention for material support.

Of course, the notions of restricted and large-scale markets refer to extremes on a spectrum that are seldom realized in their purity: "art" or "high culture" gravitates to one extreme without reaching it and "popular culture" or "entertainment" to the other. We can imagine subsystems that operate at the middle between restricted and large-scale markets—say, the regional "indie" rock of the 1980s. Whether these subsystems are called "art music" or "popular music" depends importantly on their relation to other cultural markets. "Indie rock," for all its contempt for commercialism and its tight-knit field of like-minded producers and subcultures, is nonetheless "popular music" if only because of its symbiotic ties with the mainstream music industry (distribution deals between independent record companies and the majors, for example). Some markets may be so caught in the middle that they may not be classifiable one way or the other, such as contemporary jazz, which if not for the pejorative connotations, could be called "middlebrow culture."

Throughout this book, I use the term "avant-garde" roughly to denote any high-cultural production of a modernist or postmodernist kind, in opposition to traditional high culture. In Baudelaire's terms, traditionalists prize "eternal" beauty and a barely shifting canon, whereas avant-gardes are enamored with the continually shifting "contemporary" beauties and are constantly fomenting revisions in the canon.[17] The avant-gardes—artists, critics, producers, patrons—constitute a restricted market characterized by recurrent turnovers in the ruling orthodoxies and in the values through which products and agents are endorsed and consecrated. In France I situate the birth of the modernist avant-garde sometime in the middle of the nineteenth century, best codified by Baudelaire's "Painter of Modern Life," though one could with plausibility go back to the second-generation romantics (Gautier, Nerval) in the 1830s and their invention of "art for art's sake." Not by chance, the rise of the avant-garde coincides with the rise of mass culture—mass newspapers, poster advertisements, the professionalization of popular song—and begins in subtle ways immediately to interact with it. This was not by chance, because the restricted market of the avant-garde, driven by fashion and constant turnover in symbolic value, mirrored the mass market better than any other restricted cultural market (e.g., the traditionalists market).

VI   In speaking broadly and imagistically about "interactions," "engagements," "alliances," and "border crossings" between the art world and popular music, I am referring to a heterogeneous array of aesthetic practices that it would now be useful to distinguish. Perhaps the most obvious of such practices is the appropriation by avant-garde composers of popular music's formal devices (e.g., the jazz scale, the blues form) or popular music's doing the same to art music (e.g., the Beatles' appropriation of *musique concrète*). But there are a variety of types of appropriation, not all of which indicate much of an alliance or a rapprochement. It is a banal fact about classical musicians that they frequently borrowed materials, such as fishmongers' tunes, from popular sources. But this no more constitutes an alliance or a breaching of barriers, than composers inspired by birdsong can be said to have transgressed the human/animal boundary or have allied themselves with birds. The popular material disappears in the seamless suturing of the composition and retains only a private biographical relation to the borrower.

Of more interest is explicit formal appropriation, that is, an appropriation that reveals itself, that highlights the borrowed material, quite often in a purported transgressive manner. This may take the form of musical collage, quotation, parody and pastiche, camp, synthesis, attempts by "art" music to elevate the "lower" music, to explore its unrealized aesthetic possibilities, or attempts by a popular music to "join the club" of art music through mimicry. But even here, simply by examining the musical text in the absence of concurrent practices, it is not easy to tell whether a self-revealing formal appropriation on the part of high culture constitutes a friendly overture to popular culture. How friendly to popular music is Stravinsky when he introduces a musical sequence called "Ragtime" in his *Histoire du soldat*? Doesn't the ragtime form here simply provide Stravinsky with material on which to apply his inventive talents? Does it not merely represent an event narrated by the composition, namely, the soldier's playing a ragtime piece on his fiddle while others dance? Can we conclude from this alone, without situating this work in other avant-garde practices of the time, that the composer has a loving attachment to ragtime and other popular musical forms?

If formal appropriation across the boundaries does not assure an effective alliance between high and low, neither does its absence entail the nonexistence of such an alliance. In fact, those avant-garde composers we consider most friendly to popular music in modernist Paris—Stravinsky, Milhaud, Ravel—produced only a few compositions appropriating its formal devices. Are we to conclude from this that the high/low engagements in modernist Paris were intermittent and evanescent? On the contrary, they were a never-ending preoccupation of the avant-garde, of which musical appropriation by composers was only one of its expressions. In fact, painters and poets were as involved with popular music, if not more so, than modernist musicians. But for painters and poets, the use of formal appropriation was not the normal way of conducting such engagements. A similar argument can be made when popular music is the initiator. In the 1960s the widespread fascination of rock musicians with avant-garde electronic music lasted only a few years (the Beatles' *Sergeant Pepper* album, the Beach Boys' *Pet Sounds*). But that by no means brought to an end rock's engagement with art and the avant-garde, which now developed in a more nuanced and indirect manner.

While not neglecting formal appropriation, we must look beyond it to make sense of the various types of rapprochement between popular music and the avant-garde. Or, to put it more generally, we must go beyond the formal characteristics of primary texts—the compositions, the recordings, of both popular and avant-garde artists—if we want to get a thick account of the interchanges between the high/low domains. This is especially germane since the primary texts famous for their border crossings have already been amply scrutinized, whereas the other modes of cross-border engagements have gotten little scholarly attention.

Where else might we look for indices of high/low alliances involving popular music? First, there are those particular institutions that were designed to bring together high culture and popular music, such as the turn-of-the-century artistic cabarets of Montmartre, where poetry and gallery spaces coexisted with popular song or, more recently, the art nightclubs of New York, led by the legendary Mudd Club, where punk/disco shared the same venue with avant-garde performance and art exhibitions. Such institutional links have recurrently played a key role even when, or especially when, they were not complemented by formal-textual links between high and low.

Second, we must pay special attention to the leisure activities of artists and musicians, as well as to their work activities, to their practices of consumption as well as production. With the advent of bohemia, many artists turned their own leisure and consumption activities into forms of aesthetic production and acts of public display, usually in sites and contexts in which symbiotic encounters with popular entertainment were almost inevitable. It is now accepted that when Warhol and his guests slummed at Max's Kansas City (a New York nightclub), they were actually involved in a form of aesthetic performance, and not merely taking a break from the rigors of the Factory. According to Baudelaire, to be a *flâneur* is an essential component of a poet's productive activity and not merely a sidelight or a recreation. This transformation of the bohemian art of living into a form of symbolic production has played an especially strong role in the history of modernism's complicity with popular music.

Such public displays of bohemia are part of a larger field of what we might call "secondary aesthetic practices"—aesthetic activities by artists not originally considered part of their "real oeuvre," but that had considerable impact on the way the "real oeuvre" was originally received. Among such activities we may include Toulouse-Lautrec's Moulin Rouge posters, modernist poems set to popular tunes for cabaret settings, and more recently "poetry slams" and rock bands formed by artists (for example, Jean-Michel Basquiat's band, Gray). Secondary aesthetic practices typically operate at the interstices of high and low, thus intertextually connecting the more austere-appearing primary products (abstract paintings, experimental poetry) to the garish world of mass culture.

Next, we must not overlook the important role of critics' discourses, as well as those of the general press, in defining and stimulating high/low engagements. We know that new movements in the arts typically require apparatuses of criticism to explicate and promote them. The cubists had Apollinaire; the abstract expressionists, Clement Greenberg; and pop artists, Lawrence Alloway. Significant movement across the cultural borders has also depended on critical discourses to give them a public identity. In jazz and rock, the transition from entertainment to art was accompanied by the rise of the institutions of jazz and rock criticism. The apparatuses of criticism will often provide extensive articulation to high/low interactions that are only schematically adumbrated by other media.

Finally, in the texts or primary works themselves, what gets appropriated by high from low culture (or vice versa) is more often a particular aesthetic posture than some formal device, especially when cross-media appropriations are involved. For example, it can be assumed that the "punk art" movement of the early 1980s appropriated its aesthetic stance from punk rock (else why call it "punk art"), though we may be hard put to note any formal commonalities between the former and the latter. Aesthetic appropriation is usually simply a matter of shared attitudes or postures, quite often only decipherable through critical discourse.

Thus, a full account of friendly encounters between popular music and the avant-garde requires that attention be given to a variety of practices relating the two domains: attitudinal as well as formal, institutional as well as textual, secondary as well as primary, consumption-related as well as production-related, and critical-discursive as well as musical or painterly. These associations between high and low are rarely equal or mutual, more often one-sided, and sometimes evoke hardly a response from the other party. An institutional connection requires considerable interaction by inhabitants on both sides of the cultural border. Contrarily, an alliance set out in the discourses of one party (for example, the modernist discourse of jazz critics) may initially impinge very little on parties on the other side of the divide.

VII   During the modernist period in Paris, when the avant-garde almost exclusively took the initiative in high/low interchanges, all the above types of connecting practices came into play. But in the postmodernist period, when popular music took the primary initiative, discourse became all-important. First, because critical discourse had many more duties to perform in supporting the initiatives of popular music toward high culture than it had in supporting previous initiatives of the avant-garde toward low culture. Second, because the other types of high/low interaction were less available to popular initiatives than they had been to avant-garde initiatives. This stems from the fact that popular music, in its earlier overtures to high culture, was operating from a much lower base of cultural capital than had the avant-garde in the reverse situation.

Consider the case of bebop and the birth of modern jazz in the mid-1940s. In addition to performing its usual functions of interpretation and promotion of particular artists and movements, critical discourse had to persuade the general culture at large as well as the jazz constituency that with bebop, jazz had moved from being mere entertainment to being an art form and that this was a good thing. It also had to develop, almost from scratch, a specifically jazz aesthetic, which would legitimate jazz as an art form while preserving its specificity in the face of other types of art music. Unlike cubism, which—however disruptive and novel—had emerged in an already established art field with an underlay of aesthetic theory, the bebop movement had to give rise to such a field—the field of "modern jazz"—where previously no articu-lated aesthetic theory had existed. This required a volume and a variety of legitimating discourses never needed by cubism or other avant-garde move-ments.

At the same time, most of the nondiscursive types of high/low interaction were less available to popular initiative than they had been to avant-garde initiative. For example, at the inception of bebop, the jazz world did not have the cultural capital to entice the modernist avant-garde into its institutions. What possible interest could have drawn painters, poets, new dramatists, and so on, to perform or display their work along with the lowly jazz musicians in gritty and noisy clubs, steeped in booze and drugs, oftentimes run by shady characters? Unless, of course, they had reason to believe they could take over the aesthetic agenda, but this no doubt would have been heatedly resisted by the bebop musicians and their promoters, struggling to prevent further ero-sion in their paying public. And why would the bebop musicians have placed their own developing aesthetic specificity, still insecure in its boundaries, at risk of being absorbed into the homogenizing discourses of high culture? Thus, the sort of institutional linkage between high and low best exemplified by the Parisian artistic cabarets was not an attractive means for jazz to initi-ate a dialogue with the high-cultural avant-garde.

Nor was it a live option at this stage for modern jazz musicians, not yet fully recognized as artists, to turn their lives of consumption and leisure into public aesthetic spectacles. In general, the jazz world at this time could not easily engage in secondary aesthetic practices involving high culture if there was still considerable doubt in the cultural world at large about the aesthetic legitimacy of jazz's primary products. We do associate bebop today with what may have been the first mass-culture bohemia, the hipster subculture. But hipsterism did not achieve aesthetic legitimation as a bohemia until it was later appropriated in the old-fashioned way—that is, from top down—by the 1950s avant-gardes, the beat poets, and other intellectual "white Negroes." Initially, hipsters were nebulously perceived (if they were perceived at all) less as bohemians than as marginally criminal hangers-on in the bebop universe, the more ominous successors of zoot-suiters and swing's "jitterbugs."

Thus, there will be a decided shift in orientation and methodology when I take up the postmodern era in high/low interactions—a shift from a multi-faceted analysis of institutions, scenes, musical appropriations, and so on, to a single-minded focus on the discursive formations so crucial to the cultural accreditation of jazz and rock. This exclusive preoccupation with discourse is, however, only temporary, since as jazz and rock moved up the cultural hierarchy, new avenues previously closed opened up for engagements with high culture. Indeed, by the late 1970s New York's new wave rock subculture had sufficient cultural capital to dictate conditions of engagement with the art world. Thus emerged the fashionable nightclubs merging punk and disco with painting and performance art, such as the Mudd Club, which though reminiscent of the Montmartrian cabarets, were securely lodged on pop music's cultural turf and defined in its terms. Perhaps more impressive was the power of the punk/new wave bohemia to set the terms for all bohemian practice in New York and other cultural centers. It was in fact the only bohemia in town, joined en masse by both artists and rock fans—a remarkable reversal from the early pop bohemias, such as the hipster bohemia, which only gained credibility when appropriated selectively by a later avant-garde.

VIII   This book may be perceived as aligning itself with the recent though amorphous calls for a return to aesthetics. In both literary theory and cultural studies of the past few decades, the very idea of aesthetic theorizing has been a contentious issue. If anything, an "anti-aesthetic" attitude has prevailed in these arenas, exhibited as often by an absence of aesthetic discourse—a "flight" from aesthetics—as by a polemic against the aesthetic. In literature, this was exemplified by the turn from "work" to "text," from concern with the aesthetic underpinnings of the chef d'oeuvre to the preoccupation with the psychoanalytic, political, and deconstructive ramifications of the "text," whatever its honorific status.[18] In cultural studies the prevailing populism viewed the application of aesthetic concepts to popular music as the infusion of elitist notions into a realm where they clearly did not belong.[19] These connected trends in both literary theory and cultural studies have seriously inhibited the discussion of aesthetics in academic work on popular music.

Now there is a reaction afoot, a call for a return to aesthetics, no doubt motivated in some quarters by a conservative impulse to redress the perceived excesses of poststructuralist, postcolonial, and feminist readings of literary texts and cultural practices. The erstwhile tabooed topics of beauty and genius seem to be coming back in fashion, as are speculations on what constitutes the true great work, the real chef d'oeuvre.[20] Without discounting these new efforts, I am taking a different tack, which is to move aesthetics beyond its traditional confines of high culture into the domain of the popular, with all the theoretical transformations that this will entail. There are increasingly more of us who think that the flight from aesthetics in studies of popular culture was a mistake, that a "popular aesthetic" is not the oxymoron that both populists and elitists seemed to think it is. In fact, as this book reveals and explores at some length, popular music has been saturated with public aesthetic discourses emanating from outside academia for decades, during the very period when academic populists were studiously avoiding the aesthetic. This permeation of the aesthetic within the popular music industry taken broadly is something that academic theory needs to take account of, whatever its ideological proclivities.

Two academic theorists, from different fields, have recently made promising attempts at working out an aesthetic of rock music, or more generically "pop" music. Approaching his subject matter from the point of view of the "ontology" of the art object, Theodore Gracyk has argued that any rock aesthetic must take as its point of departure the fact that rock exists primarily as *recorded* sound and must be evaluated as such. Simon Frith, operating within a sociological framework, is more interested in tying the value of pop to its social functions, such as its role in the construction of identities and the shaping of popular memory. These valuable approaches to a pop/rock aesthetic need, however, to be complemented by studies of those rich aesthetic discourses that surround the pop recording and mediate its social functions, where indeed the major aesthetic ideas of pop are forged. Taken by themselves, the ontological and social-function approaches can easily fall prey to essentialism and excessive abstraction. On the other hand, any attempt to theorize those heterogeneous, convoluted, ever-changing discourses emanating from mainstream journals, fanzines, liner notes, and so on, will altogether discourage any essentialist account of pop music aesthetics or any abstract formulation blind to its many layers. What the scholar looks for in these archives are not universal pop values, but certain enduring discursive formations that constrain how the game of aesthetic evaluation is played, what conceptual oppositions prevail, and so on.

I have already argued that an account of the discourses of criticism emanating from within the popular music field is indispensable to any adequate theorizing of the postmodern condition in high/low interactions, when characteristically popular music takes the initiative aggressively in its encounters with the avant-garde. To this I add now that such discourse analysis is also indispensable to any attempt to decipher the aesthetic values at work in the popular music field. Thus, this book, by fulfilling its main objectives, will in effect provide as an extra bonus the outlines of an aesthetic of contemporary popular music that is grounded in concrete historical practices. In it I develop a methodological model for analyzing the plethora of aesthetic discourses within the pop music field—a model that is sensitive to their historical specificities and fluctuations, but that at the same time provides us with tools for discerning those more enduring discursive formations that frame and regulate them. In effect, this book should function as a "prolegomenon" to a future full-fledged theory of pop aesthetics, the attainment of which so far has been elusive.

POP INTO ART
FRENCH MODERNISM

A. Cabaret Artistry (1840–1920)

FIGURE 1 Cover of the magazine promoting Le Mirliton, a popular artistic cabaret. A passerby views a Toulouse-Lautrec poster displaying the owner and star, Aristide Bruant (1893).

CHAPTER 2
THE SONG OF MONTMARTRE

IT WAS IN LATE-NINETEENTH-CENTURY PARIS, then the European capital of both entertainment and art, that a sustained alliance of modernism and the popular music industry was first visibly and successfully deployed. French modernism is usually ascribed a relatively early birth, sometime in midcentury with the work of Baudelaire, Flaubert, and Courbet, just at the time that the French popular music industry was taking shape. But there were no quick meetings of minds across these cultural barriers, no natural affinities that immediately and unproblematically brought modernism and popular music together. Such a remarkable alliance was forged only as the result of decades of institutional and legal changes, urban transformations, political upheavals, aesthetic controversies, and the growth in the power and visibility of bohemian culture. It was finally through the emergence and flowering of the artistic cabarets of Montmartre in the last two decades of the nineteenth century that popular music joined forces with art and literature in a synthesis of high and low cultures that has since rarely been equaled. In the next two chapters, I detail the rise, triumph, and demise of the artistic cabaret and analyze the historical conditions that made it possible.

In Europe the high/low cultural opposition has long preceded the nineteenth century, going back perhaps as far as the flowering of Greek civilization. Such a cultural hierarchy has been endorsed consistently by philosophers from Plato to Kant, with only occasional dissent by the likes of a Rousseau — a reflection of the fact that in Europe the economic class system has always been accompanied by a cultural class system.[1] However, the almost simultaneous rise of modernism and mass culture in France in the middle of the nineteenth century radically transformed the old high/low cultural dynamic, most characteristically by initiating a recurrent series of breachings of the boundaries between high and low without ever eliminating these boundaries. The institution of the artistic cabaret was the culmination in the nineteenth century of such forays over the high/low divide.

Cabaret Aesthetics

The legendary Chat Noir, founded in 1881, was the first Montmartrian venue to bring together the mix of ingredients that became the mark of the artistic cabaret: a potpourri of popular song, poetry reading, arty provocations, and modernist experiments, overseen by artists turned impresarios in spaces insistently decorated with the recent work of local artists and publicized by in-house journals. The Chat Noir's immediate and dramatic successes engendered a proliferation of artistic cabarets, which by 1890 dominated the nightlife of Montmartre, transforming it from a seedy neighborhood of dance halls and bars into an international center for the trendy consumption of culture and pleasure.

The institution of the artistic cabaret was itself deeply beholden to a number of venues and haunts of the bohemian world that had preceded it and from which it appropriated many performative devices and atmospheric tones: the *cafés-concerts,* those lavish repositories of "vulgar" commercial song depicted in seemingly countless "modern" paintings; the bohemian cafés where regular clienteles of poets and painters put their eccentricities informally on display; poetry clubs, dedicated to performances that made the new poetry more palatable and safely exhilarating for a young and upwardly mobile public; and the defunct *goguettes,* or workers' singing societies, which continued to function at the level of nostalgia in the surviving sites of cultural entertainment. Though these institutions had been negotiating the boundaries between entertainment and art for decades beforehand, none had succeeded in effecting the clear and stable synthesis of high and low culture that would later be the staple of the artistic cabarets. Nonetheless, these institutions, through a slow, tortuous process, generated the conditions that made the artistic cabaret possible and without which it cannot be understood.

By the turn of the century, the artistic cabaret disappeared from Montmartre almost as suddenly as it had appeared two decades before, abandoned by a fickle public for the slick extravaganzas of the Moulin Rouge and other music halls. The demise of the artistic cabaret in France was immediately followed, in the first decade of this century, by its rebirth in other outposts of European modernism. Undergoing mutations along the way, it spread quickly from Barcelona to Munich and Vienna, reaching out as far as Kraców and Moscow. But it was in the sleepy Swiss city of Zurich that the artistic cabaret reached its cultural apogee, when in 1916 the émigré artist Hugo Ball went to a local tavern owner to "beg" him, quite innocently, to let him "start an artists' cabaret."[2] What resulted was the Cabaret Voltaire, the founding venue of the dada movement and probably the most mythologized site of twentieth-century avant-garde practice. This brief aesthetic triumph was also the last hurrah for the artistic cabaret as a major player in the turbulent history of modernism. It continued to exist, but only as a nostalgic vestige of what it once was.

This chapter will trace the convoluted path that led from the bohemian café, poetry club, and *cafés-concerts,* to the early triumphs of the legendary Chat Noir and the irruption of the "song of Montmartre." The next chapter, after a brief account of the full flowering of the artistic cabaret in Montmartre, narrates its sudden decline and death, its equally precipitous rebirth and spread outside of France, and the final outburst at the Cabaret Voltaire. The point of these narratives is to highlight the artistic cabarets' important but underappreciated role in the constitution and reception of modernist and avant-garde aesthetic practices. Going beyond the past tendencies in the literature to treat artistic cabarets as quaint objects of nostalgia, amusing historical sideshows, or merely sociological correlates to the grand dramas of cultural modernity, I will be construing them as bona fide sites of modernist aesthetic practice, operating in the same aesthetic field as salons, art galleries, *cénacles,* studios, and other emblematic venues of modernist production.[3]

I place under the category of the aesthetic not only the "serious" production of paintings, poems, symphonies, and drama, but also the apparently more frivolous, semi-leisure activities and performances of songsters, artists, and literati in these cabarets. Of course, these practices and products of artistic cabarets have generally not received the accreditation or status from the sanctioning institutions of high culture that has been bestowed on modernist paintings, poems, and symphonies. So, we might say, the cabarets engaged only in "secondary" aesthetic practices, in contrast to the "primary" aesthetic practices taking place in galleries, official salons, and poetry journals. But this distinction is as much a reflection of conventional biases and hierarchical orderings as it is of relevant aesthetic differences in the practices themselves. Indeed, the modest secondary practices of the artistic cabarets, sharing the same intertextual space, participated quite significantly in determining the public reception of the "primary" modernist products, and hence in the constitution of their public meanings.

The notion of secondary aesthetic practice, however, is not so loose as to accommodate the practices of any venue of entertainment that might have crossed paths with nineteenth-century modernism. Rather, this notion is restricted to noncanonical and marginalized cultural practices that nonetheless either used the formal devices of modernist art (e.g., "artistic" posters and cabaret decor), or benefited from the modernist penchant to aestheticize everyday life (e.g., the "aesthetic" dress of dandies and bohemians), or were habitually programmed side by side with primary practices, thereby absorbing the modernist aesthetic by osmosis. The notion of secondary practice also includes the placing of the products of primary practices in sites of secondary aesthetic practice (e.g., paintings in cabarets and poems in cabaret newsletters). In general, a form of performance, ritual, or representation would not count as a secondary aesthetic practice of modernism unless it was thickly enmeshed intertextually with its primary aesthetic practices.

Among the institutional loci of secondary aesthetic practices, none had a greater impact on modernism and its reception in the nineteenth and early twentieth centuries than the artistic cabarets. They were among the most important aesthetic mediators and synthesizers in European modernist culture at the turn of the century. By connecting a formally aloof and somewhat inaccessible modernism with the new and vibrant commercial culture of song, they were highly instrumental in attracting an alternative broader public for modern artists and literary figures who were cut off from the traditional publics catered to by academies and salons. Indeed, the putting of the modernist art world on display as a spectacle accompanying commercial song was itself a mildly shocking form of popular entertainment, a transformation of this art world itself, in its public posturing and manifestations, into a glossy commodity. Secondly, the cabarets succeeded better than any other institution in transforming, updating, and systematically consolidating the great array of secondary aesthetic practices associated with bohemian life, which had previously appeared inchoately and informally in literary cafés, poetry clubs, and the *cafés-concerts*. Finally, the artistic cabaret also performed important mediatory functions within the sphere of high culture itself, in helping to negotiate the transition from the supposedly self-enclosed, "autonomous" art of the fin de siècle, with which it was initially allied, such as impressionism and symbolism, to the confrontative outward-looking avant-gardes of the early twentieth century, such as dada, for which it provided a crude beginning model.

Some recent writing, with the support of museum exhibits, has attempted to redress the marginal aesthetic status to which the artistic cabarets have been historically consigned.[4] The songs of Montmartre cabarets, the posters, decors, the "shock" tactics, the shadow plays—all these, it is being argued, should be treated as works of art in their own right and given the proper acclaim. In effect, this revisionist move, typically postmodern, seeks to canonize the works of artistic cabarets, to win recognition for them as products of primary aesthetic practices. I have no objection to this form of revisionism, but it needs to be distinguished from the perspective I am taking. In this and the next chapter, my interest is in determining what position the artistic cabarets occupied in the aesthetic field of their time, rather than advocating any change in their placement in today's canonical hierarchy. In my view, traditional scholarship has erred not in consigning the aesthetic practices of artistic cabarets to the sphere of the secondary, but in greatly underestimating the importance of secondary aesthetic practices to the development of modernism. One of the features that, I will argue, clearly distinguishes French modernism from the art that preceded it is a near-constant symbiosis between primary and secondary aesthetic activity. In France modernism emerged in midcentury at the very time when a tradition of secondary aesthetic practices, primarily in the form of bohemianism, was also emerging. These were not merely adventitious happenings, but from the beginning systemically connected. The foregoing sections detail this historical background to the emergence of artistic cabarets.

The Bohemian Café (1840–80)

When Rodolphe Salis, a none-too-successful con man in art world dealings,[5] founded Le Chat Noir in late 1881 in Montmartre, he had nothing more ambitious in mind than a drinking establishment catering to artists, an updated version of the bohemian cafés that for forty years had been a hallmark of the emerging modernist culture of Paris. Though the Chat Noir would soon transform itself, somewhat accidentally, from a bohemian café into the first artistic cabaret, such an idea had not yet crossed Salis's mind at the moment of the founding, and indeed would not crystallize until after the fact.

The bohemian café was any drinking establishment with a regular clientele of artists and hangers-on, who lived on the fringes or appeared to and who constituted a "scene" consumable by curious onlookers. According to the usual accounts, the bohemian café emerged in the 1840s as a symptom of major economic dislocations in the art world, caused by the breakdown of the patronage system and the hostility of the traditional aristocratic salons to modernist aesthetic practice. In response to these developments, "modern" artists and writers, excluded from the cozy confines of official culture, were forced to find new sites for convivial meetings, serious aesthetic interchanges, as well as for preening and display.

First came the alternative salons of the second decade run by renegade aristocrats, eccentric bourgeois, or radical literary figures, such as Victor Hugo, away from the town houses and lush courtyards of the aristocratic salons. This was only an intermediate step to the almost complete abandonment of the salon system by the second generation of romantics (Théophile Gautier, Gérard Nerval) who organized themselves into a small, somewhat secret, highly ritualized, and geographically mobile social group. Initially conducting their meetings at various private apartments, the "Jeunes-France" (as they called themselves) later founded a live-in colony in an elegant but dilapidated town house where the constant comings and goings assured an almost uninterrupted agenda of meetings, stray discussions, and literary and musical performances.[6]

In the 1840s, however, as economic opportunities for nonestablishment artists declined even further, young modernists, barely living at a subsistence level in cold, claustrophobic garrets clearly inhospitable to finely tuned get-togethers and rituals, turned to cheap drinking establishments for their interactive public life and small creature comforts, spending hours on a shared cup of coffee. It would be a mistake, however, to construe the bohemian café, which thus emerged out of these practices of necessity, as merely an artifact of the changing socioeconomic conditions of the art world. There were aesthetic imperatives also at work, which had first manifested themselves in the rites of the Jeunes-France and continued to hold sway in the dank confines of the bohemian cafés.

The Jeunes-France had brandished an aggressive commitment to "art for art's sake," which found an outlet in their private and public leisurely life as well as in official artwork. On the one hand, this particular aesthetic required a separation of art from life, in the sense that the raison d'être of art was not to come from any goals outside of art, whether religious, political, or moral. Art is an end in itself and thus generates its own values. But by sanctifying art as a high and pure end in itself—in effect, turning art into a quasi-sacred practice—the Jeunes-France could not easily separate art from life in another sense, that is, could hardly desist from introducing the "pure" values of art into the very conduct of their leisurely lives. In effect, they turned life into a form of art. "Art for art's sake" was thus both a separatist movement (art withdrawing from subordination to moral, political, or religious imperatives) and an expansionist movement (art colonizing the rituals of life).

As an aesthetic phenomenon, bohemianism was simply the most visible and outrageous expression of the emergence in the nineteenth century of such specific "arts of life" associated with the production of art. Put more analytically, the purified primary aesthetic practices of "art for art's sake" inevitably gave rise to a profusion of secondary practices under the guise of an aestheticization of everyday life that gradually came to be classified as "bohemian." In fact, it might be hypothesized that it was only with the advent of the "art for art's sake" movement that secondary aesthetic practices emerged on the historical stage as major forces in the public contextualization and reception of the primary artworks. We might even go so far as to assert that the systematic emergence of the phenomenon of secondary practices in the world of high culture— identified with the rise of bohemianism—was the first symptom of the birth of "modernity" in the arts and literature. Such a view coheres with the themes of that first great classic on modernity in art, Charles Baudelaire's "Le Peintre de la vie moderne," appearing two decades after the heyday of the Jeunes-France, which contends that the modern artist is distinguished as much by his [*sic*] mode of living as by the nature of his work, for example by his tendency to wander through the city exposing himself endlessly to the shocks of its sights, sounds, and jostling crowds, by his general willingness to experiment with the fragmentation and "vaporization" of his senses through drugs, and so on. That is, for Baudelaire, cultural modernity, in contrast to the premodern, is inherently characterized by a unity of "art" and "life," of production and consumption, *within* the sphere of the aesthetic.

In the case of the Jeunes-France, the "bohemian" aestheticization of life found expression primarily in singular and provocative dress codes, self-consciously scripted séances and parties, and a stylized manner of snubbing their noses at bourgeois society.[7] Gautier and his entourage set off a craze for medievalesque clothing, reintroduced the beard to France, and turned smoking into an act of getting "drunk on dreams" and searching for "oblivion."[8] These young romantics transformed the typical unruly antics of privileged young males into spectacles reputedly brimming with a subversive aesthetic, such as nude displays, graffiti proclaiming "Vive Hugo!" and dancing around flaming punch bowls while improvising verses.

This carefully scripted aberrant behavior was not lost on the "bourgeois" press, such as *Le Figaro,* which reported that the typical follower of the Jeunes-France covered his walls with poisoned daggers, drank his punch "from the skull of a much-loved mistress," and enjoyed "visits to cemeteries or dissecting rooms."[9] However committed the "art for art's sake" movement of the Jeunes-France was to the production of "pure" art, and however repelled it may have been by "paltry vaudevilles," the mass press, and other popular entertainments of the bourgeoisie, it nonetheless produced its own impure brand of amusements for the bourgeoisie through its secondary aesthetic practices.[10] From the very beginning, the duality between primary and secondary practices found expression in the duality between pure art and popular entertainment, thus displaying an inherent complicity of the most "autonomous" of art movements with the garish worlds of show business. "Ever since their simultaneous emergence in the mid-19th century," says Andreas Huyssen, "modernism and mass culture have been engaged in a compulsive *pas de deux.*"[11]

The flippant bohemianism of the Jeunes-France was replaced in the 1840s by the conspicuous destitution of the Société des Buveurs d'Eau (Society of Water Drinkers), whose members were understandably less equipped or energized for theatrical display and sartorial excess. They whiled their hours away at the Café Momus on a decrepit street near the Louvre, more for cheap coffee and an escape from the rigors of garret life than because of any inclination to entertain or to shock the bourgeoisie. But this did not stop the bourgeoisie,[12] who were looking in at the Momus in increasing numbers, from construing the poverty of this new bohemia as an altogether voluntary act of refusal and defiance against its world and values, thus evoking in them the titillations of voyeuristic outrage.[13] Willy-nilly and despite itself, this new impoverished bohemia found itself informally cast as a performing troupe for the thrill-seeking segments of the bourgeoisie.

Bohemia Emigrates (1860–80)

By the 1860s, however, the mystique of bohemia subsided somewhat, as the modest bohemian cafés—located on nondescript side streets passed by in Baron Haussmann's massive transformations of the Parisian landscape—gave way as objects of public curiosity and fascination to the brazen new musical entertainments of the *cafés-concerts,* which became a hallmark of boulevard life during the Second Empire. The bohemian café might have died as an institution, or become altogether inconsequential, if it were not for a major demographic shift in the Parisian art world in the 1860s, initiated by a group of young modern painters who, united by their alienation from the salon and academic art, began an exodus to Montmartre, motivated by the brighter and less expensive lodgings and not inconsequentially by its proximity to the burgeoning gallery scene immediately south on the rue Lafitte. Though still somewhat bucolic in character, spotted by vineyards and windmills and only recently legally absorbed in the city of Paris, Montmartre already had a reputation as a center of cheap entertainment—workers' drinking places (*gingettes*), dance halls (Elysée-Montmartre), and brothels. This was obviously a draw for the impressionists, with their predilection for slumming in, and depicting, the new commercial pleasure haunts of the working classes.

Mythically, Montmartrian bohemia begins in 1866 when Manet and some of his associates—Whistler, Zola, and later Degas, Renoir, Monet, and Pissarro—were meeting at the Café Guerbois on the western boundary of Montmartre, close to their own ateliers, to engage in serious discussions on art and beauty. After the demise of the Commune, they shifted their headquarters to the Nouvelle Athènes at the Place Pigale, made legendary by some remarkable paintings by Manet (*Au Coin du café*) and Degas (*L'Absinthe*),[14] after which they relocated to the Café de la Grande Pinte, also in Montmartre. The latter move signaled a small mutation in the evolution of bohemian cafés that facilitated the emergence of the artistic cabaret.

The owner of the Grande Pinte, a small-time art dealer, was not only warmly receptive to a regular clientele of bohemian artists, but aggressively displayed their paintings and drawings on the walls of his café and hired them to do painterly decors for his windows. In effect, he transformed the traditional minimalist bohemian café into a *café à décor,* a miniature gallery for publicizing modernist work.[15] The outcome was to expand the secondary aesthetic role of the bohemian café beyond the informalities of dress, rituals, and eccentricities, to the organized and semi-institutionalized secondary practices of placing primary products, such as paintings, in "alternative" sites, such as the café, away from their "proper" loci for display—the salons, galleries, and the living quarters of the bourgeoisie.

Rodolphe Salis, an habitué of this café, had initially conceived of the Chat Noir as primarily a *café à décor* on the model of the Grande Pinte. Strategically locating the Chat Noir on the boulevard Rochechouart in the neighborhood of the Grande Pinte, he immediately went in search for his own stable of painters. He first hired Adolphe Leon Willette to produce the initial decor, a sign representing a cat on a lamppost and paintings on window panels representing the mythical triumphs of Salis and his new cabaret. He also put on display the paintings by Willette previously refused by the Salon. Willette would later produce his cabaret chef d'oeuvre (*Parce domine*) for the Chat Noir—an allegorical painting apocalyptically, but also enticingly, depicting the rush toward self-destructiveness of a decadent bohemia.[16]

What was initially missing at the Chat Noir for it to make the transition from *café à décor* to the invention of the *cabaret artistique* was the key factor of organized performances by artists and literary figures and other cohorts of the art world—that heady mix of poetry, song, and publicity gimmicks that would give the Chat Noir its mythic identity. What was needed was a revolutionary metamorphosis of secondary aesthetic practices from informal, somewhat unscripted, and unintended forms of entertainment—from mere "arts of life" on display—to explicit involvements and entrepreneurships by artists and literary figures in the institutionalized and large-scale world of popular entertainment.

Salis might never have conceived of this possibility had he not accidentally met the Latin Quarter poet Émile Goudeau, another modernist impresario on the make, just days before the opening of the Chat Noir.[17] Goudeau came with quite a reputation, not so much for his poetry, but for having founded, and presided over, the spectacularly successful Club des Hydropathes in the Latin Quarter, which had turned poetry performances into uproarious entertainments. It was when, under Goudeau's prodding, Salis introduced and inevitably transformed the aesthetic practices of the now-defunct Club des Hydropathes into the novel spaces of his *café à décor* that the artistic cabaret was effectively created.

Poets on the March (1875–78)

The Club des Hydropathes emerged amidst a growing determination among young poets in the 1870s to reclaim a public space and a public meaning for a modernist poetry that had become inaccessible, privatized, and academicized.[18] It seemed that the sometimes facetious complaint, made by advocates of *l'art pour l'art,* that the modern poet is inevitably misunderstood had turned out to be a self-fulfilling prophecy.

Upon his arrival in Paris in the mid-1870s, Goudeau frequented the well-established bohemian cafés in the Latin Quarter, where he witnessed the by then hackneyed rituals of the art world, the endless disputations about art and life, the display of eccentricities, a certain aura of moral deviance, and the inevitable excesses of absinthe and caffeine. But he sensed that the young poets—tired of merely displaying their leisure patterns and lifestyles for a voyeuristic public while their works languished in obscure journals read only by other poets—yearned to experience the immediate gratification of performing their poems before large and enthusiastic audiences. He found evidence of this desire for showmanship at the Sherry Cobbler, a café on the boulevard St. Michel, where young poets, overcoming professional reserve through alcohol, had gotten into the habit of leaping upon tables to recite their poetry while "gesticulating wildly and shaking their hair."[19] More was needed, however, than these awkward displays and untutored excesses to create a crowd-pleasing poetic vaudeville that combined titillation with aesthetic edification.

Though he was initially unclear on how to do this, Goudeau's ideas began to crystallize after he encountered Latin Quarter poets who were developing innovative performative repertoires. Already at the Sherry Cobbler, he had met the "illustrious Sapeck," a part-time poet, author, and illustrator, who would, however, achieve celebrity status as the one who brought *le rire moderne* (modern laughter) into modernist performance, by transforming the pranks and practical jokes of young male initiations into forms of secondary aesthetic practices. A typical exploit by Sapeck was to board a cable car that did not allow dogs, and then, upon seating himself, to imitate in blood-curdling fashion the squeals of a small dog whose tail had been stepped on, causing the conductor to stop repeatedly to search for the suspected contraband. Merely the distribution of a card announcing "Sapeck will go out tomorrow at 3 o'clock" would bring out a huge throng on the boulevard St. Michel at the appointed hour, where, for example, Sapeck would appear carried by four attendants and dressed in a resplendent multicolored "Turkish" costume.[20]

Sapeck, and the growing number of his supporters, would soon introduce these *fumisteries*—these practical jokes, literally the "blowing of smoke"—into the sacred confines of literary performances at the Club des Hydropathes and the Chat Noir. By combining rank silliness with the auras of bohemia and art, these *fumisteries* could legitimately appear onstage as comic relief alongside the most abstruse of modernist poetry readings. They were the first of an array of entertainment practices used to package poetry for larger audiences with shorter attention spans. It was thus inevitable that *le fumisme,* despite its overt light-headedness, would soon be encumbered with its own aesthetic mystique, its own place in the symptomology of modernist alienation. Goudeau defined *fumisme* as a deep inner "scorn for persons and things," an "interior madness," translating itself into an "imperturbable buffoonery" of "burlesques, farces, and con-games." Goudeau's generation, "which had every reason to be pessimistic, turned to [this kind of] gaiety in [its] fight against boredom and the blues."[21]

But it was insufficient merely to surround modernist poetry by modernist pranks in order to secure a larger market for it. Modern poetry itself had to be dressed up more attractively. One obvious answer was to drape it in song, a type of song easily accessible and yet evocative of the deep stirrings of modernity, a type of song that gave a sense of shock without going much beyond titillation. At a seedy bistro not far from the Sherry Cobbler, Goudeau discovered Maurice Rollinat, the singer-poet who would bring about this mild revolution, by turning the tortured poetry of modern neurosis into pleasantly inflammatory song. There, at the entreaty of friends, Rollinat accosted the house piano with his "wild" and "dreadful" chords, and sang sonnets by Baudelaire and himself set to his "practically religious" melodies—evoking "confused" and "poignant" emotions in the small coterie of writers and painters in attendance, as "faces turned pale and eyes filled with tears."[22]

This quite dramatic reception prefigured the acclaim that Rollinat would later receive from critics after he had left the squalid confines of Latin Quarter cafés for the cozy settings of bourgeois salons. His "incredible" music was later described by critics and other observers as "painfully evocative" and "strangely nostalgic," giving "wings of fire" to his verses. His voice, so "strident" and "caustic," so full of "wild mewings" and "gripping" bass notes, seemed not to come from human organs.[23] His lyrics were cluttered with images of "coffins, suicides, specters," and "insanity"—of "horrific nightmares," "satanic evocations," and "terror-stricken hallucinations."[24] Shaking his thick hair with his "fatal head," letting his "long locks brush softly against the piano keys," he would suddenly turn toward the audience with "flaming eyes" and a "savage expression" on his "ravaged" and "tormented" face, and then "twist his mouth" into a "satanic grin" while "his hands feverishly ran up and down the piano."[25] Through "spasmodic gestures," his whole body "accented the rhythms of his verses."[26]

Clearly not an "art" singer in the manner of the Conservatory nor a popular singer, Rollinat was introducing a new genre of middlebrow performance, which made modernism accessible to wider audiences, in part by dramatizing to excess and exploiting the mythology of modern madness, psychic fragmentation, and the pale alienation of modernist poets. He was shaping a kind of secondary practice that, rather than merely coexisting as entertainment alongside high art, attempted to synthesize the abstruseness of modernism with the show-business flair of popular culture. By wedding the poetry of morbidity and alienation to the somewhat spastic and exaggerated body gesticulations then in vogue among popular singers, Rollinat was signaling the emergence of popular song as the most important medium through which this synthesis of high and low would be carried out in the secondary aesthetic practices of nineteenth-century modernism.[27]

Rollinat and Sapeck did not achieve the celebrity that would gain them entry into the high-profile artistic cabarets and upscale bourgeois salons until the advent of the Club des Hydropathes, which provided them with their first general public beyond a narrow coterie and their first publicity machine. Goudeau's major innovation, in organizing the Club des Hydropathes, was to bring together in one performance space and under a unified rubric, the previously fragmented and diffused experiments in modernist entertainment that had flickered here and there in informal café settings.

Showbiz at the Poetry Club (1878–80)

In his attempt to institute a "system" in which "singers of rhymes would hurl themselves at the public," Goudeau ran into stiff resistance from poets, excessively timid or worried about the loss of their "pontifical dignity," who could not imagine themselves "declaiming their verses before more than three or four persons" and without the comforting backdrop of "the salon chimney and the piano they could suavely lean on." Despite these trepidations, a small group led by Goudeau and Rollinat was meeting regularly in the fall of 1878 for the purposes of declamation and song, at a nondescript café in the Latin Quarter that had the "indispensable" piano and easy chairs. When this informal arrangement proved unworkable—too much interference from unruly students and hostile regulars—Goudeau and his small circle managed to secure the private use of the hall and piano at the Café de la Rive Gauche every Friday night, by guaranteeing an audience of at least twenty potential consumers of drink. A surprising number of seventy-five showed up on the first Friday, overflowing out of the hall into the nearby billiard room, clearly evincing "a cruelly felt need" for collective action in these "most backward times."[28]

Before indulging in the "gambols authorized by the muse," they officially formed a private club. Resisting the various "serious names" proposed for the new organization, with their implication of activities that "bored to death," Goudeau won approval for the name "Club des Hydropathes," taken from the title of an obscure musical composition, which because of its inane connotations had the advantage of not compromising "future doctrines" or "possible apostasies." Unlike its legendary predecessors, such as the Jeunes-France and the Parnassiens, the Club des Hydropathes would not function as a poetic sect with a unified aesthetic intransigently adhered to. Its solidarity was a pragmatic one, oriented around marketing strategies rather than ideological agendas. According to Goudeau, the mission of the Club des Hydropathes was to "penetrate the brains of those young students destined to join the ranks of the *haute bourgeoisie* with the notions of art and poetry," and conjointly to turn reclusive poets into activists "knocking at the seignorial portals" of this potential new royalty. In the face of the declining resources of the aristocracy and the intransigent hostility of state-supported cultural institutions, Goudeau viewed the Club des Hydropathes as an agency for creating a new public, not from the ranks of the general citizenry—the realm of "universal suffrage"—but from the more "restrained suffrage" of semiprivileged youth on the way to bourgeois success who populated the various educational institutions of the Left Bank. To garner such an audience on a large scale, it was imperative according to Goudeau for the Club to free itself of all "literary jealousies," "school disputes," and "coteries," and to become a "theater of poetry" open to all, even "bad poets."[29] This strategy was eminently successful, as evidenced by the surprising and rapid growth of the "membership" audience, from seventy the first week to five hundred at its peak, which necessitated a number of moves to larger cafés, all in the neighborhood of the Sorbonne and the boulevard St. Michel.

From the beginning the Club des Hydropathes was an "inextricable jumble," a "bouillabaisse" of "diverse and opposite tendencies." There were the "young political men who dreamed of transforming these get-togethers into political conclaves, the modernist poets who could not tolerate the romantics"; the amateurs who sought to titillate with their "risqué" songs and "spicy monologues"; the "old-fashioned" who dared declaim the most cheesy poetic nuggets; the young actors, some of whom never strayed from the

Racine and Corneille repertoire; while others, "with better taste and more deft," took on the work of Coppée and Hugo. A few "elegiac Catholics" volunteered "hymns to the Blessed Virgin," while some old "loony" would risk being ridiculed by imposing his "strong Italian accent" on the verses of Hugo.[30]

In this "miniature Chamber of Deputies," in the face of such a "heterogeneous, fiery, and tumultuous" crowd, the performances never proceeded for long without a rising hubbub of "exclamations, invective, and disputes"— "inextricable free-for-alls" that transformed the modest meeting hall into a "battlefield."[31] "The musicians wanted to monopolize attention, while the agitated, long-haired poets could scarcely tolerate those awkward chromatic scales." The politicians "expressed great indignation at the absence of any discussion of the rights of man and the patriots wanted to disallow the playing of any German sonatas." For their part, the *fumistes*, "under the leadership of the redoubtable Sapeck, were interested only in mocking everything, which further provoked the committed hieratics to demand that the President firmly uphold the flag of art."[32]

The drunks, tramps, and professional rowdies were quickly escorted out, and the politicians were told in no uncertain terms that they would be admitted not as conspirators, but only as "makers of fine words" who agreed to meet exclusively under the aegis of "literature, the fine arts, and the perpetual piano." The other disputes and disturbances, operating broadly within the aesthetic realm, were not only tolerated but accepted as part of the normal processes of Hydropathic performance. Indeed, such partisan and humoristic audience convulsions proved to be as entertaining, and as much of a draw, as the serious and self-conscious performances onstage. "Happily, it was youth and laughter which overcame" the tumult, or at least made it sufferable, especially when such youthful mirth was channeled through the antics of the *fumistes,* who despite all their "cheek," were ultimately "smitten" with art.[33] Sapeck worked his *fumisteries* both in the audience by helping organize and sometimes contain the catcalls and tirades, and onstage by reading poetry with hands cupped over his nose and mouth, emitting "ghastly sounds capable of rousing a whole neighborhood from sleep."[34]

In early 1879, a few months after its founding, the Club published the first issue of its biweekly journal, *L'Hydropathe,* which functioned as much as an organ for publicizing the Club's activities as a repository of its poems for posterity. Goudeau had long bemoaned the sad fate of the small poetry journals of the 1870s, which disappeared almost as quickly as they appeared, undone by their high solemnity and narrow commitment to "absolute doctrines." In contrast, *L'Hydropathe*—neither sectarian nor very serious—mixed satire, caricature, whimsy, and the snide put-on with its casual forays into poetic invention.[35] Each issue featured a caricatural drawing of one of the Hydropathes with an outlandish apocryphal biography, followed by jocular and somewhat pointless prose articles—for example, a pseudoscholarly history of *fumisme*—interspersed among the inevitable poems. The journal simply mimicked the mix of "seriousness" and provocative silliness that was already a trademark of the Club, simultaneously combining pure art with the publicity apparatus for showcasing it.

By 1880, just two years after the founding and not long after the peaking of its euphoric triumphs, the Club des Hydropathes began to unravel and quickly met with its demise. According to Goudeau, the "gang of *fumistes*" that "at the beginning had saved the institution," later proved to be its "ruin."[36] Apparently, as time went on, the *fumistes* became more aggressive, rebelling ever more "vigorously against the discipline which the President attempted vainly to impose" on the meetings. With their final practical joke—the setting off of fireworks in a yard contiguous to the meeting hall that precipitated a panic inside—Goudeau left the Club vowing never to return, thus initiating its demise.

Between Club and Cabaret

Though the Club des Hydropathes is given only the smallest of places in French literary history, understandably because it was not associated as an institution with any important school of poetry, it should nonetheless be recognized for its revolutionary impact on the history of secondary aesthetic practices, and thus at least indirectly for a not insignificant role in the shaping of modern literary culture. By converting secondary practices from informal bohemian aestheticizations of life into components of organized and aggressive theater, where they either cohabited with primary practices (e.g., *fumisteries* followed by "serious" poetry readings) or were effectively synthesized with such primary practices (e.g., pure poetry sung in a vaudevillian manner), the Club des Hydropathes greatly enhanced their role in shaping a public for modern poetry. It thus entails that it greatly enhanced the role of secondary practices in determining the *received* meaning of modernism, that is, in determining what it meant at that time to be a "modern" poet or artist. By institutionally conjoining primary and secondary practices in one setting, the Club had a considerable impact on the formation and development of aesthetic modernity in France. This it accomplished not as a sect producing shockingly new kinds of texts, but as a contextualizing agency determining how the shockingly new would be publicly construed.

The increased intimacy between primary and secondary practices brought with it inevitably a new intimacy between popular culture and high culture, and a consequent empowerment of popular culture in the constitution of the meaning of high-cultural production. The key innovation in this regard was the extensive use of the inflections of popular song in attempts by Hydropathes to make an otherwise intransigently sober poetry palatable to rowdy and easily distracted crowds.

Nonetheless, however close it came and however much it paved the way, the Club des Hydropathes never completed the revolution that finally reached fruition in the *cabaret artistiques*. It remained first and foremost a poetry club, where secondary practices were clearly tethered to primary practices and altogether subordinated to the promotion and celebration of purist modernist poetry. Song as entertainment was used only to the extent that it fulfilled this goal, and even then often grudgingly. It was only in the more congenial settings of the Montmartre art world that popular song and other secondary practices acquired their own autonomy and indeed took center stage away from poetry readings and other more serious primary practices. The older bohemia of the Left Bank—alienated, petulant, instantly repelled by anything that smelled of aesthetic political incorrectness—could not take this next step toward the full commercial liberation of secondary practices that the newer and less tradition-bound bohemia of Montmartre, nonchalantly living in the midst of dance halls and cheap drinking establishments, would not hesitate to assume.

Many former members of the Hydropathes, caught in this cultural halfway house, tried repeatedly to organize new poetry clubs based on the original model or to bring the original one back to life, with only limited and short-term success. Though sometimes drawn into these attempts, Goudeau partook only sporadically and without enthusiasm, perhaps sensing the self-defeatism in these constant returns to origins. Unsatisfied and confused, he wandered from job to job until in December 1881 he found his way to Montmartre and the Grande Pinte, where he met Rodolphe Salis just before the opening of the Chat Noir. Whether by sheer luck or an astute reading of the art world, Goudeau enthusiastically took the step initially refused by many of his Left Bank colleagues and threw in his lot with the formation of the artistic cabaret.[37]

The Early Chat Noir (1881–85)

In January 1882, only one month after the inception of the Chat Noir, Salis asked Goudeau to initiate and edit a house journal loosely modeled on *L'Hydropathe*. Named the *Chat Noir*,[38] the journal pursued a policy of cheerful eclecticism, having as its only directive from Salis "to amuse and generate laughs." Though even more flippant in its posturings than *L'Hydropathe*, the *Chat Noir* provided a nonsectarian forum for the proliferating new schools of poetry, including the nascent work of the decadent and symbolist movements, such as Verlaine's "Langueur," notorious for the bracing opening line "I am the Empire in its decadence."[39] Of course, in the journal as in the venue, poetry had to coexist with the visual arts, which had already established squatter's rights. Thus, a full page out of four was devoted to illustrations by local artists, as a complement to the predictable fare of poems, tales, songs, reviews, and cabaret anecdotes. In the relatively long run of the *Chat Noir,* over ninety artists joined the "house" stars Willette and Théophile Steinlen in the production of satirical drawings laced with a playful morbidity and world-weariness that was quickly becoming the fashion of the time. With a splashy format combining the aura of sinful Montmartre with the latest stirrings of modern art and poetry, the *Chat Noir* had would-be bohemians all over France daydreaming of a pilgrimage to Montmartre, this new capital of French art and pleasure.[40]

Taking note of their former leader's new escapades, a number of the more adventurous Hydropaths, still ensconced in the Latin Quarter, hopped the "shaky" streetcars to join Goudeau at his new faraway site of aesthetic ferment. Seizing the opportunity, Salis offered them the private use of his back room on Fridays to reconstitute their weekly performances of poetry and song. The reincarnated Hydropathic events quickly acquired a new notoriety in this new cultural territory ripe for exploitation. Salis responded by first opening the Friday performances to the public and as successes mounted, scheduled them more frequently, until they became daily fare and the trademark of the Chat Noir. It was initially through this alliance of bohemian *café à décor* and Hydropathic performance, of Montmartre art and Latin Quarter poetry and song, that the artistic cabaret was born.[41]

But the Chat Noir quickly transcended the narrow Hydropathic repertoire of entertainments to suit the atmosphere of gaiety and insouciant bohemianism that distinguished Montmartre from the more academicized and somber Latin Quarter. This resulted in two important changes in the original Hydropathic performance mix that would become the permanent hallmarks of the Chat Noir through its various reincarnations, as well as of the artistic cabarets that followed upon it: the creation of a new kind of popular art song—*la chanson à Montmartre*—which with time became the chief attraction, and the institutionalization and domestication of *le fumisme* within a sophisticated system of publicity.

At the Club des Hydropathes, the *fumisteries* had occurred in a somewhat spontaneous and disorderly fashion, coming mainly from the audience in an atmosphere of imminent rebellion. In contrast, at the Chat Noir, Salis incorporated *fumisme* into an official agenda of his administration, a scripted array of performances, *blagues,* and publicity stunts emanating mainly from the top. It first entered into his repertoire as compensation for his ineptness in the usual performance mix of poetry and song. Not being satisfied with the self-effacing role of master of ceremonies, he begun to indulge in long, but obviously unserious, harangues against the audience, berating them and provoking them, though not so much as to discourage the consumption of beer. Not long after, he was resorting to high jinks on a grander and more utilitarian scale. He had himself proclaimed "King of Montmartre" at a famous Montmartrian dance hall, with sword in hand and a retinue of artists and poets spouting royalist cheers along with republican chants. His most memorable practical joke was to have the *Chat Noir* announce his death by suicide, with an invitation to all to attend the funeral services at the cabaret. Salis appeared that day as the grieving brother accepting condolences from all.[42] No longer just a form of outrageous entertainment, *le fumisme* quickly became the key device of an elaborate publicity machine that served to advertise the Chat Noir as the entertainment center for the new Montmartrian art scene. The cabaret, in fact, quite vigorously promoted *fumisme* as its own trademark, an interesting overdetermination where advertising advertises itself. Its marquee proclaimed the Chat Noir to have been "founded in 1154 by a *fumiste,*" while the journal celebrated it as a "museum of *fumisteries.*"[43]

La Chanson à Montmartre

But the Chat Noir's most celebrated legacy, as exhibited by the many nostalgic chronicles that have appeared since, is the invention of a new genre of song, *la chanson à Montmartre* (the song of Montmartre), supposedly rooted in the "popular" and yet nuanced by "art," and the showcasing of a new generation of singer-songwriters, some of whom would reach the pinnacle of stardom.

Initially, Maurice Rollinat, with his wild displays of the neurotic and the macabre, was the star singer of the Chat Noir. But he was somewhat untypical of *la chanson à Montmartre* and fit more comfortably at the soirees of upper-bourgeois homes, where he later achieved the epitome of his fame. While Rollinat sought to make art song more accessible, and thus more "popular," the other singers at the Chat Noir, working in the opposite direction, sought to give popular song a more artistic and modernist appearance. That is, while Rollinat's brand of middlebrowism was a descent from above—setting high-flown poetry to the "hooks" of feverish and spastic melodies—the more typical fare of middlebrow art song at the Chat Noir was an ascent from below. The music appeared to be "of the people," driven by populist stirrings and imbued with a streetwise authenticity, and yet displayed the folkloric ambience, self-conscious irony, and conservatory sophistication enabling it to pass as "art." As a result of this shift, the performance of song with a popular inflection acquired its own autonomy within secondary aesthetic practices, no longer needing to serve as a vehicle for poetry in order to appear sufficiently "artful." Songsters were no longer merely poets dressed as entertainers, but operated side by side with the latter. They soon became the chief drawing cards of the Chat Noir, pushing the indomitable poets into the dim recesses reserved for a supporting cast.

These singer-songwriters gave vent to the new "arty" populism in a variety of different ways. For Jules Jouy, it meant to sing about the poverty of the urban masses and the future comeuppance of the upper classes, in a biting voice free of any other inflection. With a cigarette stub hanging precariously from his lower lip, he accompanied himself on the piano with the same two chords repeated indefatigably. Arthur Marcel-Legay, despite his conservatory training, made his reputation as a Montmartre street-corner singer accompanied only by his harmonium. Even at the height of his Chat Noir successes, he would return to the streets for an occasional performance, giving an urban musical grit to the poems, and even the prose, of the young modernist writers whose words he sang. Victor Meusy took the route of topical songs, specializing on Parisian locales, such as the Moulin Rouge, Montmartre's boulevard Rochechouart, and even the Stock Exchange. He was most famous for a scathing broadside against the Sacré-Coeur Church, the religious monument of the anti-Communards. Maurice Mac-Nab introduced a certain element of wry humor and happy irreverence to populist song, exploiting the fad for passive-aggressive laughter that was becoming a hallmark of Montmartrian modernism. He had previously honed these skills by composing and performing advertising ditties about portable stoves and ointments for removing corns.[44]

But it was Aristide Bruant who more than anyone achieved the reputation—and financial success consequent upon it—of being the "true" singer of "the people," though he clearly did not come from "the people." After years of dandyism and mainstream popular singing, Bruant abruptly changed his garb and musical style. Donning the bohemian costume later made famous in the Toulouse-Lautrec posters—a black corduroy jacket and wide-brimmed hat, a red flannel shirt draped by a scarlet scarf and black cape—he began to sing about the downtrodden and the marginalized in their own barely comprehensible argot. This "poet of the streets" populated his songs about the poorer outlying neighborhoods of Paris with the voices of petty criminals, prostitutes, the homeless, and even stray dogs. Thus, rather than merely exploiting the topicality of the disenfranchised, he gave the overwhelming impression, through intonation, dialect, and an artfully crafted performance persona, of directly embodying their own perspectives and pangs in his singing. It was the perceived "authenticity" of Bruant's vernacularized songs that sanctioned the view of him as a genuine artist and not merely a popular singer. Bruant soon replaced Rollinat as the star of the Chat Noir and achieved a popular fame that the latter never even approached.[45]

In effect, the Montmartrian system of song invented at the Chat Noir acquired its unity not from any stylistic or formalistic commonalities, but from certain coded devices designating the "popular"—topicality, argot, regionalism, flippancy, wisdom of the streets, themes of urban oppression, class-based militancy—invariably accompanied by certain marks of high art: an undisguised literacy, the occasional use of modernist poems, a folkloric authenticity, and, perhaps most importantly, the fact that such songs were performed in an artistic cabaret, in the midst of artworks and literary performances. In short, the songs of the Chat Noir were united more by the "myths" that they connoted and the environment within which they were framed than by the aesthetic or formal qualities they displayed.

In ceding center stage to the songsters, the painters and poets of the Chat Noir were not thereby acquiescing to any victory by popular culture. They were clearly exploiting the new song of Montmartre to bring in large and diverse audiences for their poetry readings and exhibits, which they could never have drawn had they been left to their own literary and painterly devices, however titillating or shocking. For anyone who just came to the Chat Noir for song had also to put up with the poems and the paintings, which were on the same bill. One of the great achievements of the Chat Noir, and the artistic cabarets that followed upon it, was to create an alternative public for modern artists and writers bereft of traditional patronage, the size and affluence of which surpassed even the most ambitious dreams of the Club des Hydropathes.

There were also political factors that favored this turn to popular song. The modernist habitués at the Chat Noir still harbored the vestiges of a left politics, which took form as a nostalgia for the Paris Commune and hatred for the censorious Third Republic. By aligning themselves with a kind of "popular" song, however aestheticized, they were symbolically expressing their political solidarity with *le peuple* against the bourgeois regime. At this time popular music, more than any other medium, was crucially targeted in political and cultural contestations over the meaning and value of the "popular." What was at issue, in particular, was the opposition between the "popular" as the "commercialized" and "vulgar," on the one hand, and the "popular" as the "authentic" and "subversive," on the other.[46] Two institutions of popular song had emerged in the nineteenth century, long before the Chat Noir, to emblematize these opposite constructions: the semiclandestine *goguettes,* with their workers' songs of defiance, and the *cafés-concerts,* whose singing stars were the most visible expression of the massive success of the new culture industry. The Montmartrian song of the artistic cabarets, clearly influenced by both, positioned itself quite advantageously between the song of the *goguettes* and the *cafés-concerts*. While inheriting the aura of political correctness and cultural authenticity from the now-defunct *goguettes,* artistic cabarets could nonetheless compete at the level of commerce and entertainment with the *cafés-concerts,* to whose "vulgar" and "reactionary" fare they sought to provide a more aesthetically and politically acceptable alternative.

This entanglement further illustrates a running theme of this chapter, which is that the artistic cabaret's identity was determined by the way that it took up, and transformed, the agendas of other cultural institutions. We have already seen how cabaret dealt with the vestiges of the high-culture institutions of the bohemian café, *café à décor,* and poetry club, thereby reconfiguring the practices of bohemia. Now we can turn to cabaret's peculiar synthesis of the "lowly" and contrary traditions of *goguettes* and the *café-concert* and the effect this had on the distinctive "popular" character of the *chanson à Montmartre.*

"Popular" Roots: The *Goguettes* (1818–48)

The history of *goguettes* and *cafés-concerts* was overdetermined by two incessant factors of French cultural life during the eighteenth and nineteenth centuries, interrupted only by spasmodic moments of revolutionary upheaval. The first was the government-authorized monopolization of theater, which prohibited any private commercial establishment not only from using the repertoire of the official circle of small theaters in its entertainments, but also from producing musical plays of more than one act with spoken dialogue, or even using costumes and sets.[47] This restriction became all the more encompassing once the circle of official theaters was expanded in 1807 beyond the elite *grands théâtres* (e.g., the Comédie-Française, the Opéra), to include certain popular *théâtres secondaires* (e.g., the Théâtre du Vaudeville and the Théâtre des Variétés), and thus to take away from the public commercial domain, in one fell swoop, a vast repertoire of popular entertainments that included vaudeville songs, skits, and dance. Until this monopoly was broken (1867), the *cafés-spectacles* (entertainment cafés) of Paris could not aspire to being anything more than highly limited *cafés-chantants* (cafés of song), initially restricted to a folkloric repertoire or to the compositions of itinerant musicians following the various fairs.[48]

More daunting, however, than this form of discrimination was the incessant system of official censorship and repression that befell the *cafés-spectacles* and other would-be purveyors of popular song. Indeed, before the advent of the *café-concert* in 1849, *cafés-spectacles* were more often than not legally prohibited from entertaining with song. But even when permitted to showcase song, they were subject to a most meticulous system of censorship that survived almost intact through a variety of regimes until it was repealed in 1906. Until then the various groups who succeeded each other in power—whether aristocratic or bourgeois, Bourbon or Napoleonic, revolutionary or reactionary—all shared the very entrenched belief that the circulation of popular song was a particularly dangerous conduit of subversive doctrines and morally suspect attitudes, as an alternative to the print media for the largely illiterate working-class populations.[49] During those eras when cafés of song were in effect prohibited, singer-composers and lovers of song would sometimes form private associations that met regularly for dinner and convivial singing in the back rooms of drinking establishments or wine merchants. The first of these, calling itself the Dîners du Caveau (Dinners of the Vault), was founded in 1733 by a group of literary lions and bourgeois intellectuals, for the purpose of singing their songs of sensuous pleasure—the usual topics being sex and drink—in the course of the consumption of a sumptuous meal. Their composed lyrics were usually affixed to well-known melodies from seventeenth-century courtly airs or eighteenth-century vaudeville. Soon, "caveau" became the generic term for any such dinner association devoted to epicurean song. Though generally suspect by the authorities for their "libertine attitudes," the caveaux thrived especially during the waning years of the ancien régime and, after falling out of favor during the heady days of the Revolution, reappeared in full force during the Directory and Empire, when the rigors of revolutionary communitarianism gave way, at least among the elites, to the attractions of individualistic hedonism. They fizzled and virtually disappeared during the Restoration despite, or perhaps because of, the loving embrace of the authorities, who were most pleased by the lack of any political content in their songs.

The caveaux were replaced by the goguettes, whose pugnacious songs of resistance seemed more appropriate after the reimposition of the hereditary monarchy than the faded epicurean fare of their predecessors.[50] Though also private associations of song, the goguettes were made up almost exclusively of artisans and industrial workers meeting and eating in the back rooms of modest cafés in the largely working-class areas of the northeast quadrant of Paris or in the suburbs outside the tariff walls where wine was cheaper. They emerged during the Restoration (1818–30) and peaked during the July Monarchy (1830–48), when it is estimated their number exceeded four hundred. The goguettiers sang about the dignity of labor, the high price of bread, anger against machinery, and the joys of communitarian living—like the caveaux adjoining new words to familiar vaudeville tunes. These lyrics, along with a verbal identification of the melody but no musical notation, were published at a very cheap price, as a tool for enlivening the collective and militant spirit of worker movements.[51]

As would be expected, the *goguettes* were subject to increasing surveillance, harassment, and repression by police agents and government spies, and were finally forced to go underground. Many changed their meeting places every fifteen days or disbanded temporarily, while their leaders were faced with the constant threat of incarceration. The *goguettes* nonetheless survived the enmity of the Restoration and July Monarchy, and figured prominently at the barricades during the 1848 uprising. They would perish not long after, at the hands of the Second Empire's much more effective apparatus of repression and cultural management.[52]

"Popular" Roots: The *Cafés-concerts*

When the regime of Louis-Napoléon banned all *goguettes* and other *sociétés chantantes* in 1852, it wisely decided to allow alternative politically innocuous institutions of popular song, which would provide sufficient distractions for the newly displaced and disoriented masses flooding into Paris. Thus, rather than suppressing the commercial *cafés-chantants* that had reemerged during the liberal days of the 1848 revolution, the new regime submitted them to a complex system of surveillance and regulation while integrating them in a modernized and smoothly functioning culture industry. Under the constraints of this twofold strategy, the generic *café-chantant* was transformed into the now-legendary *café-concert,* the most visible, successful, and phantasmagoric component of the Parisian entertainment industry in the latter half of the nineteenth century.

The anchor of this new entertainment institution was a seamless and everwatchful apparatus of censorship that assured the production of banal and politically vapid songs suited exclusively for amusement. All singers had to submit their repertoire to the minister of the interior, and all *cafés-concerts* had to clear any change in their program with the same office of censorship. "La Marseillaise" was proscribed, as were any songs dealing with revolution, controversial religious and military issues, repression, the miseries and aspirations of the working populations, or political engagement.[53] The topics of *café-concert* songs were predictably oriented around romance, the petty conflicts of everyday urban life (with concierges, bureaucrats, or in-laws), comic situations (e.g., the cuckold), or novelties (e.g., the songs "I'm Ticklish" and "The Bearded Lady").[54]

The bureaucratized censorship of song was complemented by a second and equally important system of controls, which was the professionalization and market rationalization of popular song, the turning of popular song into a legally protected commodified property. By fully supporting and enforcing the royalty rights of the members of the newly formed (1851) Society of Composers, Lyricists, and Music Publishers, the government of Louis-Napoléon added a further legal obstacle to the survival of the *goguettes* while giving itself an apparently benign excuse to further intensify its surveillance over the production and dissemination of popular song. The musically illiterate lyricist-composers of the *goguettes,* for example, could no longer affix new words to well-known melodies without paying what were for them exorbitant royalties. In addition, the professionalization of popular song intensified and rationalized the division of labor between singer and songwriter, and the separation of performance from spectatorship, thus undermining the communitarian practices that had sustained the *goguettes*.[55]

The increased costs due to the commodification of song required greater capital investments, the applications of economies of scale, with the consequent development of sophisticated apparatuses for publicity. In contrast with the traditional *cafés-chantants* or the *goguettes,* with their small and confined seating capacities, the major *cafés-concerts* would accommodate up to 1,500 customers, and even the more modest ones averaged between 400 and 500 seats. Located on the new or refurbished boulevards of Haussmann's Paris, the elite *cafés-concerts*—with their sumptuous, orientalized facades, their ornate columns, statues, multiple mirrors, gilded moldings, allegorical paintings, and fake marble and velvet—played upon the stereotyped "paradisic" imagery of the exotic and far-off, while exploiting the growing reputation of Paris as the European pleasure center.[56]

With a publicity machinery proportionate to its grandiose phantasmagoric objectives, the *café-concert* pioneered the development of the modern star system in France. It produced the dominant personality of the nineteenth-century entertainment industry, the singer known simply to her audiences as Thérèsa. The public's image of Thérèsa as a somewhat unfeminine parodist and absurdist—with an oversize mouth, exaggerated body movements, and a charismatic expressivity—was constructed out of a confluence of promotional media: the illustrated covers of song sheets, gossipy newspaper articles, caricatures and cartoons, colorful advertising posters, products named after her—such as liqueurs, dresses, and soups—and even a rags-to-riches autobiography that appeared within two years of her ascension to fame.[57]

However, in their pursuit of fantasy and the exotic, the *cafés-concerts* were initially severely restricted in their stage settings by the government-supported monopoly of the official theaters: there could be no costumes, no sets or decorations, no dance, pantomime, or mixture of declamation and song. This assured that pure popular song would reign supreme, unencumbered by competition from other vaudevillian-style entertainments. In 1867 the government ended the monopoly of the official theaters, thus allowing the *cafés-concerts* all sorts of entertainment, dress, and sets. However, the practice of popular song, by this time strongly entrenched, continued to dominate the programs. This conservatism would later prove to be the undoing of the *cafés-concerts* at the hands of the music halls, which would fully exploit the variety of entertainment fare and stage settings made possible by the freeing of the theatrical markets.[58]

Modernists at the *Café-concert*

The flamboyant commercial successes of the *cafés-concerts* forced even the cultural elites to take note, with a predictable mix of outrage and fascination. Soon modernists as well as traditionalists from the world of high culture could be seen slumming in these hotbeds of low culture, most notably the Goncourt brothers, appalled but also thrilled by the distinctive displays of "idiocy," "rottenness," "profound and perfect ineptitude," and "vulgar and corrupt caricatures" performed according to the "standards of taste of the gutter."[59] By the 1870s the impressionists were appearing on the scene, to add paintings of *cafés-concerts* to their growing portfolios representing the new Parisian sites of cut-rate pleasures and leisure activities. Though of course drawn by the fleeting play of light and movement served up by the newly gas-lit *cafés-concerts,* the impressionists were equally interested in exploiting the new forms of sexualized visibility of women, either humble servers (Manet's *A Bar at the Folies-Bergère*) or famous performers such as Thérèsa (Degas's *La Chanson du chien*).[60]

We can be sure that the *café-concert's* enormous appeal to the popular imaginary was not lost on the modernists of the Club des Hydropathes and their Right Bank allies, in their search for a large alternative public to compensate for their effective exclusion from the official salons and academies. The artists who slummed at the margins of the *cafés-concerts* may have fantasized about having their own establishments and being the objects of other people's slumming—in effect of putting modernism on parade in the manner in which *cafés-concerts* had put the "popular" on parade. The Chat Noir and other artistic cabarets following upon it, whether by design or accident, fulfilled this fantasy, by effectively serving as an alternative entertainment setting for a bourgeois public titillated by the hedonism and raucousness of the *cafés-concerts,* but repelled by their unrestrained vulgarity and mindlessness.

Though posing as sophisticated alternatives, the artistic cabarets from the very beginning interlocked incessantly with the commercial world of the *café-*

concert. Even the Chat Noir's radical-in-residence, Jules Jouy, produced songs for Thérèsa and other stars of the *café-concert.* As a highly prolific song-writer—his new songs "appeared like apples on trees"—he benefited enormously from the copyright system put in place in connection with that institution. Aristide Bruant, the "authentic" spokesperson of the disenfranchised, began his career at the *cafés-concerts* and returned as a star, after his excursus through the *cabarets artistiques.*[61] Yvette Guilbert, a legendary latter-day star of the *cafés-concerts,* got her start at artistic cabarets.

The Chat Noir's innovations can be read as attempts by the modernist art world to appropriate and aesthetically transform the *café-concert's* successful commercial devices. The organized *fumisteries* of the Chat Noir corresponded to the less self-conscious irreverences and bombastic provocations of the *café-concert,* while the artists' paintings and decor in the former replaced the faux-opulent kitsch of the latter. The *Chat Noir* journal provided the needed publicity that the *cafés-concerts* received either freely or by advertisement in the mass newspapers. The *café-concert's* crucial role as model might also explain why the Chat Noir supplanted the Hydropathes' middlebrow strategy of making modernist art song more accessible by that of making popular song more aesthetically modernist.

But at the same time, the artistic cabaret felt the need to distance itself emphatically from the *cafés-concerts,* as much because of the latter's perceived collaboration, under the pressures of censorship, with the hated regimes of the Second Empire and the Third Republic, as because of the perceived coarseness and idiocies of their entertainments. This political reading was further reinforced when after the demise of the Commune, the *cafés-concerts* significantly expanded their repertoire of patriotic and militaristic songs. The Chat Noir countered by reinscribing in its own practices the performance motifs of the long-suppressed *goguettes*: the reemergence of singer-songwriters, the argot of the masses, audience participation, and the song of protest. Jules Jouy was himself admitted to one of the few remaining and by now politically vapid *goguettes,* the Lice Chansonnière, and organized a supper club that had the ritualistic look of a *goguette.*[62]

This reinfusion of political critique at a cultural level, typical of the early years of the artistic cabarets, was as much due to legal changes as to a new-found militancy. In 1878 a new law freed all drinking establishments from the requirements of prior authorization and censorship, with the lone exception of the *cafés-concerts,* thus placing the yet-to-emerge artistic cabaret in a more permissive legal category. The *Chat Noir* journal was to benefit at its inception from a new law radically expanding the freedoms of the press from government intrusion.[63]

The government did not seem as concerned about the cynical and politically oppositionist, but altogether playful, urbane audiences at the artistic cabarets, as it was about the rough mix of lower *"couches sociales"* at the *cafés-concerts*. This attitude seems to have been justified, since the politicizing of song at the artistic cabarets, unlike previously at the *goguettes,* was unconnected with any militant activity in the political arenas and certainly not with any bravura at the barricades. In effect, the artistic cabarets "aestheticized" the discourse of political resistance, by confining it safely to the rituals of modernist middle-brow entertainment. As agents of change, the Chat Noir and its imitators were more crucially involved in the mediation between modernist high culture and the new forms of mass culture, than in any resurgence of political radicalism. Put otherwise, the political mythology of the *goguettes* functioned only as mythical packaging for that grand synthesis of bohemian café, poetry club, and *café-concert,* which was effected by the artistic cabaret.

Transition

The alliance between popular music and modernist practice, brought about by the artistic cabaret, was thus no easy or simple matter, by no means the direct coming together of binary opposites inexplicably attracted to each other. It required decades of cultural work and preparation, depended on the vagaries of institutional changes in both the art and entertainment fields, and was made possible by sudden shifts in the migratory patterns of the art world. Popular song had to put on a new face in order to be so emplaced and had to take on a variety of functions, of which the provision of publicity and the drawing of new crowds were only the most obvious.

The next chapter, opening with the Chat Noir's move to new quarters, traces the ultimate triumph and spread of the artistic cabaret in Montmartre followed by its sudden demise. Did this mean the abandonment of this unique experiment in merging high and low through popular song? What, if anything, filled the vacuum left behind by the artistic cabaret? After a discussion of the resulting Paris scenes of art and entertainment—the garish music halls of Montmartre, the vituperative *cénacles* of the Latin Quarter, and the fashionable new bohemian cafés of Montparnasse—I will turn to the rebirth of the artistic cabaret with a somewhat different agenda in modernist centers outside of France, such as Barcelona and Frankfurt. I will conclude with the final and fleeting outburst at the Cabaret Voltaire in Zurich, where the artistic cabaret reached its cultural apogee as an aesthetic practice of modernism, before finally receding to the ranks of the dimly nostalgic.

CHAPTER 3
THE BLACK CAT GOES TO THE CABARET VOLTAIRE

The Second Chat Noir (1885–89)

In one of his most theatrical acts of *fumisterie,* Rodolphe Salis, at the stroke of midnight on a June evening in 1885, led a long procession full of pageantry from the original quarters of the Chat Noir to its new resplendent and spacious location, just a few blocks away.[1] This change of scene ushered in the grand but short-lived triumphal era of the artistic cabaret, as venues following the lead of the Chat Noir multiplied along the boulevards of Montmartre and monopolized its nightlife. The Chat Noir's more spacious and sumptuous quarters made possible the accommodation of a new and even larger public, mainly bourgeois and touristic, which complemented but did not supplant the originally select audience of artists and their bohemian hangers-on. There was inevitably an increase in the variety and the scale of the programs, and indeed an overall change in the tenor and nature of these entertainments, made possible by the greater number of rooms in the Chat Noir's new three-story structure.

The most palpable manifestation of this change was the gradual displacement of the older minimalist programs of alternating poets and singer-songwriters by the extravaganzas of the shadow plays that became the rage of Paris. Introduced merely as a novelty for one evening by the painter Henri Rivière, the shadow play, involving the use of intense light from behind a screen to project the shadows of cutout figurines, drew such an enthusiastic response that it soon became nightly fare in the Chat Noir's largest and most sumptuous entertainment room. Prodded by Salis's constant encouragement and financing, Rivière gradually replaced the typically primitive production materials of shadow plays suitable for home entertainment into an elaborate and dazzling technological apparatus. Audiences thrilled at such novel special effects as the introduction of color and three-dimensional perspective to the meticulously choreographed play of forms on the screen, made possible by an intricate multitracking system in the wings.[2]

The shadow theater made ample use of the talents of the Chat Noir's artists-in-residence, who produced the scripts, sang, declaimed, composed the music, painted the scenes, sculpted the figurines, designed the stage, and provided the decor for the room. Salis did not hesitate to go outside the Chat Noir when the desire for extravaganza required it, hiring machinists, art singers, choral boys from the opera, and professional organists. In effect if not in intention, the shadow play was the Chat Noir's answer to the call for the *Gesamtkunstwerk* (the complete artwork) that was then in fashion.[3] The well-positioned theater journalist Jules Lemaître, in a "dithyrambic" review of the shadow plays, introduced a still largely unsuspecting Paris to the very notion of the artistic cabaret and its new brands of entertainments. At his summons, a whole new crowd came to experience the thrill of shocking encounters with a deviant art world that previously had for them only been a dim fantasy but that—they were assured by Lemaître—was a "tranquil bohemia and properly dressed," though "a bit neurotic."[4] The fact that the most mainstream, or even retrograde, conventional celebrities of all sorts were in attendance—financiers, politicians of all stripes (including the notorious General Boulanger), academicians, and various foreign emperors and kings—was a clear sign that even the traditional social elites were becoming increasingly receptive to the shocks of modernist confrontation. With the emergence of the shadow plays and their new public, "the Chat Noir ceased being a *cénacle* and became a worldly theater (*un théâtre mondain*)."[5]

The new kinds of entertainment did soften the blow somewhat for the new consumers. At the first Chat Noir, the song-and-poetry shows, peppered by Salis's confrontations with the audience, had constituted a kind of bipolar middlebrowism, in which the popular and modern art elements stood out in marked contrast with each other. With the shadow plays, the second Chat Noir presented a more blended and homogeneous middlebrowism, in which the high and the low were sutured into such an evenly textured whole that they were no longer recognizable as separate and somewhat discordant elements. The result was a third species of aesthetic production clearly delineated from the low and the high, and located solidly in between—tasteful, witty, sometimes "deep," easy and accessible, conspicuously technological and in its own way utterly modern.

The shadow play's "popular" character derived principally from its genealogical roots in the traditional novelty entertainments of pantomime, marionettes, prestidigitation, and dioramas. The "artiness" of the shadow plays stemmed from the known fact that they were produced by the Chat Noir's in-house artists and occasionally inspired by texts with "literary" value (e.g., a popular Flaubert novel). But none of these modernists' primary work appeared in these productions. The shadow play's modernist character came almost exclusively from its performative inscription in the modernist world, rather than from any explicitly shared aesthetic experiments with the primary works. For their part, the *chansons à Montmartre,* softened in content and slicked up in form, were integrated in the *Gesamtkunstwerk* of the shadow play as *entre-actes* or sound tracks.[6] The old crowd could still find the original fare of song and poetry in a smaller room, which was easily circumvented by the tourists and the celebrities. For all that, the shadow plays were nonetheless no less authentic as secondary practices than the more conspicuously adventurous and jagged performances that had preceded them, in no small part because they greatly widened and diversified the supportive public for whom modernism was increasingly becoming an object of desire, bringing in especially the well-heeled, who were willing to buy as well as observe.

Other features of the aesthetics of the new Chat Noir reflected this turn to the homogeneously blended middlebrow. Erik Satie, a house pianist at the Chat Noir, developed a new kind of sophisticated cabaret music for this establishment but did not perform there the *Trois gymnopédies* or any of the other innovative art music that he was composing at the time.[7] The house artists were being asked less to provide paintings than to produce functional decors for facades, signs, and windows, mostly representations of black cats and glorifications of the cabaret. In general, the modernist paintings on the walls of the second Chat Noir, other than the large and legendary *Parce domine,* were lost in a busy array of bric-a-brac, pseudocollector's items, emblems, and ornamental self-advertisements.[8]

The mainstreaming of the Chat Noir reached its apogee in the 1890s with its highly successful tour of the provinces, followed by later incursions into the outposts of Francophone culture in Belgium, Switzerland, Tunisia, and Algeria. But mainstreaming, and thus loss of fashion status for consumers on the cutting edge, was quickly followed by decline. No longer able to pay its rent, the Chat Noir went out of business in 1897, replaced by a soap boutique.

Cabaret Spreads (1884–90)

Predictably, in the wake of the Chat Noir's newfound status as favorite nightspot for trendsetters, a whole spate of venues claiming to be *cabarets artistiques* appeared on the boulevards and side streets along the southwestern slope of Montmartre. The most renowned and prosperous of these was the Mirliton (the Reed Pipe, but also translatable as the Doggerel), which was founded in 1885 at the abandoned site of the first Chat Noir by its former star

Aristide Bruant. Operating on a minimalist scale, with himself as the only star attraction, he drew audiences as much for the stylized abuse he heaped on them as for his singing. According to myth, on opening night Bruant launched into a torrent of insults and provocations against the dismally small crowd that greeted him, which, to his surprise, was more titillated than offended. From then on, as his audiences grew larger and hungrier for abuse, he perfected a particular style of colloquial proletarian invective, which he turned into a self-conscious performance complementing the self-conscious street argot of his songs. Thus, the practice of verbal provocations against audiences, initiated by Salis at the Chat Noir simply as a form of *fumisterie* to compensate for a lack of conventional performance skills, was transformed by Bruant into a formalized aesthetic practice that later would prove to be a powerful instrument of disruption and shock in the hands of the futurists, dadaists, and other confrontative avant-gardes. Bruant's song-and-invective spectacles achieved such notoriety that one of the most elegant and fashionable *cafés-concerts* of Paris, Les Ambassadeurs, reconstructed a set of the Mirliton on its stage, from which Bruant gave samplings of his performance style. This revue, stage set and all, later went on a triumphant tour of the provinces.[9]

By the end of the century, close to forty *cabarets artistiques* had appeared (and disappeared) in Montmartre. Each attempted to thematize its uniqueness through a mix of performance gimmicks and decorative motifs. The Abbaye de Thélème, with its high Gothic interiors, presented itself as a Rabelaisian *cénacle*. At the Auberge du Clou (Inn of the Nail), waiters dressed as country folk sauntered along walls studded with wooden coat-hooks and covered by naive-looking paintings depicting traditional scenes. There were the inevitable *chinoiseries* at the Divan Japonais: bamboo chopsticks glued on a red-and-white pool table, small bells dangling from red lights, and large silk panels on the walls. Perhaps the most dramatically thematized of these venues was the Taverne du Bagne (the Penal Colony Tavern), decorated as a prison housing former members of the Commune—the owner having been one of the many imprisoned Communards. Customers, gaining entrance at the command to "let another bunch of convicts in," were served in a mock-up prison refectory by waiters dressed as convicts with ball-and-chain attached to their feet and could only exit upon presenting a "certificate of liberation," which attested to the good conduct of the "released convict."[10]

Each of the Montmartrian artistic cabarets would accentuate only certain aspects of "cabaretness" at the expense of others. The Mirliton stressed performance over decor, whereas Le Tambourin (The Castanet) underscored its role as a gallery space for its artistic clientele, including special shows organized by Vincent van Gogh. Some, but only a minority, took on the serious and wearying task of producing a journal. The Taverne du Bagne specialized in song and invective suitable for the rigors of prison; the Auberge du Clou, in elaborate shadow plays on traditional themes (e.g., the star of Christmas); and the Abbaye de Thélème, in poetry readings conforming to the spirit of Rabelais. The Divan Japonais resorted to a more aestheticized version of *café-concert* entertainment in the person of Yvette Guilbert, who went on to become the most renowned popular singer in fin de siècle France. In general, though the *chanson à Montmartre* appeared on virtually all the programs of venues calling themselves "*cabarets artistiques*," it varied considerably in its importance, dominating some programs while only marginal in others.

Ultimately, the system of the artistic cabaret was much less resilient or stable than the number of venues suggests, which is confirmed by the fact that the new cabarets produced very little new talent. They relied mainly on malcontent impresarios, songsters, and artists from the Chat Noir, who left after spats with the parsimonious and authoritarian Salis. Goudeau, indefatigably discontent, founded the competing Cabaret du Chat Botté (Puss-in-Boots), thus not even straying from the by now hackneyed feline themes. By the end of the century, less than twenty years after its inception, the artistic cabaret was a dead form in Paris. The few that survived became hybrid venues steeped in nostalgia, complementing the traditional cabaret fare with stripteases and revues.

The cabaret could hardly survive the rigors of fashion change, at that time especially rapid, and a concomitantly very fickle public. But also, precariously positioned between the worlds of high and mass culture, it ended up not being able to satisfy either. In Montmartre, cabaret was quickly overwhelmed by the Moulin Rouge and the new music hall phenomenon, unable to compete with their opulence and derring-do. Meanwhile, it failed to spread from Montmartre into the more purist bohemia of the Latin Quarter, where it was deemed too slick and inauthentic to give expression to the "revolutionary" poetry schools, which resorted to their own brand of secondary practices and promotional ploys.

The Moulin Rouge (1889–1905)

The Moulin Rouge opened in 1889 in Montmartre just when the artistic cabaret was at the height of its popularity. The original owner—an investor in such ultra-modern urban enterprises as a racecourse, a roller coaster, and a combination circus/nightclub—had conceived the Moulin Rouge as a means of exploiting the international tourist market engendered by the Universal Exposition. In order to overcome the language barrier, he devised a program that highlighted dance over song. He transformed the *quadrille naturaliste,* an energetic working-class dance form associated with the dance halls of Montmartre, into an aggressive and sexually charged spectacle under the new name of "French cancan." The cancan quickly became the trademark of the nightlife of Montmartre, now an international center of tourism.[11]

There was little place for the decidedly French and comparatively modest artistic cabaret in this glossy new system. Indeed, a number of artists were lured by the commercial opportunities opening up at the Moulin Rouge. Willette, the former house artist and decorator at the Chat Noir, designed the Moulin Rouge dance hall, the outside café, and the mock-up windmill with movable sails on the roof. Toulouse-Lautrec left the Mirliton to produce his acclaimed Moulin Rouge posters celebrating the stars of the cancan. In 1893 the students of the École des Beaux-Arts shifted the scene of their annual costume ball, the Bal des Quatr'z'Arts (the Four Arts' Ball), to the Moulin Rouge. The appearance of a nude Cleopatra borne on a canopy at that year's ball elicited a heated protest by a local society for the protection of decency, leading to legal prosecution and minor fines. It was ultimately a victory for the accused, since the annual Bal des Quatr'z'Arts, now quite renowned as a consequence of this publicity, would continue its annual titillating provocations at the Moulin Rouge with little further legal harassment.[12]

The Moulin Rouge would, however, sever its somewhat tenuous connections with the art world by the turn of the century when it changed its identity from populist dance hall to resplendent music hall. Because the prohibition against skits, costumes, and sets outside of the state-supported theaters was not rescinded until 1867, the music hall system (what we call "vaudeville") appeared much later on the French scene than it did in England and the United States. It was within this vacuum that institutions unique to France, like the *café-concert* and the *cabaret artistique,* were able to thrive. Conversely, once music hall with its multifarious performance practices took hold, it was inevitable that these older institutions, much less colorful and eclectic, would be pushed aside.[13]

Music hall, as a set of entertainment practices, grew out of the "review" traditionally performed in popular theaters, which in its early incarnations was a loosely connected series of short sketches satirically "reviewing" the political, cultural, and social events of a given season. In the music hall, the review was totally recast as a sequence of visual spectacles, brimming over with special effects and highlighting "movement, color, flesh," thus reducing to a minimum the elements of verbal play and satire. The *chanson,* having lost its central place, gave way musically to the constant gyrations of the orchestra cuing changes of scene and underscoring body movement. The imagery of desire and fantasy was accentuated by the appropriation of "*les girls*" from American burlesque and the presentation of sumptuous and elaborate sets whose visual power often dwarfed the performative impact of the singers, dancers, jugglers, comedians, and animal acts. There was a certain generic and eclectic international flavor to the musical hall review, which was packaged initially as English-style entertainment and which introduced a succession of dance crazes from abroad, such as the cakewalk and the tango.[14]

In 1903 the ownership of the Moulin Rouge, under the pressure of these powerful new trends, aggressively remodeled and reformatted the club, transforming it from fading dance hall into the most grandiose and extravagant music hall of Paris. A critic called it "a calm luxurious modernity" and "the handsomest place of entertainment in the world." He predicted that the Moulin Rouge's first review would "eclipse all the others by its dazzling scenery," which included "castle walls at Elsinore" and "a huge staircase" with "no fewer than 92 steps," and "one hundred women dressed in sumptuous costumes and adornments."[15] In the midst of this fanfare and excess, the art world was decisively pushed aside as former equal partner in Montmartre's entertainment industry. In the music hall system, artists (e.g., Toulouse-Lautrec, Seurat) were reduced to being nothing other than voyeuristic consumers scavenging for new aesthetic devices.

The Politics of Poetics in the Latin Quarter (1881–89)

The artistic cabaret might have survived the onslaught of music hall had it succeeded also in implanting itself in the Latin Quarter, whose entrenched and truculent bohemia was altogether inhospitable to the incursions of music hall. There had been initially a sustained though uneasy alliance between Left Bank and Right Bank bohemias during the first few years of the artistic cabaret, nurtured by a constant trafficking to and fro. Few Latin Quarter poets could resist the temptation, at least occasionally, to spotlight their declamatory abilities before the larger audiences of the Chat Noir. But these interchanges, waning with time, were not sufficiently strong to support cabaret's emigration across the Seine. It was not the crotchety purism of the Latin Quarter's older bohemia, suspicious of any sign of accommodation with the bourgeoisie, that constituted the main obstacle. Rather, the publicity needs of the new generation of Latin Quarter poets were sufficiently different to require quite distinctive institutional arrangements and types of secondary practices, where poetry and its subtleties would not have to take second billing to popular song. For the Latin Quarter in the 1880s was brimming with talk of poetic revolution and engrossed in its own convoluted sectarian warfare, which was more easily acted out ultimately in the exuberant proliferation of little magazines, after repeated attempts to resurrect the poetry club.

In August 1881 a small coterie mainly of former Hydropaths started a new poetry club called the Hirsutes (the Hairy Ones), which hoed religiously and unspectacularly to the script of its renowned predecessor. The only excitement punctuating the bland and predictable replays of poetry club agendas came from the various leadership crises—a coup d'état against the authoritarian president, followed by the dramatic reappearance of Goudeau as Napoleonic savior. After a few months of firm and successful leadership, Goudeau, increasingly distracted by the lures of Montmartre and bored by the earnest and ingrown literary careerism of the Latin Quarter, finally abandoned the Hirsutes to a certain demise.[16]

The death of the Hirsutes was solemnly announced in the *Lutèce,* the first of a spate of proliferating small poetry journals in the Latin Quarter, which followed up in succeeding issues with a series of nostalgic articles on their rise and fall.[17] Rather than bringing a chapter to a close, the effect of these commemorative pieces was to stimulate further attempts at forming poetry clubs. Responding to this implied call, the Zutistes (from "*zut!*," an expression of provocation) appeared on the scene on the edges of Montparnasse to form a poetry club that fancied itself a Left Bank permutation of the new Chat Noir. "In the distant country of Montparnasse," declared the president, "a rhythmic movement will be established corresponding to the purrings of the Chat Noir . . . [Mont]Martre and [Mont]Parnasse are brothers."[18] This fantasized sibling relationship apparently was of little help to the Zutistes, who disappeared after only five months of checkered activity.[19]

After dutifully producing an obituary for the Zutistes,[20] the *Lutèce* decided to take matters into its own hands and to form its own club, the Jemenfoutistes (the I-Don't-Give-a-Fuck-ists), to whose meetings it dedicated an enthusiastic weekly column, beginning in January 1884. The Jemenfoutistes followed the by now tedious narrative of its predecessors, while the *Lutèce* did its best to trumpet up the stereotypical literary disputes that filled up the meetings.[21] Within a month the already flagging and desperate Jemenfoutistes resorted to a dramatic return to origins by renaming themselves the Hydropaths and bringing back the peripatetic Goudeau as president, by now disillusioned with Montmartre and the Chat Noir. Goudeau's implied rebuke of the experiment that transformed poetry club into artistic cabaret signaled the beginning of a schism between the musical and painterly worlds of Montmartre and the poetic avant-gardist world of the Latin Quarter.[22] Goudeau would berate the new Hydropathic audiences, in a none-too-subtle dig at the Chat Noir, for expecting a *"spectacle"* in the manner of a *"café-concert."* He insisted that there should be no preordained, rehearsed program, but that "everyone who wants to should simply step up to the stage."[23] Despite all the mystique generated by this return to origins, the reincarnated Club des Hydropathes faded away within two months, without even the benefit of a *Lutèce* obituary, ending for good the increasingly anemic attempts to revive the Hydropathic tradition.[24]

Meanwhile, the *Lutèce,* easily surviving the demise of its dysfunctional protégé, went on to initiate the heroic era of little poetry journals that would now occupy center stage in the secondary aesthetic practices of the Latin Quarter. These journals appeared as artifacts of a swelling public interest in, and outrage over, the young poets and their schools. The momentum for this remarkable turn of events was set off by the publication of Paul Verlaine's landmark "L'Art poétique" (1882), which set off a flurry of debates among critics. The *Lutèce* quickly became the site for the most vociferous *cénacle* of Verlaine disciples. In a deft promotional move, it published a Verlaine monograph enticingly called *Les Poètes maudits* (The Accursed Poets), which, by championing the barely known poetry of Mallarmé and Rimbaud, helped transform a personal cult into a movement. This stirring of the waters was only a preparation for the storms generated by J.-K. Huysmans's novel *À rebours* in the same year, which put the term "decadence" in wide circulation as an all-purpose designation of the new schools of poetry.

It did not take long for young poets and literary entrepreneurs who circled around Verlaine, Mallarmé, and Huysmans to seize the opportunity to promote their careers and poetic ideologies by further stoking up the fires of controversy. What followed were not only attacks against conventional poetic culture directly, thus provoking the mainstream critics into action, but also warfare among the young poets themselves, which further enticed the mainstream critics into endless curiosity. Jean Moréas fired the first shot with his "Symbolist Manifesto" (1886), which appeared upon invitation in the conservative and highly influential newspaper *Le Figaro.* While flaunting itself against all that was passé, this piece, by counterpoising "symbolism" to "decadentism," precipitated the first sectarian division within the ranks of the young modernists.[25] With his literary manifesto, Moréas introduced a new genre of secondary aesthetic practice that was to become a fashionably effective device of self-advertisement for the various poetic movements and sects. Over the next two decades, there would be manifestos on decadentism, romanism, naturism, humanism, unanimism, paving the way for the later celebrated manifestos of futurism, dadaism, and surrealism. Moréas founded the journal *Le Symboliste* a month after his manifesto, only to be immediately contested by the "decadents" and "instrumentists," who each produced their own journals. Thus began the proliferation of little journals, many of which did not last a year, and of the "isms" that they championed (*vers-librisme, paroxysme, ésotérisme, synthétisme, integralisme,* in addition to the other "isms" mentioned above). The symbolist and decadence movements alone generated or stimulated fifty-five journals during the last two decades of the nineteenth century, twenty-three during the key years 1884–90, and seven in 1886 alone, the year of the symbolist revolt. This created endless copy and consternation for the mainstream critics attempting to negotiate these theoretical mazes.[26]

By 1889 the excesses of factionalism began to subside as the new poetry was conquering the mainstream press. Though making few converts in established culture, the new schools were at least securing a place in the literary canon, if only because of the established critics' incessant efforts to classify and dissect them and to define their relation with the tradition. At this time a new and very affordable "little" magazine, *La Plume,* was founded with the express purpose of overcoming sectarian differences among poets and the ghettoization of poetry from the other arts, as well as lightening up the morbidly serious discourses of its predecessor publications. In the fall of 1889, the editors of *La Plume* instituted the weekly *Soirées de la Plume* in the basement of the Café du Soleil d'Or, the legendary meeting place of the Hirsutes, the Jemenfoutistes, and the Hydropathes in both reincarnations.[27] With a set program of song and poetry that included *chansonniers* from Montmartre, and an ambience of "fraternal" bonhomie, the *soirées* were the closest thing to an artistic cabaret to have appeared in the Latin Quarter. Nonetheless the Right Bank–Left Bank differences were insistently maintained. The *soirées* were the appendage of a poetry journal (not the other way around as in Montmartre) and took place in a bohemian café rather than full-time cabaret.

The *soirées* were constructed as an aesthetically more legitimate alternative to the Chat Noir, where, complained Ernest Raynaud, "art quickly turns into puffery and parody. One goes to Salis's place [like] one goes to a zoo, in the hope of encountering some strange animal. One senses behind the overt display of art and artists the hidden preoccupation with trade and lucre." Any poet desiring to recite at the Chat Noir needed a "strong stomach" and a "thoroughgoing careerist temperament" to be able to tolerate "the insolence of lorgnettes and monocles," and to seek the plaudits of "amateur snobs" and "idle socialites" in a "music hall atmosphere," where the "poet has to give way to the ham-actor." In contrast, at the *Soirées de la Plume*, one is "decidedly at home [*chez soi*]," seeing in all corners "familiar faces" who are there "for the sole purpose of taking in lines of poetry." Though *La Plume* "even welcomed song, knowing that in France only song makes things sacred," it was clear that poetry was the reason for the *soirées'* existence. Song appeared only at the beginning and the end, first to quiet the crowd and then to send it rousingly on its way.[28] The *soirées* equally left behind the *fumisteries* and the *frissons* of the Hydropaths and the other poetry clubs of the earlier part of the decade.

In conclusion, Montmartre and the Latin Quarter, despite their proclaimed alliances and lively intertextualities, constituted in the 1880s two quite distinct domains of bohemia, codified in two distinct congeries of secondary aesthetic practices. Popular song, and indeed the whole sphere of the popular, explicitly played only a small role in the Latin Quarter's secondary practices, which took the form most dramatically of manifestos, sectarian journals, and other projects of writerly provocation. Unlike the secondary practices of Montmartrian cabarets, which appeared as syntheses of high art and popular entertainment, those emanating from Latin Quarter poetry circles seemed primarily to operate only at the level of high art. But this opposition is misleading, for these high-art provocations and controversies were inevitably entertaining, as secondary practices are wont to be, and, though less transparent, were not essentially different from the more flagrant publicity stunts and promotional gimmicks devised at the Chat Noir. With the advent of the *Soirées de la Plume*, when tempers had subsided and modern poetry was securely entrenching itself, secondary aesthetic activity took on the allure of calm celebratory performances fashionably showcasing the young stars in an atmosphere of unruffled entertainment.

From Montmartre to Montparnasse (1900–15)

The lively opposition between a Right Bank and Left Bank bohemia, and the discursive imagery used to embellish it, did not last long after the demise of the artistic cabarets. Montmartre, overwhelmed by tourism and garish entertainment, rapidly lost its cachet in the modernist art world, while the newly urbanized Montparnasse on the Left Bank became the new center of Parisian modernist life in the first decades of the twentieth century. This was accompanied by the triumphant reemergence of the bohemian café and the dominance again of unscripted, informal secondary practices—modernist bohemians on display—at the expense of the formalized, scripted fare of cabarets and poetry clubs.

By 1900 the spread of the new music hall entertainment industry along the boulevards of Montmartre, with the consequent infusion of tourists and rise in rents, was forcing a new generation of artists and writers to migrate up to the hill of Montmartre ("*la Butte*"), where workers, anarchists, and petty criminals lived in an uneasy coexistence in ramshackle residences interspersed with seedy bars and cafés. This transitional period in the demographic and geographical history of the Parisian art world has achieved legendary status, still feverishly promoted by the Montmartrian chamber of commerce, because of the now-famous artists and writers who lived on *la Butte* during this period or frequented its nightspots: most importantly Picasso, living in the Bateau Lavoir, along with Juan Gris, van Dongen, and André Salmon; but also Modigliani, Braque, Dufy, Utrillo, and such visitors from the Latin Quarter as Apollinaire and Max Jacob. Tourists still pack the Cabaret du Lapin Agile at the top of the Montmartre *Butte,* for its nightly shows of nineteenth-century popular song and liberal doses of nostalgia for the days when Picasso and his "gang" were in regular attendance. But the Lapin Agile was hardly the full artistic cabaret that these reconstructions make it out to be. It was rather a very downscale mix of bohemian café, cabaret, local bar, and diner, more an expression of the deterioration of the artistic cabaret movement than its apogee. The Lapin Agile did, however, have a firm pedigree in the artistic cabaret system. It was founded in the 1880s, under the name of Cabaret des Assassins, by André Gill, the legendary humorist-*fumiste* who had been a major player in the Hydropathes and the Chat Noir scenes. The next owner, seeking to parlay this reputation, renamed the cabaret the Lapin à Gill (Gill's Rabbit), in reference to Gill's rabbit painting still on the marquee. Later, with the phonetics intact, the name was changed to the Lapin Agile (the Agile Rabbit).

After years of desultory existence and questionable clienteles, it again became a meeting place for artists when purchased in 1903 by Aristide Bruant, now a wealthy former cabaret star turned businessman, who then hired as manager Frédéric Gérard (Frédé), a former bar owner and fishmonger and a friend of Picasso. Picasso and others (e.g., Utrillo, Valadon) did donate some paintings, but primarily to help Frédé in his feeble attempts at decoration and not to promote art. Virtually all the formal entertainment was provided by Frédé, singing the standard fare of bars, sometimes followed by students from the Latin Quarter "braying" their "inept songs." Occasionally a desperate poet would be allowed to recite and pass the hat, but the promising writers in attendance (Apollinaire, Jacob) thought it beneath themselves to read their work before this motley crowd of "marginal" types and drunken students. Picasso himself showed up primarily for the warm atmosphere and the cheap fare, and not for art or entertainment.[29] The Lapin Agile was at best only a pale imitation of the artistic cabarets that had preceded it and that on occasion it tried clumsily to evoke.

Picasso left the Lapin Agile after three years (1905–7) as a regular, just as he was beginning to accumulate followers and admirers and his income was beginning to rise. He abandoned the desultory conditions of the Bateau Lavoir for a spacious apartment down the hill on a Montmartrian boulevard, where he attended the Medrano circus and the cinema. But this itself proved to be only an intermediate step on his way to the more affluent confines of Montparnasse. While an habitué at the Lapin Agile, Picasso had begun taking the long excursion to Montparnasse for the weekly poetry readings at the Closerie des Lilas, the first of the great coffeehouses in that district, and for Gertrude Stein's weekend dinners.[30] By the turn of the decade, he had moved to a resplendent sunny apartment near the Montparnasse Cemetery, as part of a major art world migration from *la Butte.*

Montparnasse was becoming the major magnet attracting the populations of the art and literary worlds, with its new boulevards, its recent and well-crafted housing stocks, its especially designed studios for artists, and its attractive new bohemian cafés.[31] This demographic shift to Montparnasse co-incided with the increasing commercial and public successes for the modernist art world—the dramatic impact of the fauves at the Salon d'Automne, of course, but also the emergence of enterprising art dealers altogether committed to modernist art (e.g., D. H. Kahnweiler). By World War I Picasso, van Dongen, Matisse, and Braque, among others, were on the verge of achieving a level of affluence unheard of in modernist circles.

The new bohemian cafés of Montparnasse, particularly the Dôme and the Rotonde on the corner of the new boulevard Raspail and the boulevard Montparnasse, were considerably more upscale than their forebears of the 1840s and 1850s. They became the showcases of triumphant modernism, lionized by eccentric intellectuals and adventurous aristocrats, and functioning as refuges for artists from Eastern Europe and havens of exile for alienated American writers.

These cafés firmly displaced the artistic cabarets, which had done their job of helping to generate a new public for modernism but were apparently no longer needed in an era when modernism had found a niche in Parisian life as cultural laboratory, touristic wonder, commodity for the well-heeled, and source of endless surprises and shocks. The Rotonde or the Dôme cafés did not need organized entertainment to draw crowds or to acquire mythic significa-tion. The mere presence of Picasso and the notorious cubists achieved that objective quite well. In that sense, the new bohemian cafés, like their forebears, though not conceived as places of entertainment, unwittingly turned into popular spectacle.

Cabaret Outside of France (1897–1916)

Just as cabaret died in Paris, it spread to other European outposts of modernism—no surprise, given Paris's special status as center of art world fashion. The first such venture was the Quatre Gats (Four Cats) of Barcelona, a showcase for the Catalonian turn-of-the-century renaissance, which appeared in the year that the Chat Noir went out of existence (1897) and was clearly modeled on it. It exhibited many of the usual marks of the artistic cabaret but is now best remembered for having a then unknown Picasso as one of its habitués. It suffered the usual short life, going out of existence in 1903.[32] At the turn of the century, the artistic cabaret was migrating eastward, first to Munich and Berlin, respectively at the Elf Scharfrichter (Eleven Executioners) and the Schall und Rauch (Sound and Smoke), and then to Vienna's Fledermauss (Bat), Kraców's Zielony Balonik (Green Balloon), and Moscow's Letuchaya Mysh (the Bat). Though it would soon fade away elsewhere, the artistic cabaret remained active in German cultural life well into the 1920s, in part because it successfully transformed itself to address specific problems facing German modernism not present to the same degree in France. This is clearly evident in the formation of the Elf Scharfrichter, the most impactful and mythologized of the founding artistic cabarets of Germany.[33]

The Elf Scharfrichter drew its lineage from the Chat Noir. One of its organizers was a displaced Frenchman[34] who had professedly partaken in Chat Noir productions as *chansonnier* and *conférencier* and who now avowedly sought to integrate French cabaret innovations into German theatrical life. In addition, the recent vogue for *"deutsches Chansons"*—German modernist poetry put into song, in obvious imitation of French practices—emerged just in time to acquire a central place in the Elf Scharfrichter programs.[35] This musical middlebrowism from above was complemented, as it had been at the Chat Noir, with a middlebrowism from below, namely, the inflection of popular song with the devices of art. Only in this case the materials and inspirations came not from the *café-concert,* a pure idiosyncrasy of France, but from vaudeville and music hall, which by the turn of the century were fully developed in Germany. The song format at the Elf Scharfrichter was designed to provide a suitable populist alternative to the "dullness" and "exaggerated tasteless sentimentality of music-hall."[36]

But in a striking departure from the Chat Noir, the founders of the Elf Scharfrichter aimed to turn cabaret into a laboratory for "serious" theatrical experimentation rather than letting it merely function as a promotional sideshow for modernist practices taking place elsewhere, in part because there was no "elsewhere." At the turn of the century, theatrical innovators like Frank Wedekind could find no venues for their work in the normal outlets, in the face of the stuffy conservatism of official German culture and the viciously restrictive censorship system, which found "indecency" in virtually anything that was aesthetically avant-garde. As a "private club," the Elf Scharfrichter was able to parry, and even to contest, the worst onslaughts of the censorship system, while an ultra-modern stage and receptive audiences provided its playwrights and performers with congenial opportunities for honing their innovative skills. In response to the specificities of cabaret, these theatrical experimenters tended to produce playlets rather than full-length plays, to indulge in satire, parody, and provocations against the censorship system, and in general to incorporate the energy and physicality of music hall. With the constant threat of confrontation with the censors, there were sufficient *frissons* without having to make use of the lighthearted and apolitical *fumisteries* of the Parisian artistic cabaret, whose shock effects would have paled in comparison.[37]

But these practices at the cutting edge, however thrilling for their political audacity, were only the opening acts for the star attraction of the Elf Scharfrichter, the singer Marya Delvard, whose saturated displays of angst and world-weariness made her seem to rise above the banality of music hall. According to reports, she appeared onstage "as if arisen from a coffin" and so "frightfully pale" that "one thought involuntarily of sin, vampirically parasitic cruelty, and death." "She sang everything with a languid monotony which she only occasionally interrupted with a wild outcry of greedy passion."[38] Delvard in effect created a new performative role, the highly refined but jaded, and sometimes emaciated, cabaret "*diseuse*" who typically represented popular culture in bohemian theatrical settings alongside men who represented avant-garde art—a role later acquired by Emmy Hennings at the Cabaret Voltaire and Lotte Lenya in *Threepenny Opera* and *Mahagonny*. Originally marginalized or outrightly excluded in the secondary aesthetic practices of the bohemian world (e.g., at the Club des Hydropathes and the Chat Noir), women initially gained entry primarily at the "popular" end of the high/low linkages. Later Marlene Dietrich turned the Delvard look and routine into a legendary cabaret act, which became a paradigm of "Germanness" at a time when cabaret, having exhausted its avant-garde functions, was no longer anything but cabaret.

The Elf Scharfrichter went out of existence in 1903, two years after its inception, partly out of production exhaustion and the erosive harassment of the censors, but also because the modernists, like Wedekind, were "fed up to the teeth with ballad singing," which they considered "playing the fool and groveling in the dirt." They "longed" to return "to the path of weighty, serious dramatic art." It was admitted that cabaret had proved to be "a very valuable intermediate step" for young artists negotiating their way from the "poverty of the cultural proletarians" to the havens of "recognized literature."[39] But by redefining the function of the artistic cabaret, by "upgrading" it and making it their only locus for avant-garde experiments, albeit only temporarily and out of necessity, the founders of the Elf Scharfrichter created a new kind of apparatus that would be exploited and further modified by later avant-gardes. The Elf Scharfrichter was the intermediate step connecting the Chat Noir to the Cabaret Voltaire.

Cabaret in Zurich (1916)

In 1913 the underemployed dramaturge Hugo Ball met the "*diseuse*" Emmy Hennings at the Simplizissimus cabaret in Munich, where she sang on a program faintly and modestly reminiscent of the Elf Scharfrichter. There they initiated a personal and professional partnership, uniting high and low, that was to last a lifetime. Ball's absorbed studies of Nietzsche had led him to a total preoccupation with theater as instrument of redemption.[40] Hennings had already garnered a reputation, as singer and actress, for an "electrifying" stage presence that drew raves in nightclubs all over Eastern Europe. In the (obviously male) press, she was lauded for her erotic "infinities," qualities intensified rather than diminished by her "many yeared and ravaged" look "hypnotiz[ed] by morphine," and a voice that "hops across the corpses" and "mock[s] them." It was asked: "Who can prevent this girl that possesses hysteria, that incendiary quality, the brain-tearing intensity of the literati, from swelling to an avalanche?"[41]

At the start of World War I, Ball and Hennings fled almost penniless from Germany to Zurich, where Hennings immediately took up singing in cabarets, while Ball to his chagrin could only find work as a pianist for a vaudeville troupe. Here, in a world that must have provided the most distressing contrast to his previous, culturally upscale theatrical experiences, Ball acquired a number of skills that were to prove invaluable at the Cabaret Voltaire, such as "working" an audience, training performers for constantly changing parts and songs, molding "banal activitie[s] into theater piece[s]," as well as maintaining a constantly high level of enthusiasm and energy.[42] He sampled the cultural lowlife of Zurich—a "fat negress" from Singapore "with arms like loaves of bread" sitting and "shivering" in a bar, and the tattooed lady who displayed her body art to the melodies of her husband's zither.[43]

Finally, seeking a financially rational alternative to these coarse cultural activities that would allow him to put his fulminating aesthetic ideas into practice in a city, however, bereft of any vital modernist tradition but teeming with refugee artists and writers, Ball turned to that tried-and-true cultural institution, which in this case seemed to provide the only solution. He placed a notice in a local paper in early February 1916, announcing the formation of the Cabaret Voltaire, "whose aim is to create a center for artistic entertainment," and to which "the young artists of Zurich, whatever their orientation, are invited to come along with suggestions and contributions of all kinds."[44] This rather laconic invitation, as it turned out, was the founding act of the dada movement.

Thus, at a moment when the artistic cabaret seemed on the verge again of lapsing into comatose nostalgia, it was suddenly swept into what is thought to be one of the most radical aesthetic irruptions of this century, thrust into the very center of the avant-garde vortex. It was turned on its head, transformed from a paradigmatically secondary aesthetic site into an unequivocally primary site, and not merely *faute de mieux* as at the Elf Scharfrichter. This means that the formerly secondary cabaret fare—provocations, popularly inflected song, even publicity stunts—were now resituated in the midst of avant-garde work and thus themselves transformed with suitable mutations into primary practices. Not merely a "space" or a "context," the Cabaret Voltaire itself was dada's *Gesamtkunstwerk,* an effective fusion of cutting-edge high culture and vaudeville-style entertainment.

The Cabaret Voltaire opened on February 5, 1916, to a crowd of "painters, students, revolutionaries, tourists, international crooks, psychiatrists, the demi-monde, sculptors, and police spies on the lookout for information," in a room crowded with paintings by Kandinsky, Léger, Matisse, Klee, etchings by Picasso, and futurist posters.[45] The Zurich students, who from then on constituted a major part of the audience, brought "their long pipes with them"—"their way of irritating the bourgeoisie"—and sat "around tables with their feet up on the boards."[46] On that first night, Tristan Tzara, Marcel Janco, and Hans Arp appeared on the scene to join forces with Ball, thus forming the nucleus of what would be the Zurich dada group.[47] Richard Huelsenbeck, the final member, arrived two weeks later.

The fare for the first night displayed the heterogeneity and eclecticism that was to earmark the short life of the Cabaret Voltaire. As Ball remembered it, "Mme Hennings and Mme Leconte sang, in French and Danish. Mr. Tristan Tzara read some of his Rumanian poetry. A balalaika orchestra played popular tunes and Russian dances."[48] In a typical evening in the early days of the Cabaret, audiences would be regaled with poetry readings by Ball or Tzara from the works of Kandinsky, Max Jacob, Blaise Cendrars, and Alfred Jarry, among others; the piano music of Bach, Brahms, Liszt, Rachmaninoff, and Debussy, usually interpreted by Ball; a host of Russian and Serbian folk songs sung by a Russian chorus; popular French songs (e.g., Aristide Bruant's "À la Villette") interpreted by Mlle. Leconte; and, most importantly, Hennings's repertoire of nightclub strains and antiwar songs. There were French, Russian, Swiss, and African soirées, and even an evening taken over by somewhat incompetent "Dutch boys," who with their mandolins, banjos, and "eccentric steps," acted "like perfect fools" and turned "the place topsy-turvy."[49]

Amidst this potpourri of modernist rites and popular entertainments, the dadaists, as they were beginning to call themselves, were slowly introducing the avant-garde innovations that are today canonically associated with them.[50] On March 30 Janco, Huelsenbeck, and Tzara recited the first dadaist simultaneous poem, "L'Amiral cherche une maison à louer," in French, German, and English. On May 24 Janco brought in his masks, which not only "immediately call[ed] for a costume" but also "demanded a quite passionate [dance] gesture, bordering on madness," which the dada group obligingly provided. For his pièce de résistance, Ball staged his first piece of sound poetry on June 30, clad in his now-famous "cubist" cardboard costume, the effect of which was to make him look "like an obelisk."[51] Huelsenbeck had all along been mouthing pseudo-African words in his "negro chants," backed by the banging of his big drum.[52]

But none of these avant-garde extravaganzas could match, for sheer audience drawing power, the popular singing of Emmy Hennings, who the dadaists admitted was their only "professional cabaret performer."[53] According to the local newspaper, Hennings was "the star of the cabaret." Though it found her "no longer as exuberant as a flowering shrub," the review allowed that she still "presents the same bold front and performs the same songs with a body that has since then been only slightly ravaged by grief."[54] Huelsenbeck admitted that it was on her "success or failure as a singer [that] the existence of the cabaret hinged"—an interesting admission given that she was never included by the dadaists as a member of their group.[55] Perhaps it is because the dadaists thought her songs, which "subsist[ed] on refrains and popular music," to be "low" at the "intellectual level," "though not unpleasantly so." But happily for the dadaists, the audience liked listening to Hennings's songs, which "created the 'intimate' atmosphere of the cabaret." "The students rocked in their chairs," and "the landlord stood in the doorway swinging to and fro." And the dadaists had to give her "credit" for singing Ball's "aggressive [antiwar] songs with an anger" that they had "scarcely thought her capable of."[56]

The Cabaret Voltaire quite literally died of exhaustion six months after its inception. But it did leave a legacy of the "slum atmosphere," of "music hall performers," "magicians," and "fire eaters," which never disappeared from the dada performances of the future.[57] It is normal in the literature to extirpate the canonically recognized formal innovations of the Cabaret Voltaire (simultaneous poetry and sound poetry, for example) from the rest of the performances at that venue (the French soirées, Hennings's nightclub performances, Kandinsky's poems, Debussy's music, etc.), and to treat the latter as mere appendages or accidental concomitants to the real and pure dada occurrences. But this reflects more the academization and museumization of dada today than the eclectic way that dada constituted itself in 1916 and the years immediately following. For in 1916 the Cabaret Voltaire was dada. There was no alternative institution or site that could disentangle "pure" dada from its mere accompaniment, the high from the low, the primary from the secondary, nor was any such site desired. The dadaists and their futurist forebears, as is well known, were out to destroy the institutions of high art, not finally to "graduate" to them after years of cultural exile. If they ever made use of traditional art spaces, it was only to commit outrages in them.

This is not to say that the dadaists did not think some practices were more central to their enterprise than others. But at the same time, they clearly resisted any attempt to segregate their formal experiments from their other practices operating more at the level of entertainment and provocation. Thus in the practice of the Cabaret Voltaire, there was an inherent intertextual connection between nightclub song and simultaneous poetry. At the level of reception, the cultural meaning of each was infected by that of the other, and inseparable from the other. Emmy Hennings's jaded song was integrated with the rest of the dada performances, effectively if not always intentionally, in a way in which Marya Delvard's had never been at the Elf Scharfrichter. If there was a difference between the "serious" and the "popular" at the Cabaret Voltaire, the crowd did not know it. What furthered this hierarchical confusion was the element of vaudeville, of slapstick showbiz that informed even the now-canonized "serious" dada performances, such as the wearing of funny costumes when declaiming experimental poetry. As Ball put it, "The ideals of culture and of art as a program for a variety show—that is our kind of *Candide* against the times."[58]

After Cabaret: Dada Vaudeville (1917–23)

The artistic cabaret achieved its aesthetic apogee at the Cabaret Voltaire. With the demise of the Cabaret Voltaire, the artistic cabaret disappeared as the defining site of dada performance, as did popular song. Dada, however, did continue to operate in nonstandard or "nonappropriate" sites with performance practices that, however formally at the cutting edge, were always laced with entertainment components held in disdain by high culture. Dada had used the established and somewhat jaded form of the artistic cabaret temporarily to help it hone its own peculiar performance devices and systems. The dadaists would not, however, abandon in subsequent work their obliteration of the distinction or institutional separation between primary and aesthetic practices that they initiated at the Cabaret Voltaire.

In particular, dada would consistently exploit the formal and dynamic features of the more recently fashionable music hall and variety theater, such as the short skit, radically heterogeneous programming, the sustained onslaughts of energy, jagged transitions, and deliberately crass publicity stunts. They probably drew a page from Marinetti's paean to music hall, where, he claimed, "you find an ironic decomposition of all the worn-out prototypes of the Beautiful, the Grand, the Solemn, the Religious, the Ferocious, the Seductive, and the Terrifying, and also the elaboration of the new prototypes which will succeed these." He "exalt[ed]" music hall for flaunting a "dynamism of form and color," for provoking the "audience's collaboration," for the "unexpectedness of its discoveries and the simplicity of its means," and for cooperating in the "Futurist destruction of immortal masterworks, plagiarizing them, parodying them, making them look commonplace by stripping them of their solemn apparatus as if they were mere attractions."[59]

Nine months after the demise of the Cabaret Voltaire, the Zurich dadaists opened up the Galerie Dada, where Ball claimed contradictorily both to be continuing the "cabaret idea" and to be "surmount[ing] the barbarousness of the cabaret."[60] In point of fact, the Galerie Dada was no longer a cabaret and not yet infused with the music hall aesthetic, but more a combination of art gallery, café, and avant-garde salon—anemic by dada standards. The component of popular song had dropped out, with Hennings now consigned to poetry readings and acting roles. For the moment, Ball's serious commitment to the aesthetics of "total art" was prevailing somewhat over Tzara's strategy of incessant provocation. The Galerie Dada, remembered Huelsenbeck, was "a little art business," a "manicure salon of the fine arts."[61] There were educational lectures (e.g., Ball on Kandinsky), retrospective gallery shows (e.g., the *Sturm* painters), and a hodgepodge of modernist performances: abstract and experimental dance, the obligatory poetry readings, and Schoenberg's piano music. The good-natured eclecticism of the dadaists was nowhere better exemplified than by the presence of Hans Heusser as "house composer," whose creations, with titles like "Danse triste" and "Humoresque turque," hardly went beyond the boundaries of nineteenth-century salon music.[62]

With Ball's departure in 1917, Tzara was finally free to make the vaudevillian turn toward an incendiary and yet jocularly provocative theater. He ended his performing days in Zurich with a rousing production, the "Dada soirée," in which shock and confrontation assumed a more pronounced presence in the midst of the sober modernisms previously associated with the Galerie Dada. Thus the crowd, while sitting patiently through dance performances set to Schoenberg's and Satie's music, serious speeches about abstract art, and Heusser's sedate compositions, broke out into "shouts, whistles, chanting in unison, laughter," in response to a simultaneous poem by Tzara, "performed by twenty people who did not always keep time with each other"—"all hell broke loose." "The tension in the hall became unbearable" when a young anarchist performer, after setting flowers in front of a headless dummy to smell, began to read a manifesto with his back to the audience. "The catcalls began, scornful at first, and then furious . . . until the noise almost drowned out [the performer's] voice." "The young men leaped out on the stage," brandishing "pieces of the balustrade," and chased the performer "into the wings and out the building," after which they "smashed the tailor's dummy" and "stamped on the bouquet."[63] This first entry by dada into avant-garde vaudeville was developed into its extreme when Tzara brought dada to Paris.

The dada provocations in Paris began scarcely one week after Tzara's arrival in January 1920, where he was received as a cultural messiah by André Breton, Louis Aragon, and other young literary adventurists. During the next four months, the Paris dadaists produced seven different manifestations at a feverish and exhausting pace. The programs for these manifestations were almost exclusively made up of short skits, up to fifteen in number, designed primarily to goad and outrage the audience with little or no pretense at serious art. In order to draw crowds at their manifestations, the dadaists did not hesitate to resort to "shameless publicity" and "lies," announcing, for example, that Charlie Chaplin would appear onstage, that "all the dadas will have their head shaved in public," that there would be "sodomistic music," "immobile dances," and the display of the "sex of dada." Though they delivered only on the "sex of dada"—a phallic cylinder of white cardboard resting on two balloons—they managed to provide enough other "insults" and "provocations" to engage their audiences fully.[64] The musical fare included *No Endive,* a piano piece composed according to the laws of chance, which caused "an extraordinary uproar"; Tzara's *Vaseline symphonique,* a "cacophony of sounds" by ten people shouting the syllables "cra" and "cri" on a rising scale; and a fox-trot sacrilegiously played on the grand organ of the Salle Gaveau that had been designed for the highest of art music. The overflowing audiences followed the expected script, by booing, jeering, whistling, making animal noises, disrupting the performances, and causing the lights to go out. They threw coins, tomatoes, turnips, and even beefsteaks "for the first time anywhere in the world." They brought in instruments to harass the dadaists and dropped copies of the anti-dada journal *Non* from the balconies.[65]

But the need continually to find new means of shock before audiences who were becoming increasingly blasé and jocular began to wear the dadaists down, who themselves could not always tolerate the cacophony they produced. The later falling-out between Breton and Tzara further assured that dada's avant-garde vaudeville would soon exhaust itself. The last performance occurred in late 1923, just when surrealism was emerging out of the ruins of dada, but was too "serious" politically to reconstruct a vaudevillian theater of provocation. In effect, surrealism would not take up the alliance of high art and popular culture, and the fusing of primary and secondary practices, that dada had nurtured and never abandoned.

Conclusion

After the war the artistic cabaret made a few fitful starts in the hothouse atmosphere of Berlin's politicized avant-garde. The Berlin dadaists did perform on opening night at the resurrected Schall und Rauch cabaret. They put on a puppet show, filled with the mixture of brazen political invective and slapstick so characteristic of Berlin dada. But this was the exception, since they preferred the streets or their own rented spaces for manifestations and "happenings." This was so despite the effusive proclamation by one member that "Dada is the cabaret of the world, just as it, the world, is the cabaret DADA"— which proclamation, however, was not made at a cabaret. For all practical purposes, the artistic cabaret was gone from the Berlin scene by 1923.[66]

Of course, cabaret in the generic sense continued to play a very visible role in the nightlife of the Weimar Republic in the 1920s. Collectively, the terms *"Kabarret," "Cabaret,"* and *"Amüsierkabarett"* refer to any small-scale and intimate venue that combines entertainment with drink and perhaps food and that operates on the boundaries of either legitimate theater, avant-garde performance, vaudeville, agitprop, or even nude "girl" shows. In this broad disjunctive sense, cabaret did become a stylish emblem of the "decadence" of Weimar Germany, mythologized internationally by Marlene Dietrich in *The Blue Angel* and Lotte Lenya in the Brecht-Weill collaborations. But this was a far cry from the distinctive tradition of the artistic cabaret.[67]

The forty-year history of the artistic cabaret—in the booms and busts, in the migrations and transformations, in the ephemeral experiments and the desperate promotional schemes—strikingly illustrates the many-sided vicissitudes that befell the first full-scale alliance between modernist high culture and popular song. As the narrative of this and the previous chapter has relentlessly underlined, this was a highly insecure and unstable alliance, fitful and incessantly mutating, with recurrent bouts of triumphant shockingness followed by seedy obsolescence. It had taken decades of development in bohemian secondary practices for the concept of such an alliance to emerge clearly, and it required unrelenting effort and adaptation to implement it effectively. The insecurity and instability of this alliance was in large part determined by the volatility of the fashion scene within high-cultural bohemia, where trends in secondary practices shifted even more rapidly than the notoriously tumultuous style changes in the primary practices of art and literature and where the fluctuating imperatives of promotion recurrently dictated new strategies.

As the passive component in this alliance, popular music exhibited in an even more pronounced fashion the vulnerabilities of secondary practices, disappearing from the artists' venues and then reappearing, sometimes centrally and sometimes marginally, as poetry put to music, as aestheticized street song, as satire and *fumisteries,* or as jaded world-weariness. In the modernist context prevailing before World War II, it was always high culture that initiated the alliance and used it for its own ends. The popular music of *cafés-concerts* and music halls was valued more often as instrument or weapon by modernists than for its own intrinsic aesthetics. The few "fans" of popular music among them tended to approach it as a *divertissement* or as the mildly thrilling expression of lowlife transgression. Virtually all the "popular" singing stars of the artistic cabarets came from the art and literary worlds or their appendages (Jouy, Rollinat, Delvard, Hennings) and transformed popular song to fit these high-cultural contexts. The popular music industry proceeded on its own, with its own imperatives and problems, with very little notice of these alternative goings-on or participation in them.

The end of the artistic cabaret as the innovative center of secondary practices did not spell the end of attempted alliances between popular music and high culture in modernist Europe. Indeed, at the moment when the artistic cabaret was enjoying its last hurrah in Zurich, a new Parisian avant-garde, led by the irrepressible Jean Cocteau, was turning to jazz and ragtime to energize its provocations, spectacles, and aesthetic experiments. The next two chapters will address themselves to the new cultural entanglements that defined the Jazz Age in Paris.

B. Paris in the Jazz Age (1916–25)

FIGURE 3   Darius Milhaud and Jean Cocteau hovering benignly over Billy Arnold's Novelty Jazz Band (1921).

CHAPTER 4
JAMMING AT LE BOEUF

"Ah! How I wish I were well enough to go once to the cinema and to the Boeuf sur le Toit."

— MARCEL PROUST[1]

"And The Creation of the World," *Alias cried out, "Did you see* The Creation of the World?"

— MAURICE SACHS[2]

Jazz Age Slumming

Darius Milhaud's *La Création du monde* (The Creation of the World), produced in 1923, is remembered today as one of the major attempts to incorporate early jazz into modernist compositional practice. When it first appeared, it was this but also much more. As the score for the ballet of the same name, choreographed by Jean Börlin of the Ballets Suédois, with sets by Fernand Léger and text by Blaise Cendrars, Milhaud's *Creation of the World* was the key component of a glittering and stunningly successful avant-garde spectacle, at a time when avant-garde performance was at its most fashionable, its most outrageous, and its most entertaining. It was produced at the Théâtre des Champs-Elysées, where Stravinsky's *Rite of Spring* had provoked the first of a series of "*scandales.*" Firmly situating itself in the tradition of Erik Satie's *Parade* (1917), *The Creation of the World* relied for its success on a predictable mix of formulas, such as representations of the exotically primitive, the exploitation of popular culture, and the collaboration of celebrities from different media.

In this chapter I want to focus on Milhaud's appropriation of jazz in *The Creation of the World* as part of a rousing new movement in modernism's recurrent alliances with popular culture. The staging of this work was perhaps the crowning event in the Parisian art world's sustained preoccupation with jazz, which had begun almost as soon as this music had burst on the international scene six years before. For avant-garde artists and writers, this new music was an elaborate metaphor for cutting-edge modernity and the robust vulgarity of America, at the same time that it evoked the deepest stirrings of "primitive" Africa. Jazz stimulated the creation of a new bohemia and was an essential ingredient of the Parisian Roaring Twenties (called *"les années folles"*), in which the cream of Parisian modernism was conspicuously implicated. This was, of course, the Jazz Age, when, it seemed, no sector of culture was immune to the infective power of jazz or unembroiled over its jarring sounds and raw sensuality. There was one avant-garde circle in this swirling activism of postwar Parisian modernism that, more than any other, took it upon itself to promote jazz as the badge of its own identity. Jean Cocteau, the poet turned impresario, was the titular head of this unapologetically bourgeois and manifestly upscale movement, which included at various times Picasso, Stravinsky, Erik Satie, and a group of young composers known as *"les six"* to which Milhaud belonged. The high points of this circle's jazz-related activity were the inauguration of Cocteau's trendy jazz club, Le Boeuf sur le Toit (The Ox on the Roof) and the performance of *The Creation of the World*. From the very beginning, Milhaud was incessantly involved in the whole gamut of the activities of the Cocteau avant-garde, in play and work, in spectacles and intimate performances, in publicity stunts and art world entrepreneurship. *Creation,* coming rather late in the game, was easily perceived by the public as altogether of a piece with the rest of the practices and discourses of the quirky Cocteau avant-garde, and thus was imbued, despite itself, with the mythology of "jazz" that this circle had engendered.

There was consequently much more to the jazz content of *Creation* than the timbres, rhythms, and chord changes that Milhaud had borrowed from what he had heard as jazz music. This is not to discount the importance of Milhaud's achievement at the purely formal level. Perhaps no modernist composer before him had so explicitly and lovingly incorporated major components of popular music into his or her work. Of course, art musicians have always exploited popular tunes as compositional raw material. But it is one thing for them to be influenced by popular music and to integrate it seamlessly into their compositions. It is something else to do what Milhaud did, which was musically to highlight rather than submerge the jazz components in his composition, to speak the musical language of jazz unequivocally and approvingly and make explicit use of its formal devices. Nonetheless, to focus only on the formal appropriations of jazz in *Creation* would be to miss all the jazz-related signification it acquired by virtue of being deeply enmeshed in a panoply of practices and discourses within which "jazz" functioned as a crucial signifier. Most of Milhaud's public, though it "heard" *Creation* as a jazz composition, was quite illiterate about the formal jazz components. Thus, in this chapter I will pay special attention to the dense intertextual space within which this composition was situated, that dense array of texts that affected, or constrained, its reception in 1923. This included anything that could be "read," not merely the printed word, but also performances and spectacles, escapades and publicity stunts. Ultimately, this intertextual space was filled by the "texts" consciously or unconsciously brought to bear on *Creation* by the public that attended the performance or heard about it and talked about it, a public that had eagerly frequented the spectacles and manifestations of the Cocteau avant-garde, while also slumming in jazz bars and attending the movies of Charlie Chaplin and Fatty Arbuckle.

Multiple Modernisms

By renewing the avant-garde engagement with popular music in France, the Cocteau-Milhaud circle was not merely reproducing the aesthetic practices of the previous generation of cabaret poets and painters. A new modernism, a radically new kind of popular music, and strikingly different contexts inevitably led to a new set of relations between high and low with only some overlap with the past. One of the driving hypotheses of this book is that there is no such thing as a modernist essence that underlies all the "modernist" movements and from which we can deduce certain postures of attraction or repulsion toward mass culture. By itself, "modernism" is a vague allusive term—evoking at various times the equally vague notions of self-referentiality, experimentation, avant-garde, shock of the new, the painting of modern life, and so on. It does not have the specificity and tautness to function as a theoretical term from which certain aesthetic conclusions or imperatives can be drawn. But it does serve as a useful coded expression for a whole array of different movements and practices that exist as an extended family with multifarious and partial resemblances and differences, but not sharing any core aesthetic that makes them one.

In his classic *After the Great Divide*, Andreas Huyssen, for example, distinguishes between two distinct and incommensurate "trajectories of the modern"—"high modernism" and the "historical avant-garde"—which exhibit two opposite stances toward mass culture.[3] Roughly, "high modernism" refers to a variety of formally experimental but politically unengaged aesthetic practices that are sufficiently inaccessible to be not easily appropriable by the culture industry. The historical avant-garde is a politically engaged art that directs its fire at high-cultural institutions in its effort to overcome the separation of art from life. The high modernists are described as unreconstructedly opposed to mass culture (Joyce, Eliot,[4] Kafka, Schoenberg) and the historical avant-garde (dada, surrealism, and Russian constructivism) as engaged in a nonadversarial "hidden dialectic" with mass culture. But, as Huyssen allows,[5] this distinction between "two trajectories of the modern" does not encompass all the types of modernist practices and concomitant relations to mass culture that have proliferated since the mid-nineteenth century. The Cocteau circle belongs neither to the high modernist or historical avant-garde camp, although it shares some of the characteristics of each. Like the former, the members of this circle were politically unengaged and committed to aestheticist goals. But like the latter, they resorted to shock and scandal and were friendly to mass culture. Furthermore, neither the Marxist avant-gardism of Brecht and Heartfield, nor the nineteenth-century modernism of Manet or Toulouse-Lautrec (and thus the aesthetic of the artistic cabarets), can be easily subsumed under the dichotomy of high modernism and historical avant-garde.

Among the different modernisms, there are gradations of friendliness toward mass culture and gradations of hostility. Relatively friendly ones include the impressionists, Toulouse-Lautrec, Satie, Picasso, Stravinsky, Brecht-Weill, and so on.[6] Relatively unfriendly ones include Schoenberg, the later Krenek, perhaps Kafka and Valéry, though I suspect that much of this unfriendliness comes less from artists than from the "modernist" theorists and critics (e.g., Adorno, Greenberg) who have championed them.[7] The friendly modernisms can further be distinguished by their ways of engaging with mass culture: through direct appropriations or implicit intertextual allusions; institutional alliances or rapprochements in discourse; shared formal devices or attitudes; in primary or secondary practices; in work or leisure.

In following Milhaud's aesthetic itinerary through the Cocteau avant-garde, we encounter much of the pluralism that has graced the history of modernism. Itself a happy but unstable hybrid of all sorts of modernist tendencies, the Cocteau avant-garde indulged in almost every kind of friendly connection with mass culture that can be imagined in modernist practice. I will begin more narrowly with Milhaud's own discourses and practices concerning jazz, as they led to the conception of *The Creation of the World,* before examining how the surrounding antics of the Cocteau circle concerning this music impinged on the reception of this work.[8]

Milhaud in Harlem

According to his autobiography, *Notes without Music,* Milhaud first encountered jazz in the summer of 1920, when he heard Billy Arnold's Novelty Jazz

Band "straight from New York" at a Hammersmith dance hall in London.[9] He was quickly won over and, along with Cocteau, later promoted the career of the Billy Arnold band in Paris avant-garde circles. Milhaud discovered jazz and its precursor, ragtime, somewhat later than other members of the Paris avant-garde. Not long after its appearance in Parisian clubs in the early 1900s, ragtime was incorporated into the compositions of Debussy (*Golliwog's Cakewalk*, 1908), Satie (*Parade*, 1917), and Stravinsky (*Histoire du soldat* and *Ragtime pour onze instruments*, 1918). Due especially to the impact of black American military bands, the jazz craze, initiated in America by the 1917 recordings of the Original Dixieland Jazz Band, quickly spread to Europe. The Paris avant-garde was introduced to jazz in 1918 at the comte de Beaumont's *fête nègre*, and at the Casino de Paris, where, in the words of Cocteau, they were exposed to the "hurricane of rhythms" and "domesticated cataclysm" of Harry Pilcer and Gaby Deslys's band.[10]

Though Milhaud missed out on all this activity because of his two-year sojourn in Brazil (as secretary to Ambassador Paul Claudel), he quickly resolved, after finally being exposed to jazz, "to penetrate into the arcana of this new musical form whose techniques still baffled [him]."[11] He was impressed at first primarily by its formal and technical innovations in instrumental sonority as well as rhythm. He has spoken at some length about the "new music's" "extremely subtle" use of timbre, for example, about the "languorous" trumpet with its "mutes" and "megaphones," the "lyrical" trombone with its "glissandos," the saxophone "squeezing out the juice of dreams," the piano's "dryness" and "drum-like precision," the banjo's "nervousness" and "resonance," and the violin's "slender and sharp" voice with the "largest vibratos and the least rapid slides."[12]

Milhaud went further than most modernist appropriators of popular culture by viewing jazz not merely as cultural raw material for modernist experimentation or avant-garde shock tactics, but as an innovative art form in its own right, indeed the "absolutely appropriate" musical art form for North Americans. This, to his consternation, went unbeknownst to the American musical establishment, which "relegated [jazz] to the dance hall," to the constraints of "ragtimes, fox trots, shimmies, etc."[13] It was thus incumbent on European composers, according to him, to move jazz to the next stage of its evolution by creating chamber or symphonic works that "utilize the [instrumental] combinations peculiar to [jazz] orchestras," and thus appropriate and extend its sonoric and rhythmic innovations for a concert setting. European composers who had previously incorporated elements of jazz failed in his eyes to exploit its potentialities, both because they used it primarily as a signifier for popular dances (the "Ragtime" of Stravinsky's *Histoire du soldat*), and because they restricted themselves to traditional symphonic rather than jazz combinations of instruments.[14]

Milhaud did not receive his first exposure to African American jazz until his 1922 visit to New York, two years after hearing the Billy Arnold band, when a friend took him to Harlem, which, in his words, "had not yet been discovered by the snobs and the aesthetes." In a club where they "were the only white folks," he encountered a music that was "absolutely different from anything [he] had ever heard before." He was most astounded by the "negress" singer whose "grating voice" seemed to originate "from the depths of the centuries" and who, "with despairing pathos and dramatic feeling," sang the same refrain "over and over again to the point of exhaustion."[15] Though he does not use the term, we can assume from his description that this "negress" was singing the blues, since the rage for women blues singers, initiated by the wild success of Mamie Smith's "Crazy Blues" (1920), was just gathering momentum during Milhaud's stay.

This formative experience moved him from an exclusively formalist and experimentalist preoccupation with jazz to one tempered by a strong interest in its lyricism and primitivism. Such "authentic music," he was sure, had "its roots in the darkest corner of the negro soul, the vestigial traces of Africa."[16] It is in this "primitive African side," this "savage" "African character," "still profoundly anchored" in black North American music, he wrote, "that we find the source of this formidable rhythmic, as well as of such expressive melodies, which are endowed with a lyricism which only oppressed races can produce."[17]

Milhaud starkly contrasted the archaic lyricism of Negro blues with the hypermodernity, worldliness (*la mondanité*), and mechanicalness of white jazz. The best white jazz bands leave "nothing to chance" in constructing "with a minimum of means" a "perfectly adjusted" music that operates with the "precision of a well-oiled machine."[18] Negro jazz, on the other hand, allows a much larger role for improvisation, and with it, a "much greater ease of performance" and "a play of [simultaneous musical] lines of oftentimes disconcerting complexity."[19]

Having been so "overwhelmed" by his Harlem experience that he "could not tear [himself] away," he was more than ever "resolved to use jazz for a chamber work."[20] His opportunity was soon forthcoming with Rolf de Maré's decision, as the director of the Ballets Suédois and a frequent visitor to Africa, to commission a ballet loosely based on the African creation myths collected in Cendrars's *Anthologie nègre*. The scenario for the resulting production, *The Creation of the World,* was quite simple, consisting as it did of successive representations of the creation of plants, animals, birds, and insects from an unformed mass under the supervision of three giant gods, followed by the creation of Man and Woman, who end the ballet with a dance of the kiss. For Milhaud, the archaic lyricism of Harlem jazz made it an ideal medium, despite its recent provenance, for a symphonic enactment of these primitive African myths.

Though not recognizably a jazz or blues piece, the score for *The Creation of the World* does make liberal use of the blues scale (in which the third and seventh notes on the diatonic scale are "bent"). The famous fugue from *Creation* best exemplifies Milhaud's attempt to synthesize his interests in blues and classical musical forms. At that time he was involved in exploring the harmonic possibilities of counterpoint, of which the fugue, with its overlapping voices repeating the same melodic strand, is an emblematic form. Each of the fugal voices traces out the first six bars of a typical twelve-bar blues song, shifting to the next voice at the point of resolution from the subdominant chord (rooted in the fourth note of the scale) to the tonic chord (rooted in the first note), thus highlighting the subdominant-tonic tension that is so characteristic of the blues. As the jazz scholar André Hodeir has observed, except for a few brief changes in measure, the whole piece is in the 2/2 time typical of 1920s jazz bands and is studded throughout with syncopated formulas.[21]

The Authenticist versus the *Bricoleur*

Above all, Milhaud seems to be claiming a relationship of authenticity toward his jazz sources. He purports to have carefully studied the most genuine articles of jazz and to have been true to its nature when appropriating and transforming it for symphonic purposes. Allegedly, this not only preserves and underscores the expressive primitivism of jazz, but also realizes the experimental potentialities in it rarely explored in dance music. Unlike Stravinsky, Milhaud clearly does not treat jazz as some interesting foreign musical component to be incorporated in his compositions for reasons of purely formal play, satire, caricature, humor, shock, stylistic masquerade, or parody.

Stravinsky, of course, is the great scavenger of twentieth-century music, always "casting about," in the words of Stephen Walsh, "for fresh models to use as 'subjects' or stylistic material," whether it be Russian folk song (*Rite of Spring*), banal popular song (*Petrushka*), ragtime (*Piano Rag Music*), or "the ghostly forms" of past European art music (*Pulcinella*).[22] For example,

Stravinsky uses the occasions of his formal experiments with ragtime rhythms to satirize the "tonic-dominant clichés" of that idiom by, among other things, having the chords push "relentlessly" but unsuccessfully toward a tonic resolution. Here Walsh describes him as "detaching clichés from their usual context, combining them obliquely, in the manner of a cubist painting, while at the same time deriving from them new meanings which may pointedly contradict the old ones."[23]

Hodeir has disputed Milhaud's claims of authenticity with respect to jazz, stressing that the latter had been exposed mainly to the "distortions and degradations" of "commercial counterfeits," rather than to "authentic jazz."[24] What are we to say of someone who sang the praises of Paul Whiteman, Billy Arnold, and Irving Berlin, but who could not remember the name of any of the blues bands he heard in Harlem and who knew nothing about what really counted as jazz in 1923, namely the New Orleans style as represented by King Oliver's Band? While the melodic lines at least "are faithful to the letter if not the spirit of the blues," Hodeir contends that not one of its rhythms, "syncopated or otherwise, has more than any similarity to the good jazz of the period." The polyrhythmic devices of *Creation*, he argues, are "hardly amenable to swing," in part because they destroy the tension between syncopation and the "steadiness" of the basic pulse "which is the lifeblood of the jazz rhythm." Stravinsky, according to Hodeir, despite his greater predilection toward caricature, "shows a distinctly more highly developed sense of jazz," his formulas attaining "a rhythmic flexibility that makes them resemble the riffs of jazzmen."[25]

Hodeir's criticism, however, is marred by an inadmissibly essentialist construction of "authentic" jazz. Milhaud's usage of the word "jazz" was quite typical of his generation, for whom it referred very loosely to any syncopated dance music with African American influences. In recent decades "jazz" has been used more restrictively to signify primarily an African American art music characterized by "swing," improvisation, and blues scales, among other things. It has been quite "natural" for jazz historians to read these defining traits back into early jazz, thus excising from its history much of what had previously been called "jazz." What remains of early jazz in these historical reconstructions are the New Orleans style of the 1910s and 1920s and the big band swing music of the 1930s. We can understand this exclusionary rereading of history as part of a decades-old struggle to establish jazz as a genuine art music, indeed as "America's classical music."[26] Recent histories of jazz have bypassed those early types of nominal jazz that do not fit into the trajectory leading to modern jazz or give sense to its aesthetics; it is not that they have succeeded in separating the genuine from the counterfeit. Accordingly, we should not accuse Milhaud of virtual nonacquaintance with "authentic" jazz. Much of what he called "jazz" is no longer part of the canon of jazz history.[27]

Ultimately, the question about authenticity is not germane to the explication of Milhaud's interplay as a modernist with popular culture. What is more interesting than his doubtful *authentic* relation to jazz is his undisputedly *authenticist* posture toward it, which contrasts vividly with Stravinsky's stance as a *bricoleur* (whether in the form of parodist, satirist, or caricaturist). Nonetheless, the fact that Stravinsky did not strike an authenticist pose is quite compatible with his having produced work more in accord with the spirit of "real" (i.e., canonical) jazz. This is because the difference between authenticism and *bricolage,* in this case, is reduced largely to style or posture—the former sober, deferential, studious, and scrupulous, the latter playful, irreverent, somewhat detached, and nonchalant—and is not a matter of the presence or absence of some unmediated relation to an originary source. Authenticism may involve a different set of intertextual relations with jazz than does *bricolage,* but the former are no less contrived or arbitrary than the latter.

The *Flâneur*

In effect, the similarities between the modernist authenticist and *bricoleur* are more significant than the differences. However much their postures diverge, Milhaud and Stravinsky ultimately both approach jazz in the manner of the Baudelairian *flâneur*, who is more akin to the tourist, the slummer, and the fashion plate, than to the ethnomusicologist or folklorist. Milhaud's authenticism tends to converge with the *bricolage* of Stravinsky when contrasted with the authenticism of the jazz scholar, or the faithful interpreter of the jazz repertoire, or even the consummate fan.

Baudelaire has described the *flâneur*—that metaphorical prototype of the modernist artist—first and foremost as one whose "passion" and "profession" is "to merge with the crowd," indeed "to move through the crowd as through an enormous reservoir of electricity." "Curiosity," he wrote, "is the starting point of [the] genius" of the *flâneur,* who "breathes in with delight all the spores and odors of life" and who "takes a lively interest in things, even the most trivial in appearance."[28] Baudelaire was already adumbrating in 1860 the aesthetic practice of bohemian slumming that was soon to be the hallmark of the impressionists, whose domains were the *cafés-concerts,* dance halls, and other cut-rate venues of petit bourgeois pleasure. Milhaud and his circle continued this tradition with their constant forays into the *bals musettes*, fairs, and circuses of Paris. By the turn of the century, the local dens of popular culture had become the primary terrain for the modernist *flâneur's* adventures in curiosity and assimilation.

What distinguishes the *flâneurs* of Milhaud's generation from Baudelaire's contemporaries, however, is a growing pursuit of, and absorption in, the exotica of foreign lands. The notion of the *flâneur* applies not only to the "man of the crowd" but also to the world traveler (Gauguin, Cendrars), the collector of the strange and the sundry (Picasso, Braque, Apollinaire), and the browser in obscure libraries or bookstores (Cendrars). As Baudelaire put it, not restricted to the streets and cafés of his own city, the "lover of life makes the whole world into his family, like the lover of the fair sex creates his from all the lovely women he has found." "Away from home" and yet "at home," "at the very center of the world" and yet "unseen of the world," the *flâneur* goes on his way "forever in search," "always roaming the great desert of men," "an ego athirst for the non-ego."[29] It is this preoccupation with cultural Otherness that partially explains the high-cultural *flâneur's* indiscriminate attraction to the popular, the folkloric, and the primitive. (Since the Baudelairian concept of *flâneur* is obviously gendered—the *"flâneuse"* being the equivalent of a streetwalker—I will restrict myself to the use of the masculine pronoun.)

Milhaud's autobiography, *Notes without Music,* is preponderantly a tale of a world traveler and slumming artist whose creations are substantially enriched by what he picks up along the way. His encounters with jazz are squarely situated intertextually within the discourses of travel (New York, London) and slumming (Harlem, Hammersmith). The narrative for his first major trip, a two-year stay in Brazil during World War I, is a chronicle of awed childlike impressions and assimilations of the exotic and the primitive. Arriving during the middle of Carnival, he tells us that he was "fascinated" by the "frenzied dancing" of the street musicians, who succumbed to the "hypnotic" effect of the "never-ending chorus and its insistent rhythms," while one "negro" among them licked a big sherbet "with his pink tongue in time with the music." Milhaud's description of an Afro-Brazilian "voodoo" ceremony in the Bahia is laced with references to "paroxysms," "trances," "sorcerers," and "screaming and foaming at the mouth." He reports that he practiced playing "maxixes and tangos" until he had mastered to his satisfaction "the typically Brazilian musical subtlety" of "imperceptible pauses in the syncopation" and "careless catches in the breath."[30]

The Baudelairian *flâneur* represents the consumption side of modernist aesthetic practice. In Baudelaire's words, he is constantly looking for that "indefinable something we may be allowed to call 'modernity,'" which is "the transient, the fleeting, and the contingent." His aim is "to extract from fashion the poetry that resides in its historical envelope," in its "essential quality of being the present." The cost of neglecting this "transitory fleeting element," this "beauty of circumstances," is falling "into the emptiness of an abstract and indefinable beauty."[31] In effect, the modernist *flâneur* is a compulsive consumer of the new, the not yet fashionable, the outré, the evanescent on the margins of culture. As a consumer, he constantly subjects himself to the "shock of the new" at the same time that, as an artist, he unremittingly subjects others to such shocks. Or more precisely, his being an aesthetic purveyor of the "shock of the new" is parasitic on his being a consumer of these shocks. The modernist, at least in the mode of Stravinsky and Milhaud, is like the small manufacturer who, in order to be constantly changing his product line, must forever be in search of new raw materials or design ideas. Since his home market, the institutionalized art world, is not sufficiently well endowed to provide the necessary raw materials for his continued need to reproduce the new, he must typically venture outside this world, to nearby flea markets or cheap nightclubs, or even to the carnivals and folk rituals of distant countries, in search of the transient, the shocking, and the soon-to-be fashionable. In his role as *flâneur,* the modernist always finds himself away from home, the difference between the alienness of the Montmartre music hall and the Brazilian Carnival being only one of degree. Primitivism, like colonialism for the industrial producer, becomes a determinant factor when those spaces (such as Montmartre), located outside the art world but within European national boundaries, no longer provide the requisite new materials and stimuli. Accordingly, Milhaud's appropriation of Brazilian music was doubly shocking: first the shock to Milhaud's own system of musical expectations, and then the quite different shock to the Parisian audiences of his Brazilian-inspired music. (Similarly, Picasso's traumatic encounter with African masks in the Musée d'Ethnographie du Trocadéro paved the way for the public discomfort that greeted *Les Demoiselles d'Avignon,* the painting that first incorporated the design principles of these masks.) Milhaud himself has described the "sudden shock" and "abrupt awakening" experienced by the Paris avant-garde in its "jarring" encounter with the "brusque" rhythms of Harry Pilcer and Gaby Deslys's jazz band at the Casino de Paris in 1918.[32]

In Milhaud, furthermore, there is a strong element of self-deception in his being both an enthusiastic *flâneur* and a sober authenticist. The *flâneur's* shallow knowledge and capricious attachments undermine the authenticist's claims of expertise and postures of reverence. Given his never-ending pursuit of the fleetingly new, the *flâneur* must constantly shift the objects of his gaze. And no deep knowledge is required simply to grasp the object in its newness, in its ability to disrupt the perceptual patterns of the art world, or to become a defining element of future fashions. The *flâneur's* level of knowledge and commitment is of the same order as that of the avid tourist, the buff, or the dandy.

Milhaud's interest in Brazilian music lasted just two years and his interest in jazz just three. Already in 1924, merely a year after *Creation,* he asserted that "the influence of jazz, which impressed itself so strongly on French music during the past six years, is now disappearing" and "no longer has a hold" on young composers.[33] A few years later, he added that "the influence of jazz has already passed by, like a salutary storm after which the sky is purer, the weather more reliable," so that now "renascent classicism" can replace "the broken throbbings of syncopation."[34] Milhaud had spread consternation in a recent trip to the United States by announcing that he "was no longer interested in jazz," "which had now become official," and that "even in Harlem, the charm had been broken," now that "snobs in search of exotic color" "had penetrated to even the most secluded corners."[35] Always at the cutting edge, the *flâneur* abandons his favored objects once they become commercially fashionable and turns to something else.

Thus, the inadequacies in Milhaud's understanding of jazz are traceable less to his own personal shortcomings or idiosyncrasies than to his mode of modernist discourse. If we construe him as a prototypical modernist *flâneur,* we can more easily make sense of his excessively formalistic approach to jazz, his underestimation of performance at the expense of composition, his limited exposure to the wide variety of jazz bands, his simplistic schemes of classification ("mechanical" white jazz vs. "primitive" black jazz), and his virtual ignorance of the cultural and social context of jazz. We will be less surprised by his facile appeal to the most banal stereotypes of black music and culture, as when he traces jazz to "the darkest corners of the negro soul," to "savage" Africa (though he knew nothing of African music), or incorporates into his writing the stock imagery of "frenzy" and "paroxysm," mournful sounds and lazy rhythms, and childishly comical behavior.

Enter Cocteau

Milhaud spoke of jazz almost exclusively as something *signified* by his own cultural discourse, and rarely as a *signifier* circulating within that discourse.

That is, he treated it virtually solely as a phenomenon to be represented, as an essence to be explicated textually and exemplified musically, rather than as something coming to him already laden with socially constructed meaning. As a *signifier,* jazz is the assemblage of representations commonly read into the music, and into the accompanying styles of performance, argot, and clothing at a particular historical juncture. It is obvious that the same musical performance—the same "token" of jazz—would have quite different connotations, would in effect assume a quite different symbolic role, if it took place in a Parisian avant-garde club rather than in Harlem. Indeed, the symbolic role of jazz in 1920s Paris was decisively affected by the way it circulated as a signifier in debates among modernists, and between modernism and traditional culture. We can assume that this connotative function of jazz within avant-garde discourse impinged quite forcefully on the reception of any openly jazz-inflected composition, such as *The Creation of the World.* Indeed, by appearing in *Creation* also as a signifier, the jazz component brought with it a substantially more intricate and densely populated intertextual space than if it had only functioned as a signified.

Milhaud had much less influence on the construction of jazz as an avant-garde signifier than his ally and sometimes collaborator Jean Cocteau, who without much musical knowledge managed to turn his consumption of jazz into the well-recognized emblem of his own brand of avant-garde practice. Milhaud became connected with Cocteau primarily through his membership in *les six,* a group of young French composers (including Arthur Honegger and Francis Poulenc) united more by friendship and shared performance spaces than a common aesthetic. Nonetheless, once they were labeled *"les six"* by an enterprising newspaper reporter and once Cocteau seized upon that label to publicize the agenda for avant-garde music outlined in his manifesto *Le Coq et l'arlequin* (1918), they found themselves willy-nilly implicated publicly in a movement, inspired by Erik Satie and expounded by Cocteau, to create a French music freed of German and Russian heaviness as well as of Debussy's luxuriant impressionism. Despite their constant complaints and their published accounts of serious differences with Cocteau and among themselves, they did not resist his proposals to do group concerts or to provide musical scores for his attempts to revolutionize dance theater. Thus, Cocteau was able to give substance and flesh to his proposals for a new avant-garde, while creating a circle of apparent followers and coconspirators. Milhaud's work during this period was altogether overwhelmed intertextually by Cocteau's aesthetics, even when his intentions were opposed and Cocteau himself was not explicitly involved. The latter could plausibly have claimed to have been the real (i.e., intertextual) author of *Creation.*

While doing more to promote jazz than any other Paris modernist, Cocteau at the same time sought to position it in a cultural space clearly segregated from that reserved for high-cultural aesthetic production. Why he did so becomes obvious when one connects this to his attempt to form a new avant-garde movement taking a middle path between the "artistic left" and the "artistic right."[36] Primarily this meant appropriating the formal innovations and the performance tactics of the historical avant-gardes (futurism, dadaism) while dispensing with their politics. Cocteau, like the high modernists, was altogether committed to the ideal of autonomous art, to the purist articulation of the beauty underlying the different transformations of modernity, and thus had no sympathy for the historical avant-garde's confrontations with "institution art," their dismissal of Art with a capital "A," or their blending of art and political activism.[37] He had concluded, however, that his own purely aestheticist goals could be most effectively achieved by borrowing from the tactics of the historical avant-garde, such as shock and scandal, collaboration between artists from different media, the exploitation of publicity, and the exposing of the art world to the sounds and sights of everyday modern life—the machine, the skyscraper, the circus, and especially the jazz band. But the latter move had to be especially tempered if the integrity of European (and particularly French) autonomous art was to be preserved.

The solution was to separate modernist consumption—the domain of the *flâneur*—from modernist production, and to relegate the sounds and sights of modern life to the former activity. Statements by Cocteau like "The music hall, the circus, and American negro bands, all these things fertilize an artist just as life does" and "The *café-concert* is often pure, the theater is always corrupt" have led critics to impute to him "an aesthetic of the music hall," or an aesthetic "that fluctuates between cubism and vaudeville."[38] But this is to miss the point: for Cocteau the usefulness of popular culture to avant-garde practice is due more to its sheer psychophysical power than to its aesthetic quality. As he puts it, "To turn to one's account the emotions aroused" by jazz and the music hall, by producing a work of modernist high culture, "is not to derive art from art," but merely "to stimulate" it "in the same way as machinery, animals, natural scenery, or danger."[39] Like machines, skyscrapers, sirens, and other components of the urban landscape, jazz is a "life force," "a brutal disorder," a "domesticated cataclysm," an artificial "cyclone," that provokes and stirs up the modernist *flâneur,* rather than an aesthetic model that guides his work. Indeed, the "Negro" jazz band, in Cocteau's words, "can be construed as the very soul of all these [modern urban] forces, which culminate in it and sing their cruelty and melancholy through it." The word "modern" brings to mind the image of "a negro prostrate before a telephone."[40]

Though their encounter with jazz has jarred them away from obsolete aesthetic practices, modernists, according to Cocteau, must resist the temptation to imitate jazz or appropriate it—"It is useless to badly pastiche the fox trot"—just as they should avoid letting their aesthetics be dominated by the machine. French artists may learn a number of things from their encounter with jazz, such as attention to rhythm, economy of means, simplicity, and unpretentiousness, but any attempt on their part to absorb its imputed formal principles will inevitably undermine the cultural and national integrity of their works—"Imagine a skyscraper in the Place Vendôme." It is clear that, except as a temporary tactic, Cocteau rejects the posture of the *bricoleur* as well as that of the authenticist. For the Cocteau *flâneur,* the consumption of jazz functions as brute stimulant of, rather than as an aesthetic exemplar for, the modernist production that follows upon it. "The shower from this noise has woken us so that we can now produce a different noise."[41]

Thus, according to Cocteau, the French modernist will transform the shocks of modern urban life into an altogether different aesthetic object, which is nonetheless equally modern, despite its "smallness," "delicateness," and "intimacy," partly because it succeeds in "[seizing] the spirit of the age." "An artist must swallow a locomotive and bring up a pipe." And Picasso's pipe as well as "Braque's fruit bowl" and "Derain's nymph" are "as modern as the typewriter."[42] The latter shocks through its physical aggressiveness, and the former through their aesthetic audacity.[43]

Jamming at Le Boeuf

As the "soul of all these [urban] forces," jazz was for Cocteau the proper signifier of modern life in its postwar embodiments, and thus the proper object of the *flâneur*'s gaze. It combined speed, noise, vulgarity, aggression, America, the inner city, danger, transgression, the exotic, the Negro—all stock images celebrating the mystique of modernity. In effect, jazz became the paradigmatic object of the avant-garde slummer, the new signifier for bohemian life. The concepts of jazz and *flâneur,* in their European setting, became for a period inextricably interlocked.

Though Cocteau tried to exclude jazz from primary aesthetic production, it would inevitably reappear with his blessing in the secondary aesthetic production of the Paris avant-garde, given its intimate involvement with the new slumming practices of the latter. As an impresario of the first order, Cocteau was quite aware of the importance of secondary aesthetic production for publicizing and contextualizing the "real" or primary works. He thus set about creating and spectacularizing a new bohemia that would reflect and support the aspirations of his depoliticized avant-garde movement. This bohemia was put on display at the spectacularly successful restaurant-bar Le Boeuf sur le Toit, named after the ballet by Cocteau and Milhaud, but quickly eclipsing its acclaimed namesake in notoriety and mystique. "Of all the restaurants, of all the bars that fashion makes and unmakes, none was more in vogue in those days than Le Boeuf sur le Toit," said Maurice Sachs, the major chronicler of the postwar avant-garde in Paris.[44]

Consistent with Cocteau's aesthetics, the bohemia fashioned at Le Boeuf was a sharply depoliticized variant of those that had flourished in the turn-of-the-century cafés of Montmartre and the Latin Quarter. First, the erstwhile bohemian culture of poverty and social marginality gave way to an atmosphere of upscale pleasure and fashionable consumption. Cocteau had previously expressed his desire "to persuade the cubists . . . to abandon their hermetic Montmartre folklore of pipes, packages of tobacco, guitars, and old newspapers" for the "sumptuous decorative aesthetic of the ballet," to become more "attuned to the taste for luxury and pleasure," and to enter the world of "gloves, cane, and collar."[45] At Le Boeuf, Picasso and Picabia could converse with the countess of Noailles or King Ferdinand of Rumania, while the very refined Marcel Proust dined on "excellent" roast chicken, though the service, he noted, was not as good as at his cherished Ritz.[46]

Second, what emerged at Le Boeuf was a pared-down version of the old bohemia, the bearer of that tradition now being virtually limited to the role of artistic *flâneur*. Though essential to it, *la flânerie* was always only one among many components of bohemian practice. The organizers of Le Chat Noir had produced manifestos, organized street demonstrations, harassed political institutions, performed songs of political satire, and insulted their audiences. Whereas in Montmartre bohemians had featured themselves in a variety of innovative spectacles, at Le Boeuf they were reduced to being *flâneurs* on display. The public came to watch celebrity artists and musicians who were merely engaged in the act of slumming. According to Sachs, this public consisted mainly of "young people, dazed and charmed, look[ing] wide-eyed at celebrities who drink like everyone else but whose names make them shake with admiration." What partially accounted for Le Boeuf's success was "the opinion that spread quickly through Paris that one could see there all the [cultural] celebrities of the city."[47]

And, in turn, what these new bohemians were slumming to was a pared-down version of jazz, performed mainly by members of Cocteau's avant-garde circle. Jean Wiener, a composer and an organizer of the most up-to-date concerts, played the latest tunes by Gershwin, Youmans, and Henderson on the piano, occasionally accompanied by Cocteau himself on a drum set borrowed from Stravinsky. For a touch of authenticity, they advertised for, and got, a "negro" saxophonist and banjo player, Vance Lowry, whom Cocteau judged to be "delicious" and a "demon of harmonies." Paul Morand said to him: "Vance, play some more, since the night is really the daytime for negroes."[48]

Le Boeuf sur le Toit became so intimately connected with images of jazz in Paris that even today the expression *"faire le boeuf"* is used to mean "have a jam session."[49] Le Boeuf was in effect the middle term of a syllogism linking the signifier "jazz" to the aesthetics of Cocteau's centrist avant-garde movement. It provided the framework for secondary aesthetic practices of immense popularity that reflected, bolstered, and in turn helped to configure the primary production of this movement. As an essential though subsidiary component of these secondary practices—what was being watched by those who were being watched—jazz as a signifier became seriously implicated in the depoliticization and the upscaling of the avant-garde. It was complicit in the transformation of bohemian practice into pure sumptuous slumming, and the corresponding restructuring of the sights and sounds of modern urbanity into mildly shocking objects of fashionable consumption. Finally, it functioned as a signifier not only to help define and legitimate this new avant-garde, but also to help construct a new system of publicity for it.

There is a bit of irony here. The usual discussions of the involvement of modernism with popular culture proceed along two lines of possibility: either popular culture provided an impetus for transgression or it led to co-optation of modernism by the culture industry. In the case of jazz and the Paris avant-garde, neither of these things happened. Indeed, here it was a modernist movement that co-opted jazz in its attempt to depoliticize the avant-garde. Though not inherently a subversive musical phenomenon—nothing really is—jazz can be argued to have been potentially transgressive insofar as it could have been transformed into a signifier that served as an instrument of transgression. What Cocteau and his colleagues did was to construct a signification for jazz that served the opposite purpose of undermining the radical import of avant-garde practice, as pursued by the dadaists and the surrealists, who quite interestingly made much less use of jazz. By turning the issue of co-optation around, and thus by undermining the bias toward high culture that operates even in the work of those who, like Benjamin, speak for the subversive role of mass culture, we may be in a position to come to terms with some of the more intractable issues that have confounded the high culture/mass culture debates.

Finally, *The Creation of the World*

Cocteau was altogether uninvolved in the production of *The Creation of the World* and indeed had returned to Paris only a few days before the performance on October 19, 1923. Milhaud was trying to make his own independent contribution to a movement in which he so far had only been a supporting player. But what he thought to be a major breakthrough—the first symphony for a jazz orchestra—turned out to be only a minor and late development in this already well-articulated movement. Jazz had already saturated the discourses and secondary practices of the Paris avant-garde, who by now were beginning to tire of it as Le Boeuf was being overrun by tourists. Rather than unleashing a whole new formation in European music, Milhaud unbeknownst to himself was simply giving jazz due formal recognition for the extensive cultural work it had already done within avant-garde discourse, but whose usefulness was now coming to an end. Not surprisingly, hardly any Parisian composers followed Milhaud's lead as the interests of the avant-garde began to scatter in a variety of new directions—the exception being Ravel.

In addition, by foregrounding jazz in his own work, especially given his membership in the Cocteau circle, Milhaud opened up his work to the infusion of the connotations associated with jazz as signifier, thus imbuing it with all the implications of Cocteau's aesthetics. Of course, he was in agreement with much of what Cocteau had argued for, although he was somewhat weary of *scandales* and wanted his music simply to be listened to and taken seriously. However, his intention to appropriate jazz formally as serious art music ran squarely against the avant-garde construction of jazz as music purely for artistic slumming and avant-garde play. On the plausible assumption that Milhaud's own intentions did not prevail over the power of the signifier in determining reception, we can conclude that Milhaud's public constructed its experience of *The Creation of the World* as an act of slumming not altogether appropriate for the concert hall and the performance itself as a hybrid of cultural high-mindedness and bohemian amusement. Milhaud

complained that "the critics decreed my music was frivolous and more suitable for a restaurant or dance hall than for the concert hall."[50] To avoid this,
Milhaud would have had to do battle with the jazz aesthetics emanating
from Le Boeuf, where along with Cocteau he had done his share of jamming
and slumming.

FIGURE 4 Pablo Picasso in his studio, flanked by his African art collection (1908).

CHAPTER 5
NEGROPHILIA

THE PARIS AVANT-GARDE'S ENGAGEMENT WITH JAZZ was really a double engagement, representing an infatuation with two quite distinct objects: popular music, particularly American, and "primitive" cultures, particularly African. The raging fashion for Charlie Chaplin films, circuses, and *bals musettes,* among celebrity modernists and their followers, was counterpointed by a raging fashion for *l'art nègre,* for African masks and Brazilian sambas, both of which converged on, and were amplified by, the jazz craze. The Cocteau circle was especially conspicuous in its simultaneous and indiscriminate promotion of both trends, and the ballet *The Creation of the World* was perhaps the most explicit among high-profile performances to attempt a synthesis. The last chapter, in focusing on jazz as a popular music, did not do full justice to the "negrophilia" components of this cultural synthesis, though "primitivist" issues came up regularly. For the preoccupation with things Africanesque went considerably beyond jazz, finding expression in almost every sector of French culture, from painting and dance to music hall and furniture design. This chapter means to right this imbalance, by examining the history of this negrophilia fad and its various expressions, with an eye always to the peculiar twist it gave to the reception of jazz by the Parisian avant-garde. *The Creation of the World* will again loom large in the narrative, but in this case I will be referring to the total work of art—including Blaise Cendrars's libretto, Fernand Léger's sets, and the Ballets Suèdois's dance performance—and not merely Milhaud's score.

The Cakewalk Comes to France

In his fond recollections of the Nouveau Cirque (the New Circus), Jean Cocteau describes how he was witness there, when only thirteen, to a "theatrical event of historic proportions," the first arrival of "rhythms from America." He is referring to the musical review *Les Heureux nègres* (The Happy

Negroes, 1902), which brought the cakewalk to France—making "everything else turn pale and flee"—and which gave Parisians their first popular introduction to African American musical performance.[1]

As the audience vented its "delirium" by "stamping its feet," the stars of the show, "Mr. and Mrs. Elks," appeared on the stage and began to dance to an "unknown music" that the brass instruments "attacked" with vigor. As Cocteau vividly recollects it:

> They danced: skinny, crooked, beribboned, glittering with sequins, spangled with gaudy lights, hats raked over their eyes, their ears, knees higher than their thrust-out chins, hands twirling flexible canes, wrenching their gestures from themselves and hammering the artificial floor with taps on their patent leather shoes. They danced, they glided, they reared, they kicked, they broke themselves in two, three, four, then they stood up again, they bowed. . . . And behind them the whole city, the whole of Europe began dancing.[2]

Cocteau's fix on these "rhythms" from black America evinces none of the romantic primitivism later displayed by his colleagues (especially Cendrars, Milhaud, and Paul Morand). There is no allusion to the primordial, the exotic, the magical, to lazy rhythms, smooth undulations, childlike innocence, or natural frenzies. What he accentuates are sharp angularities, flinty protrusions, broken rhythms, irregular pulsations, dismemberment, discontinuities, gaudiness, mechanical violence, and modernity. Indeed, it is the city and the machine that are being evoked here, not the jungle or the fetish. This is altogether consistent with Cocteau's general take on jazz.[3]

Of course, we can assume that these thoughts were not floating full-blown through Cocteau's head at the age of twelve, when he was excitedly following the gyrations of Mr. and Mrs. Elks. The above recollections were published in 1935, when his views about African American culture had already hardened into dogma and his negrophilia had long been left behind. In fact, African American musical performance did not gain a strong foothold in French cultural production until World War I. The dramatic entry of Mr. and Mrs. Elks was not duplicated by other black Americans for a decade, although there were occasional sightings of black vaudeville acts (the "Colored Girls" at the Moulin Rouge) and anonymous ragtime pianists.[4]

The only established African American performer to precede Mr. and Mrs. Elks in Paris was Chocolat, who with the Englishman Footit formed the most famous clown team in Paris during the fin de siècle. At the age of five, Cocteau was taken to the Nouveau Cirque to see the "unfortunate Chocolat," a "stupid negro," who served as the butt of Footit's jokes, cuffs, and hazing. Cocteau clearly preferred Footit's "flash," "charm," and "suppleness."[5] But as a construct of the nineteenth-century white imaginary, Chocolat was a vestige of the past, of minstrel shows and blackface, whereas the Elks had introduced a novel form of African American performance, which was to become a key component in the formation of postwar negrophilia. Even years before the war, Debussy had already, though somewhat meekly and tentatively, incorporated in *Golliwog's Cakewalk* (1908) some aspects of the rhythms that *Les Heureux nègres* had brought with them to France.

The Collectors

The second key phenomenon paving the way for postwar negrophilia also emerged in the first decade of the century, though independently of the first, when Picasso had his by now mythologized encounter with African masks at the Musée d'Ethnographie du Trocadéro. In the most recent version of the story, Picasso went to the Trocadéro in June 1907 to look at plaster casts of Romanesque sculpture, when he was still struggling with the "Iberian" version of his *Demoiselles d'Avignon*. In a "purely serendipitous" act, he pushed through the wrong door and found himself in the African room of the ethnographic wing.[6] His first impression was one of "disgust." "The flea market. The smell. I didn't leave. I stayed. I stayed." Picasso felt "that something was happening [to him] . . . that it was very important." He felt "shock," a "revelation," a "charge," a "force" emanating from the objects of this "frightful museum." His interest in the masks, as he insists, was not purely formal. He construed them primarily as "magical things," "mediators," "intercessors," as well as "tools" and "weapons" against "threatening spirits." This experience energized Picasso to resume his work on the *Demoiselles,* and to transform it from a narrative study to an "exorcism" picture, primarily by reconstructing the faces of two of the *Demoiselles* in a style reminiscent of the African masks.[7]

Though there is some dispute over who was the first among them, Picasso, Vlaminck, Matisse, Derain, and Braque all began avidly to collect African sculptures and masks at about this time. They combed the various flea markets of the city, such as Emile Heymann's Au Vieux Rouet (At the Old Wheel), which advertised its "curiosities," "antiquities," and "weapons of savages" (*armes de sauvages*).[8] African artifacts had been on display in Paris for decades before Picasso's discovery and had been especially highlighted, in a glorification of the French colonial empire, at the Universal Expositions of 1878, 1889, and 1900. But it is only with Picasso and his colleagues that they began to circulate as works of art and not merely as fodder for the burgeoning ethnographic sciences.

It was not long before the more adventurous members of the institutional-ized art world—young art dealers, critics, and collectors—followed the lead of the artists by slowly creating spaces in their discourses and practices for the flow of artifacts from Africa. The all-purpose expression "*l'art nègre*" was first codified in 1912 in an article predicting that tribal art would replace Greek art in the training of young artists. By the early 1910s Paul Guillaume, a clerk in a rubber tire firm, was gaining access to "fetishes" regularly ac-quired by his employer. With the guidance of Guillaume Apollinaire, who was also beginning to acquire African artifacts, he left the colonial corporate world sometime before 1914 to start an art gallery specializing in African art. Between the two world wars, he was to become the most prestigious dealer and collector of African art, and its most enthusiastic spokesperson, with such pronouncements as "The intelligence of modern man ought to become negro" and "Negro art is the fructifying seed of the spiritual twentieth cen-tury"—or, even more hyperbolically, "We who think we have a soul will blush at the poverty of our spiritual state before the superiority of blacks who have four souls, one in the head, one in the nose and throat, the shadow, and one in the blood."[9]

Modernists and *L'Art nègre*

The mild sensation caused by *Les Heureux nègres* and the early engagement of a few artists and would-be dealers with African objects, though laying the groundwork for it, did not yet exemplify the phenomenon of negrophilia that materialized in the waning years of the war and peaked in the mid-twenties, because these events even when taken in conjunction lacked three character-istics crucial to this phenomenon.

First, negrophilia completely conflates African and African American cul-tural production, and the states of mind underlying them, while eliding all but the most superficial differences. Needless to say, it also elides the differ-ences within African culture and African American culture (e.g., sculptures of the Dongo and poetry of the Fang, Brazilian maxixes, and American rag-time). It treats these quite distinct cultural products as mere expressions of "negroness" and speaks glibly of a universal *art nègre* or *âme nègre* (negro soul). "In the 1920s, Paris was flooded with things *nègre,* an expansive cate-gory that included North American jazz, syncretic Brazilian rhythms, African, Oceanean, and Alaskan carvings, ritual 'poetry' from south of the Sahara and from the Australian outback, the literature from the Harlem Renaissance, and René Maran's *Batouala* (subtitled 'veritable roman nègre') which won the Prix Goncourt"—all of these, says James Clifford, instances of "the negrophilia that was sweeping avant-garde music, literature, and art."[10] On the other hand, neither the young Picasso or Debussy, nor their peers at the turn of the century, had sought to subsume under one concept the cakewalk of the Nouveau Cirque and the Dan masks of the Ivory Coast.

Clifford's statement alludes to a second characteristic of negrophilia, which is the rapid and conspicuous circulation of things *nègre* in the system of cultural production and consumption—in effect, the pronounced commodification of "negroness" by the culture industry. According to Jean Laude, author of the classic *La Peinture française (1905–1914) et l'art nègre* and major articulator of the notion of *negrophilie,* "up to 1914, negro art is collected and interrogated only by a small circle of innovative artists, writers, and their admirers. . . . [After the war] negro art leaves the flea markets. Specialized galleries open up. Collections fill up. Fashion seizes the movement." "Negro art thus enters into the public domain and commercial circuits."[11] Indeed, it could be argued that negrophilia was the most widespread fashion movement in Parisian cultural life between 1918 and 1925, cutting across the divides of high culture and mass culture and wending its way through the various modernist sects, while making its presence felt in all the media—painting, dance, music, theater, and literature.

But—and this is the third characteristic of postwar negrophilia—one must recognize the primary role played by the avant-garde and its allies in the commodification of everything that was called "negro." Because publicity and advertisement are usually associated with mass culture, it is sometimes forgotten how skillful and enthusiastic the modernist avant-gardes had been in exploiting the instruments of self-promotion—shock and *scandales,* manifestos, posters, demonstrations, conspicuous slumming, vociferous controversies, catchy names (e.g., futurism, dadaism, vorticism)—and indeed how they pioneered those very techniques and ploys that constitute what we familiarly call the "publicity stunt." By zealously promoting the virtues of "negro" art and music, the avant-gardes sought not only to widen their own public, but also to contextualize their aesthetic practices within the discourses about the "negro," thus adding to the apparent transgressiveness and exoticness of their work. "Already by 1919," says Laude, "the public mind was forming a connection between the art of innovative painters and that of the Africans," though there were no longer any external resemblances between them. Thus, "[Robert] Delauney would venomously attack what he called the 'neo-negro,' which according to him characterized cubism."[12]

At its peak in the 1920s, the negrophilia phenomenon found its most exemplary expression in two of the major cultural spectacles of the 1920s, the ballet *La Création du monde* in 1923 and the popular musical review the *Revue nègre* in 1925. These were made possible by a sudden new flow of "negro" culture into France during and after the war and an exuberant and almost immediate reaction to it by the Paris avant-gardes.

The Influx of "Negro" Culture

Negrophilia perhaps would never have emerged when it did, had it not been for the tumultuous demographic changes that a world war inevitably precipitated. Paul Morand, the novelist reputed for his "sensational exoticism and notorious slumming," wrote: "Before 1914, did the negro exist? Occasionally in the universal expositions, one would find a negro village. The negro was something ludicrous or exotic, as in *Robinson Crusoe*. The only negro in Paris . . . wore a watch on his stomach, which marked our time not his."[13]

But the war brought many units of black soldiers to France, from the colonies as well as from the United States. There were 163,952 black Africans stationed in Europe under the French flag, of whom 30,000 died for the "*patrie*" and many of whom remained after the war as occupying forces on the Rhine.[14] A large percentage of the 370,000 African Americans who had joined the armed forces were stationed in France, though they were restricted by the United States Army to "labor and transport details, unloading ships and burying the dead" and were not allowed to fight or even to fraternize with the French troops.[15] Having found life in France more congenial, many African Americans stayed after the war. Thus, in 1928 Morand observed:

> France now finds herself at the head of millions of negroes . . . not only in its colonial empire, but on the Rhine, at the Cote-d'Azur, in the factories, in the bureaus, at the ports; and if that was not enough, here they are landing from New York . . . , from New Orleans, Brazil, Haiti, Charleston. And let's not forget the mulattos, half-breeds, and mixed-bloods of all types.[16]

Not surprisingly, the African Americans brought to Europe a whole variety of musical and performance styles, but especially the new jazz fad that swept through America in 1917 with the Original Dixieland Jazz Band's recording of "Livery Blues." In 1918 James Reese Europe, the leader of the most famous black society dance band in America, was assigned by his regiment in France (the Harlem Hellfighters) the task of assembling "the best damn brass band in the United States Army." Europe put together a unit with maximum versatility, which could do anything from classics (e.g., Brahms or Grieg overtures) to cakewalks, marches, "plantation melodies," commercial blues, popular songs, comedy sketches, dance numbers (by Bill "Bojangles" Robinson), as well as the freak instrumental effects and barnyard imitations then associated with jazz. The Hellfighters, as they were called, traveled thousands of miles throughout France, mainly to towns where troops were stationed, evoking the most exuberant responses wherever they played, such as that "of an old [French]woman [who] all of a sudden started doing a dance that resembled 'Walking the Dog.'"[17] These successes quickly opened the doors of Paris night-clubs for civilian African American bands, such as Louis Mitchell's Jazz Kings and Will Marion Cook's Southern Syncopated Orchestra, who displayed the same kind of eclectic diversity. Maurice Sachs, the young chronicler of the Paris avant-garde, recalls the "negroes in orchestras" with their "agonizing and terrible howls, soft lamentations, and cries of children; jazz shakes up the craziest and most moderate of bodies."[18]

Nonetheless and not surprisingly, the French avant-gardes got their initial experiences of "jazz" primarily from white interpreters. The first musical event in Paris to be identified as "jazz" was the review *Laisse-les tomber* (Let Them Fall), starring Gaby Deslys and Harry Pilcer, which opened in December 1917 at the Casino de Paris. Deslys, a veteran French music hall singer, had discovered the young (white) "rag-time" dancer Pilcer in America and had brought him back to France with his brother's band, Murray Pilcer's American Sherbo Sextette. The review created a sensation, as everywhere people were raving about the "jazz-band" and "jazz-dancing."[19] Cocteau, who was in attendance, spoke of "this hurricane of rhythm and beating of drums, a sort of tame catastrophe which left [Deslys and Pilcer] quite intoxicated. . . . The house was on its feet to applaud, roused from its inertia by this extraordinary turn which, compared to the madness of Offenbach, is what a tank would be side-by-side with an 1870 state-carriage."[20] For the next decade, it became the rule for French music hall stars to pepper their shows with at least the appearance of jazz sounds (as in Mistinguett's *Paris qui jazz*).

While in London in 1920, Cocteau and Milhaud made the acquaintance of Billy Arnold's Novelty Jazz Band, a white American-British ensemble somewhat in the style of the Original Dixieland Jazz Band. This was the first experience of jazz for Milhaud, which quite overwhelmed him and set him off on the whole series of musical explorations discussed in the last chapter. Back in Paris, Cocteau and Milhaud brought the Billy Arnold band to the attention of Jean Wiener, the impresario of avant-garde concerts, who scheduled them on the same bill as a player piano rendition of Stravinsky's *Le Sacre du printemps* and a sonata by Milhaud. Says Wiener: "All the musicians in Paris were there. . . . As soon as the [jazz] musicians began playing, [Albert Roussel] got up and ostentatiously left the room and slammed the door." Maurice Ravel exclaimed after the concert: "You did very well to have us hear these musicians. It was wonderful!"[21]

The fact that for the Paris avant-garde all jazz was coded as "negro music" no matter who played it made it possible for white jazz bands to contribute significantly to the growth of negrophilia while at the same time reinforcing the view that with a little practice, Europeans could master anything that was "negro." Milhaud was the first, in a major article on the topic in 1923, to sharply distinguish black jazz from white jazz, with a clear preference for the former.[22] From then on, white musicians no longer played a significant role in the spread of negrophilia.

Milhaud was not the first modernist, however, to write a critical essay on jazz. Already, Cocteau had written "Jazz-band" for the newspaper *Après-midi* (1919), which asserted that "art is made more virile by these savage contacts."[23] In the same year, Ernst-Alexandre Ansermet, the conductor most closely associated with Stravinsky, wrote his now-famous review of the Southern Syncopated Orchestra, with a special eulogy of the clarinetist Sidney Bechet,

> that clarinet virtuoso who is, so it seems, the first of his race to have composed perfectly formed blues on the clarinet. . . . What a moving thing it is to meet this very black, fat boy with white teeth and that narrow forehead, who is very glad one likes what he does, but who can say nothing of his art, save that he follows his "own way," and when one thinks that his "own way" is perhaps the highway the whole world will sing along tomorrow.[24]

In 1920 Robert Goffin, poet and major propagandist for jazz, founded the journal *Disque Vert* for which he wrote critical articles on jazz and a series of poems called "Jazz-band." The first serious book on jazz, *Le Jazz: La Musique moderne,* appeared in 1926, coauthored by the ethnomusicologist André Schaeffner, who four years later was to take part in a mammoth ethnographic mission to Africa.[25]

Modernist Negrophilia Takes Hold

The postwar avant-gardes did not restrict themselves merely to being aficionados, mere consumers, of "negro" art and music, but quite actively brought their negrophilia to bear in a variety of ways on their own aesthetic practices. They appropriated "negro" culture, parodied it, and subjected it to pastiche and *bricolage;* they exploited its formal properties and tapped its alleged spiritual powers; they claimed to synthesize it with European culture, to explore its roots, to reveal it in its authenticity, and to fulfill its hidden potential; they exhibited it, shared their aesthetic spaces with it, publicized it, and capitalized on its shock value.

We can date the beginning of negrophilia with the performance of the ballet *Parade* (1917), not only because Erik Satie's score includes a "Ragtime du paquebot" (Steamship Rag), but also because it set in motion the formation of the Cocteau circle, the avant-garde group that was to be most implicated in negrophilia. Cocteau wrote the script for *Parade,* Picasso designed the sets, and a group of young composers, later to be known as *les six* (notably Milhaud and his colleagues Poulenc, Auric, and Honegger), sat in rapt attendance, now enthusiastic followers of Satie. The circle would also include Paul Guillaume, Milhaud's collaborators in *Creation,* and even the dying Apollinaire as he was grudgingly ceding the role of impresario to Cocteau. In 1916 Apollinaire helped his protégé Paul Guillaume set up an exhibit of "twenty-five negro sculptures, fetishes from Africa and Oceania," in a studio that was being used primarily for concerts and poetry readings, and coauthored with him the first catalog focusing on *l'art nègre.* Equally groundbreaking was the fact that this "alien" art was being exhibited alongside paintings by Picasso, Matisse, and Modigliani, and being viewed by audiences who were simultaneously listening to poetry readings by Cocteau and Cendrars, or to concerts by members of *les six.*[26] It was becoming a standard practice of the postwar avant-garde to create such motley and heterogeneous assemblages of performances and exhibitions, oftentimes incorporating "negro" artifacts or imagery.

At one of these concerts, Poulenc introduced his *Rapsodie nègre,* the ultimate in negrophile chic, which was inspired by a mock book of African poetry written in pseudo-African dialect. Poulenc used some of this dialect for the vocal interlude of his piece and created a *ronde* that played on Parisian stereotypes of tribal dance.[27] This piece was performed again at the comte de Beaumont's "great Negro *fête*" (1918), which also included "jazz performed by American negro soldiers." Cocteau, who was vacationing in the sun, was disappointed that he was unable to attend. "Yes, everybody tells me about the gold and silver trombones of your negroes in the rue Duroc," he wrote to Beaumont. And to Poulenc, "I'm beginning to be dark enough to be in the band."[28]

Milhaud also tried his hand at burlesquing African American music with the composition "Caramel mou" (1920), a "shimmy" danced by "Graton the negro," who also sang lyrics composed by Cocteau. Graton's "indecisive shuffling," despite his having been hyped by Cocteau as a great performer, eliminated any doubt that this composition was anything but avant-garde farce.[29]

In 1919 *l'art nègre* finally made the transition from cult to fashion object with Paul Guillaume's wildly successful First Exposition of Negro Art and Oceanic Art, held at the chic and luxurious Devambez Gallery. To celebrate this achievement, Guillaume staged his own *Fête nègre* at the Théâtre des

Champs-Elysées, at which his typically hyperbolic comments about *l'art nègre* were followed by dance and musical numbers based on African tales and legends.[30] These performances were described as "bamboula burlesque"—the word "bamboula" connoting the European stereotype of African dance as "libido whipped up collectively by the sorcery of the tom-tom."[31]

No one, however, was quite as nonchalant and lighthearted in his negrophilia as Cocteau. Did he not say that "if you accept the Jazz Band you should also welcome a literature that the intelligence can savor like a cocktail"?[32] But this insouciance disguised a certain diffidence, for (as was explained in the last chapter) jazz in Cocteau's view is not an art but a "brutal disorder" that stimulates art and thus not something to be appropriated or imitated in modernist primary practices.[33] Or as his friend Cendrars put it, *"Le jazz hot* is not an art but a new way of living."[34] This did not prevent Cocteau from staging the ultimate of negrophilian pastiches, the ballet-pantomime *Le Boeuf sur le toit* (The Ox on the Roof, 1920), with music by Milhaud. "Still haunted" by the memories of a two-year stay in Brazil, Milhaud had decided to write an orchestral piece inspired by the carnival in Rio, which he was to name *Le Boeuf sur le toit,* after a samba that a "band was playing [one night] as all the negresses danced and danced in their blue dresses." "[He] assembled a few popular melodies, tangos, maxixes, sambas, and even a Portuguese Fado, and transcribed them with a rondo-like theme recurring between each of them."[35] Upon hearing this piece, Cocteau thought it would be perfect for a "farce" that he had been planning, a pantomime situated in a North American bar during Prohibition, with a mix of black and white characters, a "negro boxer smoking a cigar as long as a torpedo," a "negro dwarf," a decapitated policeman, a red-haired woman, and a barman "all pink and white." To further enhance the sense of haphazard cultural *bricolage,* Cocteau hired the famous Fratellini clowns to play each of these characters and directed them to dance extremely slowly in "deliberate disobedience" to the quickness of the music. It was, as he put it, "an American farce written by a Parisian who has never been in America."[36]

The success of *Le Boeuf sur le toit* was substantial enough to lead to the formation of the equally successful bar with the same name, at which Cocteau played host to his peers and admirers and occasionally performed on drums in a rather makeshift jazz band that included the concert impresario Jean Wiener on piano and the African American Vance Lowry on saxophone and banjo.[37] Later in the same year at an exhibition of Francis Picabia's work, Cocteau (now known as the *"poète-orchestre"*) performed on snare and bass drums, castanets, drinking glasses, toy flute, and the klaxon, in a "Parisian jazz" band including also Auric and Poulenc.[38]

Yet only a few months after the performance of *Le Boeuf sur le toit*, Cocteau boldly announced the end of the fad for things *nègres*. In response to a survey on the topic by the magazine *Action*, he proclaimed rather peremptorily that "the negro crisis has become as boring as the *japonisme* of Mallarmé."[39] At about the same time, he and his ally Georges Auric (of *les six*) were strenuously pushing an anti-jazz and anti-America aesthetic line in Cocteau's journal *Le Coq*, as expressed in the slogan "Return to poetry. Disappearance of the skyscraper. Reappearance of the rose." Auric wrote that though he had been "moved to tears" by such American jazz pieces as "Hindustan" and "Indianola," it was now time to "reinvent nationalism. Jazz woke us up: from now on let's stop our ears so as not to hear it."[40] This view was the subtext for his composition *Adieu New York*, a fox-trot bidding adieu to the fox-trot.

The Creation of the World, Again

Cocteau was soon forced to eat his words, since negrophilia, far from dead, had yet to unveil its main events. *The Creation of the World*, staged with stunning success by the Ballets Suèdois in October 1923, was the most thoroughgoing and systematic expression of negrophilia thus far to be attempted by the avant-garde. It also marked a shift from parody, play, and *bricolage* to a posture of authenticity, a demeanor of studious loyalty to African and African American sources and an apparent blending of art and ethnography. Part of the glitter of this performance was due no doubt to the collaborative participation of four major celebrities of the Paris avant-garde. By bringing together a script based on African folk tales of creation, taken from Cendrars's *Anthologie nègre,* and a musical composition rooted in the jazz that Milhaud heard in Harlem clubs, this ballet articulated in the most explicit fashion the tenet, so central to negrophilia, of a common "negro soul" bridging the geographical, temporal, and cultural divides of ancient Africa and contemporary America.

Cendrars, Milhaud, and Börlin (as well as the director of the Ballets Suèdois, Rolf de Maré) were already well-known negrophiles, in contrast with Léger, for whom the "negro" themes of the ballet were merely a fortuitous occasion to apply his own principles of spectacle and theatrical dynamism. For Milhaud, the preoccupation with things *nègres* was to last only a few years, while for Börlin and de Maré it was part of a larger interest in all "folk" cultures. Cendrars was the only one for whom it was to prove a lifetime obsession. "I would love to be this poor negro and while my time away," he once wrote. "For then those beautiful negresses would be my sisters."[41]

By 1923 Cendrars was already widely esteemed for his "admirable knowledge of the negro soul"—in part because of the authority of his *Anthologie nègre,* a collection of African tales and poems, but also because of his reputation as an incessant traveler to "unknown lands" and a tireless reader of exotic books. Already by 1919, before the publication of the *Anthologie,* Cocteau had proclaimed Cendrars as the "one among us who best embodies the new exoticism. Mix of motorcars and black fetishes. . . . He has travelled. He has seen. He has witnessed."[42] Michel Leiris said of the *Anthologie* that "more than a book, this is an act." Morand noted how in this book the "negro appears just as we know him: impulsive, childish, gentle, eager for destruction" —a not surprising construction, given Cendrars's preoccupation with tales and poems dealing with "fetishes" and magic. Since then the French literary establishment has canonized him as the paradigmatic negrophile—the poet who "most loved and understood blacks for themselves."[43] There was, however, nothing very original about Cendrars's anthology, which was put together, rather haphazardly and sometimes inaccurately, from a variety of ethnographic anthologies, many of which were also derivative. For the scenario of the ballet, Cendrars proposed from his collection a Fang story of creation (from the Gabon), according to which "animals, insects, birds, and finally man and woman emerge from a shapeless mass in the presence of the three giant deities of creation."[44]

Responding to the "murmur of the infinite," Rolf de Maré, like Cendrars, also traveled through the continents of Asia, Africa, and Europe, "remaining in a particular country as long as it interested [him]," where he was "drawn especially to the popular arts in all their manifestations."[45] Having a second home there, it is not surprising that he would want to make Africa a topic for the Ballets Suèdois. Börlin had already choreographed and performed a solo dance called "Sculpture nègre" in 1919, quite possibly at Guillaume's *Fête nègre.* Once Cendrars and Léger were brought in, the dance company devoted itself to "extremely serious" documentary research at ethnographic museums on "black civilizations," thus discovering and implementing some "hardly known principles" such as "dancers on stilts" and dancing "on all fours like animals."[46]

It may be surprising that, given their studious concern for authenticity, de Maré and Börlin did not seek Fang music to accompany their Fang tale, or at least a musical score that was generically or eclectically African. But there were no avant-garde composers in Paris who knew that music, nor any group of symphony musicians who could have played it. Luckily, Darius Milhaud was just back from New York, where he had just discovered "negro" jazz, which he had no doubt was rooted in the "depths of the centuries," in the "darkest corner of the negro soul, the vestigial traces of Africa."[47] Thus, he could offer his Harlem-based "jazz" composition as the perfect complement to the deep Africanisms of the *Creation* libretto, choreography, and sets. He was in effect claiming authenticity at least at a second remove for this musical commentary on African myths: first the somewhat problematic relation of his own symphonic score to Harlem jazz, and then the rather speculative connection between the latter and African musical culture (about which, of course, he knew nothing). His friend and collaborator Paul Collaer had no doubt about Milhaud's success in this regard. According to him, Milhaud "has brilliantly transposed" jazz and "raised [it] to a superior plane," where "the blues and rag themes take on characteristics of depth and grandeur." The real world of "negroes," that of "lush, humid, and warm forests," is musically captured through a whole "gamut of emotions" from "pastoral peace" to "gasping passion."[48]

Revue nègre

As the vehicle for Josephine Baker's debut in Paris, the *Revue nègre* (1925) has quite understandably become the best known of the negrophile spectacles of the postwar era. But it was arguably the last to have a significant impact, not so much in shaping negrophilia as in moving it into the cultural mainstream, no longer the preserve of the fashion vanguards and tastemakers.

The fairly sharp differences between the *Revue nègre* and *The Creation of the World*—popular culture versus high culture, modern black America over and against mythical Africa—were softened by a shared public, close institutional connections, and the homogenizing effects of negrophilia. After disbanding the Ballets Suèdois (1924), Rolf de Maré transformed the Théâtre des Champs-Elysées—where *The Creation of the World, Le Boeuf sur le toit,* and Guillaume's *Fête nègre* had been showcased—into the Music-Hall des Champs-Elysées, now a mecca for popular entertainment interspersed with some high-cultural dance events. His first successful venture was the *Revue nègre,* imported from New York and put together along the lines of *Shuffle Along, The Chocolate Dandies,* and other Harlem reviews. The first audiences included de Maré's close avant-garde colleagues—Léger, Cocteau, Milhaud, Guillaume—all of whom of course raved enthusiastically.[49]

But before it could be performed, the *Revue* had to be redesigned to fit French expectations.[50] Altogether appalled by the lack of "authenticity"—"Precision dancing he thought might be appropriate for German or English girls but not for blacks"—the French producer devised a new final act, called the "Danse sauvage" (Savage Dance), in which Josephine Baker was dressed in feathers and went into a "stomach dance" on the floor, a presage of later performances in her banana costume. This urban woman from St. Louis, resituated in the imaginary jungles of Paris, was constantly described as a "magnificent animal" (e.g., a "bird of the forest") and photographed in poses clearly reminiscent of the African statuettes that had been circulating in France for the past few decades. Thus, as the Africaneity of the *Creation* was African-Americanized by the tonalities of jazz, the African American entertainments of the *Revue* were Africanized by the interventions of the French imaginary.[51]

After the *Revue nègre*, but not because of it, the negrophilia phenomenon went into decline, though strong remnants of it remained ensconced both in mass-cultural entertainments and in decorative commodities for the well-heeled (e.g., art deco furniture). In large part, this was because the avant-garde movement, which had most enthusiastically advanced it, was simultaneously falling apart and turning its interest away from things *nègres*. Had not Milhaud announce in 1927 that he was abandoning "the broken throbbings of syncopation" for a "renascent classicism"?[52] Meanwhile, Satie died, Cocteau converted to Catholicism, the Ballets Suédois was dissolved, the Théâtre des Champs-Elysées became a cinema, Rolf de Maré withdrew into private life, "and Francis Picabia moved to the Cote d'Azur to produce tedious decorative art."[53] The surrealists, who were still quite active, directed their primitivism toward Oceanic and Native American artifacts, and largely stayed away from jazz primarily because of André Breton's general abhorrence of music.

More importantly, the increasing sophistication of ethnography (Michel Leiris and later Claude Lévi-Strauss) was slowly undermining the myths of exoticism and the universal "negro soul," and the developing complexity of jazz elicited an audience much more culturally specific in its tastes for things *nègres*. And, quite crucially, Francophone black writers from the Antilles and Africa began to intervene in the white French discourse about the "negro," as did also the émigrés in France from the Harlem Renaissance. Of course, French discourse about African, African American, Brazilian, and Antillean culture did not abate with the decline of negrophilia, nor did it necessarily always become more "progressive." It simply took on a host of different, historically specific forms that also need to be studied.

ART INTO POP
AMERICAN POSTMODERNISM

A. Jazz at War (1942–50)

FIGURE 5   Jazz Street: Fifty-second Street, New York City (mid-forties). Courtesy of William Gottlieb.

CHAPTER 6
MOLDY FIGS AND MODERNISTS

The Postmodern Turn

The historical transition of jazz from an entertainment music to an art music, initiated by the bebop revolution in the mid-1940s, set in motion a fundamental transformation in the way in which the barriers between high and mass culture would henceforth be negotiated.[1] Before then the interchanges between high and low were decidedly one-sided, as modernists eagerly appropriated materials and devices from a more passive mass culture that was hardly aware of being pilfered or hardly cared. With the bebop movement and since, mass culture has been more the aggressor in this interchange, though high culture has continued also to be active (e.g., pop art). Rock music, film, MTV, and advertising have liberally scavenged from a whole storehouse of avant-garde devices and practices. But no form of mass culture seems to have crossed the boundary between "entertainment" and "art" as early, decisively, or irreversibly as jazz, which has since achieved an almost sacred position in American culture.

As I have already argued,[2] the postmodern era in high/low interactions emerged when popular culture abandoned its previously passive, almost unwitting, engagement with high culture, to become an initiator and even an aggressor. As the first popular entertainment to transform itself into an avant-garde art form, jazz gets credit for inaugurating the postmodernist era of high/low interactions. This undertaking on the part of jazz musicians and critics occurred at a time when jazz was no longer a favorite child of the European avant-garde, having been abandoned by its patrons (e.g., Milhaud) before the 1920s came to an end. A lone exception, Stravinsky's *Ebony Concerto* (1946), written for the Woody Herman Orchestra, had little impact at the time. By the 1930s the little attention bestowed by the avant-garde on jazz tended to veer toward rank hostility—Theodor Adorno, of course, but also such an erstwhile aficionado and appropriator as Ernst Krenek, the composer of the 1920s "jazz" opera *Johnny Spielt Auf.*[3] But this proved to be a blessing in disguise. For jazz musicians could launch their own raids on the avant-garde without any meddling from high culture.

This section explores bebop's crucial role in setting in motion the transition from modernist to the postmodernist eras in high/low interactions. The bebop revolution did not occur in a vacuum, but was born in the midst of one of the most divisive disputes in the history of jazz, between the partisans of the swing bands and the Dixieland revivalists who wanted a return to early jazz. This chapter analyzes this revivalist controversy and the new aesthetic discourses it generated, which set the stage for the reception of bebop and made possible the construal of it as an avant-garde music. The following chapter will narrate the rise and fall of bebop as proclaimed, interpreted, and influenced by the jazz press.

Deciphering the transition from modernism to postmodernism in high/low engagements requires a significant shift in focus and perhaps methodology. In modernism such crossings of the divide took place along many registers, in music and critical discourse, of course, but also along institutional frontiers (the artistic cabaret, Le Boeuf sur le Toit) and in the slumming and secondary aesthetic practices of artist-bohemians. In contrast, for the postmodern turn, discourse was necessarily the dominant medium in enabling popular music initially to connect with, and appropriate, avant-garde concepts and practices.[4] The discourses of critics were, of course, crucial for alerting an otherwise unsuspecting public that jazz, for example, was undergoing a transformation from "entertainment" to "art." But such discourses were equally responsible for *constituting* the new jazz as an avant-garde music, for collectively forging an interpretive template that was foisted on still indeterminate and eclectic musical practices. As Scott DeVeaux has shown, the practices of bebop musicians initially were considerably more many-sided, considerably more enmeshed in both entertainment and art, than the jazz canon would have us believe.[5] Discourse's crucial role in the postmodern turn is further amplified by the fact that none of the other traditional options of contact between high and low were easily available to popular musics in their initial excursions across the divide. In the mid-1940s, jazz did not yet possess sufficient cultural credentials to draw high art into joint institutional ventures (e.g., a jazz club/art gallery), nor given its cultural vulnerability was it necessarily desirable for it to do so. And what could it have meant for bebop musicians to generate secondary aesthetic practices by "slumming" in high-cultural haunts? What I have said about jazz also holds for rock's transition from "vulgar entertainment" to "art" in the mid-1960s, which I will narrate in the next section. Later both jazz and rock will have accumulated sufficient cultural capital to enact successfully such extra-discursive alliances across the high/low divide. But, for the time being, the aesthetic discourses of jazz and rock must take center stage.

Warring Factions

The jazz world in the 1940s was embroiled in two major factional wars, two schisms in which spokespersons for the new were set off against those for the old. During a period spanning less than a decade, it twice reenacted the centuries-old battle between ancients and moderns so endemic to Western culture. Swing music, the music of the big bands that had dominated jazz and the popular charts since 1935, was deeply implicated in both disputes, in one case supported by modernists and in the other by traditionalists. The first of these conflicts pitted swing against the newly revitalized New Orleans jazz that it had previously supplanted, and the second against the bebop avant-garde movement that threatened to make it obsolescent.

The seeds for the first jazz war were sown in the late 1930s when a few nightclubs, defying the big band boom, began to feature small jazz combos playing in the abandoned New Orleans style of the 1920s, today popularly referred to as "Dixieland." Such a mild turn of events would not have led to a Dixieland revival without the enthusiastic participation of the aficionados and cultists of the old jazz , who collected out-of-print records and exchanged arcane discographical information. These purists were driven not only by nostalgia but also by a revulsion toward the swing music industry, which by shamelessly pandering to the mass markets, had in their eyes forsaken the principles of "true" jazz. A spate of small sectarian journals appeared on the scene, to give vent to these revivalist views and concerns. They set themselves off as the only authentic alternatives to the two dominant mainstream jazz journals, *Down Beat* and *Metronome,* which were altogether beholden to the swing phenomenon.[6]

In 1942 *Metronome* fired the first shot of the modernist-revivalist war with a vigorous attack on the exclusionary purism and incessant carping of the revivalists, whom they derisively labeled "moldy figs."[7] Over the next four years, in a continuous barrage of editorials and articles, *Metronome* would castigate New Orleans jazz as technically backward and "corny," and the writers of the revivalist journals as hysterical cultists and musical ignoramuses, against whom it positioned itself as the defender of modernism and progress in jazz. The revivalists counterattacked with charges of crass commercialism, faddism, and Eurocentrism.

By 1946, just as this war was scaling down, a second battle of jazz ancients and moderns was beginning to heat up. Modernism was now being represented by the bebop school, most notably Dizzy Gillespie, Charlie Parker, and Bud Powell, while swing music suddenly found itself relegated to the company of New Orleans jazz, on the side of the traditional and the tried-and-true. Bebop's opponents complained about the inaccessibility and undanceability of the music, the "wrong notes" and excessive musical acrobatics, the elitism, hostility, and avant-garde posturing of the musicians and their unconventional dress and morally suspicious lifestyles. Bebop triumphed in 1948 and died in 1950, only to be reclaimed later in the canon of jazz history. It was abandoned even by its modernist supporters, who laid in wait for the next phalanx in the triumphal march of modern experimental jazz.

Aesthetic Discourses and Musical Revolutions

The bebop revolution has since been enshrined in the jazz canon as a contest of epic proportions, occurring at the major fault line of jazz history. Bebop is given credit for having transformed jazz from a popular dance music, firmly ensconced in the hit parade, to a demanding, experimental art music, consigned to small clubs and sophisticated audiences. In contrast, the Dixieland war is usually construed as a retrograde sideshow, a rearguard skirmish that temporarily delayed the avant-garde advances initiated by bebop.[8]

I will be contesting this too tidy a view of what admittedly has turned out to be the most significant permutation within jazz history. What will especially have to be rejected is the severe contrast drawn between a backward-looking Dixieland war and a forward-looking bebop war. In point of fact, both contests were fought on much of the same discursive terrain—the same field of concepts, issues, aesthetic standards, and opposing theories. Indeed, the Dixieland war, as it waned, transposed itself so subtly into the bebop war that many contemporaries failed to distinguish between them.

This suggests that the apparently retrograde Dixieland war played a significant role in the transformation of jazz from an entertainment music to an avant-garde music. I am not asserting, however, that the New Orleans revival was, or was ever meant to be, an avant-garde musical movement, nor denying that bebop made the key musical innovations that ushered in the era of modern jazz. What I am accentuating, rather, is the crucial role that the Dixieland war played at the level of discourse, at the level of talk and patter, in magazines, books, and radio shows, in preparing the way for the emergence and acceptance of a jazz avant-garde.

The debates between swing modernists and New Orleans revivalists sufficiently reconstructed the issues, alternative characterizations, and standards for discoursing about jazz, to make it possible, and indeed to make it seem very natural, to refer to jazz as an "art" music, and to construe certain genres of jazz as "modernistic," "experimental," "formally complex," and "avant-garde," even before bebop made its appearance. In effect, what was being constructed in these debates was an aesthetic discourse for jazz, which was later to legitimate its breaching of the "great divide" between mass culture and art.[9] By "aesthetic discourse," I mean here not a set of agreed-upon claims about the artistic merit of various jazz styles, but rather a grouping of concepts, distinctions, oppositions, rhetorical ploys, and allowable inferences, which as a whole fixed the limits within which inquiries concerning the aesthetics of jazz could take place and without which the claim that jazz is an art form would be merely an abstraction or an incantation. The revivalists and modernists were slowly and collectively shaping and honing this new aesthetic through their acrimonious disagreements rather than in spite of them.

Thus, my purpose is neither to contest the canonical accounts of the revolutionary changes in jazz musical form in the 1940s, nor to rehabilitate the Dixieland revival, but rather to highlight the crucial role of what Foucault has called "discursive formations" in the constitution of jazz modernism.[10] I will show how the Dixieland war, as a war primarily of words, indeed a profusion and superabundance of words, engendered a new mapping of the jazz discursive terrain—a new construction of the aesthetic discourses of jazz—which was only to be amended, rather than radically transformed, by the bebop revolution.

The new aesthetic discourses, by no means pure, were laced with the idioms of commerce, politics, gender, and race. These idioms must be treated as integral to the newly emerging jazz aesthetic, rather than as mere intrusions or add-ons. Any attempt to extirpate them, in order to reveal the "pure" jazz aesthetic of that period, would leave us only with a uselessly inchoate and abstract residue, shorn of any historical specificity. This applies especially to the issue of race, which constantly surfaced in jazz writing during the 1940s despite, or because of, the fact that virtually all jazz journals in that period were owned, edited, and composed by whites and sold primarily to a white readership. At this time blacks entered into the revivalist-modernist field of discourse primarily in the role of musician-subjects, interviewed to settle some score between white critics. Quite clearly, the newly emerging "official" discourses of jazz aesthetics only codified the preferences, styles, and practices of the primarily white sector of the jazz world. But these codifications were nonetheless skewed, in very intricate ways, by the pressing anxieties of racial contact.

In the following sections, I will reconstruct the new discursive formations generated in the Dixieland-swing debates—in effect, the new official jazz aesthetic—by examining in sequence the following clusters of concepts, networks of arguments, and groups of oppositional terms that played key roles in these debates: (1) genres and brand names; (2) art and commerce; (3) folklore and European high culture; (4) progress and the new; (5) standards, technique, and schooling; (6) affect and antics; (7) fascists and communists; and (8) black and white.

Genres and Brand Names

Wanting the word "jazz" all to themselves, the revivalists sought to hammer out a precise formula that would clearly oppose jazz to swing. Though they bickered incessantly about the fine details of the proper definition, they agreed that no music could be called "jazz" that was not collectively improvised and whose melodies, rhythms, phrasings, and timbres were not primarily derived from African American sources. The not-so-subtle upshot of this was virtually to identify jazz with the New Orleans style of the 1920s and to treat it as the very antithesis of swing, which replaced collective improvisation with written or "head" arrangements and African American folk themes with "poorly invented" Tin Pan Alley tunes.[11]

Metronome's two ideologues of swing, Leonard Feather and Barry Ulanov, responded to this "moldy fig" charge in a surprising manner, by saying not that the umbrella of jazz is broad enough to cover the admittedly distinct genres of New Orleans and swing music, but that the two terms "jazz" and "swing" actually refer to the same thing, "the same musical idiom, the same rhythmic and harmonic characteristics, the same use of syncopation." In short, "swing" is "just a different word" and "not a different music from jazz."[12]

In a deft tactical ploy, they interviewed a number of musicians who concurred with their view—most notably Louis Armstrong, a favorite of the revivalists, who jocularly entered the fray:

> To me as far as I could see it all my life—Jazz and Swing is the same thing. . . . In the good old days of Buddy Bolden . . . it was called Rag Time Music. . . . Later on in the years it was called Jazz Music—Hot Music—Gut Bucket—and now they've poured a little gravy over it, called it Swing Music. . . . Haw Haw Haw. . . . No matter how you slice it—it's still the same music.[13]

This strange debate—with one side claiming that swing and jazz are completely *identical* and the other that they are completely *opposite*—was rooted not in any factual dispute, but in two very different construals of the semantics of the term "swing." For the revivalists, "swing" was a generic term denoting an easily definable species of popular music. The *Metronome* modernists, on the other hand, seem unreflectively to have been using it as a brand name. Brand names differ from generic names in not being susceptible to definitions, because their meanings are determined less by the class of objects they refer to, than by the necessarily hazy, unarticulated, and frequently revised imagery with which they are irretrievably associated in advertisements and promotions. The word "swing," in its 1930s beginnings, also exhibited the nebulous, inarticulable suggestiveness typical of brand names.

Even before Benny Goodman's legendary performance at the Palomar Ballroom in December 1935, which inaugurated the Age of Swing, the word "swing" was already gaining currency in the midst of hype and euphoria as an oblique signifier for the anticipated boom in the music industry that would follow the depression and the ending of Prohibition.[14] In a somewhat convoluted and inchoate way, "swing" was the new word being associated with a revival, and modern updating, of the more "torrid" and "brassy" "hot jazz" of the past, to suit the lively and fun-loving urges of a new affluent generation, who in their "celebrating mood" would naturally "want to pep things up."[15] At the peak of the swing craze, the media were predictably seeking, but failing to find, a definition for this elusive brand name. From musicians and aficionados they elicited answers to the question "What is swing?" that ranged from the silly to the empty, such as "syncopated syncopation," "rhythmically integrated improvisation," and "two-thirds rhythm and one-third soul."[16] Meanwhile, the word "jazz" fell into temporary disuse, stigmatized as a "corny word" standing for a music whose "time had passed." Indeed, what had previously been called "jazz" was now being reclassified as "early swing."[17]

Thus, like a brand name, the word "swing" originally had no clear denotation, being associated with a whole variety of hazy images and allusions about markets, fashions, attitudes, emotions, entertainment, *Weltanschauungen,* musical tradition, and musical innovation. But the brand name would soon evolve, at least partly, into a definable generic name. For at the same time that the industry was pursuing musical change in its incessant attempts to tailor the product to new audiences, it was also attempting to stabilize these new consumption patterns by seeking to standardize and congeal the new musical styles. As standardization gradually overcame change, the generic functions of "swing" would overtake its brand-name functions, making it more open to definition and categorization.

The revivalists would contribute to this process of standardization and codification, by reintroducing the word "jazz" in the discursive stream as a definitional counterpoise to "swing." Meanwhile, the *Metronome* modernists, harkening back to the days when "swing" functioned more as a brand-name replacement for "jazz," resisted any such attempts at definition, precise categorization, and conceptual contrast.

However, the revivalist-modernist debate over the question "Is swing jazz?"—though floundering on semantic confusions—did reflect real differences. Whereas the revivalist "moldy figs" wanted to identify jazz with particular musical structures and practices that would set the standards for all its future developments and evaluations, the swing partisans, in their unremitting commitment to the new and up-to-date, did not want to be associated with any particular genre or style, and expressed no particular undying commitment to big bands over small combos, or arrangements over improvisations. *Metronome* was first and foremost committed to "modern" jazz and to swing only so long as it remained modern.

Art and Commerce

Nothing seemed to offend the sensitivities of revivalists more than the enormous commercial success of the swing bands and the blatant spirit of commercialism with which *Down Beat* and *Metronome* happily contributed to this success. No previous form of jazz had come even close to the immense popularity of the swing bands, which thoroughly dominated the hit charts during the years 1936–45, to an extent rarely if ever equaled by any other subgenre of popular music.[18]

For the "moldy figs," this was a sure sign of the impurity, corruption, and mediocrity of swing as jazz form. They further looked upon the modernist critics as mere "stooges" of this commercial music, who could not help acquiring the "crass and callous" values of the "whole stinking commercial structure." *Metronome,* in particular, despite its pretensions, had "no more critical significance than a publicity blurb."[19]

The modernists made no apologies about either the commercial success of swing or their own complicity with it. In a 1944 editorial, *Metronome* admitted that indeed it was "commercially minded" and asserted "furthermore that the best in jazz has been and always will be successful, commercial." This happy coincidence between art and commerce meant that "much music that finds popular approval will find critical acclaim in *Metronome* and that by critical acclaim in *Metronome* more jazz will meet with popular approval."[20]

Under the pressure of criticism, the modernists soon had to qualify their facile claims about the convergence of art and commerce. Denying that he ever said that "music pays off according to its merit," Ulanov admitted only to asserting that "good jazz as all good music will find a supporting box office level several notches above starvation and subsistence living."[21] With this qualification, the *Metronome* modernists were implicitly distinguishing between two jazz markets, a primary market constituted by the most commercially successful jazz hits, normally of a lower quality, and a secondary market of higher-quality jazz with less, though still significant, commercial success. This enabled them to allow for some discrepancy between artistic and commercial achievement, while asserting that good art is normally commercially viable. Thus, Feather could distinguish those swing bands that "make minor concessions to popular taste"—the secondary market—from those who "devote seventy-five per cent or ninety per cent of their time to straight melody, conventional crooning, vocal groups, comedy routines, and novelty numbers."[22]

However, Feather's text, written in 1944, was already betraying a certain malaise about the sphere of commerce, and about the future of jazz, absent from the boosterism of earlier articles. For we are warned that "even among the best currently active swing bands, . . . practically none can be relied upon to offer real jazz, or swing music, at any given time." He might also have been sensing the end of the boom era for swing, and indeed for jazz in general.[23]

Folklore and European High Culture

If the modernists were forced to allow some distinction between art and commerce—admittedly a distinction existing within the sphere of commerce—the revivalists would be at pains to construct successfully a notion of the *non*commercial that applied to the original New Orleans music and its current reincarnations. The opposition of art to commerce, in this case, could not be interpreted in the usual way as the opposition of elite culture to mass culture, of high versus low, refined versus vulgar. The revivalist writers were quite unhesitant, and indeed quite proud, to admit that the music of Jelly Roll Morton and Louis Armstrong, was, in an important sense, a "vulgar" and "low" art. Indeed, it was as important for them to oppose New Orleans jazz to high art as well as to the hit parade, and to attack swing for its symphonic pretensions as well as for its commercialism.

Not surprisingly, some revivalists turned to the then fashionable concept of folk music, to distinguish Dixieland both from swing and European art music—not surprisingly, because the ternary opposition of folk/mass/high culture had already become one of the clichés of twentieth-century aesthetic discourse, and because the political left of the 1930s, with which many of the revivalists were associated, had already appropriated the notion of folk music to mark off truly progressive music from its bourgeois counterparts. It was thus easy for many "moldy figs" to slip into the assertion that "real" jazz "is instrumental folk music"—"the music of the American proletariat"—which "began as a folk culture of the illiterate negro." For them, the transition from New Orleans jazz to swing represented the disintegration of an authentic folk culture into a "cliché culture of the masses."[24]

Nonetheless, the claim that New Orleans jazz is folk music could not be maintained without trivializing the very notion of the folkloric. A particular cultural product counts as "folk music," in the strong sense of that expression, if it has been produced and transformed anonymously over generations, outside of any modern culture industry, by artists or craftspersons un-schooled in any prevailing academy. Of these three criteria, only the latter seems to be satisfied by early jazz. With its own stars and auteurs, New Orleans jazz and its midwestern derivatives were hardly produced anonymously. Showcased in nightclubs, disbursed through records, and promoted in newspaper advertisements, this brand of jazz was clearly produced within the confines of, and transmitted by, the culture industry—and thus incontrovertibly a commercial music, though admittedly belonging to a less successful secondary market.

Quite advisedly, some proponents of the folkloric paradigm settled for the less ambitious claim that New Orleans Jazz is *based* on, rather than *is,* a folk music, that it is rooted in a "whole store of Negro folk music[s] from spirituals and folk songs, to hollers, street cries, play party songs, and nursery rhymes." But, in so doing, these revivalists were shifting the issue away from commerce and art, production and consumption, to that of musical content and training. That is, the implied critique of swing was no longer that it was too commercial, but that it was too European, too much a "dilution" of the "traditional framework" with "foreign elements." It was alleged that by abandoning the blues for Tin Pan Alley tunes as the primary source of melodic material, the swing musician turned away from the "folk ancestry of the jazz idiom," toward the "alien" devices "of vaudeville, music hall, music comedy, and synagogue."[25]

But nothing more sabotaged the African American tradition in jazz, it was argued, than the replacement of simultaneous improvisation by the European artifact of written arrangements. West Africans, according to the revivalist Ernest Borneman, prefer "circumlocution" to "direct naming," "direct statement," and any "form of abstraction." "What prevented even the highest civilization of Africa from committing its [musical] language to paper was not lack of intelligence," but the taboo against precise denotation and a "deeply rooted faith in ambiguity as the criterion of man's freedom and spontaneity."

Thus, any attempt to commit "the jazz idiom" to the "rigidity of written language" would "vitiate" rather than "preserve" it.[26]

Nonetheless, by the mid-1940s a number of swing musicians were experimenting with new harmonic patterns associated with modern composition and presenting concerts in venues previously reserved for symphonic music—most notably the Duke Ellington concerts at Carnegie Hall.[27] The modernist critics were in the forefront in encouraging the new musicians to learn to "read and write music," to inform themselves "about harmony and counterpoint," and to seek "proper" instruction "so that their instrumental technique may become as accurate and reliable as that of academically trained musicians."[28]

For revivalists, these attempts at "raising jazz to the level of symphonic music" could only result in "lowering it to the level of a musical hybrid," "doomed to look like parodies of the real things," since the European tradition, with its "head start of five centuries," had developed "all alternatives of scored music to such peaks of perfection."[29]

Progress and the New

With typical hyperbole, Feather proclaimed that "never before has any branch of music made such rapid progress" as jazz, and that "never before have there been so many superlative jazzmen, or so many first-class bands."[30] This, it was emphasized, is no mere incremental progress, resulting from continued refinements in instrumental prowess, but as well involves substantial and sustained advancements in musical style, tone, and harmony, spurred on by "the most emphatic experimentation" and the "most courageous investigation of new sounds."[31] The *Metronome* editors seemed to envision wave upon wave of future avant-garde innovations, which they expected to "like even more" than "what is being played today."[32]

For the modernists, it was no happenstance, but a matter of historical necessity, that jazz should have progressed so far and so consistently from those "badly dated relics" of "the crude early stages of New Orleans jazz."[33] This optimism seems to have been occasioned less by reason and evidence than by the sway of "boom euphoria," that unreflective, giddy conviction, in the midst of spiraling growth—in this case, the "swing craze"—that there is nowhere to go but up.[34] This faith in inevitable progress was further buttressed by the expected Europeanization of jazz, which would make available a centuries-old storehouse of musical resources for gradual appropriation.

To "moldy figs," this "euphoric illusion of progress" merely reflected a desperate and "ceaseless search for novelty," which "has kept [swing] faddishly changing, hectically striving to avoid being out of date." In effect, a "reactionary music which [sacrificed] the truly modern tendencies of polyphonic jazz," swing could claim to be "no more modern than styles in women's clothing."[35] The historical transformation from New Orleans to swing was "not an evolution" but "a drastic stoppage of the whole evolutionary process."[36]

The revivalists themselves were in disagreement whether this decline of jazz since the 1920s was reversible. Ralph Gleason had no doubt that it was. He exhorted his revivalist colleagues to stop merely talking to each other and to reach out to the "big, wide audience," by "usurp[ing]" *Look, Esquire,* and other "fountainheads" of mass information.[37] This solution, of course, did not catch on, being so blatantly at odds with the purist image of the revivalist movement.

According to some revivalists, the decline was inevitable, since the material and cultural conditions that had called forth the "real jazz" in the 1920s no longer existed to sustain it. Appealing to an improvised version of Marxism, Borneman argued that it was the increased "concentration of capital" accompanying "the growing opulence of the music industry" after the depression that sealed the fate of New Orleans jazz and led to the rise of swing, by dramatically transforming the manner in which jazz was produced and distributed.[38] In the face of this unprecedented "industrialization" of songwriting and "cartelization" of theaters and nightclubs, with its elaborate system of "hanger-ons and go-betweens," the musicians found themselves "enmeshed" in a "closely woven net of financial strings" from which they could hardly escape. To pay for the "vast new overheads," the music "had to be tailored to a much wider public than jazz had ever been able to attract." Swing music provided the ideal solution, based on the "simple recipe" of mixing the heat of the old jazz with the smooth commodified sound of the "sweet" bands (e.g., Lombardo).

The "Marxist" revivalists were not thereby resigned to continued musical decline. There was hope that changing material conditions would lead not to a "rediscovery of New Orleans music" — "musically speaking, history does not repeat itself" — but to new "forms which would be as rich and satisfying as New Orleans music." The revivalist critics were thus exhorted not only "to write and argue about jazz but to work for a social development that would keep our music alive."[39]

Standards, Technique, and Schooling

No issue area provoked more concentrated energy, or more straining of intellectual resources, than the debate over the proper standards for evaluating jazz. Given their progressivist bent, the modernists opted for standards "as objective as our background and equipment permit," going so far as to say that the "modern standards" in terms of which all musicians, past and present, were to be judged were based on "absolute values."[40] They thought that an objective evaluation would easily come by attending to "the tone [a musician] drew from his instrument, the accuracy of the notes, the originality of the variations played upon the chords or melodic figures at hand." Thus, allegedly, it was primarily because of its superior "precision" and "finished technique," that the work of the younger swing musicians was deemed to be decidedly superior to that of their New Orleans forebears, with its "dull clichés," and "fumbling," "inept," and "uncertain" procedures.[41]

In the writings of the "moldy figs," the modernists professed not to see any standards at work, but only an appeal to "vague emotions," "nostalgia," and "historical associations," with "absolutely no analysis," "explanations," or presentation of "actual musical details." The "old time jazz lovers" are only concerned "with the music as part of a cult, a social scene," sometimes "even a political movement," or in its "relation to their own lives."[42] This absence of musical standards, this "blind prejudice" on the part of the "moldy figs," is allegedly "based on their complete lack of musical education," and particularly their inability to read scores. These "irate gentry" would "run promptly for the shelters if you asked them for the chords of the blues, or showed them a chorus on paper taken down from a solo by one of their idols and asked them to identify it," thus proving themselves no more qualified to write about jazz than "a man who knows no grammar, punctuation, or spelling, is qualified to be a book reviewer."[43]

The revivalists responded with a counterattack against the modernists' shallow appeal to technique. "Technique has nothing to do" with jazz, which as "a free art" cannot "be ruled by music books and music teachers."[44] They maintained that swing musicians, caught up in "the vanities of solo playing," were driven to "develop instrumental bravura techniques" and acrobatics "in precise ratio to the loss of the music's basic structure." Trumpet players now were flaunting their "high notes," saxophone players their "sustained breath and rounded tones," pianists their "speedy runs," and percussionists their "fast and complicated drum solos," played "as loudly as possible on the greatest possible number of side drums."[45]

Even worse, the vaunted techniques of the normal swing band, the revivalists asserted, "are largely mythical." What was being packaged as artistic virtuosity was mere "dexterity," "showmanship," and flashy display, on the same level as the "ability to make faces" or "to talk glibly."[46] No technical device of swing music incurred more opprobrium from the revivalists than the "meaningless," "idiotic," and "empty" riffs.[47] The riff is a rhythmic melodic fragment, normally used repetitiously in answer to a lead melodic phrase or to another rhythmic fragment. It was perhaps the most pronounced stylistic marker of the swing band, which frequently used riffs to answer other riffs— as in the case of brass instruments answering reeds. With the development of swing and the expansion of its market, the riff became so dominant that the typical swing piece, for example, "Tuxedo Junction" and "In the Mood," appeared to be nothing but a series of repeated riff patterns. The riff was, for the revivalists, the most offensive and blatant symptom of the glorification of the "groove beat as an end in itself" and the triumph of arranged music at the expense of "spontaneous improvisation." The "riffing style" is the "definite opposite of pure creative music," since in "riff music," one knows "exactly what is coming next for a whole chorus."[48]

This focus on the riff by the revivalists displayed, at the same time that it concealed, a certain ambivalence in their standards for critiquing swing. On the one hand, the riff, perhaps more than any other musical device, revealed swing to be a simplistic, standardized, consumer package loaded with hooks and operating with the imperative insistence of a military march.[49] On the other hand, the swing arranger would sometimes use a wide variety of different riffs in one piece to create a complex musical montage, generating an experimental, avant-garde sound, which glaringly excluded such pop requisites as a recurrent and easily recognizable melody (e.g., Jimmy Lunceford's "Stratosphere.") In criticizing the riff, the revivalists were thus also complaining about swing's "over-elaborate and complicated phrases . . . stripped of all meaning," its "search for out of chord notes" or more recondite chords, in general, its pretensions at modernist experimentation and formal play. They even resorted to the stereotyped lowbrow complaint of there being "no melody at all."[50]

Affect and Antics

For their part, the modernists were most irritated with the revivalists' excessive preoccupation with the expressive and emotional side of music. Revivalist writing was replete with claims like "Jazz is either the transmission of emotion or it is nothing," and "The deeper and truer the feeling, the deeper the jazz."[51] The "moldy figs" excoriated the swing musicians for performing "in a slick, mechanical, and unfeeling manner," as if governed by a "slide rule," in contrast to the practitioners of the New Orleans style, who value "simple honest emotional expression" over "conscious intellectual exercise."[52]

The modernists adamantly rejected the use of "emotional symbols" and were especially repelled by the "emotional ecstasies" or "orgasms" of "non-musical writers," which served only to express "personal and narrow prejudices." They feared that the explicit glorification of the emotive in jazz was merely a cover for advocating the "merely nostalgic, aphrodisiac, and cheaply melodic," at the expense of musical risk and experimentation.[53] This devaluation of affect on the part of the modernists constituted quite a radical revision of the swing image, which originally had been constructed more around the perceived emotional excesses of the "swing craze," than the dry formal innovations imputed to swing arrangers. The expression "swing craze" called to mind wild new acrobatic dances, such as the jitterbug; crowds pressed against the bandstand transported by every trumpet high note and drum solo; flashy zoot suits with the attendant body mannerisms; and a new array of slang expressions, such as "corny," "screw-ball," and "See you later, alligator." That is, rather than denigrating emotion, the swing movement seemed to outside onlookers to be producing too much of it.[54]

The revivalists, however, dismissed this appearance of unbridled affect among swing fans as merely phony emotionality—a "spurious" and commercially constructed "frenzy," which is merely the "superficial mechanics of an emotion." Swing, to them, was nothing but "a highly organized form of instrumental noise devoted to the super-inducement of a wholly unnatural excitement" deserving "psychiatric study." This excitement, which was "instantaneously" released by "the first notes or the drum blows," quickly took on the form of "mass auto-hypnosis," venting itself in "anarchistic, orgiastic, and dangerous excitement."[55]

Fascists and Communists

Quite frequently the revivalist texts were tinged with the metaphors and insinuations of left-wing political discourse. There was a certain self-congratulatory implication of political correctness—a proper mix of nativism, antifascism, and Marxism—which underlay many of the arguments espousing New Orleans jazz over swing. It is within this larger political frame that the revivalist construals of New Orleans jazz as noncommercial folk music, or music of the proletariat, can best be viewed. We should thus not be surprised, for example, by one revivalist's complaint that "modernist" black musicians have "sold their birthright for a stale mess of European pottage," a clear evocation of Marx's own famous evocation of the Bible.[56] Nor should we be surprised by revivalist proclivities for cultural pessimism, and in particular by their tendency to blame the degradation of popular culture on the mo-nopolization and cartelization of capital, a view then in vogue among other left-wing cultural critics, including Clement Greenberg and Theodor Adorno.

Also, like these theorists, many of the revivalists began to see signs of creeping fascism even in the cultures of the most formally democratic of cap-italist countries. When some "moldy figs" claimed to find the imperatives of militarist discipline lurking in the swing riff or packaged "frenzy" and "mass auto-hypnosis" appearing as swing affect, they were indirectly pointing to fascist tendencies within the confines of swing itself. As it was put, "Swing is a form of *rabble rousing* that elicits . . . the same *blind idolatry* the dema-gogue or the dictator receives from the mob." In short, swing is "nihilistic, cynically destructive, reactionary."[57]

The modernists, in keeping with their politically "liberal" posture, tried as much as possible to keep musical discourse separate from political dis-course—which explains in part their preoccupation as critics with technique and other internal features of jazz music. When finally goaded by the revival-ists into the arena of politically nuanced charges and countercharges, they tried to restrict the discourse of "left" and "right" to the practices of music performance and music criticism alone.

Thus, they imputed to the revivalists a reactionary aesthetics, not a reac-tionary politics. In their most virulent and inflammatory articles—particu-larly Leonard Feather's—they went so far as to accuse the "moldy figs" of "musical fascism." They variously vilified them as the "right-wingers of jazz," "the voice of reaction in music," a "lunatic fringe" of musical criticism with its "ill-tempered and abusive outbursts," in effect, the "vanguard of jazz re-actionaries."[58] The "moldy figs," understandably irate, labeled this a form of "yellow journalism" more "raw" than anything achieved by "Hearst in his palmiest days," which in particular exposed Feather as the real "fascist raving maniac of the music business."[59]

This mini-controversy over "cultural fascism" was situated in a larger net-work of discourses that constructed jazz as the very negation of fascist cul-ture. These were generated by the banning of jazz in fascist countries and stimulated by war patriotism. *Down Beat* took pleasure in reporting on Nazi attempts to eradicate jazz as a reminder to musicians in the home front of "what you cats are doing to the supermen of the Third Reich."[60] The well-known French jazz discographer Charles Delauney reported to *Down Beat* that the German occupation stimulated "an overwhelming burst of enthusiasm by Frenchmen for jazz" as a "symbol of," and "last tie with, the outside, free world." Said Delauney: "By 1941, I was able to lecture on hot music to farm villages."[61]

Black and White

By the mid-1940s, the virtually all-white jazz journals were boasting of their progressive racial attitudes, as well as that of white musicians, while denouncing Jim Crow practices in nightclubs, record companies, and the rest of society. *Metronome* argued, for example, that since "musicians as artists are traditionally above bigotry and prejudice"—"artists go where bigots fear to tread"—the music business should follow the example of the "rank and file of white musicians," who long ago had "thrown aside prejudice" to "play side by side with their colored brothers."[62]

In 1945 the editors of *Metronome* announced with fanfare that due to their incessant "fight against racial prejudice," their readers were now voting "automatically without regard to color" in the annual balloting for the all-star jazz band.[63] The numbers did support the editors' euphoria: 74 percent of the musicians voted into the all-star band of 1944 were black, contrasting markedly with previous readership polls when African Americans garnered less than 25 percent of the positions.

Metronome's Feather had orchestrated a similar breakthrough, a year before, with a group of selected critics, in the first annual *Esquire* jazz poll. This poll, however, provoked a surprisingly hostile and racially tainted counterattack from the revivalist press. By convincing *Esquire* to sponsor an annual yearbook on jazz, Feather had scored a major coup that sent ripples throughout the jazz world, it being the first time that a general mass publication, and a "serious" one at that, had devoted such space and attention to jazz music. Since Feather had a major hand in selecting the writers and the critics, the impression quickly circulated that the 1944 *Esquire's Jazz Book* was largely a purveyor of the *Metronome* line—a bias that the revivalist press was quick to try to expose.

None of these responses was quite as puzzling as Jake Trussell's essay "Jim Crow—Upside Down,"[64] which accused the *Esquire* poll's critics of reverse racial discrimination, due to their excessive preoccupation with the "fight against Jim Crow." Trussell had discovered to his horror that the *Esquire* critics gave only 28 percent of their first- and second-place votes to white musicians in selecting the all-star band—"a most startling case of race prejudice in cold, analytic figures." This article reflected a split on racial matters within the revivalist community itself. Some were partisans of the classic black jazz of New Orleans (e.g., Louis Armstrong), while others were more partial to the white midwestern derivatives of this tradition (e.g., Eddie Condon). Of course, the revivalist movement, whatever its racial tastes, was initiated and propagated only by whites with an almost exclusively white audience. The overwhelming tendency of younger black musicians to join the swing movement irritated even the most vociferous supporters of black music among the revivalists, like Rudi Blesh, who complained: "How tragically the negro trades his own music for only another sort of slavery!" For swing music, he insisted, "is an abandonment of the truly Negroid elements of jazz in favor of white elements more intelligible and acceptable to white society. Thus, swing, outwardly the symbol of [Negro] triumph, is inwardly the failure of emancipation."[65]

However, even *Metronome,* the self-proclaimed champion of "Negro" rights, was not immune from engaging in some racial bullying of its own, when it severely admonished a small and short-lived black jazz magazine, the *Music Dial*—"an ill-spelled, shoddily-printed rag"—for its "strong political line," carried "regardless of its relevance to music," and its "narrow" preoccupation solely "with the interests of the colored musician." "Music magazines should concern themselves with music, and that's all."[66] The response was swift. While white "progressives" critiqued the *Metronome* editors vaguely for their "snide" and "reactionary" attitude, *Music Dial* quite pointedly identified a fascist strain in their tendency to treat music as a "fetish" or an "opiate."[67]

These local, racially defined conflicts in the jazz press were symptoms of a much larger, more generalized anxiety about racial destabilization and violence in the music industry. There was much to feed this anxiety: the movement of southern whites and blacks to northern industrial cities; racial tensions in the armed services; increasing physical attacks on black musicians; the race riots of 1943; continued and sometimes intensified segregation in the music industry; increasing black militancy. This was reflected in recurrent *Down Beat* headlines during the mid-forties, exposing egregious cases of racial discrimination, in voices that expressed outrage, fear, and sometimes puzzled hysteria, such as "Racial Hatred Rears Ugly Mug in Music," "Jim Crow Stuff Still Spreading," "Vagrant Chicks Blamed in Part for Racial Row," and "Sarah Vaughan Beaten up by [White] Gang."[68]

Conclusion: From Swing to Bop

In 1945, not long before the emergence of bebop as a publicly identified movement, *Metronome,* sensing the imminent demise of swing, was speculating that postwar jazz would be characterized by a profusion of different and increasingly adventurous modernist approaches, identified more with individuals than movements.[69] It committed itself fervently to the "support of the musicians who stand for the most emphatic experimentation, for the most courageous investigation of new sounds, for musical daring and integrity."

When *Metronome* first introduced Dizzy Gillespie to its readers, it portrayed him not as part of any movement, but as a somewhat idiosyncratic stylist with an array of imitators, one of many modernists experimenting within the expanding boundaries of swing.[70] Even later, in 1948, when bebop appeared to be the heir of swing, it was consistently portrayed by the jazz press as only one of many alternative modernist tendencies, which included also the work of Stan Kenton and Lennie Tristano.

In point of fact, during bebop's years in the limelight, and despite the major musical changes that it wrought, the jazz press continued to apply, with only minor modifications, the same self-styled "modernism" discourse to it that it had used years before to differentiate the more adventurous tendencies in swing from Dixieland. Bop was pigeonholed as only the most recent wave of modernism to oppose itself to the traditionalism of New Orleans. This is none too surprising since virtually all the main defenders of bebop were veterans of the revivalist war and former proponents of swing. The revivalist-swing war so subtly transposed itself into the bebop war that many of the criticisms, once directed against swing by the "antimodern" revivalists, were now being leveled against bebop, though in different circumstances and with different inflections. Like their swing forebears, bebop musicians were accused of fetishizing technique, of introducing excessive harmonic and rhythmic complications, and of being too mesmerized by the devices and concepts of European art music. They were reprimanded for their preoccupation with showmanship, their undignified publicity stunts, their mannerisms and argot.

Thus, the bebop revolutionaries were confronted at the outset not only with a recalcitrant musical legacy, but also with a new but already entrenched discursive formation, fashioned and configured during the Dixieland-swing war. Although the bebop movement significantly transformed that musical legacy, it made the smallest of dents in the reigning discursive formation. The jazz critics' claims and counterclaims concerning bop, however outrageous, were constrained and delimited by a particular configuration of allowed topics, concepts, contrasts, argumentative styles—what I have called an "aesthetic discursive formation"—that was formed in the heat of the revivalist-modernist debates of the swing era.

The unity of this new aesthetic discourse was a "unity in dispersion," to use Foucault's phrase—that is, a unity that propagated discursive opposition, that created points of discursive repulsion. As such, it was organized primarily around a group of interconnected binary oppositions: art/commerce, authenticity/artificiality, swing/jazz, European/native, folk culture/refined culture, technique/affect, modern/traditional, black/white, fascism/communism, and right wing/left wing.

The centrality of these binaries to the new aesthetic discourses virtually assured the existence of diametrically opposed aesthetic views that nonetheless belonged to the same discursive world. When the revivalist war shaded into the bebop war, the same unified set of binary oppositions was available, with small modifications, to sharply define the conflict of bebop partisans and their enemies. These binaries did not operate separately, but were densely entwined, accounting in part for the remarkable entrenchment of this discursive practice, despite its relative newness. For example, the anticommercial stance of the revivalists played into, and reinforced, their promotion of authenticity, folklorism, tradition, and affect, set against a vaguely left-wing, antifascist background.

Such a tight interconnection is no accident, since the binaries were not created from scratch, but lifted out of the various European avant-garde and modernist discourses. The jazz aesthetic generated by the revivalist war was not original in its constituent binaries, or its imagery and rhetorical devices—which were by now clichés of aesthetic modernism—but in the way in which these binaries, images, and devices were brought together as a unified whole to satisfy the requirements for legitimating jazz as an art form, and in particular for fueling the revivalist-swing debate through its twists and turns. This means that in the broad sense of "modernist" that applies to European art discourse, the revivalists were as much "modernists" as were their swing adversaries. They simply accentuated certain tendencies of the modernist impulse at the expense of others. We need to remember, for example, that the concepts of the folkloric and the primitive were crucially involved in the "modernist" practices of Picasso, Bartók, Milhaud, and the surrealists, while the notion of reactionary and the art/commerce dichotomy entered crucially into the avant-garde terminologies of opprobrium.

Finally, to say that bebop was defined, explicated, defended, and criticized—in general, "received" in the jazz world—in terms of the aesthetic discursive formation previously generated by the revivalist war is not to deny that the bebop war did indeed effect some modest changes in the configurations of this discourse. Certainly, as jazz receded from the hit parade into the secondary markets—bebop never entered the *Billboard* pop charts—there would be inevitable changes in the way in which the binary art/commerce would function in the musical debates and connect with the other binaries. Also, the concepts of argot, ritual, and lifestyle would loom more centrally and threateningly in the contestations over bebop.

Since then and until recently, the attention given to the revivalist-swing debates had dwindled to almost nothing—the occasional cursory chapter in a "comprehensive" jazz history book, which typically approaches its topic as if it were an embarrassment, as belonging to a dark age.[71] Even if it were true that the 1940s produced no "great" jazz critics—a highly contestable point —the discursive formation, collectively and unwittingly generated by these allegedly minor voices, had a formative and enduring impact on the way in which jazz history got constructed and jazz as an art form got legitimated.[72] The first jazz war cleared the discursive field for modern jazz, to which the next chapter addresses itself.

A triumphant Dizzy Gillespie on Fifty-second Street (mid-forties). Courtesy of William Gottlieb.

CHAPTER 7
BEBOP UNDER FIRE

THOUGH THE IDEA THAT JAZZ IS A MODERNIST ART FORM appeared in full force in the revivalist-swing debate, it is bebop that gets credit in the jazz canon for being the first modernist jazz, the first jazz avant-garde, the first jazz form in which art transcends entertainment. In that respect, it should get credit also for representing the entry of postmodernism into American art. There is no paradox here, for the appropriation of "modernist" or "avant-garde" devices by a "popular" art is itself a "postmodern" act. This chapter focuses on the original reception of bebop, during its brief period in the sun, in order to reconstruct how the "modernity"—the "avant-garde" character—of this now-legendary musical transformation was constructed in the swirling discourses of the jazz press. These discourses were as driven by controversy and antagonism as the predecessor revivalist debates. But, more so than the latter, they were also haunted by confusion, incertitude, and even an occasional panic, occasioned in part by the recurrent economic crises that plagued the jazz industry.

The "Dizzy Rage" (1944–46)

As the story is told, the bebop movement was born and incubated between 1941 and 1943, during the after-hours jam sessions at Monroe's and Minton's of Harlem, in relative seclusion from the jazz press, whose eyes were focused on the various nightclub scenes on Fifty-second Street.[1] In these small and modest venues, the musicians who were to be the charter members of this movement—Dizzy Gillespie, Charlie Parker, Thelonious Monk, Oscar Pettiford, and Max Roach, among others—were honing their new skills and experimenting with new harmonic and rhythmic devices, in the hothouse atmosphere of no-holds-barred competition.[2] But the full bebop sound, with the melodic, harmonic, and rhythmic innovations all working together, did not take shape until 1944–45, when the musicians had moved down to Fifty-second Street with their first combos, at the Onyx, the Spotlite, and the Three Deuces.[3] It was only then that the jazz press began to take note, though what it first heard was not a movement, but a small stream of new individual sounds joining a rising tide of modernisms, a small group of innovators who were to be added to the ranks of Stan Kenton, Boyd Raeburn, Art Tatum, Coleman Hawkins, and Woody Herman.

Alone among his co-experimenters from Harlem, Dizzy Gillespie was seized by the press as a force of his own, as the most exciting and influential jazz musician of his generation. People spoke of a "Dizzy rage," a "Dizzy movement."[4] He achieved his first publicity breakthrough in two articles by Leonard Feather of *Metronome*—"Dizzy Is Crazy Like a Fox" (1944) and "Dizzy—21st Century Gabriel"(1945)—each of which had all the earmarks of a hard-sell promotional piece.[5] Gillespie was being described in the jazz press as a unique new stylist and technical virtuoso, with a "genius for substituting and extending chords in unorthodox but singularly thrilling ways and places" and a facility for playing "incredible cascades of fast notes at breakneck tempos," while making "every note mean something."[6] While praising Gillespie, these writers were most severe in excoriating the "horde" of imitators who "sound like a grotesque caricature," and who have even "been trying to make themselves look and act like Dizzy to boot," with their "goatee beards," "ridiculous little hats," and "apathetic" "S" postures.[7]

Yet by the end of 1945, the jazz press had slowly shifted from seeing Gillespie as an individualistic prodigy to construing him as only one among many leaders of a revolutionary movement larger than him, which was also shaped by the contributions of Parker and Roach. Gillespie was now more modestly described as the "symbol" or "focal point" of this new revolution, rather than as a movement unto himself.[8] But the jazz press did not resort to the word "bebop" to denote this as yet unnamed revolution until April 1946, when a controversy erupted over the new music in, of all places, Hollywood, California.[9]

Bebop in Lotus Land (1945–46)

It is generally agreed that the word "bebop" originated during Dizzy Gillespie's first residency at Fifty-second Street in 1944 from one of the onomatopoeic scat phrases that he used to remind musicians of the opening melodic-rhythmic line of a newly invented, untitled tune. Soon customers would ask for "that bebop song" or "that bebop stuff."[10] However, the word was not used initially to designate a new musical school or revolution. The tune "Bebop," composed by Gillespie in 1944 and recorded in 1945, was not presented as the standard bearer of a movement nor was it so construed in a somewhat unenthusiastic *Down Beat* review, which simply treated it as a failed attempt at "good swing."[11]

The mainstream jazz press initially resisted the term "bebop," as did the movement musicians themselves, though for different reasons. The first found it too undignified at a time when they were trying to upgrade the image of jazz, and the second resented the naming of their movement by a term devised by white promoters and audiences.[12] Not being so constrained, some revivalists were using the term "bebop" intermittently before its appearance in the mainstream jazz press to refer quite indiscriminately to any of the most recent modernisms that they despised, even to the nonbebop music of Lionel Hampton and Woody Herman.[13] It took a controversy, inspired and disseminated by the mass media, for the name "bebop" to become firmly entrenched and for the newly designated bebop movement, finally disentangled from other jazz modernisms, to reach the center stage of public attention. In mid-March 1946 a Los Angeles radio station banned "hot jive," which it equated with "bebop," on the pretext that it emphasized "suggestive lyrics," aroused "degenerative instincts and emotions," and was "a contributing factor to juvenile delinquency."[14] This little publicity-seeking outburst might have had no repercussions, if *Time* magazine had not given it national attention in an article called "Be-bop Be-bopped." In the process, *Time* gave the first definition of "bebop" to appear in print, when it described it as "hot jazz overheated, with overdone lyrics full of bawdiness, references to narcotics, and doubletalk." It claimed that the "bigwig of bebop" was Harry "the Hipster" Gibson, a "scat" who "in moments of supreme pianistic ecstasy throws his feet on the keyboard," and that the "No. 2 man" was his partner, "Slim" Gaillard, "a skyscraping, zooty Negro guitarist."[15] This most bizarre account was not, however, totally unconnected with the facts, at least as they existed in California.

In mid-December 1945 Gillespie brought a combo of musicians, including Parker, for an eight-week engagement at Billy Berg's of Hollywood. "Be-Bop Invades the West!" proclaimed Ross Russell, the future producer of Parker records, in the monthly publicity leaflet for his Hollywood music store. While promoting Gillespie as the "rave trumpet star" who had been "making history along 52nd Street for over a year," Russell gave a short conciliatory disquisition on the "modern school," which had "dropped melody overboard" while flaunting its "brilliant technique, progressive harmonic explorations, and suspended rhythms."[16]

Gillespie's band was preceded at Billy Berg's by Harry "the Hipster" Gibson and Slim Gaillard, who had achieved considerable popularity and notoriety with their novelty songs, filled with sly allusions to sex and drugs, such as "Cement Mixer" and "Who Put the Benzedrine in Mrs. Murphy's Ovaltine?" Continuing their show on the same bill with the Gillespie band, Gibson and Gaillard quickly became associated with the new movement, more because of the profuse use of "hip" or "jive" talk in their songs than any similarity in music style.[17] This apparent alliance was further reinforced in the public eye by the burgeoning "hipster" subculture regularly in attendance at Billy Berg's, whose members, spouting their "mysterious lingo" and appearing as "high as barrage balloons," were infuriating and shocking the more traditional clientele.[18]

It was in the context of this array of events and perceptions that Radio KMPC of Los Angeles imposed the ban on bebop for which *Time* gleefully provided the subtext. *Down Beat* and *Metronome* quickly and indignantly came to the defense of their California colleagues and in the process introduced "bebop" into their official lexicon. *Down Beat* was especially outraged by the fact that the author of the ban, Ted Steele, was a musician engaged in "a vicious and slanderous attack on his fellows," rather than a mere "press agent" exhibiting "poor judgment and bad taste." However, in defending the newly named "bebop" movement against censorship, *Down Beat* was doing no more, as a trade paper, than expressing solidarity with some of its clientele. It was not interested in contesting definitions or distinguishing Gillespie's music from that of Gibson-Gaillard. It most emphatically was not endorsing bebop or its perceived lifestyles.[19] *Metronome,* on the other hand, was more concerned to correct the distorted image of "bebop" created by *Time* than to challenge Radio KMPC's act of blatant censorship. Unlike *Down Beat,* the editors of *Metronome* were strongly committed to the legitimation of what was being called "bebop," as a modernist art movement within jazz. In an interview *Metronome* pressed the censor, Ted Steele, to concede that "he had no argument with jazz," or even bebop, and was in reality only banning the "suggestive" songs of Gibson and Gaillard.[20]

Contesting *Time*'s definition of "bebop," *Metronome* asserted that beyond its musical-onomatopoeic connotations, the term was "meaningless," and that if you ban bebop, "you might as well ban the diatonic scale or the Dorian mode." This counterclaim accentuated *Metronome*'s resolution to describe the movement denoted by "bebop" in purely musical terms, in terms of harmonic, rhythmic, and tonal resources, rather than by reference to any lifestyle or verbal content (e.g., suggestive lyrics). According to *Metronome,* Radio KMPC and *Time* "had confused the frantic antics" of Gibson and Gaillard with the "intense but very different blowing" of Gillespie, Parker, "and their cohorts." The editors distanced themselves from Gibson and Gaillard, whose songs, "thick with reefer smoke and bedroom innuendo," "do all jazz musicians a disservice." Hence, "the banning of their records from the air is of little consequence." The villains in this controversy, according to *Metronome,* were not the puritanical censors, but writers and publicists who distort jazz to appear as a "degenerate's paradise" or a "fool's delight," rather than presenting it truthfully as a "serious, disciplined art."[21] The one concrete result of this controversy was the official promotion of the word "bebop" from a nonsense to a technical generic term, like "swing" and "Dixieland."

Interlude: Searching for Great White Hopes (1946–48)

The California controversy, lasting barely a month, was followed by an indecisive two-year interlude in the jazz world—a period of confusion, negotiation, economic anxiety, mild storms, and petty competitions. The bebop movement was now clearly a force to be contended with, bearing an imagery that shocked, titillated, and threatened. But the jazz world was not ready to crown it the heir of swing, or even give it priority over the other modernisms (e.g., Boyd Raeburn, Stan Kenton et al.).

During this interval *Down Beat*, *Metronome,* and the revivalist press responded to bebop each in their own distinct, complex, and somewhat inconsistent ways. *Down Beat* provided perhaps the best barometer of the changing whims of the public reception to bebop. As the self-appointed, broad-based trade magazine for band musicians, constantly concerned with the economic welfare of the music industry, *Down Beat* went out of its way to project a moderate and nonideological image of its practices. However, though apparently allowing for every tendency, this journal was clearly more wedded to the interests of big band swing musicians and looked at both the revivalists and the beboppers with a mixture of muted hostility and bemusement.[22]

Initially, *Down Beat* responded to the newly baptized bebop movement more with novelty articles that catered to the fad, with catchy titles such as "Zu-Bop Now," "Jack Goes from Bach to Bebop," and "Czechs Check Bop," than with critical analyses or substantive news reports. *Down Beat* whimsically asked, for example, "Why must you wear a goatee to play a good hot horn?"[23] Some articles, which otherwise had nothing to say about bebop, would nonetheless use the word in the headline as a hook to lure the reader.[24]

Down Beat did occasionally transcend such reportage to articulate its own ambivalent musical views about bebop, as in the response by the regular record reviewer Mike Levin to a Ross Russell letter admonishing him for his somewhat hostile reception to bebop disks. In a reexamination of bebop records produced by Russell's Dial label, Levin complained of a "constant, nerve chiseling tension," a disregard for "consistency of tone," and a propensity to "replace genuine improvisational ability with sensational technical figures played at extremely fast tempos." Unlike the followers of "Diz and Bird," he could not rate the latter "as equally important in their time as an Armstrong was in his."[25] *Down Beat* implied, by its statements and allusions, that it objected only partially to bebop and only on musical grounds. It would rise unqualifiedly in defense of bebop against global and nonmusical attacks, such as "worse-than-Uncle-Tom," racial slurs against movement musicians or gleeful pronouncements that "bebop is dead."[26]

Positioning itself emphatically to the musical left of *Down Beat* on the side of the ultra-modern, *Metronome* was unwavering in its support for bebop. But this journal also made it abundantly clear that bebop was only one, and not necessarily the favorite, among many advanced modernist movements in jazz that it would support with dedication. Indeed, Barry Ulanov, the chief propagandist for modernism at *Metronome,* seemed to prefer jazz that was more cerebral, more influenced by European avant-garde music, and, in contrast to bebop, less embroiled in showmanship, unusual argot and dress, and suspect lifestyles. Amidst a series of warm endorsements of bebop musicians, such as the selection of Gillespie in 1946 and Parker in 1947 as "Influence of the Year" and Gillespie's band as "Band of the Year" in 1948, *Metronome* scattered enough objections to imply serious philosophical disagreements.[27] With respect to Gillespie and his 1947 band, in particular, Ulanov complained of the "senseless screams," the "endless quotations of trivia," "frantic clowning," and "can-can" gyrations—all "acrid" musical effects of a "bitter" personal philosophy driven to avoid any "musical statement bordering on the exalted."[28]

In a striking 1947 article, in which he happily proclaimed the death of swing ("the Benny Goodman groove"), Ulanov called upon musicians to create a radically new era in jazz—to rid themselves of the "dead wood," the "banal harmonies," the "fascination" with "merely lush and rhythmic figures," and to study and ground their work in the modern compositions of Hindemith, Berg, Schoenberg, Ives, Cage, and Varèse. "It is time for jazz to stop looking in the mirror and fawning upon itself" and to begin "to listen to [these composers] in humble appreciation of what they have done." To accentuate this new symbiosis between jazz and European art music, he announced that *Metronome* from then on would be subtitled the *Review of Modern Music.* He commended "Dizzy and the Be-Bop crowd" for having initiated this trend. But he was also saying that bebop, innovative as it may have been, was being passed by as only the first of a whole series of transformations in jazz based on European high culture. The question for the forward-looking *Metronome* was: Who would occupy the next stage?[29]

For Ulanov, no one captured the future of jazz as convincingly as Lennie Tristano, whom he championed for three years as the one who was transcending bebop after having learned from it.[30] Tristano obligingly supported this line in two articles for *Metronome* on "what's right" and "what's wrong with the beboppers." He objected particularly to the proclivity of young beboppers toward "pseudo-hip affectations"—they "slouch" rather than "sit," "amble" rather than "walk." Nonetheless, for Tristano, bebop, though "not an end in itself," is "unquestionably an excellent means" in the transformation of jazz into an "art for its own sake"—for example, by "its valiant attempt" to replace "emotion with meaning" and by "successfully combating the putrefying effects of commercialism."[31]

Following quickly on *Metronome*'s heels in the search for a modernist alternative to bebop, *Down Beat* chose Stan Kenton, the winner of their 1947 Reader's Poll, who also proceeded to mouth formulas about the intermediary character of bebop and the relevance of European art music. Though bebop is "doing more for music than anything else," such as "educating the people to new intervals and sounds," Kenton opined, it nonetheless is "not the new jazz" but only a "hot-foot along the way," because "it lacks emotion" and "hasn't settled down yet." The jazz of the future "will dominate and swallow classical [music]."[32]

Faced with a bebop movement dominated by African American musicians, the virtually all-white jazz journals seemed always to be in search of "great white hopes"—white modernists, like Tristano and Kenton, with whom a mostly white readership would feel more at home. There may indeed have been a racial code operating in the white critics' expressed desire for a more cerebral and European modern jazz, as well as a jazz purified of any association with lifestyles, argots, or dress.[33]

The contortions around bebop, which both *Down Beat* and *Metronome* underwent at this time, were not unrelated to the sense of economic insecurity that overtook the jazz world immediately after the war, when many big bands had to break up at least temporarily, and jazz clubs on Fifty-second Street were being turned into strip joints.[34] In good or bad times, *Down Beat* never hesitated to display a blatant preoccupation with commerce, which *Metronome* camouflaged with a patina of aesthetic concern.[35] This insecurity indirectly informed the discourse and debates about bebop. *Metronome* insisted, not altogether convincingly, that bebop and other postwar modern jazz movements would create a new market to supplant the declining market for swing.[36] Still wedded to the big bands, *Down Beat* was more confused and clearly worried, despite its denials, that the public was switching its preference from "swing" music to the "gentle drip of uncontrolled sugar," typical of the "flossy" "sweet" bands.[37] Whatever its musical misgivings, *Down Beat's* attitude toward bebop would ultimately be determined by how well or badly it affected the market for jazz. During the 1946–48 interval, the results were unclear.

Interlude: The Moldy Figs React (1946–48)

If *Down Beat* and *Metronome* agreed on anything, it was that Dixieland music and its "reactionary" revivalist supporters were the natural, and most hostile, opponents of bebop. But this construal was more an invention of these media, with their predilection for simplistic binary oppositions, than a statement of fact. Insofar as they were critical of anything that was "modern," that is, anything since New Orleans jazz, the revivalists would, of course, have little good to say about bebop. But they did not despise bebop more than they did any other jazz modernisms and, indeed, had already spent most of their animus against swing, which for them was the ultimate outrage against "real" jazz.

By the time bebop became an issue, the war over revivalism had already subsided somewhat, in part because New Orleans music was succeeding in carving out a niche in the world of jazz entertainment. Of the approximately ten "moldy fig" journals that had appeared in the early 1940s, only *Jazz Record* and the *Record Changer* remained, though they spent very little time critiquing bebop.[38] Ernest Borneman, a former editor of the *Record Changer,* was one of the few "moldy figs," along with Mezz Mezzrow, to fight systematically and recurrently against bebop. Borneman's main complaint was that the bebop-inspired Europeanization of jazz would make jazz musicians permanently inferior to "legitimate" art composers. He found it outrageous to compare the harmonic experiments of bebop with those of Schoenberg and Hindemith. Measured against the achievements of the latter, "Dizzy's harmonic continuity is infantile" and "Bird's contrapuntal patterns are puerile."[39] But this aggressive vendetta was not typical of revivalists (some of whom, including Ralph Gleason, actually converted to bebop).

This did not stop *Down Beat* and *Metronome* from whipping up a publicity campaign on the supposed war between Dixieland and bebop. *Down Beat* spiced up its pages with headlines like "Police Avert Clash of Dixieland and Bebop," "A Jazz Purist Guilty of Collecting Re-Bop!" and "Bop Gets Monday Night Home in Dixie Hangout," while provoking a public argument between Dixielander turned bebopper Dave Tough—"Dixieland Nowhere Says Dave Tough"—and the revivalist leader Eddie Condon—"Condon Raps Tough for 'Rebop Slop.'"[40] For his part, Ulanov of *Metronome* organized a "Moldy Figs vs.

Modernists" radio show with revivalist Rudi Blesh, involving an "all-star" modernist band made up of Gillespie and Parker as well as Tristano. *Time* magazine, somewhat taken in by these antics, explained to its readers that "moldy fig" was "boppese for 'decadent' Dixieland jazz," though this expression had appeared in print as early as 1944, in a quite different context, before there was any "boppese."[41]

The Revolt of the Musicians (1946–49)

Perhaps the most serious challenge to bebop was the growing resentment of musicians outside the movement, mostly from swing bands, who were made doubly insecure by the threat of marginalization in an already shrinking market. The first to complain openly was Benny Goodman, who, smarting at insinuations by "modernist" critics that he was becoming passé, responded in an October 1946 interview by striking out against bebop. "I've been listening to some of the Re-bop musicians. You know, some of them can't even hold a tone. They're just faking. Bop reminds me of guys who refuse to write a major chord even if it's going to sound good."[42] He continued to snipe even after introducing bop elements into his own arrangements two years later—critiquing bebop for being more "nervous" than "exciting music" and complaining about the "morals" of the boppers, who have to be "screen[ed]" before being hired, "like [in] the FBI."[43] It was good copy for the jazz press to provoke criticisms of bebop by other musicians, and many obliged, including Fletcher Henderson, Hot Lips Page, Nat "King" Cole, Lester Young, Artie Shaw, and Benny Carter. Most were subdued and careful in their remarks, following a code of peer etiquette, unlike Tommy Dorsey, who simply blurted out: "Bop stinks. It has set music back twenty years."[44] The revolt of the musicians peaked in early 1948, when Louis Armstrong, egged on by the media and a few revivalists, launched into a sustained and surprisingly angry diatribe against bebop. After *Time* aired some of his grievances—"Mistakes, that's all bop is" and "A whole lot of notes, weird notes . . . that don't mean nothing"[45]—*Down Beat* and *Metronome* cornered him into interviews that turned stray remarks into a major controversy. The boppers, he said, are "full of malice and all they want to do is show you up."[46] He was clearly smarting against unnamed bebop "cats" who were deriding him for being "old-fashioned" and playing "too many long notes."[47] "All the young cats want to kill papa so they start forcing their tone." He also blamed bebop for the decline of the band business, particularly on Fifty-second Street, where "they've thrown out the bands and put in a lot of chicks taking their clothes off."[48]

Triumph (1948–49)

Nonetheless bebop triumphed. By mid-1948 the jazz press, and crucially *Down Beat*, followed by the mass media, concluded that bebop had acquired artistic legitimacy (however bizarre), that it had a powerful "cult" following that could not be disregarded, and was on the verge of achieving massive commercial success. Most important, it was agreed that bebop, having bested the other modernisms, would occupy the next stage in jazz history as the legitimate successor to swing.

Keenly aware of the dynamics of marketing, Gillespie did more than anyone to assure commercial success for bebop. In early 1948 *Metronome* commended him for organizing a big band with a marketable image and hiring an activist agent, Billy Shaw, from whose office "streamed reprints of articles about Diz, a steady diet of Gillespie food for editors, columnists, and jockeys." Though it had carped in the past, *Metronome* now applauded Gillespie for developing a "visual personality," imitated "all over America" by "young boppers" who "donned the Dizzy cap," "struggled with chin fuzz," "affected the heavy spectacles," and "with their own little bands began to lead from the waist and the rump."[49] Realizing the importance of cultural legitimation as a marketing device, Shaw organized a very successful Carnegie Hall appearance for Gillespie and Parker in the fall of 1947 and a tumultuous tour of Europe for Gillespie's big band in the spring of 1948.[50] Said *Time* magazine: "In Paris, zealous French zazous (jazz fans) came to blows over [Gillespie]."[51]

But what most impressed the commercially minded *Down Beat* was bebop's reinvigoration of the New York nightclub scene. After the demise of Fifty-second Street jazz, a few very lively bebop nightclubs emerged on Broadway between Forty-seventh and Fifty-second Street. The Royal Roost, a chicken restaurant, which in early 1948 had started featuring bebop sessions as a once-a-week novelty, achieved enough success to transform itself into a jazz nightclub with nightly sessions.[52] The results were spectacular. By August the Roost was drawing "the biggest jazz crowds in New York . . . many of whom outbopp[ed] the bandsmen, at least in appearance."[53] Other purveyors of bebop soon set up shop on Broadway: the Clique, Bop City, and later Birdland.[54] Bebop musicians even appeared regularly in Greenwich Village, the stronghold of the Dixieland movement.[55]

Buoyed by the surge in the bebop business, *Down Beat* happily stoked up its publicity machine in a supportive role, doubling the number of articles devoted to bebop matters and news. It exulted over the adoption of bebop styles by erstwhile swing musicians, such as Goodman, Charlie Barnet, Nat "King" Cole, Chubby Jackson, and Charlie Ventura, who also lectured on bebop on the radio.[56] It enthused over the rapid spread of bebop to college campuses, foreign countries, and even American rural backwaters (e.g., Greeneville, Tennessee).[57] It promoted the new books on bebop, introduced a series of "technical articles on bebop," and explained the bop argot.[58] Most importantly, after years of parody, *Down Beat* finally produced a few serious, theoretical analyses of bebop, which unanimously supported it as a healthy, inevitable stage in the development of jazz.[59] One article remarked that in the controversies over bebop, "history was repeating itself," since so many of the complaints against bebop—noisy, undanceable, undefinable, shocking—had once been leveled against swing. Born of the swing age, *Down Beat* was nonetheless, for the moment, allowing that the bebop revolution was as momentous as the swing revolution had once been. "Same story, different characters."[60] The peak of bebop's period of commercial success was probably reached during the critically triumphant coast-to-coast tour of the Gillespie band in the fall of 1948—from Billy Berg's to the Royal Roost. Surrounded onstage by look-alike cultists, even young women with painted goatees, the band played to enthusiastic, star-studded audiences, including Lena Horne, Howard Duff, Joe Louis, Mel Tormé, Benny Goodman, Henny Youngman, and most notably Ava Gardner, "who came out two or three times a week to hear us."[61] In their typically supercilious fashion, *Life* and *Time* took note of these commercial triumphs with feature articles anointing bebop as the musical vogue of the year. Among other fictions, *Life* photographically represented the ritual of a bebop greeting—involving the "flatted fifth" sign, the shout "Eel-ya-dah," and the "grip" that "ends the ritual," so that the "beboppers can now converse."[62]

Even the "moldy fig" press fell in line before the bebop juggernaut. The *Record Changer*, the only viable revivalist journal remaining, announced in early 1948 that it "refuses to be known as a sectarian publication." New Orleans jazz, though the "best," is not the "only" jazz.[63] Over the next two years, the *Record Changer* would give bebop a great deal of sympathetic attention, including a series of articles by Ross Russell on bebop rhythm, instrumentation, brass, and so on, which together constitute arguably the first systematic treatise on bebop.[64]

Decline and Death (1949–50)

Barry Ulanov of *Metronome* declared 1948 "the year of bop"—"the year when the Royal Roost dominated jazz life in New York, when the only jazz acceptable to young audiences around the country was modern jazz."[65] The attention and the plaudits from the press continued another six months into 1949, after which the fortunes of bebop plummeted precipitously.

Down Beat was willing to support bebop only so long as it perceived it to be commercially viable. But quite soon the bebop nightclubs, the only manifestations of bebop's commercial success, began to falter and go out of business—first the Clique and Billy Berg's in early 1949, followed by the Royal Roost in mid-1949, and Bop City at the end of 1950, leaving only Birdland, by this time no longer primarily a bebop establishment.[66] It was clear at the beginning of 1949 that the jazz industry was facing its worst economic crisis since the depression, from which it might never recover.[67] Ballrooms as well as nightclubs were folding quickly, or indulging themselves in the new country-western square-dance craze, which was causing hysteria in the jazz press—"Hillbilly Boom Can Spread Like Plague," screamed *Down Beat*.[68]

Attempting desperately to re-create consumer interest, *Down Beat* launched a highly publicized contest to replace the "outdated" term "jazz" with a new word "to describe the music from Dixieland through bop." The two winning words, "Crewcut" and "Amerimusic," never gained currency, as *Down Beat* backed down in the face of outraged opposition.[69] By the end of 1949, scare headlines in *Down Beat* announced that the prestigious "modern" bands of Charlie Barnet and Woody Herman were "Toss[ing] in [the] Towel."[70] *Down Beat* decided to take matters in its own hands in dealing with the horrendous "slump in the dance biz." It would spend all of 1950 attempting to fabricate a new dance boom, for example, by devoting a whole issue to dance music and even to conducting "a laboratory experiment with [an unidentified] dance band to discover what is wrong with the business."[71]

Meanwhile, a scapegoat had to be found, and bebop was the ideal candidate. For the remainder of 1949 and into 1950, musicians and disc jockeys, some of whom had been avid supporters, spilled their recriminations against bop on the pages of *Down Beat*. According to Chubby Jackson, jazz was "plagued" by a "cult" of young musicians causing "bizarre night club spectacles," such as "leaning against walls and staring into space like idiots." Buddy Rich fired the bop "elements" from his band. There was innuendo about the taking of drugs and other behaviors that would give jazz the reputation it used to have "before we picked it out of the gutter and made it respectable." A disc jockey pleaded: "Let's dance, I'm sick of bebop."[72] Responding to news of a funeral procession for bebop at the University of Minnesota, Charlie Ventura, erstwhile lecturer on bebop, agreed that "Bebop is really dead . . . that is, if you could ever say it was alive."[73] *Down Beat* apparently also agreed, since it reduced its coverage of bebop in 1950 to a trickle, dealing mostly with crisis and demise. But it was *Metronome,* formerly the most enthusiastic promoter of bebop, that declared it dead earliest and most decisively. In the December 1949 issue, Ulanov proclaimed "a once-strong edifice is crumbling and the decay is from within." The boppers brought their demise on themselves through the "ugly fights" over the "problem of origins"—was it Gillespie, Parker, or Monk who originated bebop?—as well as the "imitations" that became "apings," the loss of a danceable "steady pulse," and a fetish for breakneck speed. But worst were the "rotten [personal] habits" and mannerisms that "conquered every reserve of decency in jazz" and made "a joke of musicianship and japes of musicians."[74] After bop, he predicted, "we [will] have a jazz of reflection and restraint, soft statements and extended ideas," music "with mind as well as emotion"—the sure formula for the "birth of the cool."[75]

As the musician most associated with the marketing of bebop, Gillespie also suffered through the downfall of 1949–50. Fighting against the undertow, he labored to make bop more accessible to "the average guy," by featuring "more bop variations on standard tunes" and introducing a steady four-beat pulse that people could dance to.[76] However, he was rebuked by a reviewer for sacrificing "spark to get his 'bop with a beat'" and contradicted by Parker, who denied not only that bebop has any "continuity of beat," but also that it has any roots in traditional jazz.[77] (Parker's popular reputation was gaining on Gillespie's at the time and was to peak only after the bebop movement was dead.)

In mid-1950 Gillespie put together a more purist bebop band that drew rave reviews but had to break up within a month for lack of venues. The foreboding *Down Beat* headline—"Gillespie's Crew Great Again, but May Break Up"—was followed two months later by the clincher: "Bop at End of Road, Says Dizzy." In September 1950 Gillespie was "without a band, without a recording contract, and with no definite plans for the future."[78] Thus, bop had come to an end. The careers of Gillespie, Parker, and Monk would all revive in the 1950s, and bebop would be enshrined in the jazz canon as the first great wave of jazz modernism—just as *Metronome* had predicted. But the bop movement never came to life again.

Postmortem

This little narrative raises a number of interesting issues that it would take a full-length essay to do justice to, but that I will nonetheless briefly summarize here. What strikes me most about the story of bebop is the power that the "discourses of reception"—the press, advertising, and promotion—were able to wield in the construction of the meaning of the music. Though having considerable control over their musical product, the musicians seem to have had little control over its public meaning. Their own comments about their music were filtered through the jazz press, or worse the mass magazines, quoted out of context, and redistributed in the printed texts to fit the ideologies and marketing strategies of authors and publishers. The bebop musicians neither possessed their own means of discursive dissemination, nor as "mere" jazz musicians were they endowed by society with sufficient cultural credentials to offset those of the critics. Indeed, they were sorely dependent on these critics for increases in their own cultural accreditation.

This leads to the complicated and all-pervasive issue of race. By 1944, even before it had acquired a name, bebop, as an African American movement, had already migrated from Harlem into the white jazz world, performing in the downtown clubs on Fifty-second Street and on Broadway and having its message constructed by white critics. Harlem had not sufficiently recovered from the depression to support the small specialized jazz clubs and publications that bebop would have needed. The last African American jazz journal, the *Music Dial,* had died in 1945. Thus, it is not surprising that bebop got smothered in the racially coded discourses of European modernity and was constantly stigmatized by racially coded biases about lifestyles, mannerisms, and argot. Of course, some beboppers, in particular Charlie Parker, wanted to appropriate European compositional practices but ran into resistance when trying to accomplish this in their own racial and cultural terms. It seems as if even the most avid supporters of bebop, like Ulanov, were always trying to "civilize" it, particularly on the behavioral level, but also at the musical level. Of course, these critics were not racially prejudiced in any gross sense, for they were in the forefront in the fight against racial segregation in the business. But the fact that bebop got enveloped by the virtually all-white jazz-culture industry assured that this African American movement would be to a large extent discursively constructed in a way that reflected the biases of such a racial hegemony.

If swing was the child of a postdepression, post-Prohibition, wartime economic expansion in the music industry, bebop was the offspring of a postwar recession in jazz that never seemed to end but grew into crisis, and even into the threat of death for jazz, from which it would not recover until the mid-1950s. From the beginning bebop was burdened with the obligation to save jazz from its economic miseries. But there was clearly an incompatibility between the imperative to become as European and avant-garde as possible, on the one hand, and to become as commercially successful as possible, on the other. Gillespie and Parker personified this tension, the former a genius at publicity and showmanship, the latter operating at the limits of his craft.

Neither the beboppers nor the critics seemed to appreciate the fundamental changes that the music industry was undergoing—the revolutions in recording technologies; the rise of television; the decline of the live music scene, particularly nightclubs and dance halls; the emergence of studio orchestras; the increasing popularity of singers at the expense of bands; and so on. Unlike swing in its heyday, bebop never made the hit parade or infiltrated the top ten. It did not even make the "race" charts, which were being taken over by rhythm and blues, by then the dominant musical culture of Harlem but altogether unseen by the jazz world. In the final analysis, bebop never became "modernist" in the way desired by *Metronome* and never succeeded commercially to the extent desired by *Down Beat*. Thus, it was abandoned by both parties.

Although dead as a movement and a fashion, bebop would soon acquire a new life as perhaps the most venerated component of the jazz canon and performance repertory. Indeed, the emergence of a jazz modernism initiated by bebop, and thus of a jazz "art music," helped legitimatize the subsequent construction of a jazz canon in the 1950s through a spate of jazz histories and scholarly essays, many of whose assumptions and principles are still held to this day.[79] Thus, though no longer a current contending movement after 1950, bebop reentered the jazz world as an especially honored part of the perennial repertoire, existing alongside the succeeding waves of new movements and styles (e.g., free jazz). The bebop musicians continue to be revered as the icons of that great revolution in jazz that made all subsequent jazz modernisms possible. The construction of a jazz canon, following on the heels of the bebop revolution and giving pride of place to that revolution, is itself a complicated cultural event that deserves further scholarly attention.[80]

B. The Cultural Accreditation of the Beatles (1963–68)

FIGURE 7

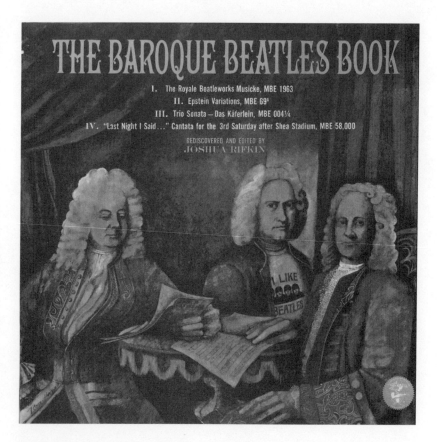

In this 1965 recording, Joshua Rifkin and a group of classical musicians put a baroque spin on Beatles compositions. Joshua Rifkin *Baroque Beatles* artwork used courtesy of Elektra Entertainment Group Inc.

CHAPTER 8
GAINING RESPECT

From Jazz to Rock

Despite the disparities in the idioms and fan base, rock music[1] has followed the same broad narrative of cultural accreditation as jazz. By "cultural accreditation" I mean the acquisition of aesthetic distinction as conferred or recognized by leading cultural authorities, which, in the case of performers, means the acquisition of the status of "artist" as opposed to "entertainer." Like jazz, rock music was initially reviled by the American cultural establishment for its rank vulgarity and sexuality, but later achieved permanent recognition as a legitimate art form. In this transformation and thereafter, rock has intensified the postmodern turn initiated by modern jazz. That is, it has intensified popular music's turn toward an activist and highly appropriative stance toward high culture. This chapter and the next sketch the processes that led to the cultural accreditation of rock during the mid-1960s and their impact on the dynamics of postmodern American culture.

There are enough interesting differences, however, between the American jazz and rock narratives to require a somewhat different approach. First, rock music's transition from pure entertainment to art took place much sooner in its lifetime and, once initiated, was completed more rapidly and compressedly. Emerging in 1954, rock music was on its way to legitimation by 1964, which it triumphantly achieved by 1967. In contrast, jazz did not irreversibly begin its climb up the cultural ladder until roughly 1942, twenty-five years after its irruption on the mass-market scene, and did not complete the process until the mid-1950s. Jazz did accumulate some cultural capital early in its infancy, due mainly to the flattering attention of avant-garde culture, whereas rock was universally vilified or dismissed by adult culture up to the point of its sudden and spectacular rise to respectability. But American jazz was unable to convert the early avant-garde endorsements—sporadic, short term, and mainly European—into a permanent fund of cultural prestige. Once abandoned by the avant-garde, jazz remained a lowly art. Only later, in the early 1940s, when it developed its own institutions of criticism, did jazz acquire the means of accumulating cultural capital to sustain a climb to a secure niche in the cultural hierarchy. This it achieved single-handedly, without any immediate help from high culture, though the lingering traces of past avant-garde approval no doubt made a contribution. In contrast, rock music's very rapid rise up the cultural hierarchy was promoted at every level of the cultural hierarchy, by literary critics and musicologists, but also by pundits from mass magazines and the nascent institution of rock criticism.

This heady mix of cultural forces acting in rapid fire over a short period of time generates a narrative of cultural accreditation considerably more jagged, tumultuous, and multidimensional than jazz's. In particular, such a narrative must deal with an increasingly complex hierarchy of cultural authority, generated by the phenomenal growth of middlebrow culture. Though still deriving much of its cultural authority from the standards and concepts of highbrow culture, middlebrow culture was at the same time becoming increasingly independent in its power to legitimate individual works as well as previously disenfranchised fields or genres, such as rock 'n' roll or film noir. By the dawn of rock 'n' roll, the field of middlebrow cultural production had become sufficiently bloated to encapsulate its own inner hierarchy, which commentators at the time characterized (perhaps too crudely) as the opposition between "high middlebrow" (*New Yorker, Vogue,* etc.) and "low middlebrow" (*Time* magazine, *Seventeen*).[2] In point of fact, during its transition from lowbrow ignominy to cultural legitimacy, rock music was entangled with a whole spectrum of "higher" cultural authorities, emanating not only from high culture *tout court,* but from "low" and "high" middlebrow culture as well.

Finally one group, the Beatles, stood at the center of rock's cultural accreditation in America like no performer(s) did during the emergence of modern jazz. Of course, today Charlie Parker looms large in any discussion of that crucial period in jazz history, but at that time his was only one of many names—including Gillespie, Boyd Raeburn, Stan Kenton, and Lennie Tristano—that circulated in the new aesthetic discourses of jazz. I am not saying that the Beatles' rise up the cultural hierarchy was the sole cause of rock music's parallel rise, although certainly it was a major factor, but rather that it corresponds almost point by point with that of the rest of rock, thus providing a useful vantage point for viewing the latter. Nor am I discounting, for example, Bob Dylan's indispensable contributions to rock's achievement of cultural legitimacy, to which I will give its due. But the story of Dylan's canonization does not coincide as neatly with that of rock as does the Beatles'. The narrative for the cultural accreditation of rock music begins, as I will show, with the Beatles' "invasion" of North America in 1964 and reaches its apogee in 1967, contemporaneously with the release of the *Sergeant Pepper* album to a torrent of accolades. On the other hand, Dylan acquired most of his prestige before joining the rock field, which, at the time of his crossing over in 1965, had already begun its rise up the cultural hierarchy. And disabled by a motorcycle accident, he was totally absent in 1967 at the moment of rock's accreditory triumph, only to reappear the next year to contribute (along with the Beatles) to a new period of modest normalcy and return to roots. Along with other important players, Dylan will appear at key points in my narrative, but the pride of place belongs to the Beatles, whose own story of cultural conquest, while quite unique and immensely interesting in itself, provides the clearest point of entry into the more convoluted account of rock's transition from mere entertainment to art.

The problem can be succinctly stated as follows: During the Beatles' first "invasion" of America in early 1964, their music was treated with utter disdain by the American cultural establishment. The massive coverage devoted to the irruption of Beatlemania focused almost exclusively on the success of the Beatles as a social rather than musical phenomenon, as an artifact of teenage hysteria and ritualistic acting-out. By 1967 all had changed. The Beatles were now praised for their brilliant musicianship—the daring studio experiments, their constant reinventions of themselves, the humorous exercises in irony and collage, and the perceptiveness of their lyrics. What could possibly have happened to bring about this radical reversal? Did the Beatles simply become better musicians according to traditional standards? Or did public musical taste undergo a massive transformation? If the latter, to what extent were the Beatles uniquely responsible for the changing public reception to their music and to what extent was the latter merely an epiphenomenon of a wholesale aesthetic reevaluation of youth culture by the established authorities of adult culture? An effective way to begin to answer these questions is to construct a genealogy of shifting discourses of aesthetic legitimation, emanating from the various authoritative levels of the cultural hierarchy, as these bear on the Beatles' rapid accumulation of cultural capital and its connection with that of the rock field in general. This chapter begins with the Beatlemania period, at the zero point of cultural accreditation, and then traces the first tentative and awkward expressions of aesthetic approbation for the Beatles, leading up to the summer of 1965, when the rest of the rock 'n' roll field also came in for some surprising if anemic approval. The next chapter will detail the correlation of the Beatles' aesthetic triumphs of 1967–68 with that of the rest of the rock field and the impact this had on the shaping of a rock aesthetic. In line with the geographical focus in this book's sections on postmodernism, I will be concentrating on the North American reception to the Beatles' music, with accompanying references where needed to the British discourses.

Beatlemania Lows (October 1963–April 1964)

The term "Beatlemania" was introduced by the British press in October 1963 to describe the allegedly riotous behavior of teenage fans outside the venerable London Palladium, where the Beatles were making their first appearance on a TV program aimed at a mass adult audience.[3] The press was not really discovering anything new, since the Beatles had been the object of a national teen adulation for six months and already had placed three records at the top of the British charts. The Beatlemania phenomenon first emerged fully when adult consternation and fascination was thrown into the already existing mix of teenage euphoria and spectacular commercial success.

The American press fully joined the Beatlemania bandwagon in January 1964 in response to the Beatles' first American number one hit ("I Want to Hold Your Hand") and the announcement of the impending American trip in February. The discourses of Beatlemania saturated the American media during February and March and continued to maintain a high profile until the Beatles' second coming to America in the fall of 1964. From then on, these discourses would wane somewhat, giving way ever so slowly to the new discourses of aesthetic appreciation, but were always on the verge of being rearoused in full force by a new Beatles tour or some controversial event.

The few and scattered observations on the Beatles' music during the period of Beatlemania were condescending, breezy, and confused. The Beatles were vacuously described as "bellow[ing] a sort of rock 'n' roll music" distinguished by being "less formalized" and "slightly more inventive."[4] Their songs, "achingly familiar" for Americans, "consist[ed] mainly of 'Yeah!' screamed to the accompaniment of three guitars and a thunderous drum." It was generally agreed that musically this "wild rhythm and blues quartet" with the "raucous big-beat sound" was a "near-disaster, guitars and drums slamming out a merciless beat that does away with secondary rhythms, harmony, and melody." Their lyrics were "a catastrophe, a preposterous farrago of Valentine card romantic sentiments."[5] The musical performances were repudiated as "high-pitched, loud beyond reason, and stupefyingly repetitive," really "more effective to watch than to hear."[6]

The British press, unlike its American counterpart, was not universally dismissive of the Beatles' music, in part reflecting the greater toleration of British high culture toward mass culture.[7] In a now-classic article, the highbrow British music critic William Mann of the *London Times* proclaimed

Lennon and McCartney to be "the outstanding English composers" of 1963.[8] He was especially impressed by their use of sophisticated harmonic and melodic devices, the "chains of pandiatonic clusters," and the "flat submediant key switches so natural in the Aeolian cadence." Pandiatonicism refers to the clustering of mainly dissonant chords that do not functionally relate to each other, that is, do not function to heighten a sense of resolution.[9] This can create in the hearer the sense that the piece is operating simultaneously in more than one key, a feature that critics since Mann have noted about some of the Beatles' early music. In using the term "Aeolian," Mann was alluding to the presence of medieval modal scales in the Beatles' music, though the Aeolian itself corresponds to the standard minor scale of Western classical music. This jargon, obviously foreign to any "Beatlemaniac" or for that matter to most readers of the *Times,* was meant to evoke how Lennon-McCartney, beneath the surface simplicity of their music, were not only transgressing the harmonic bounds of popular music in a modernist way, but harkening back to preclassical European music before the diatonic system took hold.[10]

However, Mann's musicological speculations either fell on deaf ears in the American press or evoked hostile rejoinders. A *New York Times* critic, setting himself in opposition to his "learned British colleague," countered emphatically that the alleged pandiatonicism was a mere illusion generated by the "tendency to build phrases around unresolved leading tones," which "precipitates the ear into a false modal." Despite the use of such deceptive devices, "everything" in the Beatles' music "always ends as plain diatonic all the same," that is, never strays from the well-worn harmonic clichés of popular music.[11] Ultimately, in his breezy and offhand music-theoretical praise, Mann was anticipating what within years would become the dominant aesthetic approach toward the Beatles' music. The Beatles are almost unique among rock performers to draw a plethora of arcane musical analyses seeking to explain their unusual (for rock) scales and surprising chord changes.[12]

For their part, the Beatles were willing to pay lip service to the put-downs of their music. It was thought to be part of their "peculiar charm" that they viewed their success with "bemused detachment," "disarmingly" conceding "that they have no real talent after all."[13] "We're rather crummy musicians," said George, to which Paul added, "We can't sing, we can't do anything, but we're having a great laugh."[14] This bemusement about themselves was seen as part of a larger display of wit, exhibited most vividly in press conferences —this "quick intelligence beneath their bangs" noted in countless quotes of their bon mots and incisive repartees.[15] This benevolent assessment had already been sanctioned, in the earliest days of British Beatlemania, by the royal family's surprisingly cheerful reception to the Beatles at a command performance. John Lennon's instruction to the crowd—"Those in the cheap seats clap. The rest of you rattle your jewelry"—was quoted everywhere as a surprising marker of Beatle cleverness. The Queen Mother, who "was seen clapping on the off-beat," found the Beatles "lovable," "so young, fresh, and vital."[16]

Ultimately, it was the performances of the teen Beatlemaniacs themselves, and not the Beatles, that aroused the most interest, analytic fervor, and concern among adult writers. These young girls—boys were virtually absent from the discourses of Beatlemania—were oftentimes seen as the real stars, the real force ready for incitement, for which the Beatles only provided the occasion.[17] Most of the theorizing about the astonishing success of the Beatles was concerned with the psychological and sociological roots of the "outbreak of madness" and "frenzy" that was Beatlemania. Was the Beatlemania "malady" rooted in a latent "aboriginality," in "jungle rhythms" and "tribal atavisms"? Or was it more symptomatic of the peculiar afflictions of modern youth, the "inner tensions that bedevil a mixed up psyche," the "joyless conformism" turning teenagers into "rhythmic obedients," or perhaps simply the need of a "last fling" before entering the adult world.[18] A number of respondents were, however, beginning to resist these pseudo-anthropological inanities, insisting among other things that the Beatlemania phenomenon was a perfectly understandable reaction to the dysfunctions of adult society: the "shocking death of our president," the possibility of nuclear holocaust, "racial tension," "brutality and the daily reports of Americans being killed" in Vietnam.[19] These subtle discursive shifts were the first signs of a status upgrading of youth culture and a concomitant downgrading of adult culture, which was to become one of the more glaring markers of the 1960s cultural wars.

In one respect, the media preoccupation with the "madness" of Beatlemania was simply a continuation, at a higher level of intensity, of the adult anxieties and expressions of consternation set off by the explosive emergence of rock 'n' roll in the mid-fifties. But, contrary to the early days of rock 'n' roll when the press seemed almost unanimous in its vilification, it now found itself significantly divided on questions concerning the alleged dangers and dysfunctions of Beatlemania. More significant than the fact that the adult world was now somewhat inured to the cyclical emergence of new teen idols and teen "hysteria" was the relative absence in the discourse of Beatlemania of any coded reference to fears about race, delinquency, and sex. The very Englishness of the Beatles accentuated their whiteness, marking them off quite strongly from "white negroes" like Presley and Jerry Lee Lewis. The Beatles' abandonment of black leather for Edwardian suits served to remove, at least for Americans ignorant of teddy boys, any allusion to delinquency. This perceived harmlessness was oftentimes construed in sexual terms, for example, in the obvious relief that the Beatles "have evolved a peculiar sort of sexless appeal: cute and safe."[20] Their "mop tops," reminders of Captain Kangaroo's "square hairdo," "softened" the "dividing line of sex."[21] Unlike Presley, "who made his pelvis central to his act" and evoked screams "straight from the raunch," or Sinatra, "whose Adam's apple bobbed in Morse code," "the Beatles are really Teddy Bears covered with Piltdown hair," as "wholesome as choir boys."[22]

Thus, the obvious similarities between the discourses of Beatlemania and previous public controversies and anxieties about rock 'n' roll tend to mask the significant positive shifts in adult attitudes toward rock 'n' roll and youth culture that were then emerging confusedly and tentatively. Indeed, amidst the torrent of psychologizing and moralizing theories and trivially detailed reportage, there was a small glimmer of aesthetic assessment and approbation. For the intensity of the public glare turned almost anything the Beatles did outside the privacy of their rooms—the press conferences, receptions, their comical attempts to escape the hordes of Beatlemaniacs—into public performances somewhat classifiable and evaluatable in aesthetic terms. So while in their formal musical performances they were judged to be talentless, they were heaped with praise for the inventiveness of their informal, unscripted performances. These informal displays of wit and charm were soon to be given formal, scripted expression in the film *A Hard Day's Night*, which played a crucial role in launching explicitly the discourses of aesthetic approbation.

Nonmusical Plaudits (April–August 1964)

Not long after the Beatles' return to England, while Beatlemania was still in full swing, two events subtly initiated what would later become a major reversal of the public assessment of the Beatles' aesthetic worth. The publication of a volume of John Lennon's poetry in March (*In His Own Write*) and the American release of the film *A Hard Day's Night* in August, both to surprisingly strong reviews, led to the first quite hesitant and minimal bestowals of aesthetic approval on the Beatles—however, only for activities altogether extrinsic to their music.

The low-middlebrow press, the most conspicuous respondents in America to Lennon's book of nonsense poetry, gave it a warm but perplexed and insecure reception. Indeed, *Time* and *Newsweek* seemed more interested in reporting on (and puzzling about) the very favorable response given Lennon's collection in the English highbrow critical establishment than on assessing its content. Said an amused *Newsweek*: "The British critics refused to take John Lennon unseriously," hailing him "as an heir to the Anglo-American tradition of nonsense: Lewis Carroll, Edward Lear and James Thurber," and comparing his "wordplay" with "the elaborate puns of James Joyce's *Finnegan's Wake*."[23] *In His Own Write* was not only "quoted at [English] tea tables," but "praised" in the "sometimes staid" *Times Literary Supplement*, which "concluded a jovial eulogy" with the enjoinder that Lennon "must write a great deal more."[24]

These celebratory endorsements from the more prestigious English publications provided a safe context for the American middlebrow press to indulge in its own more muted approbation, allowing that though there is "little of [Carroll's] orderly Victorian pedantry" nor "Joyce's erudite multilingual allusiveness," Lennon's work comes on "frothing with original spontaneity."[25] "In this startling collection of verse and prosery," said *Time* in the distancing discourse of "Timese," "Lennon has rolled Edward Lear, Lewis Carroll, and James Thurber into one great post-Joycean spitball." Beneath the perceived inanities and empty formulae of the Beatles music, there lurked apparently the caustic mind of an aesthete—something that, *Time* and *Newsweek* were happy to note, had totally escaped "all those jellybean-lobbing, caterwauling Beatle fans."[26] There was "an extra dimension of pleasure in a book that suggests that when John Lennon sings 'I Want to Hold Your Hand' he is wishing he could bite it."[27] Here we have the first intimations of adult cultural discourse seeking to decipher in the midst of the Beatles' teenybopper effusions a message or aesthetic aimed exclusively at adults.

The publication of *In His Own Write* was, however, only a minor event in the constitution of an adult public for the Beatles when compared to the impact of *A Hard Day's Night*. Noting the "universally fine reviews" that greeted the film, *Variety* asked in a dramatic headline whether the emergence of an "Adult Okay Endangers [the] Beatles?" Now that the Beatles were clearly "'in' with American parents and critics," *Variety* worried that they would suddenly "become 'out' with their teen and pre-teen following," who "might not dig sharing their Beatlemania with such obvious squares as their elders."

And, indeed, "all the New York daily critics" had gone "slightly ape over the film."[28] They expressed astonishment that what should have been an aesthetically worthless exploitation film turned out to be superb both as entertainment and art. Said Bosley Crowther of the *New York Times*: "This may surprise you—it may knock you out of your chair—but the new film with those incredible chaps, the Beatles, is a whale of a comedy."[29] The critic for the *Saturday Review,* a month late with his review, sheepishly admitted that due to "misguided indifference," he had "skipped the press screening" of what he expected to be "a sleazy, indifferently made exploitation picture." "I was wrong. On the advice of friends and breaking the critic's protocol, I went to a local theater, bought a ticket, and thoroughly enjoyed every minute of my first exposure to the Beatles."[30] It was now conceded that the "legitimacy of the Beatles phenomenon is finally inescapable. With all the ill will of the world, one sits there, watching and listening—and feels one's intelligence dissolving in a pool of approbation and participation."[31]

The Beatles were praised in particular for their remarkable comedic power, which was simply a cinematic translation of the wit and self-parody already displayed in press conferences. "Far from being the guitar-strumming cymbal thwacking oafs who have walked the golden path explored by Elvis Presley," the Beatles "have a neat sense of knockout comedy timing that places them somewhere between the Marx Brothers and the Three Stooges."[32] This comedic performance took the form of "a wonderfully lively and altogether good-natured spoof of the juvenile madness called 'Beatlemania.'"[33] It was this "sardonic edge to the film" that made it "surprisingly palatable" despite the fact that "of course, the Beatles sing a lot" in the film.[34] And, "of course," the film critics, however enamored otherwise with the Beatles, continued in the tradition of musical invective, complaining about the "moronic monotony" of the music, the "frequent and brazen 'yah-yah-yahing'" that is "grating to ears not tuned to it."[35]

Ultimately, however, it was more Lester's directorial use of current "art film" techniques than the comedic star presence of the Beatles that won over the critics. Found to be "much more sophisticated in theme and technique than its seemingly frivolous matter promises," *A Hard Day's Night* was praised as the *"Citizen Kane* of jukebox musicals."[36] The critics readily applied the stock formulations and fashionable hyperboles of art-movie discourse, describing the film as a "brilliant crystallization" of *"cinema vérité,* the *nouvelle vague,* free cinema, the affectively hand-held camera, and frenzied cutting."[37] The major directorial names of the trendy art movie-house scene were nonchalantly called in to certify the film's artistic credentials. In "a curious but effective fashion," the director Richard Lester had supposedly combined the "swift, elliptical, intimate style of Godard's *Breathless,*" with "semi-abstract Antonioni-ish chases," "a Fellini helicopter at the end," and "the staccato, Truffaut-like punctuations which give a semblance of syntax."[38] One critic summed it up thusly: "If [*A Hard Day's Night*] had starred anyone but the Beatles, and if it had come from France instead of England, it would have been hailed as a fascinating extension of the New Wave (which it is) and would have proceeded directly to long, albeit less profitable, runs in all the art houses."[39] Even the success of the Beatles' comedic sequences was credited as much to the cinematic achievements of the director and writer— to the "fast-flowing spurts of sight gags and throw-away dialogue" and to "such a dazzling use of camera that it tickles the intellect"—as it was to the native wit and performance abilities of the Beatles.[40] Nonetheless, coming into the film still positioned at the lower end of the cultural class system, the Beatles had everything to gain in cultural capital by bathing in the reflective aesthetic glory of the film's director and his bag of avant-garde tricks.

One film critic, Andrew Sarris of the *Village Voice,* did break with the consensus among his colleagues by asserting that he "enjoyed the music enormously" in *A Hard Day's Night,* despite the fact that "so help me I [had] resisted the Beatles as long as I could." Though "the lyrics look so silly in cold print," they "only mask the poundingly ritualistic meaning of the beat," where "the passion and togetherness is most movingly expressed." The Beatles and their fans provide "the kind of direct theater that went out with Aristophanes" and an "empathy there that a million Lincoln Center Repertory companies cannot duplicate." Sarris confessed that his "critical theories are all shook up" and that he was "profoundly grateful to the Beatles for such pleasurable softening of hardening aesthetic arteries." Sarris may well have been the first important American cultural authority to speak favorably in a sustained way about the Beatles' music, anticipating the first rush of complimentary analyses by a year.

The Summer of 1965 (I): "Baroque Beatledom"

Quite inexplicably, in the summer of 1965, there was a sudden turn of the tide, as invective toward the Beatles' music began to give way to sober analysis and praise—part of a larger movement of cultural reversal toward the whole field of rock 'n' roll music. What is especially intriguing is that this rapid reversal of attitude could not be adequately accounted for by changes in the music itself. The Beatles were still ensconced in the musical conventions of "I Want to Hold Your Hand"—"Help!" was the big hit of the summer—and had not yet recorded *Rubber Soul,* their first "art" album.[41] The two most popular rock 'n' roll sounds, Motown and California surf music, had been in circulation for a few years and quite comfortably operated in the by now conservative legacy of rhythm and blues and teen idol music. The one important new musical genre, "folk rock," which did admittedly generate a good deal of accreditory attention, only materialized as a public phenomenon later in the summer of 1965, some months after the first appearance of favorable articles on rock 'n' roll and thus, though relevant and important, could only partially account for the wholesale reevaluation initiated at that time.

Though the Beatles did not monopolize or dominate this groundswell of aesthetic approval, they did draw the most prestigious of the discourses. Theirs was the only rock 'n' roll music at this time to be favorably compared to traditional European art music and to be spoken of approvingly by highbrow celebrities. This art-musical approach to the Beatles, initiated in 1963 by William Mann but summarily repulsed at that time, now became the norm for explicating the value of their music. In August 1965 the *New York Times* in an abrupt about-face—until then it had been among the most snobbish in its put-downs—published a highly commendatory article reporting on the "almost unanimous astonishment" among "musicologists" over the way "Beatlemania has taken hold." The author Richard Freed was to spend the remainder of the year explicating in various high-middlebrow journals why "for some time musicologists have been studying the influence of the Beatles on the world of 'serious' music, and vice versa."[42]

These "musicologists"—and here the term seems vapidly to include any highbrow music expert, whether critic, composer, musician, or scholar—were evidently drawing some startlingly far-reaching "parallels" between the Beatles' works and a motley array of art-music classics, ranging from Carl Orff's *Carmina burana* (twentieth century), Charles Gounod's *St. Cecilia Mass* (nineteenth century), and even the *Locheimer Liederbuch*, "a collection of songs assembled in 15th-century Nuremberg." For example, "several musicologists" had noted "a similarity between the theme" of "I Want to Hold Your Hand" and the Credo of Gounod's *Mass,* while other "scholars" also "discerned" in songs by the Beatles a "grand simplification in the way of chord sequences and melodic development," which they "likened to the work of Carl Orff."[43] This included such "devices as the repetition of a single chord instead of an expected chord sequence" and "fragmented instead of fully developed melodies."[44]

Among the "musicologists" who expressed such "admiration for the shaggy Liverpudlians," Freed listed Leonard Bernstein and Abram Chasins, the latter an erstwhile composer and now music director of a New York classical music radio station. However, one would have searched in vain through highbrow journals or formal occasions of highbrow performance music for favorable references to the Beatles made by such "musicologists," who more readily dispensed approbations over cocktails or in chatty articles in high-middlebrow journals. Thus, the Beatles were not in any sense acquiring a formal highbrow certification, but rather a tenuous and somewhat patronizing endorsement, cavalierly doled out by highbrow agents outside of their proper venues in lower arenas of accreditation.[45]

This practice was especially well exemplified by Bernstein, the most visible and enthusiastic among the "musicological" fans of the Beatles. Having "[fallen] in love" with the Beatles "along with his children," he began to use musical quotations of Beatles songs in his annual *Young People's Concerts* on television, not for their own inherent musical value, but as a seductive means of illustrating certain features of classical music such as the sonata form—in effect, using the Beatles to get young people interested in classical music.[46] His own considered opinion on the Beatles was communicated by rumor or reported in society or homemaker pages of newspapers, far away from the music sections. An article on Bernstein's domestic activities "at home in Connecticut," for example, described a typical afternoon of leisure as consisting of "hours of tennis" followed by an "impromptu lecture on the Beatles, the Rolling Stones and the rest of pop music."[47] A captioned photograph shows Bernstein with cigarette in hand giving a "concentrated and thoughtful hearing" to a record by the Beatles. The "impromptu lecture" included such assertions as: "You're missing the whole tenor of this country if you don't follow pop music." Though "ninety-five per cent of it is unlistenable," the other 5 percent, preeminently the Beatles' music, is "more adventurous than anything else written in serious music today."[48]

There was another "musicological" event in the summer of 1965 that led to a separate Beatles boomlet in the art-music world—what was called "Beatles à la Baroque" or more generically "baroque rock." This movement was initiated by a group of classical musicians, operating as the "Barock and Roll Ensemble," who produced a record called "Eine Kleine Beatle-Musik," which offered Lennon-McCartney songs "in a graceful, almost Mozartian setting for small string orchestra."[49] Though the record, released only in England, did not garner much notice, it did set the stage, and may well have stimulated, the more ambitious and better promoted effort by the recent Juilliard graduate Joshua Rifkin, who rearranged various Beatle songs to fit a baroque orchestral format. The resulting disk, the *Baroque Beatles Book,* released in fall of 1965, includes an orchestral suite based on "I Want to Hold Your Hand," "I'll Cry Instead," and so on; a harpsichord solo ("Hold Me Tight"); a trio sonata ("Eight Days a Week," "She Loves You," etc.); and a cantata ("Please Please Me," "Help," etc.). Though sporting a humorous cover (Handel, Bach, and Telemann gazing upon a Beatles baroque music score) and tongue-in-cheek liner notes (reporting the discovery by Rifkin of this long-lost manuscript), the recording was played straight and with consummate competence. "There is no slapstick or overt comedy," Freed reported, nor apparently could there have been for "the Beatles have a firm policy against parody in the use of their copyrighted material. There is plenty of humor but it is of a fairly subtle variety, yielding most meaning to musical cognoscenti."[50]

The *Baroque Beatles Book* was reviewed widely and enthusiastically in the high-middlebrow press, most noticeably in audiophile journals, which normally paid no attention to popular music. It was proclaimed to be a "joy from first to last," with musical sounds that are "witty," "handsome," "resplendent," and "moving."[51] "Supported by admirable instrumentalists and singers," Rifkin was praised for having "produced performances of exceptional quality that are worthy to stand as models of baroque style."[52] The opening orchestral suite was performed with "ringing authority" in the "best French style of the early eighteenth century"—its overture a "six minute masterpiece complete with fugue."[53] The reviewers left no doubt that "this record should be in the collection of every baroque enthusiast." The Beatles, for their part, simply "sent in their congratulations on the results."[54]

The "common artistic impulse" apparently linking the Beatles to the baroque style led one amazed reviewer facetiously to conclude that "Jung must have been right all along: only his theories of the collective and racial subconscious can account for the phenomenon"[55]—a wry indication that the Beatles' baroquelike achievements were due less to acquired musical skill than to some strange process of musical osmosis.[56] Meanwhile, the *Saturday Review* reported with obvious approval that as the Beatles are "outgrowing the syndrome" of "persistent uses of the words 'baby' and 'yeah,'" there is a "strong movement afoot to separate them from the rock 'n' roll idiom entirely," since they are "much too sophisticated to hang around much longer in the malformed and murky depths of rock 'n' roll swamps."[57]

The Beatles themselves, with the assertive input of George Martin, would produce a number of records laced with an obvious "classical" sound, through the introduction of classical instruments played in some appropriate art-musical style—as in "Yesterday" and "Eleanor Rigby" (string quartets), "In My Life" (Elizabethan-style keyboard), "For No One" (French horn), "Penny Lane" (piccolo trumpet in the baroque manner), "Strawberry Fields Forever" (cellos and trumpet), and, of course, "A Day in a Life" (a forty-one-piece symphony orchestra). None was released early enough, however, to have elicited or influenced the accreditory discourses of 1965 linking the Beatles and classical music or the recordings setting Beatles songs in a classical or baroque framework.[58] If anything, it is more plausible to assume that the introduction of classically coded components into Beatles recordings was itself partly the result of the spread of classical or baroque readings of their work. George Martin, who himself had established a reputation as a producer of classical records before taking on the Beatles, might well have been aware of some of these discourses and some of these productions. Nonetheless, by early 1966, in the wake of *Rubber Soul,* the term "baroque rock" had gained wide currency though a very uncertain reference, evoked primarily by rock recordings that used harpsichords, trumpets, and string quartets. Like the companion expressions in vogue at the time, "folk rock" and "raga rock," it performed the small accreditory function of appending a high-prestige concept onto a low-prestige one.[59]

The question now readily asserts itself: What accounts for the sudden emergence in the summer of 1965 of favorable reviews of the Beatles' music in the American cultural press after a year and a half of unbridled invective if there had been no significant change in the music itself? Why did numbers of "musicologists" in mid-1965 finally join in a fray of art-musical analyses of the Beatles' music when in early 1964 such attempts were resisted or actively rebuked? At least part of the answer is fairly simple, although perhaps not terribly flattering for the self-conceptions of the "musicologists."

The first accrediting articles of that summer were occasioned by the Beatles' anticipated third tour of the United States and the growing realization that, contrary to earlier predictions of its imminent demise, Beatlemania was more entrenched than ever, much to the "almost unanimous astonishment" of "musicologists." What "astonished" the "musicologists" even more was the spectacular revitalization of the rock 'n' roll field that followed as "dozens, or possibly hundreds of groups" had "sprung" in the "wake [of the Beatles] on both sides of the Atlantic."[60] As one *New York Times* "musicologist" put it, "In less than two years, the Beatles have inspired an upheaval in pop music, mores, fashion, hair styles and manners. They have helped conquer a growing number of adults with their charm, irreverent wit, and musical skill. They have, in this country, provided marching songs for the teen-age revolution." The Beatles "have brought rock 'n' roll, which many have sought to describe as ephemeral since its start in 1954, to its third and greatest pitch of popularity." The conclusion: "In whatever form, rock 'n' roll appears to be with us for a long time."[61]

Thus, the reappraisal of their music by the cultural press seems to have been evoked in part by the surprisingly sustained financial success of the Beatles and their long-term stimulative effect on the rock 'n' roll industry. Interestingly it seems that most of the discourses of aesthetic accreditation in the summer of 1965, whether aimed at the Beatles or rock 'n' roll in general, were prefaced with a summary of sales figures and market shares. Queries seeking to explain the overwhelming popularity of the Beatles when posed in 1964, when Beatlemania was thought to be merely a fad, evoked issues of psychology, sociology, and anthropology. But in 1965, when the Beatles seemed firmly entrenched and their financial empire to be expanding continuously, the same queries led to issues of aesthetics. This points to a rather curious feature in the dialectic of aesthetics and commerce, not always noted by theorists. Though, as everyone recognizes, there is a constant tension in the sphere of cultural production between the achievement of financial success and the reception of aesthetic approbation, this tension seems to work irrevocably only in the face of *perceived* short-term financial success, where the work is almost universally dismissed. But as popularity and robust sales maintain themselves in the *perceived* long run, the evaluations of critics often noticeably improve and stabilize. Longevity in economic accreditation pays dividends in aesthetic accreditation.

The Summer of 1965 (II): A Plethora of Sounds

Of course, it was quite logical that the new aesthetic respectability garnered by the Beatles, induced in part by sustained economic success, should spread to the rest of the rock 'n' roll field, whose commercial revitalization, stimulated by that of the Beatles, was equally impressive. But the accreditory writings on the rest of the rock 'n' roll field took on a quite different tack than those dedicated to the Beatles. The classical music analogies were decisively cast aside, as the cultural press preoccupied itself with the complex proliferation of sounds that typified the rock 'n' roll field and the sudden influx of "meaningful" lyrics generated by the folk rock movement. Thus was initiated the recurrent tendency by the mainstream accrediting press to set off the aesthetics of the Beatles' music from that of the rest of the rock 'n' roll field. Nonetheless, given their overwhelming popularity and impact, the Beatles inevitably intruded even in those accreditory discourses that were not directed primarily at them. Theirs was a pervasive presence against which everything else in rock 'n' roll had to be measured or compared. The Beatles would in turn inevitably reap accreditory benefits from these other discourses, for the same reason. In 1965 there was no genre of rock 'n' roll whose accreditation was not inextricably connected with that of the Beatles, whether explicitly or subtextually.

On May 21, 1965, *Life* magazine issued what is perhaps the first serious attempt in an established journal to analyze and explicate rock 'n' roll as a musical form. From the outset, *Life* made no bones about the connection between the startling new economic successes of rock 'n' roll and its own reversal of aesthetic attitude toward it. The article opened with a hyperbolic announcement about

one of the most extraordinary phenomena in the history of music. Rock 'n' roll, born 11 years ago and scorned by parents who assumed it would go away if they would ignore it, has now jack-hammered its way into becoming the most widely heard music in the world today. Its driving beat and big sound consume and excite youngsters everywhere—and stirs adults into jumping like their kids at the discothèques. It is now as embedded in popular music as jazz, the blues and country songs.[62]

Indeed, in 1965 it was not merely that rock 'n' roll had gone from fad to "embedded" form that most impressed the media, but that it was now a global music that overwhelmingly dominated, in an unprecedented manner, the world market of recorded music. "Ninety percent of the 130 million single records sold last year were of the big sound."[63] Other publications chimed in breathlessly to report on these striking changes: "Now as [rock 'n' roll] flows unendingly from juke boxes, TV, transistor sets and car radios in a river stretching from the U.S. to Britain to France to the Scandinavian countries, it seems as if the world has gone mad for the music."[64] No popular music had ever achieved that status: even "Irving Berlin's songs were never international hits."[65] Since rock 'n' roll was just "not going to go away," it now seemed more useful to these writers to desist from the habitual incantations of "scorn" and "outraged complaints," oftentimes "accompanied by a vague nostalgia for the glorious, good old days of (let us say) Glenn Miller," and to start asking "where it came from and why it is so tenaciously meaningful to young people."[66]

Decisively taking up this imperative, *Life* abandoned the usual media perspective on teenage fans by addressing them somewhat as experts, as having an authoritative voice and some autonomy, rather than as troubled and manipulatable subjects to be psychoanalyzed. The interviewed teenagers happily responded by speaking more aggressively, defiantly, and confidently, asserting unapologetically that adults "do not understand [the] purpose" of rock 'n' roll, which is not "music to listen to, as they once listened to Sinatra and Como. It's music to move to, music to live by." To adults they said: "You're just jealous that you didn't have anything like this when you were young!"[67] We can assume that teenagers in the early summer of 1965 were not immune to the new militancy of the college student power movement that had irrupted at Berkeley in the previous fall.

The interviewed teenagers were especially resistant to any suggestion that they were being manipulated by the recording and radio industries. "It's got to reach down and turn us on." "There's no way they can trick us." *Life* firmly supported this claim to autonomy by appealing to the inherent unpredictability of the recording industry. "More than 800 records are turned out each week; perhaps six will really catch on."[68] Other journals concurred: because the music market is "untamed" and "chaotic," no station manager "feels confident that he can pick hits, can say for sure what the kids will like or reject. They are not only modest but awestruck, flabbergasted by the many tails of this rock-and-roll dragon." Thus, "the slightest touch of cynicism, of pandering would be smelled out."[69]

But if *Life* was successfully to initiate a move toward taking rock 'n' roll seriously, it needed to come up with an analytic framework for deciphering the imputed aesthetic components of the music, those interesting complexities that operated behind the perceived surface banalities and simplicities. It may have been obvious that the classical musical framework, with its stress on harmonic and melodic complexity, could not work to legitimate the whole rock 'n' roll field, which was still under the sway of the three basic chords and standardized song structures, as it had somewhat for the Beatles, who at least displayed some melodic and harmonic eccentricities. Nor could rock 'n' roll be aesthetically legitimated in the manner of jazz and the blues: it exhibited none of the improvisational qualities of jazz or the down-home sounds and folk authenticities of country blues.

Life's solution, which would set a yearlong pattern in the rest of the cultural press, was to shift the focus away from harmony and melody toward "sounds." No longer dismissed for its flat uniformity, rock 'n' roll was being seen as a complex and not easily decipherable field of distinct styles identified by their unique "sounds." "The student of rock 'n' roll," *Life* announced, "finds that there are now seven reigning 'sounds,' and though it takes an exceptionally trained ear to tell them apart, apparently the kids can do it."[70] These were identified as the Liverpool, Detroit, California, Nashville, New York, Chicago, and Spector sounds, the latter in reference, of course, to the producer Phil Spector.

In purely music-theoretical terms, the analysis of sounds is the analysis of timbres, the different musical tones and colors that can occur at the same pitches, which vary with different instruments and voices or different ways of using the same instrument or voice. At the same pitch, the timbre of a trumpet varies quite dramatically from that of an electric guitar, as does the timbre of baroque-style trumpet playing from that of the Louis Armstrong style. Perhaps because it does not have available to it the same imposing formal apparatus typical of melody and harmony but must resort to metaphor and vague qualitative descriptions, the analysis of timbres holds a lower status in traditional music theory than does the analysis of harmony and melody. But insofar as the discourses of timbre nonetheless have some importance in art-musical analysis, they can be used to accredit music that is claimed to be genuinely creative at the level of sounds (= timbres) even if not at the level of harmony or melody.

Ultimately, the technical analysis of timbres played only an intermittent and cosmetic role in the eclectic and confusing discourses of sounds initiated by *Life* and pursued enthusiastically by other publications. In effect, the notion of sound was blithely and inchoately expanded to refer to almost anything that could identify a style, such as the context, connotations, hooks, and even verbal themes. The few halfhearted attempts at technical timbral characterizations of sound styles laughably tended to miss altogether what these styles were really about. For example, one writer defined the "Detroit sound" (i.e., Motown) as the use of "a muffled double drumbeat with tambourine and a large brass section," although he sheepishly allowed that the "less technical definition" offered by the Supremes might work as well, who reduced the sound simply to "rats, roaches, guts, struggle, and love."[71]

But more typically, writers abandoned such meager technical "musicological" attempts and, following the lead of the Supremes, focused more on imagery and expression in defining the sounds. It being admitted that the "techniques" of the "Liverpool sound" seem to defy analysis, other than the fact that it is considerably more "toppy" than the "Detroit sound."[72] One writer resigned himself to defining it as a "buoyant, urgent, infectious rhythmic series of cadences," with an "aura of youth, channeled sexuality, and exuberance."[73] The "California sound," which received a great deal of accreditory attention in the summer of 1965, was identified primarily in terms of themes and lyrics: the preoccupation with the topics of "surfing, skateboarding, drag-racing and sky-diving," the most current example being "carburetor love songs," in which "rock 'n' roll troubadours expressed [an] undying devotion" to automobiles, couched in a "hot-rod argot, replete with background drag-race noises."[74]

This very heterogeneous discourse of sounds was inflected less by music theory than by the appellations of publicity and promotion. It was in effect a discourse of product and trend identification, which came right out of the recording and broadcast industries. As it was put quite revealingly in *Holiday* magazine, "'sound' is the word that reels triumphantly through all echelons of the rock-and-roll industry; you'd better have a distinctive one if you are to be around longer than four and a half minutes." Audiences were urged by disc jockeys "to listen not to a record but to a sound, the way a fashion house shows off a look." Rock 'n' roll stars "wear their sounds like identifying badges." Lesley Gore's sound is "spunky, ripe-apple fresh, no nonsense," the Zombies' is "tense, thin-chested, sex-frightened," and Petula Clark's is "platonically intimate," that of a "girl who feeds you broth and tides you over a bad affair." The search for new sounds, it was concluded, "goes on with the same assiduity the Pentagon uses in rooting out new weapons. Sound is the passport, the currency of acceptance."[75]

Once we see the discourse of sounds as emanating from the vernacular of the rock 'n' roll industry, we need not be surprised that it should have entered crucially into the first attempts to provide a framework for analyzing and explicating rock 'n' roll music. Nor should we be surprised that virtually the only "students of rock 'n' roll" consulted by *Life* and others in these initial accreditory attempts were record producers, promoters, radio managers, and disc jockeys. For before accreditation, and before rock 'n' roll fans found an institutional expression for their own voices, the only systematic and fine-tuned public discourse about the music came from the industry that produced it, marketed it, and attempted assiduously to decipher the taste of those who consumed it. And, correspondingly, that industry provided at that time the only locatable "serious students" who researched rock 'n' roll extensively and analyzed it minutely. However, the discourse of sounds was hazy and multifarious enough, for the most part, to camouflage its origins in the images and values of marketing and promotion and to appear to be grounded in musicological concepts. This illusion contributed significantly to whatever accreditory power it had.

Among all the types of accreditory discourses that would be spawned between 1964–68, the discourse of sounds had the distinction, whatever its limits, of being the most racially inclusive. African Americans were producers of four of the seven sounds listed by *Life* as defining the rock 'n' roll field: the Detroit, Chicago, New York, and Spector sounds. In addition, the fact that even all the white sounds of 1965—the Liverpool, Nashville, and California sounds—were clearly rooted in black music (unlike some later Beatles sounds, for example) was itself the source of some cultural approbation for rock 'n' roll from those journals heavily invested in the promotion of black music.[76] For example, *Ebony* magazine—the African American equivalent of *Life*—eagerly took part in the expanding discourses of sounds under the assertive headline "Rock 'n' Roll Becomes Respectable." *Ebony* was especially pleased with rock 'n' roll's role, through the very popular programs *Shindig!* and *Hullabaloo*, in exposing African American performance to "the great eye of television"—something quite rare in those days. Even such neglected "old-timers" such as Howlin' Wolf and Bo Diddley thereby found their way into "millions of living rooms and dens and bedrooms from Beverly Hills to Bogaloosa."[77] Martin Williams, the distinguished jazz critic at *Down Beat,* gave "one cheer" to rock 'n' roll for having drawn "attention to some exceptional [African American] blues performers such as Joe Turner, Big Maybelle, Ruth Brown, and Laverne Baker" and to have brought Ray Charles to public attention—"one of the most remarkable popular artists this country has ever produced."[78] Even *Life* made it a point to conjoin its article on sounds with a scholarly looking disquisition dealing with the African American roots of rock 'n' roll, in order to correct the "youngsters' claim" that the "big sound" is "their own discovery."[79] From then on, however, and peaking in 1967–68, the writers involved in the certification of rock as an art form would focus almost exclusively on white music, or at best would place rock on a different accreditory track than black music.

The Summer of 1965 (III): Folk into Rock

The emergence of folk rock in the summer of 1965 stimulated a third array of preliminary discourses of accreditation, to complement the art-musical discourses on the Beatles and the discourses of sounds. As the chief exemplars of the "Liverpool sound," the Beatles were obvious direct beneficiaries of the discourses of sounds. Their relations to the discourses of folk rock were more indirect and complicated, but the accreditory returns were surprisingly much greater—a point to which I will return.

The folk rock movement got its impetus in June when the Byrds' rock 'n' roll version of Bob Dylan's "Mr. Tambourine Man" reached the top of the *Billboard* charts. Roger McGuinn of the Byrds claimed to have seen "this gap, with Dylan and the Beatles leaning toward each other in concept. That's where we aimed."[80] In effect, the Byrds combined Dylan lyrics and melodies with Beatlesque vocal harmonies and the concept of the guitar rock band made fashionable by the Beatles. But the legendary big moment for folk rock, of course, occurred on July 25 at the Newport Folk Festival, when Dylan introduced his new electrified sounds to a mixed chorus of boos and cheers— creating an enduring split in the folk community between the older so-called "purists" and the younger more aesthetically adventurist and generationally confrontational members, who very soon would massively emigrate into the rock 'n' roll community. In September folk rock became a cause célèbre, when the first of its protest songs, Barry McGuire's "Eve of Destruction," reached the number one spot, in the midst of the Watts riots and the first massive buildup in Vietnam.

The entry of the hybrid signifier "folk rock"[81] into the rock 'n' roll vernacular brought with it a complex array of aesthetic and political allusions, deeply embedded in the discursive history of the urban folk music movement, which would prove in the long run to be an accrediting bonanza for rock 'n' roll. The most obvious accreditory contribution of folk rock was, of course, the infusion of "more meaningful lyrics, long a point of attack for hostile critics"[82]—an issue never addressed or successfully negotiated by the art-musical discourses on the Beatles or the discourses of sounds.

How the various cultural publications reacted to this "common law marriage" of "big-beat music" and "momentum" with "big-message lyrics"[83] depended significantly on their previous attitudes toward the politics of the urban folk movement. The more liberal high-middlebrow press—for example, the *New York Times* and the *Village Voice*—responded with genial approbation, while the conservative lower-middlebrow press—particularly *Time* and *Newsweek,* with a history of hostility toward Dylan and the urban folk movement[84]—exhibited a confused mix of grudging approval and barely concealed passive aggression. *Newsweek* referred derisively but with evident interest to the "folky rollers" and "bugged bards" who protest against "being put down" and "being hung up."[85] With tongue awkwardly in cheek, *Time* announced: "Suddenly the shaggy ones [i.e., rock 'n' rollers with Beatles cuts] are high on the soapbox," and teenagers, once "too busy frugging to pay much heed to lyrics, most of which were unintelligible banshee wails anyway, now listen with ears cocked and brows furrowed." "The rallying cry is no longer 'I wanna hold your hand,' but 'I wanna change the world.'"[86]

But the folk rock movement generated a complex barrage of accreditory discourses that went considerably beyond the simple preoccupation with "meaningful" lyrics, due largely to the rich and convoluted aesthetic controversies that followed Dylan's migration into rock 'n' roll. These controversies, it must be emphasized, had originated nearly a year before his crossover into rock 'n' roll, when he was being denounced by the folk "old guard" for having abandoned protest music for songs that were termed "surrealist," "personal," or "self-conscious," as in "My Back Pages" and "Mr. Tambourine Man."[87] For the left critics, Dylan's subsequent crossover into rock 'n' roll was simply adding a further insult—mass commodification—to the injury already inflicted by the "essentially existentialist philosophy" of his immediately preceding work.[88]

In the earlier folk protest period, Dylan had been inundated by the aesthetic discourses of authenticity. His "rough and unpolished vocal style" was seen as a conscious attempt "to recapture the rude beauty of a Southern field hand musing in the melody on his porch." Some of these songs, it was thought, "could have been composed in the back hills of Kentucky in 1824."[89] But when Dylan turned to "personal" poetry and rock 'n' roll music, the discourses shifted to the themes of romantic genius, modernism, and avant-garde transgression, which were used by the antimodernist folk purists to disparage him and by his youthful supporters in the folk community to defend him.[90] For the latter, Dylan's "authenticity" was now lodged in his being true to himself as a poet, rather than in reflecting the needs and aspirations of a mythical folk community. Against the "sad and even pathetic charges of Social Irresponsibility and Artistic Decadence" leveled by "representatives of the Thirties and the Forties," the youthful respondents couldn't "emphasize strongly enough that there must be no shackles put on any writer to force him to cover certain subject material or use certain styles."[91]

These "new left" partisans were clearly abandoning the social realism of the "old left" for an "art for art's sake" ideology, according to which artistic "geniuses," like Dylan, were to be valued not for providing the right "messages," however deep, but for constantly challenging the limits of aesthetic conventions and giving full expression to the wealth of their inner imagery, no matter how disturbing. They extolled Dylan as "the generation's most awesome talent," who succeeded in synthesizing "Guthrie's conversational folk-say with a dash of Rimbaud's demonic imagery."[92] As a "musician who breaks all the rules of song writing," thus giving his audiences the "needed doses of musical shock treatment," this "angry and passionate poet" had managed to "explode the entire city folk music scene into the incredibly rich fields of modern poetry, literature, and philosophy," in a manner analogous to Burroughs's "explosion" of the novel.[93]

These vociferous supporters viewed Dylan's entry into the rock 'n' roll field not as the commodification or dilution of his past artistic innovations, but as a new "experiment with ways to express his genius," as a new "avant-garde direction."[94] They were determined to defend this "folk-music avant-garde" against the "musical rearguard" attacks of the "old left," who sought to impose "orthodoxy" in the manner of "doctrinaire Soviet cultural organs."[95] Consonant with this mode of analysis, the young radical critics construed even the "rock" component in "folk rock" in an avant-gardist manner, by identifying it almost exclusively with "electrification," leaving aside all the other manifestations of rock 'n' roll, such as catchy melodies, hooks, standardized structures, and dance beats. That is, "folk rock" was made to signify a double avant-garde union of experiments with images (Dylan's "surrealist" poetry) and experiments with the new sounds of electricity—"the revolution of new electric music into contemporary areas of abstraction, philosophy, and poetics."[96]

The folk rock movement never lived up to these bracing modernist and avant-gardist proclamations by its most "advanced" proponents but settled in more predictably with Simon and Garfunkel's soothing poetic disquisitions on alienation and noncommunication, delicately backed up by the least obtrusive of electric guitars sounds. Contesting for hegemony in the rock 'n' roll field, folk rock held its own for a year but fell out of the competition with

supporter of free jazz and its perceived left politics, that best illustrated how vulnerable the jazz world appeared to its spokespersons. As late as 1966, the editors were adamantly reasserting their policy of "jazz only," telling readers to "look elsewhere for critiques of the other arts."[66] But by the summer of 1967, the magazine abruptly changed its name to *Jazz and Pop*, explaining that it was in the "most musically vital aspects" of "pop" that "revitalization" was "now occurring in American music." To a jazz readership shocked by such an unsightly conjunction, the editorial retorted that "jazz, pop, classical, folk" are "crude descriptive categories at best," which have more to do with "in-group exclusiveness" than to "musical sounds," where "there are no neat boundaries." In fact, "1967 has witnessed the birth of a serious American pop music which encompasses jazz, rock, folk and blues." Jazz was not to be construed "the exclusive property" of the "underground" and, "let's face it," jazz "needs popular music"—"economically as well as aesthetically." After all, in the words of Bob Dylan, "it's all music, man!"[67]

The jazz press, however, was decidedly mixed in its reception of the Beatles. A *Down Beat* article, for example, denied the Beatles any claim to be "in the vanguard of pop music": their "impact," though "staggering," was "mostly sociological and only negligibly musical." Far from being the "Andy Warhols of rock," as the "popular press" was trumpeting, the Beatles were "merely the popularizers, not the creators." The vaunted concepts and "techniques" of *Sergeant Pepper* had neither "originated" with them nor were "used by them in terribly original ways." Indeed, by the time the album appeared, it had "already been left behind by the work of other groups"—"the 'operettas' of the Mothers of Invention," "the Who's dynamic performances and advanced compositions," "Cream's brilliant experimentation," "the unique and adventuresome psychedelic experiments" of San Francisco musicians, and "the continuing excellence of the Rolling Stones."[68] This was by no means the universal view in the jazz press, as the rash of irate letters in response to the article testified, but it did presage the coming normalization of the aesthetic discourses on the Beatles, a retreat from excess and adulation.

Many rock critics rejected the idea of a jazz-rock merger. To some, jazz appeared dated and desperate, much more in need of rock than rock needed it. Jazz performance, in the words of one rock critic, wore the "fixed smile" of a "middle-aged society page matron: weary, sagging, desperately trying to be 'with-it,'" and "telling the same old 'charming' stories over and over."[69] At *Esquire* Robert Christgau concurred. Only "five or ten years" beforehand, "when jazz clubs were filled with college kids," the music "had balls." Then, he recalled, the best of jazz was filled "with dissonance and rhythmic tension" and was "physically involving." But now jazz "had lost its grab." The "old masters" seem "to repeat themselves; and what was once vibrant and compelling has become martini for Yale 56's, their necks shaved to the occiput." The only jazz that "justifies itself," the avant-garde, "is so insularized it can't expect popular support and doesn't get it."[70]

The overriding concern for rock critics, however, was that any jazz-rock merger, or indeed any attempted accreditation of rock in terms of jazz, would undermine rock's unique aesthetic qualities, making it the inevitable loser. "Rock embraces triviality," which is the "all-purpose pejorative" in jazz, "and makes it fun." Its "emotional content is out front with none of the clever ennui that came to typify jazz singing after Billy Holiday."[71] Conversely, rock, it was allowed, could not do well what jazz does best. Although the Doors, Hendrix, and Clapton have had "interesting forays into the territory of jazzlike improvisation," those who think "that any of the rock attempts at improvised solos can match those of Ornette Coleman, Milt Jackson or Cecil Taylor, would do well to compare the two kinds of music more thoroughly," said *Rolling Stone* critic Langdon Winner. At any rate, he added, rock has its own unique aesthetic values, in no way inferior to those of jazz, and thus "needs no gift pass from Dizzy Gillespie in order to enter the gates of musical immortality."[72]

The Rock Critics Take Over

By 1968 rock criticism had achieved the critical mass necessary to participate forcefully in the national debates on the aesthetics of rock, made possible by the founding of *Rolling Stone* and the spread of rock columnists through the middlebrow press. Though by this time the major battles of accreditation had been won, the need for accreditory discourses had not dissipated. For if it was by now widely accepted that rock music is a legitimate art form, there was still considerable confusion and disagreement about what kind of art form it is. With the withdrawal of highbrows from the arena of debate, it was left to the young rock critics, who now monopolized the high-middlebrow discourses, to attempt to elaborate a consensual aesthetic of rock, in effect to consolidate the gains from accreditation.[73]

Predictably, there was much more consensus and clarity among them on what was to be rejected, as part of the rock aesthetic, than on what was to be included. What most united rock critics was the opposition to attempts, typically by mainstream authorities, to legitimate rock music by appeal to the aesthetic values of other musical traditions and practices, such as Western art music and jazz. "There is no need to 'justify' rock 'n' roll by linking it to something bigger than itself—we have nothing bigger than rock 'n' roll, and nothing more is needed to 'justify' it than a good song."[74] Rock was asserted to have its own specific aesthetic, utterly distinct from, and totally irreducible to, that of other musics. "Rock is an art form in its own right with its own rules, traditions, and distinctive characteristics," said Langdon Winner.[75] It "was born with attributes not found in any other musical form," concurred Jon Landau, chief critic for both *Crawdaddy!* and *Rolling Stone*. It was "a distinctive new sound."[76]

Indeed, according to Greil Marcus, adults "over thirty" could not even comprehend this unique aesthetic, much less explicate it in terms of their values. Though, of course, older adults had the "ability" to "enjoy the Beatles" or to "think that Dylan has something to say," they nonetheless could not "be part of" rock 'n' roll, nor could it "be part of them."[77] "To be in tune with" this radically different "medium" requires years of exposure to the constant repetition of hit songs on the radio combined with a "conscious effort" to "preserve and heighten" these "experiences," to "intensify the connection between the individual and the music, between one's group of friends and the music they share." "This music is ours" and "can't belong to anyone else," not even to "the kids who'll follow us."[78]

Those rock critics who were most emphatic in asserting the uniqueness and irreducibility of rock aesthetics naturally assumed a skeptical or outrightly hostile posture toward the "art rock" bandwagon set off by the Beatles—as exhibited in the work of Clapton, Hendrix, Morrison, and, more obscurely, Van Dyke Parks. Thus the Beatles, who had been the darlings of highbrow critics, were for that reason received somewhat more gingerly in the rock press. The rock critics were especially opposed to the highbrow attempts to segregate the Beatles aesthetically from the rest of the rock music field. The Beatles were to be judged by the values of rock practice, since the ultimate accreditory commitment of rock criticism is to the field as a whole and not to any individuals or groups taken in isolation. To the extent that they veered away from rock traditions toward some post-rock avant-garde, the Beatles were to be censured. Many of the leading critics shared Richard Goldstein's deep ambivalence toward the experiments of *Sergeant Pepper* as a possibly wayward path that would undermine rock music rather than push it onward.

No one was more hostile to the apparent excesses of the art-rock movement than Landau, who was roused into discursive action by a publicity handout (for a rock group he did not name) grandly proclaiming that "the honky tonk atmosphere of rock and roll has been replaced by the opening night atmosphere of an art exhibit. Pop music has become valid. It is an art form." For Landau, this document "articulates one of the most misleading and destructive attitudes currently held by some musicians, a lot of fans, and too many critics." It is a "dehydrating and lifeless attitude" based on a serious "misunderstanding of what rock and roll is." The "core" stance of rock, taken by the "early Beatles as much as Little Richard," is altogether "antithetical" with that of "formal art." Rock, which was "never intended to be reflective or profound," cannot "withstand [the] kind of burden" imposed on it by the growing "artiness cult" within "the rock community," which has led increasing numbers to "expect of rock what they used to expect of philosophy, literature, films, and visual art." This sad "pattern" can be readily perceived in the career of the Beatles, who "managed to arrive at the complete negation of their earlier selves with 'Fool on the Hill,' a song that contains all the qualities that the early Beatles sought to deflate: it is pious, subtly self-righteous, humorless and totally unphysical."[79]

Other critics, if not quite as adamant and uncompromising, were also troubled by the art-rock phenomenon. "Rock and roll has exfoliated so luxuriously that it is frequently unrecognizable," said Christgau ruefully.[80] Having "milked every tradition in American popular music," it had now "hoked itself with classical melodies, string quartets, counterpoint, atonality, Indian raga, and all kinds of electronic trickery." But, he assured the reader, this new "rock avant-garde" has not "captured me." "If I knew more about music I might prove what I already suspect[81]—that avant-garde pop is a self-contradiction because its innovations" sound "suspiciously like middlebrow subterfuges borrowed from classical music and jazz," which are "elevated by an ignorant audience that applauds the 'new' whether it is bogus or not." "Most of the classical devotees who think about rock at all would rather it retain its folk vitality and stop dabbling."[82]

Ellen Willis of the *New Yorker* worried that the "unprecedented demand for technical virtuosity" and "complex music and lyrics" was "a trend threaten[ing] to get totally out of hand." "In spite of all the good music that would never have happened otherwise," the "increasing tendency to judge pop music intrinsically, the way poetry or jazz is judged," was "on balance" "regrettable." For it meant that "rock has been co-opted by high culture, forced to adopt its standards," thereby bringing to an end its "radical experiment in creating mass culture on its own terms, ignoring elite definitions of what is or is not intrinsic to aesthetic experience."[83] Furthermore, these initially ambitious art-rock experiments were deteriorating into the insipidities and clichés of "pop ecumenicism"—"music that reaches both the kids and the elders" and "*demands*" the "pleasant, nothing too noisy or raunchy, or too angry, or too anything." "And though these criteria do not rule out excellence—the post–*Rubber Soul* Beatles qualify most of the time—the usual formula is pap in hippie package," best exemplified by Simon and Garfunkel, whose "special gimmick" was a "rock poetry" dealing with such "cliché subjects as the soullessness of commercial society and man's inability to communicate."[84] For Christgau, this duo is most censurable for pretending to turn rock into poetry, something impossible and undesirable. Bob Dylan himself is to be praised not as a poet but as a songwriter. Dylan's "My Back Pages" is indeed a "good song, supported by a memorable refrain," but if the lyrics are taken by themselves, it is a "bad poem," loaded with out-of-date metric forms, "clackety-clack rhymes," and "scatter gun images."[85]

The Return to Origins

By mid-1968 rock critics were relieved to note that even musicians were beginning to "worry about [the] decadence" that "has infected pop since *Sgt. Pepper*," thus delaying the arrival of the "apocalypse."[86] There was apparently a discernable trend toward music that was "healthier," "less pretentious," and more "simple" than that of the "heady post-'Pepper' era," initiated "ironically" by the "very stars whose experiments inspired art rock," such as the Beach Boys, the Doors, and the Rolling Stones, who finally returned to sanity with "Jumpin' Jack Flash."[87]

The "most important figure in the anti-decadence movement," however, was Bob Dylan, just back after a two-year hiatus, whose *John Wesley Harding*, with its "acoustic accompaniments and pared-to-the-bone music and lyrics," was welcomed by rock critics as an antidote to the excesses of other rock "luminaries" too preoccupied "to find their own thing and to make sure it was heavier than anyone else's."[88] The old Beatles/Dylan opposition, articulated in 1965, was now reversed. No longer the avant-garde conceptual pioneer, Dylan was now the champion of simplicity and the preserver of roots in the face of the Beatles' excursion into avant-garde "abstract frameworks." "Instead of plunging forward, Dylan looked back. Instead of grafting, he pruned," in rank opposition to the new "Liverpool conventions." In the album the "diction is spare, traditional," and "abstract," "with no waste of materials," and the songs mercifully short. Thus, though "not a better record than *Sgt. Pepper*," "it should have better effect." "It is mature work that still shows room for rich development"—"something not easy to say of that of the Beatles."[89]

Rock critics were not alone, or even the first, in this growing advocacy of a "return to basics" but were unwittingly allied with a revivalist surge initiated within the music industry itself. Recording companies were reissuing hits from the 1950s in attractive albums, promoters were searching out and reassembling the members of defunct doo-wop groups for packaged nostalgia tours, and radio stations were introducing "golden oldies" formats into their programming. *Time* magazine, that barometer of the culture industry, took note of this trend, months before the spread of a similar revivalist discourse in the rock press. For *Time* it was actually the Beatles who, with the release of "Lady Madonna," most dramatically "captured the current upsurge of interest in 'old-fashioned' rock 'n' roll." With this rollicking tribute to the New Orleans rhythm and blues of Fats Domino, the Beatles, "instead of pushing farther out," were "glanc[ing] backward" to the "simple hard-driving style they left behind in Liverpool." The "electronic rumbles," "shifting keys," and "tempos" were left behind. "Madonna," released three months before the Rolling Stones' similarly retrospective "Jumpin' Jack Flash," may have been the first single by an elite rock band to signal the "return to roots."[90] At the end of the year (1968), the Beatles consolidated this "return" with the White Album.

In that year of the music industry's return to roots, the most influential rock critics were subscribing at least in part to a revivalist aesthetic, which evaluated current rock in terms of its continuity with the musical values of the founding "fathers," such as Chuck Berry. This was not to deny that there was "room for introducing wholly new elements into the music including seemingly arty ones"—"the Byrds and Procol Harum have succeeded in this way"—so long as these "highly eclectic sources" could be "synthesize[d]" "authentical[ly]" into "a basic rock framework." The most important contribution of the early Beatles and the British Invasion was to "resurrect the great spirits of the earlier days in rock and roll and remind everyone where it all came from," to express "affinity and a sense of continuity" with that "great early period."[91]

Clearly these rock critics were not practicing revivalism in the strict sense of the word, that is, were not calling for a return to the fifties, but rather were using the music of the fifties to help define a perennial rock aesthetic that would provide a framework for assessing new experiments. The initial attempts at such a definition were predictably sketchy and inchoate, though suggestive of the more pronounced positions that would emerge later. In general, the critics commended the early music as a "folk" music that was "direct" and "physical." Despite its blatant commercial character, early rock 'n' roll "at its best" was "unmistakably a folk-music form" in the sense that "musicians articulated attitudes, styles, and feelings that were genuine reflections of their own experience, and of the social situation which had helped to produce that experience."[92] It was perhaps because "they didn't worry about art" that "the people who ground out the rock-and-roll of the fifties" were "engaged in (unconsciously, of course) making another kind of art, folk art." For "consciousness tends to kill what is vital in folk art." Though contemporary rock could not recover the original period of innocence, it could do what Charlie Parker did for jazz, which is to combine "the vitality of a folk art plus all the complexity and technical inventiveness of the 'higher' arts."[93]

Despite its sometimes "ersatz, repetitious," and "imbecilic" character, the early rock 'n' roll music, asserted the critics, displayed "a simple vitality" unmatchable in other popular musics, "a joyfulness and uninhibited straightforwardness" that has become "such an essential side to all rock and roll."[94] "At its best," early rock and roll was "unpretentious, hard, simple, body music," expressing a "totally uninhibited" "physical style that had become fashionable all over." Not even the blues or country music, it appeared, had "engendered the kind of mass and direct communication" or responded to the music in such a "totally physical way" as in the likes of Elvis Presley and Little Richard. Rock, according to these critics, was "much more direct and immediate" than "poetry or art."[95]

Such rudimentary formulations were typical of the attempts at this time to delineate the implicit values of rock music. Both the conceptions of rock as a "physically direct" and a "folk" music, despite quite different terminologies, were adumbrating an "authenticist" rock aesthetic, according to which music achieves *authenticity* when it is rooted in a community, when it directly expresses the simple and unpretentious feelings of the performer and communicates in an unmediated way with the human body. Though the terms of discourse would shift over the next decades, authenticism would continue to drive rock criticism—or plague it, depending on one's point of view. The concept of the folkloric would find sustenance in the discourses on American "independent" rock of the 1980s, especially in its regionalist manifestations— the sounds of Austin, Minneapolis, Washington, D.C., and, of course, Seattle. With the advent of the likes of Iggy Pop and punk rock, the motif of physicality developed into a thicker aesthetic discourse, a discourse of assault and shock. Aesthetic authenticism would also find new avenues in the "stripped-down" and "minimalist" punk rock of the mid-1970s and the boomlet for "lo-fi" in the mid-1990s.

There was also a "nonauthenticist" aesthetic available for rock criticism in 1968, which earlier in this chapter I alluded to as "popism" when discussing Goldstein's McLuhanesque manifesto. Such a view blatantly and unapologetically promotes the values and practices of mass culture, even those traditionally viewed as most reprehensible and "inauthentic." Popism asserted that mass culture has its own implicit aesthetic that is equally valid with that of high culture, which it will supplant. It found expression in the tendency among rock critics to celebrate those earlier periods of rock 'n' roll when "commercial and aesthetic considerations were almost indistinguishable" and the "geniuses" owed "their greatness to the same qualities that made them best-sellers."[96] Popism valued the music of the Monkees despite (or because of) their being "hated" by "serious rock fans." Their music was "good," even though they were "lousy singers" who could hardly play their instruments." The "Top Ten" remained "an important test" if rock was to continue as "truly a popular art."[97]

In these "inauthenticist" and "popist" moments, rock critics took pleasure in glorifying those mass-cultural features of the music that traditional critics found so repugnant, such as rapid obsolescence, market saturation, constant repetition, and the merger of economics and aesthetics. "You don't listen to rock the way you listen to 'Le Sacre du Printemps,' anticipating a 20th century vision of timelessness," said Goldstein, perhaps the chief popist, in his rousing defense of rock's "willing[ness]" to "succumb to obsolescence." Pop "is like a display window; it needs changing with the season." It is meant not "to refract one moment through another, like a monument," but to seem "instantly awesome and eventually awful, like a supermarket." "This tumult of constant change is what gives rock its vitality."[98]

Despite its fresh and provocative appeal, popism could not ultimately become the dominant rock aesthetic. For the radical leveling process implicit in that aesthetic was at odds with the tendency of rock critics to claim a privileged aesthetic status for their music relative to the other "popular arts." Becoming a popist would have meant placing on the same aesthetic plane as rock all the genres of popular music, including the Tin Pan Alley tradition, "easy listening" and "elevator music," and "bland" white covers of black music. One could not accept Little Richard but reject Pat Boone while refusing to make any distinction between commercial success and aesthetic value. Nor could one easily subscribe to popism while proclaiming, as one rock critic did, that rock music "now stands as the most interesting vehicle for both composition and performance of any music in the Western stream"—"the essential musical development of our time."[99] Furthermore, popism is incompatible with the high/low bifurcation emerging within the rock field at the time, institutionalized through the distinction between "progressive album rock" played on FM radio, aimed at young, mostly college-educated adults, and the "singles" rock on AM radio, aimed at "teenyboppers." Rock journals, whose review pages focused primarily on "album rock," were clearly complicit with this new hierarchy. In point of fact, "art rock, with its implicit hierarchies," had won a permanent place in the accreditory discourses of the rock press, whatever were the misgivings. For better or worse, the "toothpaste" was "out of the tube."[100] The "popist" strain of rock criticism (e.g., articles on "bubblegum" rock) would need to exist side by side with the art strain.

Drugs, Politics, and the Aesthetics of Rock

There are certain nonmusical or nonaesthetic matters whose puzzling relations to the accreditory process require some commentary. First is the fact that there were so few references to politics and drugs in the discourses of accreditation, at a time of massive political and cultural upheavals with which rock music seems to have been complicit. Second is the overwhelmingly disproportionate attention given to white male musicians in these discourses, which goes even further than what rock 'n' roll's history of gender and racial biases would have led one to expect.

The relative inattention to drugs, at least by the mainstream accreditors, seems to have a simple explanation. Many of these writers were no doubt hostile to, or intimidated by, drug culture and barely understood the concept of a drug aesthetic. More importantly, given the hostility of the general public, connecting rock too closely to drugs would have severely undermined attempts to legitimate it as an art form. Nonetheless, the topic could hardly be avoided in the case of *Sergeant Pepper*, given the Beatles' admission to having experimented with LSD and the smattering of apparent drug references in the album. But even when they broached this issue, accreditors from *Time* to the *Partisan Review* disavowed or played down its relevance. Though allowing that the whole album is "drenched in drugs," *Time* wondered "whether the Beatles' songs" "are meant to proselytize in behalf of drugs or simply to deal with them as the subject of the moment"—particularly since McCartney's latest "pronouncement" was to advise against taking LSD, which, though it "can open a few doors," is "not any answer."[101] Mainstream critics, whether highbrow or middlebrow, denied that Lennon's refrain "I'd love to turn you on," which had sparked the BBC's decision to ban "A Day in the Life," really had anything to do with drugs. This line to them could "mean many things," such as the "desire to start the bogged-down juices of life itself."[102] According to Poirier, it proposes "quite delightfully, and reasonably, that the vision of the world while on a 'trip' . . . isn't necessarily wilder than a vision of the world through which we travel under the influence of the arts or the news media." Or, "Loving to turn 'you' on" might have been "an effort to escape the horror of loneliness projected by the final images of the song."[103] Such was the confusing combination of weak assertion and strong denial that ran through the mainstream writing on those not frequent occasions when the topic of drugs intruded on the discourses on rock.

If the rock press was even less inclined to bring drugs into aesthetic discourses, it was not due to any puritanical queasiness or any wariness about offending the readership. *Rolling Stone* clearly exhibited its enthusiasm for drug culture by offering a roach clip with each new subscription.[104] But at the same time, Jann Wenner, editor of *Rolling Stone,* unqualifiedly rejected any attempt to connect the meaning of rock to hippie lifestyles and drug cultures. The music was decidedly not to be construed as an appendage of any counterculture, but as standing on its own. This was simply to extend the consensus among rock critics concerning the aesthetic autonomy of rock from musical to social matters. In this view, the aesthetic legitimacy of rock music is as independent of outsider *social* (e.g., hippie lifestyle) values as it is of outsider *high-cultural musical* values.[105] Such a posture is by no means unique or abnormal in the annals of art but closely parallels the doctrine of "art for art's sake" that has been a mainstay of modern art since the heyday of romanticism—thus, the apparent paradox that the rock critics' very assertion of aesthetic autonomy is deeply rooted in the "outsider" values of modernist high culture.

This "art for art's sake" attitude toward rock music also explains in part the relative absence of politics in the early writings of rock critics, and especially the refusal to link rock music to politics. To the claim that "rock is valid" because "it is social criticism," the rock press had an unqualified retort: "Rock is not political theory and never will be."[106] Jann Wenner—who consistently resisted the inclusion of political material in *Rolling Stone,* even when unconnected with music—was the most emphatic in declaring rock's independence from politics, indeed its willful *separation* from politics. Having "its own unique meaning, its own unique style and its own unique morality," rock 'n' roll "wants no part of today's social structure," particularly politics, the "most manifestly corrupt form." This meant no part even of New Left politics, "which is, after all, still politics." In fact, "rock and roll is the only way in which the vast but formless power of youth is structured, the only way in which it can be defined or inspected." The "de facto spokesmen of youth" were not, according to Wenner, the New Left leaders, but "the Beatles, Bob Dylan, the Grateful Dead," who have brought with them "new ideas, new approaches, new means and new goals."[107] Most rock critics did not go to Wenner's extreme of wanting to replace politics by rock 'n' roll culture. But they tended in various ways, though not without wavering, to insist on the aesthetic independence of rock from politics.

This picture needs to be refined somewhat. First, political activists initially were as emphatic about the irrelevance of rock to politics as critics were on the irrelevance of politics to rock. Until 1968 the early political underground press—such as the *Berkeley Barb, Los Angeles Free Press,* and *East Village Other*—either maintained a hostile posture toward rock music or paid no attention to it. The cultural pages of these otherwise blistering publications were filled with placid reviews and reports about highbrow theater and string quartets, jazz concerts, and folk scenes, a reflection in part of the generational position of the editors. But it also reflected the historical antagonism of the left toward the machinations of the culture industry that were so blatantly brandished in the marketing of rock 'n' roll. As late as March 1966, a *Berkeley Barb* article predicted with some satisfaction the imminent death of rock 'n' roll, because "high school kids, rock's major market for the past several years," had "quit buying records," leaving the industry only with junior high students. But "ultimately, the death was caused by the exploitation of rock by the worst elements of the music industry, a fairly disgusting industry at best."[108]

Second, it is important to note that the accreditory processes reached their peak before the great youth-related political upheavals of the late 1960s had taken place—the events at Columbia, the Democratic Convention in Chicago, Peoples' Park, and Kent State, which galvanized a broad-based youth movement. The main year of accreditation (1967) was the year of the hippie, be-ins, and love-ins, whereas the string of just-mentioned political events ranged from April 1968 to May 1970. Not surprisingly, by mid-1968 when the political uproar was at a peak, the rigid discursive boundaries between rock and politics, erected both by the New Left and the rock press, began to break down. The burgeoning underground press, now in younger hands, was celebrating the political virtues of rock music. Though most writers in the underground press did no more than view rock as the preferred culture of the left, leaving unspecified how culture and politics are interrelated, some went further, arguing that rock music is inherently revolutionary. "Music is revolution," exclaimed John Sinclair of *Seed* magazine and manager of Detroit's MC5, "because it is immediate, total, fast-changing and ongoing." "A rock-and-roll band is a working model of postrevolutionary life."[109]

Meanwhile, *Rolling Stone* relaxed the "music only" policies of its editor, though somewhat sporadically and not without struggle, to generate articles on political issues generally in sympathy with the movement. Rock critics sympathetic to the left were themselves writing politically inflected copy for underground publications (Greil Marcus for the *San Francisco Express Times* and Jon Landau for the Liberation News Service). But though their views on the relation of rock to politics became more nuanced, they continued to subscribe to rock's aesthetic autonomy with respect to politics.

This is illustrated by their part in the spirited uproar over the Beatles' release of "Revolution" in the summer of 1968. The underground press, who already regarded the Beatles as at best anemic liberals, was quick to excoriate them for sounding "like the Hawk plank adopted in the Chicago convention of the Democratic Death party"—"a lamentable petit bourgeois cry of fear."[110] Leading rock critics joined in on the denunciations. Said Robert Christgau: "It is puritanical to expect musicians, or anyone, to hew to the proper line. But it is reasonable to request that they not go out of their way to oppose it." Lennon did, "and it takes much of the pleasure out of [his] music for me."[111]

But the issues raised by "Revolution" for rock critics were not quite so simple. According to Marcus, Lennon's mistake was not so much to give the wrong message, which he did do, but to try to give a message at all. Had he been politically correct, he would still have been criticizable for message mongering. "Message lyrics are afraid to admit the element of uncertainty that gives art—music, painting, poetry—the tension that opens up the senses." There is nothing "left to the imagination." "The words of a message song lie on the floor, dragging the music down." Happily, the musical sound of "Revolution," with its "freedom and movement," overcomes the "box[ing]" effect of the words.[112] It "takes the risks that politics avoids." Marcus, even when involved in the struggle over Peoples' Park, could nonetheless, when hearing the sound of "Revolution" in his automobile, feel the desire to press his "foot down on the accelerator" and beat his "hand on the roof and all over the dashboard." "Rock 'n' roll at its best," and this includes "Revolution," "doesn't follow orders—it makes people aware of their bodies and aware of themselves." It is not "a means by which to 'learn about politics,' nor a wave length for a message as to what is to be done or who is to be fought." But in key moments of political crisis, it is "a way to get a feeling for the political spaces we might happen to occupy at a particular time."[113]

The left press fastened on the Rolling Stones as the appropriately radical alternative to the Beatles. As the "freaks and outlaws" of rock music, in opposition to the Beatles, who "were always nice kids, a little weird maybe," the Stones were thought to stand clearly on the side of revolution, despite their own professed admission in "Street Fighting Man" to be nothing but "poor boy[s]" who can do nothing but "sing for a rock and roll band."[114] Referring to them as "our comrades in the desperate battle against those who hold power," a group of young California radicals proclaimed in a leaflet: "ROLLING STONES—THE YOUTH OF CALIFORNIA HEARS YOUR MESSAGE! LONG LIVE THE REVOLUTION!!!"[115]

Landau accepted the construal of the Beatles and Stones as political opposites, and, of course, he sided with the Stones. "The Stones strike for realism in contrast to the Beatles' fantasies."[116] But as a rock critic, he was not willing to accept the claim that their latest album, *Beggar's Banquet,* "is a polemic or a manifesto," as leftists were proclaiming. "It doesn't advocate anything." True, in this album the Stones "try to come to terms with violence more explicitly than before and in so doing are forced to take up the subject of politics." But they were turning to political themes only insofar as it allows them to "express themselves" on how "street" happenings are "affecting their lives." Though "they make it perfectly clear that they are sickened by contemporary society," they do not think it "their role to tell people what to do. Instead, they use their musical abilities like a seismograph to record the intensity of feelings, the violence, that is so prevalent now." There are, strictly speaking, no messages or "slogans" in the Stones' music. "After all, they are rock and roll musicians, not politicians, and London is such a 'sleepy' town."[117]

Clearly, the growing political activism of 1968–69 did affect the aesthetic discourses of rock critics. Positions shifted and the received views on the relation between rock music and politics were subject to considerable fine-tuning. But rock critics, even those committed in some way to some political agenda, did not depart from their basic view that rock music did not derive any of its legitimacy as an art form from whatever relation it had to left-wing politics. Indeed, it would lose much of its aesthetic power, according to them, were it to function as an instrument of political protest or as a bearer of political ideologies. At the same time, these same critics did accord rock some kind of contextualizing and expressive role in the emerging culture of political activism. But they were in complete disagreement with those enthusiastic writers of the underground press who identified rock with revolution and who were in search of "musical guerillas" — "a joke," said Marcus.[118]

Where Were Race and Gender?

That white male musicians were the primary beneficiaries of the accreditory process is no surprise since all along they were the dominant economic force in rock music. What is interesting is that they seem, on first impression, to have dominated the accreditory discourses more than they did the sales charts.[119] Put in Bourdieu's terms, white musicians' disproportionate share of total cultural capital seems to have been even greater than their disproportionate share of economic capital during the key years of cultural accreditation. Also, it appears that women and African Americans between 1965–69 did worse in the more prestigious album charts than in the singles charts.

The white male dominance among accreditees at that time was reflected by white male dominance among accreditors, especially in the rock press. The two prominent women in the rock critic ranks, Ellen Willis and Ellen Sander, operated somewhat on the outside of the circle of rock critics, despite (or because of) their prestigious positions at the *New Yorker* and the *Saturday Review,* and left the ranks of rock criticism within a few years. *Crawdaddy!* and *Rolling Stone* were virtual white male fraternities. Susan Lydon, who wrote occasionally for *Rolling Stone,* was used more often as a receptionist and copy editor. In its first twenty years, *Rolling Stone* did not hire any black writers.[120]

Crawdaddy! had "come in for criticism" for not doing "justice to Negro music," as did also *Rolling Stone.* Paul Williams, *Crawdaddy!*'s editor, conceded that "if we fail anywhere it's on spade music" but added that "the magazine is a very personal thing and we don't feel guilty about it. It's what goes in that's important, not what's left out."[121] In an early article, Williams had announced that "for the first time in the history of America, the best contemporary music is not being made by the American Negro. In fact, much of what is now called 'rhythm & blues' by the music trade . . . is watered-down formula stuff." This he thought was particularly true of Motown, where "talented groups like the Four Tops [and] The Supremes" churn out "variations on variations on themes by each other."[122]

The eminent jazz critic Ralph Gleason, soon to be associate editor of *Rolling Stone,* concurred with this view. "A curious thing" is "happening" in "Negro" music, he said: the current "Negro performers" (e.g., James Brown, the Supremes) "are on an Ed Sullivan trip, striving as hard as they can to . . . become part of the American success story." "While the white rock performers are motivated to escape from that stereotype," the "Negro performer" has moved in the opposite direction, becoming "almost totally style with very little content." "The Supremes and the Four Tops are choreographed more and more like the Four Lads and the Ames Brothers." In contrast, Gleason noted, "today's new [white] youth," unlike their white jazz forebears, who sought to "sound like a Negro," are "not ashamed of being white." Though "remarkably free from prejudice," white rock musicians were "not attempting to join Negro culture." For Gleason, this was a matter of "considerable significance," since it meant that "for the very first time in decades," something "new" and "important" was happening "musically" that did not come from the "Negro" but to which "the Negro will have to come," just as "in the past the white youth went uptown to Harlem," because this was "the locus of artistic creativity."[123]

Such views, which in effect were denying cultural accreditation to contemporary black music, were not representative of the attitudes of the most influential early rock critics, who clearly enjoyed contemporary black music and, as this chapter has shown, forcefully argued for the canonization of the African American pioneers of rock 'n' roll, in opposition to mainstream critics, who oftentimes seemed to think that nothing good had happened in rock music before 1965. Nonetheless, in the late 1960s there was in the rock press (as well as the mainstream press) a certain benign neglect of contemporary black music, which it appears was thought to be sufficiently different to require a different kind of aesthetic analysis, though few at the time inquired into what this could be. The major exception was Landau, whose long series of articles on contemporary black performers in both *Crawdaddy!* and *Rolling Stone* seemed a deliberate attempt single-handedly to compensate for this neglect.

What was going on in the rock press seemed to reflect a deepening division between the marketing and functions of white and black popular music. Before the British Invasion, the pop and r&b charts had come to overlap so much that *Billboard* in December 1963 stopped publishing the r&b charts. White musicians were crossing over into the r&b charts apparently as frequently as black musicians into the pop charts. Not only Elvis Presley and the Righteous Brothers, but even Frankie Avalon, Paul Anka, Neil Sedaka, the Everly Brothers, and the Beach Boys had appeared, sometimes with some regularity, in the r&b charts. After the British Invasion—the Beatles interestingly never crossed over—the r&b charts were reconstituted by *Billboard* (January 1965), as black music went on separate trajectories from white rock music. By the end of the decade, much of black music (mainly "soul" music) was marketed and critiqued as good-time dance music while much white rock, especially that "credentialed" as art, was viewed as music to be listened to carefully (with or without drugs). Soul music was further credited for its "sincerity," in contrast to the self-consciousness and irony of art rock.[124] Given that music to dance to has traditionally a lower aesthetic status than music to be listened to, and that "sincerity" is less prized in the art world than irony, it is not surprising that black music should have been somewhat neglected in the accreditory discourses of the late 1960s. "Album rock" became a code for the art end of the pop spectrum and "soul" and "funk" for the entertainment end. White consumers and critics who engaged in long disquisitions on the meaning of Dylan's and the Stones' songs during the day would then dance the night away to recordings by Aretha Franklin and Sam and Dave. This bias, though not racist in the usual sense and compatible with enthusiasm for contemporary black music, nonetheless led to a disproportionate diversion of the more valuable types of cultural capital toward white rock, leaving the lesser coinage for soul. This discursive bias was redressed somewhat in the 1970s, as exemplified in Greil Marcus's work and the *Rolling Stone Illustrated History of Rock & Roll,* but by no means eliminated, as future chapters will indicate.[125]

Women were even more absent from the discourses on pop music during the key years of accreditation, more so also than their minority presence on the charts would have warranted. Many suffered from the neglect given African American artists, while white women rock performers often found themselves ensconced in the folk rock and later "singer-songwriter" categories, genres that were not generally highly regarded by the leading rock critics. It was not till the punk movement that the accreditory fortunes of women began to shift somewhat.[126]

Postscript

In October 1969 the Music Educators National Conference, representing fifty-eight thousand music teachers at all levels, voted to "formally" endorse the teaching of rock music in public schools, colleges, and universities. Wiley Housewright, the president of the organization, declared with a flourish: "Art is nonexclusive. Rock music belongs alongside all music. Bach, Beethoven and Brahms move over! Make room for rock." Such bravura, in the waning days of the decade, came too late to cause much of a stir. But this belated endorsement, wrung after two years of debating and cajoling within an organization notorious for its conservatism, brought to an end any organized resistance within the highbrow community to the cultural accreditation of rock 'n' roll. As if to make up for his organization's lag with excess zeal, Housewright called upon President Nixon "to sponsor a rock music festival on the White House lawn to narrow the generation gap."[127]

Predictably, the fear of falling enrollments and the marginalization of music education had provided the initial stimulus, as early as 1967, for rethinking the music curriculum in primary and secondary education. That year at the Music Educators National Conference, participants were warned that "in an era of protest, irritation and rapid change," when "the kids are telling us that our methods and music are irrelevant, we can't just sit back like fat cats." Paul Williams, then merely a "nineteen-year-old editor," was brought in to educate the educators on "what they could do to reach their students"—such as starting a course off with "a study of the Beach Boys and the Beatles."[128] These pep talks did not inspire immediate acquiescence. Opponents reasserted the obligation of teachers "to perpetuate Western art music" rather than joining "the adolescent business of growing up."[129] There were perplexities, such as "how can you use [rock] in the seventh grade" and "what do you do with the marching band?"[130]

The final victory over these recalcitrants at the Music Educators' conference of 1969 can symbolically be viewed as the moment when the accreditation of rock music came to a semiofficial point of closure. A certain discursive calm now prevailed, as the remaining highbrow and middlebrow outsiders, their blessings given, withdrew from the debates and queries concerning rock, leaving the field to rock critics, who were still embroiled in the process of consolidation.

This accreditory calm prevailed also over the Beatles, the frantic accolades having long since subsided. The cultural media now accepted the rock critics' more modest though still laudatory assessment, which placed the Beatles squarely in the rock field, neither above it nor beyond it, and subject to its standards. There was certainly no longer any temptation to view them at the forefront of an internationally nonspecific avant-garde. Simply recognized as among the elite of rock musicians, though not necessarily the best, they had to contend particularly with competition from the Rolling Stones, whose "raw," blues-based sound was increasingly more in favor with critics than the Beatles' "arty" contrivances. In retrospect, it seems that cutting the Beatles down to size played a significant, if not indispensable, role in the cultural accreditation of the rock field as a whole.

The Beatles contributed generously to this reevaluation first with the debacle of the *Magical Mystery Tour* film, a disastrous attempt at unscripted spontaneity, which cured them as a group from any further avant-garde escapades. "'Tasteless nonsense,' 'blatant rubbish,' 'a great big bore,' howled the London critics."[131] Meanwhile, the Beatles were getting increasingly absorbed with their increasingly convoluted and acrimonious business affairs, particularly the troubled Apple empire, prompting the media correspondingly to shift its attention. In 1969, for the first time since 1966, the leading cultural journals devoted more print to the extra-musical adventures of the Beatles than to the quality of their musical output. The White Album (*The Beatles*), their minimalist attempt to "get back" to roots, received mostly qualified praise and some hostile responses. Not untypical was the rueful assessment that the Beatles were entering a "mannerist" phase "where skill and sophistication abound, but so does a faltering sense of taste and purpose."[132] In terms of their own aesthetic standing, it was perhaps good that the Beatles as a group came to an end when they did.

In early 1976 Robert Christgau, then at the *Village Voice,* produced an article proclaiming in its assertive headline that "Yes, There Is a Rock-Critic Establishment (but Is That Bad for Rock?)."[133] Certainly, the institution of rock criticism was by the mid-1970s firmly established, with hubs in Boston, New York, Detroit, and the Bay Area, and dominated by writers who had honed their skills during the pioneering accreditory-consolidation discourses of the late 1960s. Indeed, by 1976 it appeared that the period of consolidation initiated by the rock critics in the late 1960s, following upon the accreditory triumphs, had been brought to successful completion. There was now a general consensus on a rock canon, expanded to include the more recent arrivals of Elton John, Van Morrison, and Randy Newman, and the belated recognition of the Velvet Underground. The new critical establishment was agreed also on what not to like, such as the English art-rock bands (Yes, Electric Light Orchestra), most heavy metal, and disco.

The Beatles also experienced a revival of sorts in 1976: "Got to Get You into My Life" was a top ten single, while *Rock 'n' Roll* (a collection of covers by the Beatles) and *The Beatles at the Hollywood Bowl* made the top ten album charts. This hardly affected their standing among critics, who generally ignored this moment of nostalgia and had found little of interest to say about the Beatles after their departure. This was left for the die-hard fans, more caught up with the tidbits of the Beatles' former everyday life or the arcana of their recording sessions.

However, this happy period of establishmentarian unity, announced in 1976, came quickly to an end that same year with the explosion of punk and new wave. This splintered the entrenched rock press, drew in a new group of critics and journals, and provoked a fresh reentry of highbrows—in this case not musicologists, literary theorists, or celebrity critics, but from the brash new academic field of cultural studies. With the advent of punk, Beatles nostalgia was decidedly no longer hip. In the next section, I will take up this punk/new wave disruption of the aesthetic discourses of rock and the new involvement with highbrow culture that was involved.

C. New York: From New Wave to
No Wave (1971–81)

FIGURE 9 *Creem* magazine publisher Barry Kramer (*left*) and rock critic Dave Marsh (*center*) welcome Lester Bangs to Detroit (1970). Courtesy of Charles Auringer.

CHAPTER 10
PUNK BEFORE PUNK

Introduction

Nowhere in the history of rock was the dialectic of pop and art, of high and low, as intensive and convoluted as in the new wave rock movement in New York during the years 1975 to 1982. This was no adventitious fact about the new wave, but its most important trademark, emphatically foregrounded and advertised, what made it distinctively hip and exciting to its fans. Partisans of the new wave repeatedly promoted it as the rock music movement that most successfully operated on the tense boundaries between pop and the avant-garde, without doing injustice to either.

In its first years (1974–77), new wave was nothing other than the music scene at the seedy Bowery bar CBGB's. First conceived as a site for blues and bluegrass, CBGB's inconspicuously assumed its historical role when the owner agreed in early 1974 to let the new band Television use the premises for its gigs. Others, now regarded as the pioneers of new wave, quickly followed suit at CBGB's, turning this club into the center of the rock underground in New York. This included the Patti Smith Group, Richard Hell and the Voidoids, the Ramones, the Talking Heads, and Blondie.

The CBGB bands were not initially called "new wave," which as a label does not appear until 1977 and does not become entrenched till a year later. At first simply referred to as the "New York underground," these bands were in early 1976 suddenly saddled with the label "punk," much to the dismay of many. Within a year "punk" and "new wave" were being used interchangeably to denote the same movement and musicians. By 1978 "new wave" won out as the label of choice, serving as an umbrella term for all New York bands connected with the CBGB scene and its immediate successors in the East Village and SoHo. For purposes of convenience, except when otherwise indicated, I will be using the expression "new wave" generically to designate all these musical practices, however heterogeneous, which emerged in New York's hothouse atmosphere in the years 1974–82. However, at key junctures I will provide genealogies of the competing labels for this music ("underground," "punk," "new wave," "no wave," "the downtown sound"), with special attention to the aesthetic ideologies that they brought in their train.

As the New York new wave developed, young painters, filmmakers, and performance artists, mostly from the nearby East Village, were increasingly showing up at CBGB's and fraternizing with the musicians, many of whom reciprocally took a strong interest in the doings of the art world. Rock musicians went to their friends' art shows, took part in their independent film or performance projects, and began explicitly to appropriate devices of the musical avant-garde, just as art musicians were appropriating rock devices or even forming rock bands. There were explicit collaborations between established "stars" across the divide (e.g., David Byrne and choreographer Twyla Tharpe). All this crisscrossing peaked with the much-publicized "punk" and "new wave" art movements of the early 1980s amid the emergence of that legendary art-punk nightclub, the Mudd Club.

But such showcase border crossings came later and were somewhat peripheral to the more subtle dynamics of art and pop, which from the beginning were at work within the practices of the new wave itself. Beneath the flashy interchanges between it and the art world, the new wave was riddled by its own inner tensions between art and pop, which both predated and survived these extrinsic relations with the art world. This is clearly exhibited in the early competition between the labels "punk" and "new wave," the former evoking street-tough lowbrowism and the latter the avant-garde flash of Godard and Truffaut. Given these preexisting art/pop tensions within its own practices, it is no surprise that the new wave was later drawn into the art world activities occurring in its own backyard.

The art/pop aesthetic defining the New York new wave did not emerge with it but predated it in discourse. In 1971 a dissident group of rock writers—Lester Bangs, Dave Marsh, and Greg Shaw—alienated by the fashionably "arty" recordings of James Taylor, Led Zeppelin, and Elton John, developed a counteraesthetic of rock that stressed its unpretentious, unadorned, and pugnacious pop roots. They introduced the label "punk" into the rock discursive stream to identify what they thought to be the paradigms of "real" or "authentic" rock 'n' roll. These discourses of punk, though tethered to the concept of pop, somehow became complicit with certain notions of the avant-garde. So there were punk discourses, riddled with the tensions between art and pop, which were already firmly in place when the CBGB punk/new wave scene emerged in 1974. Indeed, it can be argued that these discourses provided the interpretative template according to which the heterogeneous array of musical styles at CBGB's could be viewed as all falling under one category. In the absence of such preexistent discourses of punk, there might never have been a mid-1970s movement conceptualized under the joint rubrics of punk and new wave.

Thus, the narrative of the new wave's perambulations along the high/low coordinate must look backward as well as forward. This chapter analyzes the discourse of punk that antedated the punk/new wave movement, the next deals with the "first wave" of the new wave when the art/pop dialectic was primarily internal to the music, and the final two chapters with the new wave's crossover into the art world.

Fanzine Aesthetics

We need to go back to 1970, to the founding of Greg Shaw's journal *Who Put the Bomp,* for the first inklings of a punk aesthetic. The first moment, if there was one, was an editorial in which Shaw sought to distinguish his "oldies" journal from the spate of others that had arisen in response to the recent growth of the revivalist market. *Bomp,* he declared, was not "just another [rock] magazine," but the first "rock and roll fanzine," that is, a magazine "written and produced by amateurs, for little or no profit, out of their love for their hobby." The "essence of a fanzine is participation from the readers," who not only produce "articles, reviews, drawings," but especially are active in commenting on the journal, "giving their reactions to the magazine and their contributions to whatever discussions are going on."[1]

As it turned out, *Who Put the Bomp*'s promotion of fanzine aesthetics would move in tandem with its promotion of a punk aesthetic. Indeed, since then there has been a constant correlation between the development of punk and the development of musical fanzines. In the mid-1970s the rock fanzines, such as *New York Rocker, Punk* (also of New York), *Search and Destroy* (San Francisco), and *Sniffin' Glue* (London), were the print media most emblematic of the punk/new wave revolution. In the 1980s, as "alternative" rock mutated, fragmented, and regionalized, the "zines" became an integral part of the proliferation of "anticorporate" regional networks that included independent record labels, college radio, and local nightclubs. Claims about nonpecuniary motivations, amateurishness, and participation from below have since become common currency in the mythology of fanzines. Fanzines sought to mirror, in posture and rhetoric, the perceived aesthetics of punk, which, in addition to the above characteristics, included a willful teen orientation (by writers who were far away from being teens), an adamant "pop" sensibility, and a "ranting" style of writing that is half Jack Kerouac and half "dumbed-down" imaginary street discourse (but hardly dumb).

As he himself admitted, Shaw did not invent the term "fanzine," but appropriated it from science fiction discourse, where it already had a venerable legacy. The appearance of *Amazing Stories* in 1926, the first magazine of original science fiction, had quickly given rise to national networks of discussion groups among devotees, who then founded another magazine, the *Comet* (1930), in order to publish their opinions, analyses, and communications. The latter was in effect the first fanzine, whose function it was to comment on the fictional material of "prozines" like *Amazing Stories*. The *New Republic,* commenting in 1949 on science fiction fanzine writers, observed that "they seem to be infected with a virus. They read, reread, and analyze stories with the zeal of scholars tracking down the key word in a Shakespearean play. They correspond with fellow sufferers, sometimes in letters running to twelve pages."[2] This offhand report does reveal two common features of science fiction and rock fanzines: first, an aesthetic fanaticism—a consuming preoccupation with one type of aesthetic object—that generates the most abstruse and unrelenting of quasi-scholarly activities; second, an interactive community of amateur knowledge seekers engaged incessantly in communications about common interests.

The Birth of "Punk"

Shaw also made it clear that though an oldies magazine, *Who Put the Bomp* was not interested in catering to nostalgia or merely to serve as a repository of arcane information for rabid collectors of out-of-print records. There is an edge, an articulated ideology, and an undercurrent of polemics in the typical fanzine not to be found in pure nostalgia magazines or collector guides. *Bomp* was to be forward looking as well as backward looking, using the past in order to revitalize the present. For if *Bomp* "delve[d] into the past frequently," it was only "because so little good rock & roll is being made nowadays."[3] In effect, Shaw was at the starting point of a movement among discontented critics who would be calling for a new rock 'n' roll revolution. Such was the framework within which the discourses of punk began to take shape.

Still in an inchoate state, these ideas spread quickly to the pages of *Creem* magazine, under the leadership of Dave Marsh and Lester Bangs. *Creem* and *Bomp* promptly formed an alliance. Shaw became the regular reviewer of single recordings for *Creem,* Bangs and Marsh corresponded regularly with *Bomp,* and Bangs later published in *Bomp* what would be the manifesto of the new punk aesthetic.[4] *Creem* was born an underground leftist music magazine, initially bearing the ideology of John Sinclair's White Panthers party. After

Sinclair's imprisonment for possession of marijuana and with the advent of Marsh and Bangs, *Creem* shifted from political to cultural dissidence, replacing political populism by musical populism. Though not a fanzine—more like *Rolling Stone,* a general magazine of rock criticism and feature writing—*Creem* oftentimes appropriated, in a highly self-conscious way, the amateurist and faux lowbrow discourses of *Bomp.*

Dave Marsh sounded the call to arms in the spring of 1971 against the prevalence of "fucked up" music. This was typified by Elton John, a "70s Paul Anka" who "crossed" the music of Tin Pan Alley "with pseudo-Dylan lyricism" and "watered-down Beatles music."[5] Marsh and his two allies, Shaw and Bangs, had equally unkind things to say about James Taylor (the virus of "James Tayloritis"), Led Zeppelin ("jaded fops"), and Chicago, all of whom were consigned to "the whole pompous edifice of this supremely ridiculous rock 'n' roll industry."[6] The only way to combat this new decadence, this new inauthenticity, Marsh asserted, was to rediscover "old jams just the way the old jams were rediscovered ten years ago when the Stones were rapping about Little Richard and Chuck Berry and Fats Domino and Sam Cooke." That is, a new rock 'n' roll revolution, like that spawned by the British Invasion, which brings about the new by revitalizing the old. The new rebels would have an advantage over the old in that they had "much more history to learn from," having available to them "not only the killer jams of the 50s but the killer jams of the 60s."[7]

But what "killer jams" from the past were to be evoked as models for reviving the rock music in the 1970s? Should rock musicians turn for their inspiration to the music of the 1950s, as the Beatles and the Stones had done? The decisive move by the *Bomp* and *Creem* coterie was to turn away from the 1950s to the 1960s in search of the models of essential rock 'n' roll, and in the 1960s away from the most established groups and genres toward those yet to be recognized or conceptualized. This shift initially was motivated by practical rather than aesthetic considerations. In trying to shape a distinctive "oldies" format for his magazine, Shaw faced competition from a number of oldies magazines preoccupied with fifties music, which by this time had been "exhaustively researched, discographed, and eulogized" "to a degree far beyond that of which I am capable."[8] This was "cool" with Shaw, for whom the "second cycle" of rock 'n' roll, "which took place in the mid-sixties," was "of much greater interest" and, unlike the first cycle, had been "almost totally ignored."[9]

But this turn to the 1960s raised some interesting problems, since the "decadent" music of the 1970s is rooted in some of the dominant musical genres of the 1960s, such as the psychedelic music of San Francisco to which Shaw had once been a devotee, but which he now castigated as an "outmoded hippie orientation." "Hippies are the squares of the 70's and the less they have to do with rock & roll, the better."[10] Bangs, for his part, bemoaned the unhealthy effects that the Yardbirds and the Who, whom he had greatly admired in the 1960s, had on the music of the 1970s. Though he had "especially idolized" the Yardbirds, he "eventually wised up to the fact that the Yardbirds for all their greatness would finally fizzle out in an eclectic morass of confused experiments and bad judgments." They were "just too good, too accomplished and cocky to do anything but fuck up in the aftermath of an experiment that none of them seemed to understand" and for which "the only spawn possible" were "lumbering sloths like Led Zeppelin." Correspondingly, "the Who, erupting with some of the most trailblazing music ever waxed, got 'good' and arty with subtle eccentric songs and fine philosophy"—"all this accomplishment sailing them steadily further from the great experiment they'd once began."[11]

In their search for 1960s rock 'n' rollers who were neither touched by decadence nor influential of it, Bangs and his allies searched through different makeshift categories—the British Invasion, surf music, American bands influenced by the British Invasion, such as the "San Jose groups."[12] Gradually, they settled upon a collection of not well-known 1960s bands, one-hit wonders previously neglected by critics, who combined rank amateurism with a certain pugnacity—bands such as Count Five ("Psychotic Reaction"), Question Mark and the Mysterians ("96 Tears"), the Seeds ("Pushing Too Hard"), and the Troggs ("Wild Thing"). Today we refer to them as "garage bands," but Shaw (or was it Marsh?) saw fit to name them "punk bands," a name that stuck.[13] Such was the advent of the "punk" nomenclature into rock discourse, five years before the punk/new wave revolution of the mid-1970s.

This turn to sixties "punk" bands on the part of Shaw, Marsh, and Bangs was more an act of conversion than nostalgia, since they admitted not to have liked these bands or to have ignored them when their music was current. Shaw "missed out on Sixties punk culture," since "there was always some Grateful Dead concert or trips festival or something that I deemed more important than seeing the Seeds, the Standells, and Count Five when they came to town."[14] Said Bangs: "I used to hate groups like Question Mark and the Mysterians. They seemed to represent everything simple-minded and dead-endish about rock."[15] Now, past hostility or neglect was replaced by near veneration. "Goddam, what a holy moment," exclaimed Marsh, after attending a concert by the newly reconstituted Question Mark and the Myste-rians, that "original bizarro band" who gave a "landmark exposition of punk rock."[16]

Lester Bangs: The Theoretician of "Punk"

The point was not, of course, to bring back these mid-sixties "punk" bands, but to revitalize 1970s rock with a "punk" aesthetic, itself retrofitted to adapt to what was a distinctly less innocent period in rock history with a large adult constituency. This would require some discursive work, since the category of punk was a new invention and the "punk" bands a new discovery. For this, Bangs's writings in the early 1970s proved crucial. If Shaw was the most active promoter of a punk revival, Bangs was its chief theorist. He laid out the groundwork for an aesthetic of punk in three oversize essays between late 1970 and early 1972, with a rhetorical bravado and amphetamine drive that would set a new standard for rock writing and turn Bangs into a star of sorts (now a legend). The first essay gave a rousing defense of Iggy Pop, who could be interpreted as a latter-day bearer of the spirit of 1960s "punk" bands, and the other two did the same for the barely remembered 1960s "punk" bands, Count Five and the Troggs.[17]

In the midst of Bangs's verbal barrage, three themes of a punk aesthetic emerged. First, sheer aggressiveness and loudness, the element of physical shock. The Troggs' music was "so insanely alive and fiercely aggressive that it could easily begin to resemble a form of total assault." They "churn[ed] out rock 'n' roll that thundered right back to the very first grungy chords and straight ahead to the fuzztone subways of the future." This "raw high-energy" took the form of "electro-fertility stomps," appealing mainly to sexually driven and frustrated young white males. The Troggs' lead singer wore one of the "most leering, sneering punk snarls of all time."[18]

The fact that the praise of shock and assault is now a commonplace of rock discourse should not blind us to the originality of this theme in 1971, which before then had only appeared in subsidiary contexts in the writings of rock 'n' roll. The early rock critics, operating in the late sixties, had turned to the fifties for their defining models of authentic rock 'n' roll, which, though it definitely thrilled and moved its audiences, was not designed in the main to assault them in adversarial fashion. The early rock critics did stress the "physicality" of fifties music—its direct (or unmediated) physical communi-cation—but this does not imply shock and assault. Of course, part of the aesthetic appeal of early rock 'n' roll music was that it offended parents, schoolteachers, and the clergy, but that is a different matter. In contrast, Bangs and other proponents of a punk aesthetic were promoting the practice of shocking the audience, as part of the aesthetic of the music, at a time when some rock musicians—Jim Morrison, Iggy Pop, the Velvet Underground, the Who—were becoming increasingly assaultive in performance. Richard Meltzer, a follower of Bangs's gonzo journalism, praised one band for acting as "hated badmen even to their audience," unlike earlier bands, like the Stones, who "built up their initial rep by scarin' the bejeesus out of them lil' ole ladies."[19] Given Bangs's utter disillusionment with the rock fans of his generation, it was natural for him to look to confrontative bands, like the Stooges, for "a strong element of cure, a post-derangement sanity." When "people have become this passive, nothing short of electroshock and personal exorcism will jolt them and rock them into some kind of fiercely healthy interaction."[20] The earlier rock critics, much more at one with their audiences, did not even entertain the idea of a need for such an assault.

There were two other features to the new punk aesthetic, as adumbrated by Bangs, which, like aggression and assaultiveness, produced an important shift in the discourses of rock criticism. These are minimalism and defiant rank amateurism. The mid-sixties "punk" bands, said Bangs, were "most effective" when operating "at their most bone-minimal."[21] Thus began a theme that was to become a mantra of the 1970s alternative discourses, which is that rock 'n' roll is at its best when "stripped down" to its "bare essentials"— an antidote to the increasing complexity and pretentious experimentalism besetting the music. In its purest form, this minimalism meant the use only of guitars and drums, simple riffs, a maximum of three chords, and the avoidance of long guitar solos. The pretenses of improvisation were especially anathema. Bangs praised the Stooges for resuscitating this punk minimalist aesthetic—for producing "stunningly simple two-chord guitar line[s] mechanically reiterated," which, though "nothing" by themselves, take on within the context of a song "a muted but very compelling power," "a simplicity so basic it may seem pristine." This music, "monotonous and simplistic on purpose" and certainly not "highly sophisticated (God forbid)," was nonetheless "certainly advanced." "Seemingly the most obvious thing in the world," the Stooges' turn toward minimalism was "a stroke of genius," which was "at least equal to Question Mark and the Mysterians' endless one–finger one–key organ drone behind the chorus of '96 Tears'"—"one of the greatest rock 'n' roll songs of all time."[22]

The most striking aesthetic move made by Bangs and his colleagues was to combine this minimalist aesthetic with the praise of ineptness and amateurism. Bangs had been initially "a little wary" about the "aggressive medi-ocrity" of Count Five's music, "because I knew just about how gross it would be." It wasn't till later when he found himself "drowning in the kitschvats of Elton John and James Taylor" that he "finally came to realize that grossness was the truest criterion for rock 'n' roll, the cruder the clang and grind the more fun and longer listened-to the album'd be." Some of Count Five's record-ings were "so grungy that . . . you could barely distinguish anything except an undifferentiated wall of grinding noise and intermittent punctuation and glottal sowlike gruntings." Yet this was "intrinsically" and "unqualifiedly rock 'n' roll," "fine and professional," despite its ineptitude and "grungi-ness"—"truly exhilarating music, filled with the wild pulsebeat of cre-ation."[23]

The Stooges, in their renovation of the punk aesthetic, maintained this commitment to music that sounds "simplistic and 'stupid.'" None of them had been playing their instruments "for more than two or three years, but that's *good*—now they won't have to unlearn the stuff which ruins so many other promising young musicians." They exemplified "the magic promise eternally made and occasionally fulfilled by rock: that a band can start out bone-primitive, untutored and uncertain, and evolve into a powerful and eloquent ensemble." For rock is basically an adolescent music, it "*can't* grow up." Any-body who dared "call [the Stooges' music] art" should "end up with a deluxe pie in the face."[24]

Again, as in the case of shock, it is important to recognize the important shift in the discourses of rock brought about by the aesthetics of minimalism and rank amateurism. Given their commitment to fifties rock 'n' roll as the model of authenticity, the early rock critics would not have easily been drawn to these notions. Among the canonical stars of the 1950s, one does not ascer-tain any attempt to produce a "stripped-down" music. Although the Atlantic, New Orleans, and Sun Records studios were certainly interested in "keeping it simple," there is no obvious attempt to "pare things down" to a "bone-minimum." These studios were peopled with skilled professional musicians who did not hesitate to add various ornamentations and would have been in-sulted at any well-meaning attribution of "amateurishness."[25]

Though the early rock critics, especially in their revivalist mentality, were quite emphatic about their preference for basics rather than complexities, they had a strong incentive in highlighting the performative and composi-tional skills of rock musicians. Jon Landau in particular, himself a musician, sought to inform his readers on the technical musical qualities of the music he reviewed. Said Bangs on the differences between himself and Landau: "It was just that [Landau] couldn't stand ineptitude of any kind of music, which was perfectly reasonable, while I dug certain outrageous brands of ineptitude the most!" Thus, Landau refused to print a Bangs review of Count Five's *Carburetor Dung* in *Rolling Stone*—"absolutely horrible, one of the worst monstrosities ever released." He accused the *Creem* group—"Jesus Christ, I used to have some respect for you guys"—of either "losing your minds or turning against rock 'n' roll. It's getting to where *Creem* won't even cover an album unless its either free jazz or so fucking metallic, mediocre and noise-oriented that you'd do as well to stick your ear over a garbage disposal or a buzzsaw."[26]

Punk as an Art/Pop Dialectic

The three features of the punk aesthetic that Bangs was adumbrating—assaultiveness, minimalism, rank amateurishness—were clearly meant to constitute a "pop" aesthetic, that is, an anti-art aesthetic that positioned itself in the domain of the "popular." Assaultiveness opposed itself to aesthetic edification and seriousness, minimalism to the worship of complexity, and, of course, that most anti-art of all these traits—ineptness and grunginess—to the false pretenses of instrumental virtuosity. Thus, in the dichotomy of pop and art, "pop" stood for good and "art" stood for bad. But the matter was not quite so simple.

The "popular," in this case, was construed primarily in terms of the consuming desires of teenagers—or, more precisely as it turns out, white male teens caught up with the frustrations of sex. (The sixties "punk" bands themselves were male and white, though in many cases also Hispanic.) Nothing would seem to be further than "art" than that. Bangs and his colleagues made no bones about the fact that punk music, as true rock 'n' roll, is a teen music, despite the fact that they, as post-teenagers, were addressing their writing primarily to young adults. "A big part of punk rock," said Bangs, is "the Great . . . Teen Sublimation Riff. Everybody wants to get laid 'twixt twelve and twenty, thinks about it round the clock in fact, but most of their cogitation is neurotic energy-drain stuff."[27] Early "punk" rock "overcompensate[d] for [this] teen neurosis with exaggerated displays of macho arrogance driven home by vengeful hard-on bass lines." "Punk" is the real expression of rock 'n' roll and the latter, insists Shaw, "is essentially teenage music."[28] Or, as Marsh puts it even more strongly, "TEENAGE would seem to me to be one definition of rock 'n' roll, in the first place."[29] "Rock 'n' roll"—as the opposite of "rock"—does not designate the music of a particular period (the mid-fifties), but of a particular age group. "The point is, rock & roll is not 1955–58, it's 12–17."[30]

The evocation of (white male) teenhood was part of an attack on the writers' own generation, who were seen as the main cause of the current decadence of rock music. For this "groovy, beautifully insular hip community" of older rock fans, while "certainly an improvement on the repressive society now nervously aging," exhibited its own "strong element of sickness." This generation, "caught up in the whirlwind" of its "[self-]consciousness," was unfortunately taking itself "with the utmost seriousness." Rock 'n' roll had thus become a "soundtrack" for "personal and collective narcissistic psychodramas." This "trend toward narcissistic flair" has been responsible in large part "for smiting rock with superstar virus," where "*attitudes* and flamboyant trappings, into which the audience can project their fantasies," are substituted "for the simple desire to make music, get loose, knock the folks out or get 'em up dancin.'" It was not enough for rock musicians to do this anymore. Now they had to figure out a way of getting themselves "associated in the audience's mind with their pieties and their sense of 'community,' [that is,] ram it home that [they're] one of THEM." They needed the "constant reassurance" from their "sophisticated" adult fans that what they are doing "is Good Music, more advanced or important, of so much higher quality than that alleycat racket the teens and proles wallow in."[31]

But—and this is where things get complicated—this punk pop aesthetic, which presents itself as an anti-art aesthetic, functions also as a strongly pro-art aesthetic. Being against art simply meant being against the unmediated appropriation of mainstream art notions and their pretensions into popular music—the pieties of singer-songwriters, the virtuosic convolutions of some heavy metal, and the classical music quotationalism of British art rock. Yet at the same time, the punk aesthetic was clearly incorporating avant-garde notions that came from outside the rock 'n' roll ambit. Inevitably, it appears, since the punk aestheticians, alienated from both the singles/AM and album/FM mainstreams, were forced to position themselves as a "popist" avant-garde or underground.

And indeed Bangs's key aesthetic notions—assault, minimalism, and amateurish nonvirtuosity—had already been variously adumbrated in avant-garde movements of the art world. The use of assault and shock, of course, are well-known trademarks of twentieth-century avant-gardes of all stripes, particularly dadaists and surrealists. And, of course, many avant-gardists, mostly in the dada tradition—but here John Cage's aleatory experiments are also noteworthy—made it a point to undermine the cult of virtuosity and professionalism in the arts. It would be tempting to connect the new punk aesthetic totally with dadaism—as some have done[32]—were it not for the minimalist component, which is more easily situated in the purist and inward-looking traditions of high modernism, even when it takes on a "postmodern" face.

As a label, "minimalism" entered art world discourses rather late, only in the mid-1960s, when it became a favorite aesthetic buzzword for painting and sculpture reduced to bare-bones abstraction—in the work of painters Robert Ryman and Brice Marden and sculptors Donald Judd and Robert Morris. By the early 1970s, "minimalism" was being applied to the stripped-down, repetitive pattern-oriented music of Lamonte Young, Terry Riley, Steve Reich, and Philip Glass—not to their liking, one might add.[33] By the mid-seventies New York rock criticism, operating within the hothouse atmosphere of the New York art world and increasingly receptive to Bangs's punk philosophy, was actively incorporating the art label "minimalism" into its discourses about the CBGB scene.

Thus, the punk aesthetic of Bangs and his early allies was at the same time a pop and avant-garde aesthetic, which combined the perceived ethos of male teen culture with art world concepts, largely but not exclusively dadaesque. For Shaw, sixties punk style, though as lowbrow and pop as music could get, failed to achieve much popularity because, like the avant-garde, "it was just too hard, too offensive, too insulting to all musical and social standards."[34] There was a certain (unconscious) element of underground, confrontative art in the "sneering stud arrogance" of these bands.[35] The art/pop binary, in the discourses of punk, was thus not consistently or only an oppositional binary. "Art" was both an inseparable complement to "pop" (that is, as avant-garde) as well as its unrelenting opposite ("mainstream" art). There was, dare we say, a dialectical tension between art and pop in the new discursive formations denoted as "punk." Because of this dynamic interplay between complementarity and opposition, the art/pop tension proved to be, in its unresolved state, a boon to the development of the discourses of punk—to the generation of debates, nuances, distinctions, and theoretical inflections. That is, this tension was more productive in its unresolved state than it would have been once the oppositions were overcome. For good reason, the oppositions were never overcome.

It should come as no surprise that Bangs, the populist punk philosopher, should also have been an enthusiastic fan of free jazz, the most resolutely experimental and avant-garde popular music in this century. He went so far as to propose that the woes of 1970s rock 'n' roll could best be surmounted by merging free jazz with the punk framework. There was no reason why "you couldn't play truly free music to a basic backbeat, gaining the best of both worlds." "Why couldn't you find some way of fitting some of the new jazz ideas in with a Question Mark and the Mysterians type format," thus preserving "the primordial rock and roll drive whilst shattering all the accumulated straitjackets of key and time signature which vanguard jazz musicians had begun to dispose of almost a decade before." This was the only hope "for a free rock 'n' roll renaissance which would be true to the original form," which would "rescue us from all this ill-conceived dilettantish pap so far removed from the soil of jive" and open possibilities "for truly adventurous all-guitar-group experiments in the future."[36]

Thus, rock could adventurously move forward while remaining true to itself. It would "pick up on nothing but roots and noise," thus escaping "the folk/*Sgt. Pepper* virus," the "mire" of "blues and abortive 'classical' hybrids," and "every other conceivable manner of 'artistic' jerkoff." For it is noise that connects that most primitive rock with the most contemporary avant-garde practices. "I never grew out of liking noise, from Little Richard to Cecil Taylor to John Cage to the Stooges." "Because properly conceived and handled noise is not noise at all, but music whose textures just happen to be a little thicker and more involved than usual, so that you may not hear much but obscurity the first time, but various subsequent playings can open up whole vistas you never dreamed were there." This noise tradition of rock music was displaced when the "folkies," who had previously "looked down their noses at that ugly juvenile noise called rock 'n' roll," picked up electric guitar, and "started storing all the musics in their well-educated little beans together, and before we knew it, we had Art-Rock."[37] Bangs's jazz-rock utopia (certainly different from the jazz-rock fusion that was taking place at the time) was perhaps only a passing aesthetic fantasy, but it does illustrate the intricate connection from the very beginning in the discourses of punk between a rank popism and an uncompromising avant-gardism. We cannot underestimate the importance these punk/avant-garde discourses have had on the original reception, and thus in the constitution, of the New York punk/new wave movement. There is perhaps no comparable instance in the history of rock 'n' roll where a preexisting discursive formation had such an impact on the formation and constitution of a musical genre.[38]

Punk Meets Bohemia: The Velvet Underground

While in the middle of his punk campaign, Bangs had also taken up the cause of Lou Reed and the Velvet Underground. Though separate, these agendas inevitably impinged on each other. The outcome was that the discourses of punk got infused with the imagery of New York bohemianism and Lou Reed became the "godfather" of punk. Arguably Bangs did more than anyone else to rescue the Velvet Underground from obscurity and to put them on the road to rock canonization. In their five years (1965–70) as a group, the Velvet Underground were a critical as well as commercial failure. Their two first albums peaked at number 171 and 199 on the *Billboard* charts while the final two never made the top 200. What is especially striking is the little critical attention they received during that period, despite the fact that they had recorded with an established label (Verve) and were well integrated in the Andy Warhol circles. No one reviewed the first album, and only *Crawdaddy!* in 1968 had any serious discussion of their second. *Rolling Stone,* initially quite hostile, finally tolerated Lester Bangs's 1969 review of the third album. Even in New York, their home terrain, the Velvet Underground got virtually no attention, not even from the *Village Voice.* The lone exception was Richard Goldstein's amused New Journalism article in *New York* magazine on the scene at the Balloon Farm, an East Village nightclub.

Nonetheless, according to the story now deeply imprinted in legend, a small cult was growing in the midst of the Velvets' obscurity, a number of musicians and musicians-to-be (Iggy Pop, Jonathan Richman of the Modern Lovers, Peter Laughner of Rocket from the Tombs, later of Pere Ubu), and also some writers among whom Bangs was in the forefront. The Velvet Underground cult began to spread beyond that narrow coterie in 1971, both in the United States and Great Britain, after the issuance of the last album, *Loaded,* and just at the time that the group was breaking up. *Melody Maker* made up for its past neglect during that year by retrospectively reviewing all the Velvet Underground albums, as well as shards that had appeared as bootlegs.

In the United States, Bangs led the drive toward cultural accreditation with a major article in *Creem* that, though ostensibly a review of *Loaded,* gave an album-by-album account of the musical history of the group and a narrative of their breakdown. This article was put forth as a definitive statement and was so received. Though written in the midst of Bangs's series on the 1960s "punk" bands, this piece made no attempt to tie the Velvet Underground to the punk aesthetic. But there was definitely an art/pop dialectic at work in the article, with strong emphasis on avant-garde experimentalism and bohemianism, which subtly brought the two agendas closer.

For Bangs, each of the Velvet Underground's four albums represented a different aspect of the group's aesthetics. The *Velvet Underground and Nico* was saturated with bohemian imagery, in the tradition of the beat poets. "Thematically grim," it "rendered the dark street life of New York City in a vision as fully realized as in Burroughs." The song "Heroin" is "a classic treatment that stares death in the face and comes back poetic if unresolved"—a welcome antidote to the "narcissistic, vibe-y albums" of "Woodstock Nation" groups who "are content to serve as PR squads for the youth culture's 'beautiful young people.'" The second album (*White Light/White Heat*) established the Velvet Underground "as one of the most dynamically experimental groups in or out of rock." It is "a milestone on the road to tonal and rhythmic liberation which is giving rock all the range and freedom of the new jazz."[39] The seventeen-minute cut, "Sister Ray," exemplified best for Bangs the salutary results of heeding his call for "applying the lessons of free jazz to rock." "Interested in the possibilities of noise from the start," the Velvet Underground brought to completion the project initiated by Ornette Coleman in *Free Jazz*.[40]

Quite rightly, according to Bangs, the band did not pursue this "pattern of fiendishly intricate experiments" in future albums, but left *White Light* behind "as their ultimate statement in the new musical vocabulary of electronic abstraction." For "they had more stories to tell," and any broader audience was acutely "unprepared for futuristic music." The third album (*The Velvet Underground*) brought "simplicity," "eloquence," and a "sense of universality," in such "little masterpieces" as "Candy Says" and "Some Kinda Love." Said Lou Reed: "I've gotten to where I like 'pretty' stuff better (rather than drive and distortion) because you can be more subtle, really say something and sort of soothe, which is what a lot of people seem to need right now."[41]

Bangs hailed the fourth album (*Loaded*) for being "one of the most lazily listenable since [Van Morrison's] *Moondance*"—"the Velvets do all the work for you." Such was needed in 1971, because of the plethora of albums "contrived," with their "cryptical constructions," to make consumers do all the work. "I mean it's gettin' to be fuckin' work to listen to music today, what with all those symmetrical dozens of couplets pregnant with convolutions of meaning." The Velvet Underground's "sane, healthy instincts" led them to counter this trend toward excess meaning, simply by making their music "easier to listen to." *Loaded,* however, is not just pure pop, but a "high-sighted art-statement" that is at the same time "the best affirmation yet" that the Velvet Underground is "still just a rock 'n' roll band from Long Island." This it achieves simply by "reflect[ing] Real Life rather than half-digested Soph Camp profundities."[42]

Thus, as in the case of punk, Bangs's celebratory discourse on the Velvet Underground is riddled with the art/pop binary, or perhaps more accurately, the good art/bad art/pop ternary. Nonetheless, there is no explicit reference to the 1960s garage bands, much less any attempt to show the kinship between the Velvet Underground and, say, Question Mark and the Mysterians.

And clearly, the Velvets had a distinctive, avant-garde agenda that is altogether absent in the 1960s "punk" bands. But as Bangs and his allies took up the promotion of Lou Reed's solo career, as well as that of Iggy Pop, Jonathan Richman, and other like-minded musicians, the discourses of punk began to intermingle with the canonizing discourses on the Velvet Underground tradition. There were formal similarities that encouraged the comparison—the two- to three-chord minimalism, the aggression toward the audience—but the self-conscious aestheticism and purposeful shock tactics, as well as the dashes of irony, simply put the Reed-Pop-Richman axis on a quite different plane than that of the 1960s "punk" rockers, whose stripped-down musicianship was hardly a matter of intention and whose shocking demeanor (where it existed) was not the result of a thought-through aesthetic. Nor could one with any plausibility impute amateurishness either to Lou Reed or Iggy Pop.

Still, as the discourses on the Velvet Underground tradition and punk grew in tandem, the claim of a deep connection between the two acquired almost the status of a tautology. By 1978 the critic and essayist Ellen Willis could write: "In New York City in the middle sixties the Velvet Underground's lead singer, guitarist, and *auteur,* Lou Reed, made a fateful connection between two seemingly disparate ideas—the rock-and-roller as self-conscious aesthete and the rock-and-roller as self-conscious punk." This "aesthete-punk connection," she claims, was then passed on by various "Velvets-influenced" performers (Pop, Mott the Hoople, Roxy Music, the New York Dolls) until it reached its apogee in 1977 "as the basis of rock and roll's new wave."[43] Willis's account, when it appeared, reflected an already entrenched discourse that drew a clear path from the Velvet Underground to the New York new wave through the intermediary of the concept of punk. Her account also points to a developing instability of the 1970s concept of punk, whereby it sometimes encompasses the whole art/pop binary and sometimes only the pop pole of that binary, an instability kindled by the joining of the discourses of punk with those of the Velvet Underground tradition. To the extent that it stood only for the pop component of the art/pop binary, "punk" could not function as a firm label for any movement defined in terms of that binary. Thus the later need of a complementary term expressing the art component, such as "new wave."

"Punk" Spreads (1972–73)

After the appearance of the last of Bangs's three manifestos in early 1972, the word "punk," and the embryonic aesthetic it connoted, left the informal confines of the small circle of dissidents to assume a wider, institutionalized presence—first locally, as a promotional emblem and product identifier for *Creem* and as a focus of archival interest for *Bomp*'s amateur writers and its garrulous readership. But it soon spread to New York, where it shifted from a pure retro term to a term also denoting the new.

By mid-1972 *Creem* was advertising itself as the journal that "delivers" that "unique perspective" that "our friends call 'Punkitude.'"[44] At about the same time, Lenny Kaye, a frequent writer for *Creem*—later the lead guitarist for the Patti Smith Group—assembled the now-legendary double album *Nuggets,* the first compilation of mid- to late-sixties recordings explicitly identified as "punk." In scholarly liner notes, Kaye spoke lovingly of these forgotten groups who "were young, decidedly unprofessional, seemingly more at home practicing for a teen dance than going out on a national tour. The name that has been unofficially coined for them—'punk-rock'—seems particularly fitting in this case, for if nothing else they exemplified the berserk pleasure that comes with being on-stage outrageous, the relentless middle-finger drive and determination offered only by rock and roll at its finest."[45] An enthusiastic *Creem* review of this compilation proclaimed: "Psychedelic Punkitude Lives!!"[46] Said the delighted Greg Shaw, "I never thought I would see the day when anybody'd take this music seriously."[47] In its Reader's Poll for 1972, *Creem* introduced the category of "Punk of the Year," somewhat tongue-in-cheek. The readers responded accordingly: Alice Cooper won, Lester Bangs came in at sixth, and Lou Reed at eighth—quite serious and appropriate—but then Donny Osmond came in at fifth and Richard Nixon at ninth.[48]

Meanwhile, *Who Put the Bomp* was busy assigning punk archival tasks to its freelance writers. "Lester will be doing the Seeds," wrote Shaw, "but I still need someone to write on the Tremeloes for the next issue."[49] There were discussions of "flower punk" and "acid punk," research articles on regional punk scenes of the 1960s (New Jersey, Northern California, Michigan), and features on the Standells, the Knickerbockers, the Leaves, and the Beau Brummels.[50] Between 1972 and 1974 Shaw kept up a barrage of confident assertions that a "pop renaissance" was hovering "just over the horizon." For "the real story of rock & roll is recorded on singles," and there were "enough brilliant singles on the air" to warrant this optimism. These records, "clearly designed for AM play," had the virtue of being totally at the "center of pure pop" without any of the "portentous moralizing" typical of FM album rock.[51] This rhetoric of revolutionary anticipation grew unabated in 1973–75, though it was not shared to the same degree by his allies. "I keep waiting for it to end, but the rock renaissance just keeps on growing and growing," since there is "still no stopping the deluge of great singles."[52] Shaw was still waiting for a "much higher level of teen mania" to light the fuse. The conditions seemed ripe, since "we have today a large teenage audience who have no direct memory of the British Invasion, Dylan, flower power, and all that" and thus are "ready for something fresh and exciting, something they can call their own."[53] The mid-1970s punk revolution did not occur as Shaw predicted: it was neither driven by a revived singles industry nor teenage rebellion (although many punks appealed to that myth). And when it did occur, Shaw was caught completely off guard.

"Punk" Goes to New York (1973–74)

It did not take much time for punk and its discourses to spread from Detroit (*Creem*) and Fairfax, California (*Bomp*), to New York and the pages of the *Village Voice*. "Punk" made its *Voice* debut in a June 1972 headline ("When Punk Rock Met the Vietcong"), but not in the accompanying article, which used the headline hook to announce the fact that the reissue business was now turning to the sixties. The author discussed mainly a new compilation of Jan and Dean hits, hardly "punk" in the emerging sense of that term.[54]

In the midst of other frivolous uses in the *Voice* pages, the term soon began to take on a serious and contemporary cast. There was a new excitement afoot in New York musical circles, requiring new descriptors and new labels. The New York Dolls were the main cause of all the stir—the first eruption of a particularly New York brand of a rock music since the Velvet Underground. From the beginning of their residency at the Mercer Arts Center in June 1972, the Dolls acquired a loyal and vociferous following. Critics quickly busied themselves trying to determine what was stylistically distinctive about them and in particular how this style expressed a certain "New York-ness." First of all, there was that element of glam and glitter mixed with arty bohemianism in the manner of David Bowie. The New York Dolls were "the latest entry into the drag sweepstakes," the latest expression of "deca-rock" or "transvestite rock."[55] But there was another side to the Dolls' aesthetic that the appellations "glam" or "deca" simply did not capture: a gritty edge, a certain back to basics rock 'n' roll, loud and raucous, which seemed to belie the niceties of the Bowie syndrome. "The Dolls, they [were] something else again," simply "the best get-it-on rock band to emerge from New York City since the Velvets," producing a "supertight, dynamite rock 'n' roll."[56] "Massive, thundering waves of just the right high energy chords pound through" their performances, "underpinning the group's fast developing tightness." "Avoiding solos, they hit for the gut every time and score amazingly well there."[57]

The word "punk" somewhat awkwardly entered in to capture this second side of the Dolls' aesthetic. "Theatrically," the Dolls may be "glitter cabaret," but "musically" they are "punk rock," mused a *Voice* contributor. David Johansen, lead singer of the Dolls, "is an absolutely fantastic combination of Mick Jagger and Marlene Dietrich." This "bold attempt to combine punkdom and cabaret and maintain the integrity of each" is simply "an honest reflection of the 1970s," when rock needed to strive "for higher and higher levels of artifice."[58] This dual aesthetic was ascribed by extension to other groups in the Mercer Arts scene, such as Suicide and Teenage Lust—the latter "somehow managed to combine the artful, fake punkiness of the Dead End Kids with the elegant, computerized cruelty of Kubrick's 'A Clockwork Orange.'"[59] Clearly, an art/pop binary was operating behind this dual aesthetic: "glam" and "cabaret" represented the art component, and "punk" the pop component. Quite unmistakably, "glam" and "cabaret" also represented a gay component and "punk" a traditional heterosexual component.

The art component of the Dolls' image was, in addition, reinforced by their association with the Mercer Arts Center, which was, despite its threadbare appearance and leaky ceilings, literally an art center, "a kind of downtown Lincoln Center seen through the wrong end of a telescope."[60] Reconstructed out of a dilapidated Greenwich Village hotel, the Center was a multiplex of rooms devoted to the performance arts. The old hotel kitchen, aptly renamed the Kitchen, was used for state-of-the-art multimedia performance. To raise revenues, it was decided to rent the Oscar Wilde Room to the New York Dolls and other related rock groups. Thus, the punk/art dichotomy was also expressed architecturally: avant-garde performance and "supertight," "thundering" rock 'n' roll occurring simultaneously in adjoining rooms, sharing part of the same audience. So situated, how could the Dolls avoid the aura of art?

The infusion of punk into the New York discourses in 1972–74 brought with it the various aesthetic concepts previously adumbrated by Bangs and his colleagues, but none seemed to take root as enthusiastically as the valuation of rank amateurism. One enthusiastic reviewer of Teenage Lust's performances could not get over praising them for their ineptitude. They are "raucous," "too loud," and "screamingly monotonous." It's clear that "almost anyone can play as good, including yourself." He concludes without explanation that, yes, Teenage Lust "is really not a very good group at all," and yet "from all the words I've written about them I hope you get the idea that they are terrific."[61] Paul Nelson, producer of the Dolls' first album, reminisced about the Mercer Arts aesthetic with more analytic perspicuity. The available talent at the Mercer, he fondly remembers, was "narcissistically inept": "Sheer style . . . had never been asked to do so much for so little." The groups and fans seemed "to be joyfully embracing a return trip to innocence through a kind of hopeful, energetic, vivacious amateurism." What Nelson celebrated as most characteristic and endearing about these bands was not "the bogus aura of sophisticated drugs and pathetic evil" that admittedly did pervade the Mercer, but the "bond of communal (and only somewhat deliberate) musical incompetence"—"amateur night at a very bizarre high school." Rather than a weakness, this is "the very roots and magic of rock 'n' roll."[62]

Music and Discourses

It is important to stress that however wildly and widely it circulated in New York discourses between 1972–74, the word "punk" had not yet acquired the firm status of market label or genre label, which would not happen until 1976, and so far had only entered the vocabulary of a small circle of cognoscenti. But at the same time, it is important not to underrate the growing impact of a new and alternative aesthetic discourse of rock, of which the increasing and still inchoate circulation of the word "punk" was only a symptom. This new discourse, though still needing fine-tuning, was already in place when the first bands appeared at CBGB's and constituted a decisive force in shaping the reception of what turned out to be the New York punk/new wave movement.

But these punk discourses were not an alien force imposing itself on innocent or resistant musicians. Quite the contrary. The early new wave was, out of necessity, intimately entangled with the emerging alternative institutions of rock criticism. Bereft of contracts from a hesitant record industry, they were shut out from radio play, promotional tours, or even exposure in most New York clubs, which only showcased signed acts. Initially, these musicians found in the written word of marginalized writers—the purveyors of the discourses on punk—their first source of publicity and legitimation. But the relation of music and discourse here had more than a utilitarian base. Many of the CBGB's musicians were originally not musicians, but came from the other arts, including poetry (Patti Smith, Richard Hell, and Tom Verlaine). Some had tried, or would try, their hand at rock criticism (Smith, Hell, Wayne County, and Lenny Kaye). The point is that a close alliance was emerging in the early 1970s between renegade rock critics and renegade musicians. Some of the musicians may have been present at the "salons" hosted by *Hit Parader* critics Lisa and Richard Robinson, who were also leaders of the belated canonization of the Velvet Underground. Never before in the history of rock 'n' roll had a putative movement in music been so inextricably connected with a preexistent (though still evolving) discursive formation. In the next chapter I take up this striking interchange of discourse and music, during the "first wave" of the New York new wave.

FIGURE 10   Joey Ramone on the cover of *Punk* magazine, illustration by John Holmstrom (1976). Courtesy of John Holmstrom.

CHAPTER 11
THE FIRST WAVE

Many Waves

The New York new wave, in its approximately nine years of existence, went through three different generations. First, there were the pioneering members of the "first wave" (1974–77), from Patti Smith to the Talking Heads, altogether identified with the CBGB scene. During this period the new wave only sporadically made incursions into the art world. The first wave came to an end when its members, recording contracts in hand, left the CBGB roost, which would no longer serve as the primary venue for new wave music. The "second wave" (1978–80) was led by the "no wave" avant-garde (James Chance and Lydia Lunch, for example) and such purveyors of pastiche as the B-52s and Devo.[1] During this period rock musicians and young artists in the East Village set up alliances that quickly became institutionalized. The most striking outcome of this activity was the birth of the first art/rock nightclub, the Mudd Club. The third period, in which the musical center shifted from the East Village to SoHo, ushered in the decline of New York new wave. Of this generation, only Laurie Anderson broke into the national market. In contrast, the East Village and SoHo art scenes were caught up in the euphoria of the 1980s art boom, benefiting in no small way from their association with rock. There were the trendy "punk art" and "new wave art" group shows, and resplendent art-decorated nightclubs, such as Area and the Palladium. The successful young art world continued to maintain this connection with rock culture and rock imagery some years after the decline of new wave rock music. This chapter deals with the first wave, the next with the second and the third waves, and the final chapter with the new wave art world that grew out of the rock music world.

Origins of the First Wave: The CBGB Scene (1974–75)

A dank dive with a notorious bathroom in the seedy Bowery, CBGB's was an altogether unlikely site for a major cultural movement. If it had not been for the physical collapse in August 1973 of the Mercer Arts Center, home to the New York Dolls and other alternative bands, CBGB's would probably not have left any trace on the city's cultural history. The various art organizations that had occupied the Mercer, like the Kitchen, had no trouble relocating. But unrecorded rock bands found themselves without options in a nightclub scene geared mainly to showcasing nationally recognized recorded acts.

As legend has it, the era of the New York new wave was initiated in March 1974 when the unsigned band Television convinced Hilly Kristal, owner of CBGB's, to let them play in his venue. Kristal had never conceived of his bar as a center of an avant-garde scene. His traditional and unimaginative objectives were clearly expressed in the decoding of the acronym that made up the full name of the club, "CBGB-OMFUG," which translated as "Country, Bluegrass, Blues, and Other Music for Uplifting Gormandizers." Opening only a few months after Mercer's collapse, CBGB's appeared soon enough to exploit the empty cultural space left by Mercer without having had the time to settle into its originally conceived "roots" format.

A number of other groups followed Television's entry into CBGB's. The Ramones debuted in August 1974 as did Blondie. But it was the Patti Smith Group, with an already acquired notoriety in local art and rock circles, that really set the CBGB scene in motion when they paired up with Television on a two-month residency in the spring of 1975. The Talking Heads' debut two months later completed what was to be the nucleus of the new wave in its first incarnation, though at this time the scene was still nameless. The local rock critic establishment—at the *Village Voice* and *New York Times*—was slow to respond to the goings-on at CBGB's and not enthusiastic when it first did. During the length of the first wave, the brunt of local support came from the alternative press, initially the *SoHo Weekly News* and later the fanzines *Punk* and *New York Rocker.*

The writers' initial vagueness reflected the vagueness of the original CBGB scene. But even after a year or so, when the scene coalesced and the individual groups took on a distinctive configuration, there were no stylistic or attitudinal commonalities that welded it into one. How could one stylistic rubric encompass the Ramones' "dumbed-down" lyrics and speeded-up garage-band riffs, Patti Smith's snarling streetwise poetry, the Talking Heads' spastic sounds and faux preppy lyrics, Television's meandering improvisations, and Blondie's retro girl-group posturings? Yet almost without exception, rock writers, even when expressing confusion, acted as if there was an aesthetic homogeneity underlying these oppositions, or as if the CBGB scene constituted a united musical field.

Whatever can be said about the musical diversity at CBGB's, there was clearly a unified discursive field—a discursive formation—that materialized around it and gave it the unity it might otherwise have lacked. This is not to deny that individual writings about the new wave differed considerably in the theories enunciated, the rhetoric, the biases, and the stylistic idiosyncrasies. Even those critics who liked the CBGB scene differed in which groups they chose to promote or disparage. Nonetheless, if we put all these writings together, we discover certain dominant structures, foci, and tensions. This is not surprising, since the writings on the new wave grew out of the discourses on punk elaborated in the early 1970s in conjunction with the canonizing discourses on the Velvet Underground and their followers. Within discourse CBGB's was constructed as a united musical field driven by the opposition of art and pop, a unity in opposition, in the manner of the Velvet Underground. This was evident not only in attempts to situate each group in the general scheme, but also in debates about which label ("underground" or "punk" or "new wave") best fit the CBGB scene. In the remainder of this chapter, I discuss these art/pop discursive constructs insofar as they impacted on group identities and label choices.

The Players: Patti Smith

Patti Smith was both of and not of the first wave, an originator and intermediary more than a full-fledged participant. A poet who later came to rock 'n' roll, she never shed the identity of a *poet* who does *rock 'n' roll,* an artist who explicitly combines poetry and rock 'n' roll. She went from reading poetry at St. Mark's Place in early 1971, to opening as a poet for Teenage Lust and other rock bands in the heyday of the Mercer Arts Center (1972), to forming a performance duo with guitarist Lenny Kaye (1973), the producer of the punk-retro album *Nuggets,* and finally with him to forming a rock band, the Patti Smith Group (1974).

Smith was said to have brought "rock 'n' roll rhythms to poetry," thereby having "reversed the process" initiated by Bob Dylan, who gets "credit for introducing poetry to rock 'n' roll."[2] This brand of explicit art/pop synthesis, in which the art and pop components maintain an easily differentiable presence, was not at all typical of the CBGB scene. Though the founders of Television, Tom Verlaine and Richard Hell, were poets before they became rockers, the music of Television was never perceived as the marriage of poetry and rock. And, of course, the Talking Heads, as former visual art students, did not present themselves as combining rock with the visual arts. This is not to say that the poetry and art backgrounds of these musicians did not contribute to the construction and marketing of their images and the aura of "art" that surrounded their work. But the fact remains that the art and pop components in the rest of the CBGB music scene were not so easily differentiable and separable as they were in the Patti Smith aesthetic.

Such was the intermediate character of Smith's aesthetic that as easily looked back to Dylan, or more recently to Springsteen, as it looked forward to the Ramones and Blondie. She was perhaps not sufficiently understated in her "artiness" for the CBGB scene and was already too established to benefit from inclusion in it and definition by it. Her press coverage thus made little reference to her connections with CBGB's. Not surprisingly, in the first canonizations of the new music, Smith was relegated to the role of "godmother" of punk, paralleling Lou Reed's "godfather" role, a precursor rather than participant.[3]

In the narrative of the CBGB scene, Patti Smith is more important for what she gave to the scene than what she got from it, and in what she gave, more important in providing exposure and audience than in shaping the aesthetics. For it is the Patti Smith Group, with their already established reputation, who transformed CBGB's into a cultural venue to be contended with during their two-month joint residency there in spring 1975 with Television. More significantly, they brought in a "following drawn from the art fringes," an "art-rock crowd," who quickly "cemented" a permanent relationship with the bedraggled "rock & roll crowd" already ensconced at CBGB's.[4]

Television: Verlaine versus Hell

In 1974, in the first review of any CBGB band, the *SoHo Weekly News* described Television as "loud, out of tune," and with "absolutely no musical or socially redeeming characteristics."[5] Less than a year later, *SoHo Weekly News* reported that "since their last stand at CBGB's, Television have improved considerably, tightening up their sounds and consolidating their influences into a powerfully cohesive entity."[6] Meanwhile, the two coleaders of Television, Tom Verlaine (formerly Tom Miller) and Richard Hell (formerly Richard Myers), were developing opposite aesthetic personas, which as it turned out fit neatly in the binary template of art and pop. Verlaine would occupy the art end of the spectrum and Hell the pop end—an opposition that, as it intensified, led to Hell's departure from the band.

In their self-descriptions, however, Verlaine and Hell each positioned himself on the art/pop boundary. Hell stressed the influence on him "by the twisted French aestheticism of the late 19th century like Rimbaud, Verlaine, Huysmans, Baudelaire." He even gave an artistic spin to his torn shirt and cropped hair look, soon to be imported to England as the emblem of punk.

"There were some artists that I admired who looked like that. Rimbaud looked like that. Artaud looked like that. And it also looked like the kid in *400 Blows,* the Truffaut movie."[7] Verlaine, more the musician, "started composing on the piano when I was in the fifth grade." But then he "heard John Coltrane, . . . got a saxophone," and later became "a huge fan of Albert Ayler," the free jazz saxophonist with whom he continued to identify throughout his career. On the pop side, both Hell and Verlaine were inspired by the "sort of American punk of the late Sixties that was made by the groups on Lenny Kaye's *Nuggets* Album, like the Standells, the Shadows of Knight, the Seeds." According to Hell, Television was emphatically not "in the tradition of the late Sixties worship of guitar playing, exquisite jams and precious music."[8]

But as the band developed, Hell and Verlaine found themselves, not happily, on the opposing ends of the art/pop spectrum. While Verlaine was already experienced with the guitar and worked unrelentingly on his skills, Hell was a neophyte on bass and sought to turn that into a virtue. "What I wanted to convey," said Hell, was "that anyone can go out and pick up a bass," which he admitted was "a completely different attitude toward performance" than Verlaine's. "To me, it's a total catharsis, physically and mentally," whereas for Verlaine "it's just mental." Hell "used to go really wild on stage," which he recalled irritated Verlaine, who "said he didn't want people to be distracted when he was singing." Verlaine's focus, on the other hand, was "how do I get this song to sound better?" He stated that his "whole orientation was towards music and performance rather than getting the photographs right." He "got bored" with those three-minute songs "real quick and got more into the improvisational stuff." Hell, who "really liked the Ramones" for their "short, hard, compelling and driving music," recalled that Verlaine "thought they were beneath contempt."[9]

In March 1975 Hell left Television and cofounded a new band, the Heartbreakers, with Johnny Thunders, formerly of the New York Dolls, whose "fuck art, let's rock" attitude seemed more congenial to Hell's aesthetics. But only a year later, Hell left the Heartbreakers, again because of an art/pop tension, which in this case situated him at the art end of the spectrum. Hell remembered: "It was just that the music was too brutish for me. It was clear that it wasn't gonna have any kinda musical ambition except to stomp out rock & roll which I liked, but I wanted to be able to extend it more."[10] He formed the new group Richard Hell and the Voidoids, whose continued commitment to "short, hard, compelling and driving music," according to a reviewer, proved quite consistent with Hell's poetic sensitivity and Robert Quine's highly proficient guitar chops. "The Voidoids suggest an uneasy compromise between jazzy lucidity and a tone-deaf thickheadedness that lends everything they do a dizzy mobility."[11] Thus, the art/pop tension re-appeared in Hell's own groups.

Meanwhile, under Verlaine's exclusive leadership, Television moved toward the art end of the CBGB art/pop spectrum, hardly maintaining that opposi-tional dynamic with pop exhibited by the other bands in that scene. Taking a cue from his nom de plume, reviewers turned to the mythology of French symbolism in trying to get a fix on Verlaine's aesthetic persona. He was described as the pure artist, "pallid and gaunt," with a "strain of genius," who "fus[ed] an attractive symbolist disordering-of-all-the-senses aesthetic with a rich musicality and austere personal style." Conveying "a suggestive thoughtfulness," he "lack[ed] the brashness" to "overwhelm through a more overtly violent rock and roll." This "genuine auteur," who "had sprung up in the precious soil between the cracks in the concrete," did not quite seem to belong in the rock 'n' roll world.[12] "Verlaine is too sensitive for this crummy Bowery bar," and "Television is a little too ambiguous and yes, a little too un-commercial as well."[13] From mid-1975 on there was endless speculation, even confusion, on what was distinctive about Television's fine musicianship, and how this fit in with the rest of the CBGB scene. "Television is not a band that is easily pigeon-holed."[14] By 1976 Television had ceded center stage at CBGB's to the Ramones and the Talking Heads, whose play with art and pop was more ebullient and focused.

The Ramones

The Ramones, who began to accrue critical attention by mid-1975, were the first in the CBGB underground to acquire a distinctive and strongly etched profile. They were consistently positioned in discourse on the pop end of the CBGB spectrum, which was reflected in the recurrent predictions that of all the CBGB underground bands, they had the best chance of breaking into the pop charts.

From the beginning, the discourses over the Ramones employed the full panoply of concepts associated with the punk aesthetics previously devel-oped by the *Creem-Bomp* circle—assaultiveness, minimalism, rank ama-teurism—even before "punk" became a label of preference for the CBGB scene. Their music was typically characterized as "loud, hard and relentless," as "furious, blasting rock 'n' roll" that is "intent upon piercing a hole in the ozone layer."[15] At their "fierce, assaultive best," they were like the "wild bunch" of the Peckinpah movie, "a beautiful self-destroying machine," leav-ing "nothing behind them but scorched earth"—"a perilously overheated chopper," ready to "go up in flames."[16]

These overwrought descriptions give only one side of the story. Whatever was shocking about the Ramones' music, and it was never terribly shocking, was neutralized by their charm and humor. A British critic found them "simultaneously so funny, such a cartoon vision of rock 'n' roll and so genuinely tight and powerful that they're just bound to enchant anyone who fell in love with rock 'n' roll for the right reasons."[17] For Lisa Robinson, the *Hit Parader* critic, a Ramones performance is "funny" and "couldn't be cuter." "All their songs sound exactly the same, each one is under two minutes long, they start out each number with a shouted 'one-two-three-four,' and then rush ahead at breakneck speed. Then they just stop suddenly." Another woman critic noted that the "dangerous exteriors" of these "pseudo-delinquents" conceal a "shamefully near-perfect etiquette."[18] The Ramones' supposed "assaultiveness" seems to have been more a matter of male perception.

Nobody accused the Ramones of being inept or subscribing to an aesthetic of rank amateurism. But they were, by all accounts, a limited band who knew how to work within their limits, their posture being "do what you can do, and only what you can do. Your guitar player can't play lead? Well, fuck lead. Your singer can't carry a tune? Fuck tunes. Your drummer can't play slow tempos? Fuck slow. Your bass player can't riff? Fuck riffs."[19] But this was seen as a virtue rather than a limitation. The Ramones were, in the eyes of almost all critics, the ultimate and paradigmatic minimalists. No one seemed as adept at "stripping rock 'n' roll down to the bare essentials," at "cutting rock right down to the basic ingredient" and "rebuilding from there."[20] "Each tune is built upon a few chopping, grinding chords, heavily churned out," while the rhythm section devotes itself exclusively to "capturing the three best riffs in rock and utilizing them over and over again." The Ramones' greatest virtue, it appeared, was to do without the "unnecessary icing that unduly sweetens the pie." In the Ramones' music, "the bare bones of rock and roll are delivered directly in the simplest manner with all the ugly fat stripped away. . . . Art lives in the bones of structure."[21]

In the promotional jargon for the CBGB underground, no term captured more neatly the productive dissonance of art and pop than did "minimalism." On the pop side, "minimalism" implied simplicity and adherence without ornamentation to a basic universal rock framework, which in turn implied accessibility, familiarity, and eminent commerciability. It is for this reason that the Ramones, as the purest embodiments of CBGB minimalism, were widely viewed as the band with the greatest commercial potential.[22] The Ramones were signed to a recording contract and released their first album one year earlier than any other band originating at CBGB's. On the other hand, "minimalism" is clearly an art term betokening a certain self-conscious approach to musical materials—a certain conceptuality, certain views about history and tradition, even a certain detachment. As a rock aesthetic, "minimalism" required a certain "aging" of rock 'n' roll and its fans and a sophisticated apparatus of rock criticism to identify it. John Holmstrom, the editor of *Punk*, "always thought the Ramones had a special class and intelligence, a simplicity that took sophistication to appreciate." Their "twenty minute set in those days" was "very artistic and so well executed that I had a hard time figuring out if they were really punks in leather jackets who would kill you for looking the wrong way or if they were just posing. . . . Once I met them I realized that they fell somewhere in between." According to Chris Frantz of the Talking Heads, the Ramones "were extremely arch in a musical way . . . they cared about making an artistic statement. To me, that was the essence of the Ramones."[23] The Ramones, in their purist minimalism, could be viewed more abstractly "not just [as] a band," but as "a real good idea." "I mean, conceptually they're beautiful, poised with mathematical elegance on the line between pop art and popular schlock. From your aesthete's point of view, the Ramones sound has the ruthless efficiency of a Warhol portrait."[24]

Certainly, the Ramones took an "anti-art" posture, such as their virulent anti-virtuosity, their dumbed-down lyrics ("Beat on the brat with a baseball bat," "I don't wanna go down to the basement"), and in general their refusal of "meaning." "They aren't worried about being genuinely creative," observed a British critic, "and if you told them that they provided a unique insight into anything they'd probably piss on your shoes, and you'd deserve it too."[25] But as we know only too well, highly emphatic anti-art is often riddled with art. At any rate, the Ramones' anti-virtuosity was simply the other side of their minimalist aesthetic. And their exhibition of an "earnest dumbness of an adolescent pop" more redolent of a bygone era, before an audience of artists and other sophisticates, could only take on the allure of satire and irony.[26] Of course, irony was a never-absent component of the CBGB aesthetic.

The Ramones versus the Talking Heads

As the image of CBGB aesthetics sharpened, the Talking Heads and the Ramones became the perfect foils for each other, each defined by the public in opposition to the other, the highbrows from art school versus the lowbrow dropouts from Queens, the quintessential new wavers versus the paradigmatic punks. Many who supported one of these groups tended to show contempt toward the other. Alan Vega of Suicide, who "never liked the Talking Heads," complained that they were so "studied" and Byrne's moves "were all plotted." "He didn't make any twitchy gestures without something in his head saying,

'Make a twitchy gesture now.'"[27] Whereas John Rockwell, highly enamored with the Talking Heads, tended to be dismissive at best of the Ramones, whose sets, though "pleasingly amusing" upon first hearing, became "simply crude" upon repeated exposure. Of course, "only if you have a penchant for *Mad* magazine–type humor" can "this stuff" seem "both funny and cute."[28]

On the other hand, Rockwell, from the beginning, considered the Talking Heads to be the "class of the field among unrecorded New York bands." Their unabashed artiness was a virtue rather than a vice for Rockwell, who later became a chief proponent of art/pop fusion. "The Talking Heads is a stimulating instance," he reported approvingly, of "how the art world has had an effect on local rock."[29] He opened his review of the Heads' first album with a disquisition on the relation of art and pop. "Ever since the Beatles' 'Sergeant Pepper's Lonely Hearts Club Band' album of 1967, people have been wondering about the relationship between rock-and-roll and art music." Against those rock fans who respond with "disdain to the idea that their innocent entertainment be burdened with elitist associations," he clearly sided with those "who believe that some rock is art and that all rock can be considered in artistic terms." For him, the music of the Talking Heads is the paradigm of a rock "art form" that demands interpretation in "artistic terms." Their album "is as provocative a focal point for discussion of rock as art as any that could be found."[30]

More than anything, it was the explicit overturning of rock performance styles and the obviously ironic use of the clichés of middle-class life that established the Talking Heads as a premier art-rock band. The band "is composed of four very neat-looking individuals whom any parent would introduce in polite company without a trace of nervousness." The Talking Heads offered "a fragile middle finger" to bands with "anonymous sidemen playing power-house back-up through a Luftwaffe of amplifiers."[31] They were a welcome alternative to the "notion that power and glory can be found through efficient organization around the sexiest available male."[32] "If Jonathan Richman [of the Modern Lovers] plays the kid who ate his snot, David [Byrne] plays the kid who held his farts in. He doesn't move like any rock star ever." And what was one to make of the quirky lyrics, "leaden with homilies" and "hyperventilated clichés," delivered "with the same fervor the Who always reserved for 'My Generation'"?[33]

The Talking Heads' art identity was further highlighted by their being paired in CBGB programs and tours with those emphatic lowbrows, the Ramones. The art/pop contrast between the two groups was amusingly accentuated during their European tour. The Talking Heads would get up early to go to the museums, to the surprise of the local booking agent, who was accustomed to rockers "who can't get up before four and then have horrible trouble with their bowel movements." The Ramones "hated Europe," reported their manager, and "didn't like the idea that people didn't speak English." "They hated the food and just looked for hamburgers everywhere." Meanwhile, "the Talking Heads talked to everybody in French," which made the Ramones "pissed."[34]

But, just like the Ramones, the Talking Heads displayed more art/pop complexities than originally met the eye. Aesthetically, they were closer to the Ramones, and a better fit, than any other CBGB group, a point accentuated by Tommy Ramone. "Whenever we had to find someone to play with us, we'd use the Talking Heads. Even though the Ramones played hard and raunchy, conceptually there were a lot of similarities: the minimalism." "We were so unique at the time that they were the first ones who played with us who actually fit."[35] Indeed, minimalism, with doses of irony and parody, became the recognized aesthetic trademark of the Talking Heads as well as of the Ramones. The Talking Heads were perceived as closer to the Ramones than, say, Bruce Springsteen, who otherwise shared the latter's "primitive matters and meters" and "spirit of rat-breath oblivion." But whereas "Springsteen's music brims over with Spectoresque studio trimmings," the Heads, like the Ramones, "are stripped to the chassis. Their unvarnished arrangements rattle bones. No pickles, no garnish." To this reviewer, the Talking Heads "meet the first and last criterion of the [rock] art form, which is that the music should be as hot and monotonous as a marathon fuck."[36] Put this way, the opposition between the Talking Heads and the Ramones had perhaps much more to do with style than aesthetics, the "loopiness" of the former perfectly "complementing" the "monomaniacal tightness" of the latter.[37]

There is much to be said for the pop aspect of the Talking Heads. By all accounts, they were the best dance band at CBGB's and the only one whose rhythms were rooted in African American music. Lenny Kaye said the dance factor "was a great reference" for the Talking Heads, "especially since 'dance music' had a totally different connotation for avant-garde rockers in those days. That element of blackness shouldn't be underestimated." Though David Byrne took pleasure in the fact that "writers seemed to like us very quickly," he found it to be a drawback to being "dubbed as being intellectual." "We don't think we're smarties, we just don't enjoy being stupid either. We don't get into ball scratching. . . . The term art-rock annoys me." Of course, he admitted, the Talking Heads were "very self-aware" about their mode of presentation, which could to some appear "very contrived." But there was no alternative, since "the days of naive, primitive rock bands are gone."[38]

The discourses on the Talking Heads and Ramones, taken collectively, thus became the verbal equivalent of a gestalt-switching mechanism. These two groups were sometimes portrayed both as diametrically opposed to each other, and yet with the slightest discursive shift, appeared suddenly to be completely in harmony with each other aesthetically. Discourses that viewed them both or singly as art switched quickly into viewing them as pop. None of these images were really contradictory, or only contradictory, since the discourses of art and pop, though always in tension, were always on the verge of collapsing into each other. The Talking Heads and the Ramones represented most starkly the two-headed aesthetic that was gradually being applied to the whole New York underground scene.

The Battle of the Labels: "Underground"

But the CBGB scene could not achieve security as an identifiable movement, as a new and distinctive trajectory within rock, without acquiring a label or brand name. Nothing promotes a hard sense of unity and homogeneity, however falsely, or coalesces a fragile and inchoate scene, like the evocative power of a label. The label (e.g., "cool jazz," "heavy metal") brings with it a whole baggage of connotations that catalyze and enrich discourse—a point amply corroborated in this book. Having survived over a year without a label, the CBGB scene would be buffeted during the next two years by a battle of labels ("underground" versus "punk" versus "new wave"). But this confusion of labels was no disservice to that scene nor was it dysfunctional discursively. Indeed, like the art/pop tension of which it was an expression, the battle of labels generated a rich output of discourse that contributed significantly to promoting CBGB music and shaping an aesthetic for it.

The active search for a label began effectively in July 1975 when CBGB's, in order to gain record industry recognition for its neglected brood, organized a Festival of Unrecorded Rock Bands, showcasing forty bands over a two-week period. With this event the CBGB scene finally emerged from the shadows, for the first time drawing the attention of major local (the *New York Times* and the *Village Voice*), national (*Rolling Stone*), and international cultural publications (*New Musical Express*). Amidst reviews floundering to make sense of the chaos and the eclecticism of the festival, John Wolcott's "A Conservative Impulse in the New Rock Underground" (*Village Voice*) stood out with a carefully wrought theoretical line that significantly impacted on future construals of the CBGB scene.[39] The article also put the term "underground" in circulation as its first identifying label.

Though Wolcott defined "underground" prosaically as "unrecorded," the label came in with much accumulated baggage that he exploited. An art term with combat connotations, like the term "avant-garde," "underground" emerged in the 1960s as a designation of New York experimental film—literally underground in the sense that it was initially being screened in basement apartments. By the late 1960s the term appeared in rock writing to designate a yet-to-be nationally discovered music scene or movement, operating on the experimental edges and sure to be the "next big thing." In 1966 Robert Shelton described Frank Zappa's Mothers of Invention as "the most original new group to simmer out of the steaming rock 'n' roll underground"—"a group bent on overthrowing every rule in the music book."[40] *Newsweek* and *Time* were delighted in introducing the "hippie underground" sound of San Francisco to their readers just as it was beginning to "bubble to the surface."[41]

The reigning assumption in rock writing of the late 1960s, buttressed by the myth of rock democracy and certainly justified by the facts of the time, was that the underground was a temporary way station for innovative musical movements toward mainstream success. This view shifted in the early 1970s with the emergence of the Velvet Underground cult and the stories of their nonacceptance, plus the failure of critics' favorites like Iggy Pop, the MC5, and the New York Dolls to cross into the mainstream. The idea of a permanent underground began slowly to seep in—a rock avant-garde permanently sequestered on the sidelines and permanently in revolt against the mainstream. This new realization altogether disrupted the ruling orthodoxies of rock criticism based on claims about the innate populism of the music.

The *Bomp* and *Creem* critics of the early 1970s, though proponents of the then rock underground (Iggy Pop, etc.) and themselves part of a writerly "underground," had misgivings about the excessive "arty" connotations of the term. Greg Shaw insisted that the "real rock 'n' roll underground" was materializing not in the bohemian circles of New York, but in the revivalist fanzines of the hinterland. He hoped that the resurgence of a "pop" mentality would enable critics and fans "to see through the myth of 'underground' rock.'" He went on a campaign to get people "to start thinking in terms of 'pop music' again, instead of this 'underground rock' twaddle." But to no avail since the "pop" he was most enthusiastic about was relegated to the "underground."[42] Thus, the term was ready to reemerge in full force, as it did in the Wolcott article, when the yet-to-be recorded CBGB scene became an object of attention in 1975.

In the *Creem-Bomp* tradition, Wolcott emphatically linked the CBGB underground with a return to the roots of rock. Such was the import of the title of his essay, "A Conservative Impulse in the New Rock Underground," which declared that the avant-garde movement was also a revivalist movement. For Wolcott, the new "style of musical attack" at CBGB's was a necessary "counterthrust to the prevailing baroque theatricality of [current] rock," which had become "arthritic" and "as phlegmatic as a rich old whore." The only antidote was for rock's "creative impulse" to become "conservative" rather than "revolutionary," that is, to renovate "rock's tradition." "The landscape is no longer virginal" and "exists not to be transformed but cultivated."[43]

With the label "underground" in full play, it was more natural to locate the roots of the CBGB scene in that paradigmatic underground group, the Velvet Underground, than in the 1960s garage bands. Virtually everyone who reported on the CBGB scene at the time of the Festival of Unrecorded Rock Bands made some reference to the Velvet Underground as somehow at the bottom of this all, much to the dismay of Television and the other bands who did not share this "retro" conception of themselves.[44] The Talking Heads—with David Byrne looking like "the bastard offspring" of "Lou Reed and Ralph Nader" and Tina Weymouth appearing as "a pale poker-faced Nico-esque woman"—were declared to be "closest to a neo-Velvet band" among the CBGB retinue. They represented that "distillation" of "controlled distortion" so characteristic of that legendary band.[45]

For six months after the CBGB festival (the latter half of 1975), "underground" monopolized the discourses as the label of choice for CBGB musicians. For the most part, the term was adopted by the main elite press and by the more aesthete critics, like Rockwell, who had a special interest in fusing rock with the avant-garde art world. Rockwell took note of the "scruffy" and "murky" character of the "much touted underground" at CBGB's. He spoke of Television's "effusions" of "tortured undergroundism" and perceived an "underground image" even in the dumbed-down self-presentations of the Ramones. Christgau referred to Television as the "rocking automatons of the underground."[46]

But "underground" was ultimately too generic a term to work as a satisfactory brand name, given that the CBGB scene was only the last of a series of "New York undergrounds." Thus, when "punk" and "new wave" arrived, "underground" was relegated to the role of a general descriptor for the movement designated by these new labels. However, the *New York Times* critics in particular, put off by the anti-aesthetic implications of the word "punk," held on to "underground" as a name for a while longer, until "new wave" came in to save the day.

The Battle of the Labels: "Punk"

Within six months of the CBGB Festival, two fanzines appeared that would be the main support for the New York underground and that were most instrumental in circulating the two labels that would vie for contention to name this movement. *Punk* magazine set "punk" in motion, and the *New York Rocker* did more than any other publication to support "new wave" as the proper alternative to "punk." *Punk* magazine, appearing in December 1976, developed the first distinctly fanzine style—*Bomp* had previously had the idea but not the implementation. *Punk* was self-consciously dumbed down, but by no means dumb, rather quite aesthetic, indeed helping initiate the "trash aesthetic" sensibility that would pervade the East Village art scene of the 1980s.

The editor, John Holmstrom, created the trademark look of the magazine, a comic book style rooted in the aesthetics of *Mad* magazine, which he had learned while a student of the School of Visual Arts. His associate, Legs Mc-Neil, a self-described ne'er-do-well—the "resident punk"—infused the discourse with a purposeful and charming dumbness. The first issue quickly achieved legendary status for its presentation of a Lou Reed interview in the form of a comic strip, in which Holmstrom asked musical questions about, for example, the motive behind the noise-and-distortion-driven album *Metal Machine Music,* while McNeil, when not blanking out, posed the dumb queries ("Do you eat at McDonald's?" "Do you like the Big Mac?").[47] *Punk* itself was as much performance as the performances it reported on and reflected in its own practices the art/pop tensions that pervaded the local musical field. It clearly stood out, with its unapologetically biased fandom, from *Rolling Stone* and other rock journals that, with their aura of authority and seriousness, were hardly distinguishable from other middlebrow cultural publications, such as *Esquire* or *Down Beat.*

Though McNeil gets credit for suggesting *Punk* as the magazine's name, Holmstrom, as the music aficionado, was the one cognizant of the history of the term in the discourses of rock.

> It was pretty obvious that the word was getting very popular. . . . *Creem* used it to describe this early seventies music; *Bomp* would use it to describe the garage bands of the sixties; a magazine like the *Aquarian* would use it to describe what was going on at CBGB's. The word was being used to describe Springsteen, Patti Smith, and the Bay City Rollers. So when Legs came up with it we figured we'd take the name before anyone else claimed it.[48]

Holmstrom's interest in punk was piqued by his discovery of the Dictators, a group appearing at the same time as Television (early 1974) but strangely not included in the CBGB ambit. "I picked up the Dictators' first record and went nuts over their humor."[49] What little publicity the Dictators received helped bring "punk" back in circulation during a period (1974–75) when the term indeed had been languishing in discourse. A *Voice* writer at that time anointed them "the first true punk-rockers of the 1970s," the first purveyors of "punkoid pleasure" and "punkoid arrogance."[50] Gonzo writer Richard Meltzer praised them in uppercase letters for "DESPIS[ING] KULTURE LIKE IT WAS SPINACH." Recalled McNeil: "All summer we had been listening to this album *Go Girl Crazy* by this unknown group called the Dictators, and it changed our lives." "We'd just get drunk every night and lip-sync to it." McNeil saw "the magazine Holmstrom wanted to start as a Dictators' album come to life," a "combination of everything we were into — television reruns, drinking beer, getting laid, cheeseburgers, comics, grade-B movies, and this weird rock & roll that nobody but us seemed to like." The magazine, it seemed, "should be for other fuck-ups like us. Kids who grew up believing only in the Three Stooges." The word "punk" seemed "to sum up the thread that connected everything that we liked — drunk, obnoxious, smart but not pretentious, absurd, funny, ironic, and things that appealed to the darker side."[51]

McNeil and Holmstrom, at least in their retrospective remarks, each put a different slant on the notion of punk. McNeil amplified on lifestyle, posturing, and modes of willful consumption, whereas Holmstrom zeroed in on music. Said Holmstrom: "Punk rock was rock & roll, like the Stooges and garage-rock. Basically any hard rock & roll was punk and that's the kind of music we wanted to write about, to differentiate it from Paul Simon or the soft-rock that was dominating."[52] Holmstrom was obviously beholden to the more generic revivalist conception of punk that had emerged in the early 1970s under the aegis of Shaw, Bangs, and Marsh. "The key word — to me anyway in the punk definition — was 'a beginner, an inexperienced hand.'" This is the idea that "any kid can pick up a guitar and become a rock 'n' roll star, despite or because of his lack of ability, talent, intelligence, limitations, and/or potential, and usually does so out of frustration, hostility, a lot of nerve and a need for ego fulfillment."[53]

Interestingly, the CBGB scene was not a factor in the conceptualization and formation of *Punk* magazine. McNeil: "It's funny, but we had no idea if anybody but the Dictators were out there. We had no idea about CBGB's and what was going on, and I don't think that we cared."[54] Holmstrom had only been interested in putting together "a regular rock or general magazine." It was only because "we were in New York" and "they were accessible" that "we did the New York groups."[55] Nonetheless, after the first issue of the magazine, the word "punk" spread quickly and appended itself almost immediately to the New York underground as the new label of choice.

In its short existence as the dominant label, "punk" went through a number of mutations: (1) from a revivalist term to a term denoting only the new;

(2) from an almost exclusively New York label to an almost exclusively British label; (3) from label of choice to a label under question; (4) from a lone label to being conjoined with "new wave." I will now trace these interlocking discursive threads.

"Punk": From Retro to Nouveau

Initially, the New York punk music at CBGB's was construed as a revivalist movement, just as it had been when previously saddled with the "underground" label. In effect, "punk" filled out the content of that supposed "conservative impulse" in the "new rock underground." There were constant references in the discourse of critics to the original "punks" who had made the CBGB punk movement possible. Lou Reed, portrayed only a few months before as the paradigmatic "underground" rocker, was now being touted as the first "punk." The *Voice*'s Wolcott, in an article titled "The Rise of Punk Rock," dealt almost exclusively with Reed, except at the end where he professed to find "punk humor" in the music of the Dictators, the Ramones, and Patti Smith, "in magazines like *Punk* and *Creem*, and in television heroes like Fonzie and Eddie Haskell." But, in the end, "of course the rock-and-roll regent of punkish irony is ex-Velvet Lou Reed."[56] Others traced the origins of the CBGB scene, particularly the Ramones, in "the great Midwestern punk groups of the 1960s."[57] And, of course, the aesthetic of *Punk* magazine had from the beginning a deeply revivalist component.

The Ramones were the CBGB band most easily squeezed into the punk template. The release of their first album (April 1976), in the midst of the "punk" hubbub, further connected them in promotional discourse to that term. For Rockwell, the album represented a "highly stylized extension of the [punk] idiom," and for *Cash Box*, it stood out for its "street punk stance."[58] Said Rockwell: CBGB's is "most certainly . . . the World Headquarters of punk rock," and the Ramones, "the most characteristic American punk rock band."[59]

In early 1976, a few months after *Punk*'s first issue, the retro term "punk" spread to London, appearing in the media's first attempts to define the Sex Pistols. The *New Musical Express* described them as a "quartet of spiky teenage misfits" playing "60's styled white punk rock." This designation was quickly and unthinkingly taken up by an unsympathetic press trying to get a conceptual handle on what it was about the Sex Pistols that generated such audience activism and violence. A review in April described the Sex Pistols' "lead guitarist" as another "surrogate punk suffering from a surfeit of Sterling Morrison [of the Velvet Underground]." Whatever "novelty" there was to this "tired spectacle" was "soon erased by [the Pistols'] tiresome repetition of punk clichés."[60] The Ramones' controversial English tour in the summer of 1976 further stimulated the entrenchment of "punk" in British musical discourses, as did the rise of a plethora of bands following upon the Sex Pistols. But now the label "punk" was adopted by fans and promoters of the music as well. *Sniffin' Glue,* the first British punk fanzine, appeared in July, saturated with references to "punk," including an attempted definition.[61]

But as it spread through British music discourses, "punk" went through a number of changes, the most important of which was to lose its retro and revivalist character, its connection to 1960s American punk, and to become a designator of the "new" and the "revolutionary." In her groundbreaking articles in the summer of 1976 for *Melody Maker,* Carolyn Coon emphatically denied that the "emerging British bands" had anything but the "most tenuous connections with the New York punk rock scene," the latter being "much closer musically to the Shadows of Knight, the Leaves and the other punk rock bands of the 60's." The British punk scene, "far from glorifying the past, is disgusted by it. Nostalgia is a dirty word." "We hate everything," said the British punks.[62] The "shock of the new," of course, distracts from any preoccupation with past roots.

As is well known, the London punks also introduced a political component in their music that was altogether absent from 1960s punk rock as well as from the punk discourses initiated by *Bomp* and *Creem.* The American punk writers of the early seventies, following upon the founding American rock critics in the 1960s, were caught up with the inner values of rock music and inherently suspicious of rock's reaching out to any outside forces or values, be they those of high art or politics. If there was a politics to these early discourses, it was a politics internal to music. In contrast, attacks on the welfare system, capitalism, consumer culture, and so on were recurrent themes in British punk music. Furthermore, the new British punk sported a jadedness, a world-weariness, an all-knowingness, that was barely enunciated in the more innocent aggressiveness of 1960s American punk.

This new nonretro notion of punk, uncoupled from references to 1960s bands, spread from England to North America, ultimately to dominate the discourses of punk there. Within a year "punk" would universally become a code word for a radical, fiercely oppositional break within rock musical culture, unburdened by any past tradition. What assured the dominance of the British version of punk was the mass-mediated hysteria over punk rock that burst forth in England and was later imported to North America. As early as the summer of 1976, before even the first issuing of punk recordings, punk became a cause célèbre in England, a subject of media hype and paranoia the extent to which had not been experienced since Beatlemania. In the midst of this, journalists were tripping over each other searching for the right definition for this apparently unprecedented and chaotic movement. Coon soon weighed in to provide the definitive glossary.[63]

The news about British punk music and the controversies surrounding it began to filter into the United States by the end of 1976. The trade magazines and fanzines picked up on it first, followed by the mass press, and finally and recalcitrantly by the American rock critic establishment.[64] In the summer of 1977, *Newsweek* and *Time,* with surprisingly sympathetic lead articles, brought punk dramatically to the attention of the larger American public.[65] By this time the American mass media had almost completely assimilated New York punk into the British model, noting only a few small variations. *Rolling Stone* and the *Village Voice* did not weigh in with serious articles on British punk until October 1977, months after the mass magazines had done their job. The *Voice* countered *Rolling Stone*'s highly negative assessment with an enthusiastically positive special issue, but rather late in the game actually, just a few months before the Sex Pistols broke up and the original punk scene came crashing down.[66]

The new discourses on punk, altogether absorbed with the "now," consigned the pioneering punks of the 1960s—Question Mark and the Mysterians, the Count Five—into definitional oblivion, bereft of any label. The imperatives of categorization soon led writers to invent the new designation of "garage bands" for these former "punks." No longer punk, they were now merely influences on punk.

Resistance to "Punk"

At the same time that the "punk" label was spreading, it was encountering resistance from within the so-called punk communities, particularly in the United States. Holmstrom, the culprit behind the spread of the label, was one of the first to express dissatisfaction with its new denotations. As early as the fourth issue of *Punk* (April 1976), he was complaining that "punk" had become a critics' "catchword" for "New York underground rock, most of which is not punk rock."[67] He and McNeil had originally thought of "punk" as "a general term for anything that was hard rock and roll." "But then the term got very narrowly defined." To Holmstrom's chagrin, "punk" became "the Sex Pistols and everybody who sounded like the Sex Pistols."[68] Hilly Kristal, CBGB's owner, was especially unhappy with the term's flattening out of the differences between the bands in his stable. "I think a lot of writers started the idea of punk rock, meaning there's just one specific kind of music and one attitude and what they don't realize is that they're just labeling something which isn't so. Television, the Shirts, and the Talking Heads are not punk rock."[69]

New York Rocker, the chief local press booster for the CBGB scene, was especially discomforted by the "punk" label, if only because it denied the originality of the local music, subsuming it as a satellite to what was going on in England. "Eager to pin a title on the now emerging bands of CBGB-Max's fame, many journalists/critics erroneously entitle the whole of it 'punk rock,'" complained Lisa Persky. Its allusions to "inexperienced or callow youth," "to passive homosexuality, whores and Chinese incense," hardly do justice to what it is supposed to designate. Thus, "the creators of what is New York Rock and Roll find themselves placed by the media in a category unfit to describe even the lowest of musical creatures." No broad descriptive label, she argued, could do justice to the heterogeneity of the New York bands. "The music varies dramatically from one group to another." Whatever similarities may have existed had "little or nothing to do with the politics of hate and killing, leather, safety pins or zippers." "Only the Ramones are remotely linked with these 'philosophies' and even they, tongue-in-cheek."[70]

Rocker's point of view was shared by establishment critics, who especially wanted to protect the more "arty" and complex bands, like Television and the Talking Heads, whom they tended more to support, from the "punk" designation. Rockwell and Robert Palmer contemptuously equated the "punk school" with "leather jackets," "abrasive social stances," "lyrics about drugs and sado-masochism, or screamingly loud, twanging, three-chord guitar rock." The unfortunate effect of this "punk image," they worried, was to mask "some sophisticated music," like that of the Talking Heads and Television, who "in the midst of this" stood "curiously alone." Television, for example, went beyond "punk" in "building on the raga and jazz-influenced rock of the mid-1960's in an original manner," while the Talking Heads reputedly did so by using "intersecting planes of instrumental color to create a rock equivalent of trends in contemporary art."[71] Asserted another critic: "Punk has little to do with [Television's] music," which, unlike that of the Ramones, does not reduce "the complexity of experience" to a "monotone."[72]

But it was not only critics supportive of the art side of the CBGB scene who were hostile to the "punk" designation. Surprisingly, the original punk aestheticians from *Creem* and *Bomp*—Bangs, Marsh, and Shaw—were not at all happy about the mid-1970s triumph of the "punk" label, but for opposite reasons. In this case, it was not "punk" that was the unworthy designation, but the new so-called "punk" bands that were unworthy of being so designated. Marsh was especially unremitting in his hostility. "Punk" "no longer describes style, much less music. It has become a marketing device, an excuse for decadence, often with a macho bent." The real "punk code" with which Marsh identified (e.g., in Springsteen's music) was a "simple, direct street philosophy: loyalty and self-respect are its highest values, friendship the only society it recognizes." Whereas what the current "punks" mistook "for rebellion" was "merely marketable outrage."[73]

Shaw, though not unsympathetic to the punk scenes of New York and London, found them wanting in real *punkness*. "In a matter of just a few months, 'punk' has become the most overused word in the pop vocabulary." The "similarities" between the original and contemporary punk were "only superficial." "In today's punk scene, any ignorant sod can become an idol merely by donning black leather and drooling a lot." Among the "ideal" punks, Shaw cited Chuck Berry, Phil Spector, Bob Dylan, and even the Fonz of *Happy Days*. He could not think of "anyone in today's rock scene with the audacity and strength of character to even meet" the "admittedly high standards" set by the earlier punks. "The Ramones? Bruce Springsteen? What a laugh." At the height of the spread of punk, in late 1976, Shaw announced a contest for "your favorite punk" in *Bomp* that, with the exception of Patti Smith, included only candidates from the fifties and sixties.[74]

Clearly, the former "punk" renegades of rock criticism were now part of the rock critic establishment protecting their hard-won turf. In the process they were widening the extension of the term beyond its narrow sixties base in the garage bands to include any rock 'n' roll in its pure or authentic state. Bangs, who like Shaw was otherwise quite sympathetic to both the New York and British scenes, reminded his readers that "punk rock was hardly invented by the Ramones . . . [or] the Sex Pistols," since "what at bottom" this expression means "is rock 'n' roll in its most basic, primitive form." In other words, punk rock "has existed throughout the history of rock 'n' roll, they just didn't call it that."[75] Thus, in the process of critiquing the more recent uses of the "punk" label, the *Bomp-Creem* critics in effect transformed it from a genre or style name to the universal aesthetic and moral criterion for rock music. But in contesting the right of mid-seventies punk bands to primary ownership of the name, they also took ownership away from the sixties punk bands whom they had been the first to classify and champion. This further speeded up the relegation of these bands to the "garage rock" category.

Also quite discontent with the "punk" designation, but less public about the matter, were the representatives of the record industry investing in the punk music—Sire Records, Atlantic, Elektra, and others—who thought it to be an unfortunate marketing term. By late 1976 a number of executives were suggesting alternative labels, such as "underground rock," "arrogant rock," or "urban rock." But only Seymour Stein of Sire hit upon "new wave rock," the label that would succeed "punk." There was nothing prescient about this nor did he invent the term. He was paying close heed to the situation in Great Britain, where for some months the discourses of new wave had been welling up alongside those of punk.[76]

The Battle of the Labels: "New Wave" in Britain

Surprisingly, it was in London, where there was the least discursive consternation about "punk," that the term "new wave" first surfaced, only to cross over to New York some time later. Today pop encyclopedias and consumer guides tend to identify the "new wave" as a broad range of musical styles that emerged after punk and were influenced by it but that are substantially less aggressive and more "arty." The "new wave," according to the *Penguin Encyclopedia,* resulted from a "new breed of young rockers" who "emerged with the energy of punk but with more finesse and ability."[77] It was, says another guide, a "music inspired by punk that wasn't really punk," "a punk in pop drag, allied with a postpunk musical questioning."[78] This account may reflect the way the expression "new wave" has entrenched itself in the rock canon, but it does not accurately portray its first uses. Initially, in England "new wave" was simply put forth as a complementary label for those bands and movements *also* designated as "punk." The expressions "punk" and "new wave" were nearly convergent in their mid-seventies applications and equally volatile in their definitional shifts.

All the evidence indicates that the label "new wave" first appeared in English discourses in 1976, very shortly after the entry of "punk." The Sex Pistols' manager, Malcolm McClaren, put off by the initial retro and anti-art allusions of "punk," reportedly introduced "new wave" as the appropriate label, with its obvious reference to the flashy avant-gardism of the French New Wave film movement of the 1960s.[79] Within a few months smatterings of references to the new wave began to appear in the midst of the discourses on punk. By September even the ultimate punk magazine, *Sniffin' Glue,* was proclaiming "the new wave" to be "the most exciting thing to happen in British music in ten years."[80] Carolyn Coon, the promoter of "punk" in the establishmentarian music press, also began using "new wave" as an alternative to "punk," although in a subordinate and contradictory fashion. In her November 1976 glossary of the "Punk Alphabet," she made the first attempt in print to distinguish "punk" from "new wave." Though "not a popular label," she cautioned, "punk" was now the "accepted" label for bands like the Clash, the Damned, Siouxsie and the Banshees, and the Sex Pistols "who usually play frantically fast, minimal, aggressive rock with the emphasis on brevity, an all in-sound rather than individual solos and the arrogance calculated to shock." She found "new wave" to be a more "inclusive term," used to describe a variety of bands like Eddie and the Hot Rods, the Stranglers, and Slaughter and the Dogs, who "definitely" were not "hard-core punks" but nonetheless were "part of the scene" because "they play with speed and energy" or "try hard" to. Yet, somewhat contradictorily, in that same month she referred to the "punk" band the Clash as "certainly the most politically aware of the new wave bands." "In one year the Clash, in the vanguard of the new wave, have seen their music, their attitudes and clothes influence and inspire a new generation of musicians. But because of the ban on *punk* music, their reputation has been built, somewhat precariously, on fewer than thirty gigs."[81] Here, it appears she is using the terms interchangeably, which is further confirmed by the title of her 1977 book, a collection of her articles, titled *1988: The New Wave Punk Rock Explosion.*

By 1977 these initially hesitant identifications between "punk" and "new wave" became the norm in British discourse. The Jam, who were said to have "all the outward trappings of a punk band," were also called "the black sheep of the new wave." Mick Jones of the Clash used the equivalence negatively, asserting of the band's debut single "White Riot" that "it ain't punk, it ain't new wave, it's the next logical progression for groups to move in. Call it what you want—all the terms stink. Just call it rock and roll."[82] This despite the fact that in the Clash's first album a few months later, they would "salute the new wave" and "hope nobody escapes!"[83] This is not at all untypical of the British discourses in the first half of 1977 when "punk" and "new wave" were oftentimes uttered practically in the same breath, as in the *Melody Maker* headline "Riding the New Wave; *MM* Probes the Punk Business."[84]

Clearly, in the heyday of British punk, there was a felt need for a complementary term ("new wave") that could be applied to the same bands. "New wave" appeared only a few months after "punk" and became its equivalent "other" in less than a year. Its function by this time was not to replace "punk" or to designate bands that were not "punk," but to capture in punk bands what the designator "punk" left out—the arty, avant-gardish, studied, and ironic dimension that accompanied the streetwise, working-class, and raucously "vulgar" dimension.

Originally, neither term, it seemed, could do without the other. But by the summer of 1977, "new wave" was threatening to replace "punk" in England as the name of preference for all groups involved in the scene that was once called "punk." In late July *Melody Maker* announced a new "series on the up-and-coming new wavers" ("On the Crest of the New Wave"), with articles on

Ultravox, the Adverts, and Generation X, among others. This may have been a symptom of the fact that some bands, like Ultravox, were going beyond "punk," abandoning the streetwise dimension but holding on to the avant-gardish and ironic side. Compilation albums of new wave music began to appear, with samplings from the Ramones, Patti Smith, the Damned, the New York Dolls, the Dead Boys, and the Talking Heads, thus lumping under that one category groups that the rock canon today would definitely segregate into the distinct categories of punk and new wave. By the end of 1977, "new wave" had definitely triumphed in the United Kingdom as the proper label for the then-contemporary underground music, just when the media in the United States were at their peak in their uproar over "punk." McClaren, true to his outsider posture, now reversed himself, referring to "new wave" as "establishment language, more descriptive of a new hair style than anything else."[85]

The Battle of the Labels: "New Wave" in America

"New wave" crossed over to the United States only a few months after its emergence in England, but in America's year of punk (1977), it was initially shunted to the sidelines. Like "punk," it first appeared in fanzines, spread next to the generic mass press, then finally was taken up by the established rock press. American writers initially applied "new wave" exclusively to those British bands that were also referred to as "punk" rather than to American bands. *New York Rocker* was the first American journal enthusiastically to seize upon "new wave," as it was among the first publications extensively to cover British bands, seeing them as possible allies, but also as possible threats, to the CBGB movement. In December 1976 the magazine was praising the Clash as "the most devastating of the new wave British bands." "Categorization-happy music papers over here have labeled it 'punk rock'—how can you dredge a word from the past to describe a movement aimed at the future?"[86] But at the same time, *Rocker* was sowing confusion by peppering the same texts with the two contending names, as if it did not know which was appropriate for what. A column entitled "New Wave Records" discussed the Damned's "contrived punk posing," the Vibrators' admitted leap "onto the punk-bandwagon," and identified Chris Spedding's "The Pogo Dance" as the "first punk gimmick single."[87]

It did not take long for *Rocker* to extend "new wave" to the increasingly vulnerable New York scene, which it had taken upon itself to champion against neglect at home and competition from abroad. This magazine was keen to emphasize that the Ramones, Blondie, "along with most of the rest of the new wave, constantly disavow the punk-rock tag."[88] This new baptism occurred just when ominous signs were appearing about the future of the New York scene. "Now, finally, with the dawn of a new 'new wave' upon us," worried one writer, "it looks like New York will again be buried," in this case, by the "tidal wave" of the "English new wave, with their more extreme politics, sounds, and costumes."[89]

Perhaps no one welcomed the new label more than the Talking Heads and their fanzine promoters, who were now anointing them "one of the most prestigious and respected bands in the elite company of the new wave scene." In their struggles with "questions of image," the Talking Heads sometimes wondered whether "we should be a lot punkier and then we'd make more money." But, said keyboard player Jerry Harrison, "people are fed up" with musicians posing as punk. "And they know that we're not posing," but "try to be honest" with them. Of course, commented the interviewer, the Talking Heads "isn't punk" but "must be ranked among the few originals in rock today" as well as "one of the most subversive bands in America—far more subversive than punks, who are after all the latest chapter in a great American tradition." Indeed, it was the Talking Heads' "concern with directness and truth, more than anything else," that connected them "to the rest of the new wave."[90] "New wave," in contrast with "punk," seemed thus to be a marker of originality, the refusal to pose, and a liberation from the musical weight of the past. The Talking Heads became the paradigmatic new wave band of the late 1970s.

The new label left the marginal confines of fanzines in the summer of 1977 to enter the discourses of the mainstream media, on the occasion of *Time* magazine's first full-blown account of the punk explosion that, coming a year after the fact, was also liberally laced with the label "new wave." "More and more," said *Time,* "the punkers find themselves being referred to as members of yet another New Wave," which to the magazine seemed "an apt catch-all label for the energetic and varied music that has emerged in recent months from some of the young American bands."[91] The establishment rock press finally chimed in with "new wave" toward the end of the year, initially using the term exclusively as an alternative reference to British "punk," but then also extending it to the New York scene. In England, announced Richard Goldstein, "native punk" is called "new wave music, because of working-class allegiances, and because (like the new wave cineastes) it presumes a connection between intimacy and art." "England," proclaimed Christgau, is "the land of the Sex Pistols and home of 'new wave.'"[92]

By 1978, when "new wave" finally settled in as the label of preference in the United States, the first wave of CBGB bands was leaving its nest and the new music of London, New York, San Francisco, and so on, was diversifying and expanding. It was then that the label "new wave" began to take on a decisively postpunk aura, referring to bands no longer as aggressive and shocking as the first wave, bands that were more sophisticated and arty but still committed to minimalist, speedy music. Meanwhile, the label "punk" came back to life to designate retroactively those groups (the Ramones, the Dictators, the Sex Pistols, the Clash, etc.) in the New York and London scenes, which in point of fact best satisfied the criteria adumbrated in the *Creem-Bomp* discourses on punk. There was clearly an aesthetic significance in this bifurcation of the labels. "Punk" accentuated the pop side, and "new wave" the art side of the art/pop dichotomy that was at work both in British and New York new music and the surrounding discourses. The triumph of "new wave," and its gradual dissociation from "punk," was a palpable expression of the fact that by 1978 the art side of the New York musical scene was getting an edge over the pop side. This was noted early in 1978 by Roy Trakin, a writer who was to become a major promoter of this new trend. Though conceding the "admittedly hair-splitting distinction between punk and new wave" and the "journalistic oversimplifications" in the "use of either word," he insisted that "taken as two sides of a constantly fluctuating and dynamic equation, these terms help describe what is so fascinating about the current renaissance in rock 'n' roll."[93] What made "new wave" especially pertinent to labeling the "local scene" were "the ties that join the New York art community with the rock 'n' roll world. Three-chord rock has been taken in an entirely distinct direction by ostensibly new wave bands" than it had by "more conventional punk rock groups." In the next two chapters, I turn to this dramatic next phase—this "second wave"—when New York rock music established an alliance with the art world, the likes of which had not been seen before or since.

FIGURE 11 James Chance, leader of the no wave band the Contortions, looking menacingly at his audience (c. 1978). Courtesy of Roberta Bayley.

CHAPTER 12
NO WAVE

New Wave Anxieties

In spring 1978 it was clear something was amiss at *New York Rocker*. Born in early 1976 as a fanzine dedicated to promoting the CBGB punk/new wave scene, the magazine seemed to be suffering from uncertainty and disorientation. The founder, Alan Betrock, left the magazine with no advance warning to the readership. The new publisher-editor, Andy Schwartz, announced this change in an editorial that was forcibly upbeat but barely repressing a tone of impending crisis. He admitted that the music scene was vastly different and more difficult to decipher in 1978 than it had been two years previously at the founding of *Rocker,* when "some of America's best rock 'n' roll bands were playing at CBGB's every week." But "after what seemed like a long time," the record labels finally signed "the best bands of that first wave," who now "transcended the New York 'scene' and CBGB's and the boundaries implied by words like 'punk rock.'"[1]

Did *Rocker* still have an agenda, now that the first wave had left its nest? Yes, affirmed Schwartz, perhaps with a bit too much conviction. First, *"New York Rocker* [would] continue to pick tomorrow's hitmakers today from among a flock of contenders in New York's new wave." He was wagering that a second wave of the new wave was poised in readiness to fill the vacuum left by the first wave. He was assuming that the new wave was an ongoing process, a kind of permanent revolution within rock that, not reducible to any one style, could accommodate a variety of stylistic changes. But just in case this did not happen, he promised that the magazine would also look beyond the New York scene, even to "mainstream" rock 'n' roll. So, despite the fact that 1978 was "a great time to be alive and in love with rock 'n' roll," Schwartz was clearly hedging his bets.[2]

That *New York Rocker* was no longer putting all its chips on the New York scene was clearly accentuated by the cover photo of the Clash (the first non–New Yorkers on the cover). By the end of 1977, it was obvious that British punk/new wave was stealing the thunder from the New York new wave. Further, Schwartz made no mention in his editorial of the disappointing showing of the first wave of recorded New York artists in the national market. *Talking Heads '77,* the most successful of the first wave debut albums, peaked at number 97 on the *Billboard* charts. The Ramones' first album only went to number 111, and neither Blondie's nor Television's nor Richard Hell and the Voidoids' even cracked the top 200.

So Schwartz had good reason, beneath his upbeat evocation of a new era, to deliver a decidedly mixed message. It was no surprise when, a few months later, *Rocker* declared in a splashing headline ("Rock 'n' Roll 78: Is There Life after Death?") that the new wave was in crisis, to which it devoted much of the issue (number 14, September). Local representatives from the music industry were brought in to diagnose what was wrong.[3] Why had the new wave failed to build sufficient momentum to enter the mainstream market? Why was it still confined to the small select group of artists, bohemians, intellectuals, the small hip scenes of major cities?

Clearly, the immediate problem was the absence of support from radio and only anemic support from the record industry, mainly from smaller labels, some of which were independent and some appended to the majors (e.g., Sire, Elektra). The latter seemed to be pulling out, since according to one, "We signed a tremendous number of new bands during one year. A year and a half later, we see that the 'wave' or the fad did not come to fruition." The local independent record companies, which had emerged in support of the new wave—Red Star, Jem, Private Stock—were never able to establish a toehold, like their British counterparts, Stiff Records and Rough Trade. It was in "the wonderful world of radio" that the *Rocker* survey garnered "the least optimistic responses."[4] "It's ultimately depressing," contributed Ken Barnes, "to realize [that] most of the new wave records don't have a chance in hell of getting any radio air play."[5] But "more disturbing yet" was the fact that even those radio stations that "took the chance found their phone lines flooded with complaints."[6]

The majority of the correspondents in the *Rocker* survey did seem to agree that "the new wave had peaked," that it was "slowing down," and that "the term 'new wave' is kind of passé." Some, like Lester Bangs, put much of the blame on the music itself. "Listen to most of the music; it is so oppressive, so anti-sexual, anti-emotional, and anti-feeling. It's the flip side of disco. Disco's going 'Whee, the world is one big party' and punk's going 'Uhh, we're so bored.' What shit!" Punk/new wave "only went half way" in the right direction, saying, "'This all stinks' but forgetting to say 'However, we have a better idea over here of how to do things.'"[7]

New York Rocker's crisis was not merely a misfortune of local relevance, a typical trial suffered by a small magazine overly invested in a narrow cultural movement. This was the first sign of an emerging rift within rock culture between criticism and commerce. Heretofore, it had been an almost universal assumption of rock criticism that whatever was well received by critics tended also to sell well, not because criticism determined sales, but because critics, committed to the idea of rock as a democratic art, could not imagine liking a brand of rock that was not potentially liked by the general rock public. The converse did not hold true, of course: critics did not expect to like all the brands of rock liked by the general public (e.g., disco).

So a general malaise could be discerned in the critical establishment by 1978 when punk/new wave did not seem to be catching on, even though it had won the critics' war. To most, this seemed to be merely a temporary aberration, due mainly to the intransigence of the music industry. Perhaps a second wave of the new wave would overcome this resistance as well as avoid the mistakes of the first wave. In 1978 no one yet perceived that the split between critical accolades and sales charts would persist and deepen into the 1980s and 1990s, after and beyond the new wave movement, a split later to be marketed as the opposition between "alternative" and "mainstream" rock.

No Wave

Just at the time that the *New York Rocker* was declaring a crisis, a second wave of new wave bands was beginning to draw attention. Some were simply carrying on the tradition of the first wave's fast, loud minimalism, such as the Fleshtones and the Cramps. Others picked up on retro-rock irony and pastiche—the B-52s, Devo, later the Lounge Lizards—exploring a performance domain already pioneered by Blondie. But at the moment of crisis, no one among this second wave more galvanized the hopes of *Rocker* and other new wave media than a decidedly avant-garde group of bands that made their dramatic appearance not at CBGB's or some other seedy bar, but at a cutting-edge art space. These bands, soon to be labeled "no wave," were inaugurated as a movement in May 1978 at Artists Space, a not-for-profit alternative SoHo gallery, as part of a five-day festival of relatively unknown new wave bands. The roster of no wave bands at Artists Space included Teenage Jesus and the Jerks (led by Lydia Lunch), James Chance and the Contortions, D.N.A. (led by Arto Lindsay), Mars, Theoretical Girls (led by Glenn Branca), Tone Deaf, and the Gynecologists (including Rhys Chatham).

Though there had been no previous aesthetic alliance among these bands, no proclamations, manifestos, or other expressions of artistic solidarity, they were immediately seized upon as collectively representing a new musical vision. Clearly in the ambit of the new wave, they were nonetheless severely testing its art/pop equilibrium by moving aggressively toward the art end of that spectrum. The label "no wave" caught on quickly to express this surly second wave transformation of new wave. The no wave bands seemed to go just far enough left on the art/pop spectrum to sit on the boundary between art and pop, neither strictly art nor pop, yet both art and pop, belonging to both worlds. This was, it seemed, a true borderline music, a true art/pop fusion, going beyond anything attempted in the first wave of the new wave. This aesthetic in-betweenness gave no wave its product identity, its promotional hook, its legitimacy as a revolution within the new wave revolution.

John Rockwell, the guru of art-rock fusion, was quick to proclaim this turn to borderline aesthetics. First, he noted that the musicians performing at the Artists Space festival originated as much from the art as from the rock world.[8] These included poets (Lydia Lunch of Teenage Jesus, Adele Bertei of the Contortions), experimental filmmakers (James Nares of the Contortions, Margaret Dewys of Theoretical Girls, Arto Lindsay of D.N.A.), avant-garde dramatists (Glenn Branca of Theoretical Girls), visual artists (Pat Place of the Contortions), sculptors (Robin Crutchfield of D.N.A.), and art-music composers (Jeffrey Lohn of Theoretical Girls). James Chance came out of the free jazz loft scene in SoHo.[9]

Equally striking about the Artists Space festival, according to Rockwell, was the fact that a space "heretofore reserved for overt, foundation and government-supported art work" was "opening [its] doors to young rock bands."[10] This, he felt, was not an isolated event. The no wave bands were altogether complicit with that new set of art institutions, called "alternative spaces," which had only recently taken root in the SoHo/TriBeCa areas. Roughly, the institutional art world in mid-1970s New York was split along highly coded binaries, first between uptown and downtown, the former standing for establishmentarian modernism (Fifty-seventh Street galleries, Lincoln Center, etc.) and the latter, in SoHo and TriBeCa, for the cutting edge, the new movements, or those still incubating.[11] But downtown was rent by its own binary, between the for-profit galleries, catering to the rising stars in painting and photography, and the not-for-profit alternative spaces, originally located in lofts and storefronts, which provided an opening to the unknown and more adventurous artists and which were especially responsive to the growing interest in performance art and video. In the mid-1970s the best known of these alternative spaces was the Kitchen, formerly of the Mercer Arts Center, where it had existed side by side with underground rock, but now located on Broome Street in SoHo. Though initially promoting primarily the video arts, it grew quickly into one of the most active centers in the country for musical minimalism and other such adventures in musical avant-gardism.[12] Though the Kitchen gradually opened its doors to new wave music, it is Artists Space that gets credit for having produced the first "exhibit" of rock bands in an alternative space.

The emergence of no wave at Artists Space effectively initiated a long-term institutional alliance between New York popular music and the art world, which outlasted no wave and has become a trademark of New York musical culture. The no wave bands were at the borderline between art and pop, not only demographically (in terms of membership and audience), but also institutionally, insofar as they trafficked back and forth between art institutions (the alternative spaces) and seedy rock clubs. Such sustained crossover activity between avant-garde and pop institutions was altogether unprecedented in the history of rock music or any American popular music, for that matter. In previous interactions between popular music and the avant-garde in America, "high" and "low" appropriated from each other in their own institutional domains. The bebop revolution took place in jazz nightclubs. The Beatles and the Beach Boys carried out their experiments in electronics for the same recording labels and within the same marketing and distribution structures that had sustained their teen anthems. The first wave of the new wave never transcended the CBGB's/Max's ambit of live performance and sought entry only in the pop media of recording, radio, nightclubs, and packaged tours. As a rare exception, the Velvet Underground did traffic in the mid-1960s between the rock world and Warholian performance sites, but this lasted little over a year with no long-term institutional transformations.

No Wave Aesthetics

Teetering *institutionally* and *demographically* between the art and pop worlds, no wave music was quite naturally perceived by its media devotees as also teetering *aesthetically* between these two worlds, that is, as incorporating avant-garde components and rock components equally into its musical practices, and thus itself *musically* neither strictly avant-garde nor rock, really a new mutation. In the promotion of no wave, it was thus important, in the face of its fervent excursions into the avant-garde, equally to assert its pop connections and sensibilities. All seemed to agree that this pop component was nothing other than the first wave itself, especially in its extreme punk manifestations. That is, punk, which had previously been encumbered with its own inner art/pop binary, now became the pure pop component in another binary, itself only a subordinate unit in a larger musical scheme. No wave, it seemed, was simply punk meeting the avant-garde on the aesthetic boundaries between art and pop.

Punk's role in this partnership, according to critics, was to provide the firm musical and cultural framework within which the no wave bands could take their liberties and conduct their experiments. In rooting itself in "punk rock basics," no wave apparently was simply appropriating the by now familiar tripartite aesthetic of shock, minimalism, and rank amateurism—what the critics were now calling "organized noise," "anarchy and amateurism," and the reduction of rock 'n' roll "to its common denominators."[13] It was also taking up, in a modified form, some of the nonmusical practices of punk, the "lifestyle," "sartorial tradition," and "the way you think about the world in general."[14]

But, it needed to be emphasized, punk was not the whole of no wave, only the pop starting point that was to be transcended in avant-garde fashion. What no wave was especially keen to jettison, according to the critics, were the rigidified pop formulas that had survived unabated in punk music: "the rhythms of rock and roll," "regular chord exchanges," and "songs with conventional verse-chorus-verse structures."[15] No wave "took those arbitrary categories apart, piece by piece," as it adopted a "deliberately experimental" attitude toward punk's materials, a "slightly intellectual approach" not found in punk. No wave was driven, it appeared, by a "kind of thinking that says, 'What would happen if I did this?'"—much different from punk's more conventional kind of thinking, like "Oh, this is a good lick, let's try this one out, bang it around a bit."[16]

How, according to their promoters, did no wave bands transcend the pop limits of punk? Most frequently they did so simply by pushing to the limits the avant-garde undercurrent implicit in the otherwise populist punk aesthetic of noise/shock, minimalism, and amateurism, never fully exploited by the first wave, which was still encumbered by the rigid conventions of pop. That is, the no wave bands stayed within the punk aesthetic to transcend punk, moving it toward the art end of its art/pop spectrum, and for the most part avoiding the importation of avant-garde components foreign to punk. Or so it was perceived. For example, the no wavers seemed to "reduce rock to such [extreme] minimalism that to some it might seem there's nothing there at all," as in pieces made up of only "one chord strummed in a light percussive accompaniment."[17] Teenage Jesus, with their "brutal simplicity," were hailed as "the most rigorously minimal 'rock' band in the world." "Lydia Lunch [the leader] chants her words in a bratty monotone, . . . reinforced by one-note-per-beat bass playing and time kept on a single drum."[18] D.N.A. characteristically used "simple repetitive riffs" on keyboard, "roboticized" patterns that were nonetheless "wonderfully resonant," backed up by a drummer functioning as a "human metronome."[19] Thus, not mere minimalism, but an "extreme," "brutal," "rigorous" minimalism, reduced almost to nothing.

No wave minimalism was quite frequently associated with no wave amateurishness, given that as artists trained in other fields, many of the musicians were new to rock instrumentation. Such amateurishness in turn provided the perfect occasion for these avant-gardes to explore in an unconventional manner the sonic possibilities of their instruments. Arto Lindsay, who performed with D.N.A. only a month after having taken up the guitar, produced "a scraping, crackling buzz" out of the guitar box. "Hand positions and directions seem dictated almost as much by what feels and looks right as by what sounds are called for."[20] When James Chance of the Contortions first appeared in the jazz loft scene in SoHo, "his saxophone playing sounded as if he had just picked up the instrument." But "his assortment of squeaks and noises was uncannily effective."[21] The no wave "singers" similarly used their untrained, "unmusical" voices for timbral and sonic exploration. Such were the effect of Chance's "screams" and "tortured lyrics," Lunch's "gratingly loud" and "tuneless wall-of-hate vocals," and Lindsay's "anguished neurotic screams."[22] Lindsay "snaps and barks and drools the syllables, grins and grimaces, pokes his glasses back up above the bridge of his nose."[23] In no wave, amateurishness was apparently neither good in itself nor an intended mere expression of the democratic do-it-yourself ideology of rock music. It was rather an occasion for experimentation and the play with cutting-edge timbres and noises.

It was clear that the no wave bands were using these sonic and timbral experiments also for purposes of shock and disruption.[24] In effect, at an avant-garde level, they were combining the punk aesthetics of amateurism with that of adversarial confrontation. Lydia Lunch could be "morbidly witty, cruelly cynical, trashily shocking, downright terrifying, . . . an affront to the world." "Her assaults on mankind have always had all the thrill of a splatter film."[25] Chance outdid his punk forebears in his aggressions. Going beyond sneers, insults, and gobbing (spitting), he would physically attack the front-row onlookers, "as he snarled and smirked with unmerciful obnoxiousness."[26] This aesthetics of violence was not well received by establishment critics. Rockwell complained about Chance "cuffing and slapping people" and engaging in "repartee right out of a grade-school recess yard."[27] Christgau rose out of the audience to refute Chance physically. He got into a "fierce imbroglio with James Chance" and "admirably acquitted himself by pummeling the lead Contortion into bloody submission." "Talk about abandoning your critical stance," observed the *New York Rocker* critic.[28]

The alternative press interpreted Chance's antics in a more benign light, giving it a dada spin. Chance was described as a multimedia performance artist, whose "unsettling" behavior simply went along with the "unsettling" music. "Music and menace are thrown at you in an atmosphere of such unresolved tension that if the thunder don't get you, the lightning will." Chance was out to "push people into admitting their passivity, uniformity and lack of imagination," forcing them to become "member(s) of the show" and to realize that they are but "tacit participant(s) in an insult . . . aimed" at them. In the accompanying interview, Chance was only too willing to support this dadaesque interpretation. "Art? I hate Art. It makes me sick. My whole idea is anti-Art. And as for SoHo, it should be blown off the fucking map, along with all its artsy assholes." By physically attacking them, he was simply trying to undermine the nonchalance of the hip New York audiences. "In New York they just sit and stare at you. . . . New York people are such assholes—so cool and blasé. They think they can sit and listen to anything and it won't affect them. So I decided I just had to go beyond music, and *physically* assault them."[29]

There was occasionally a fusion aspect to no wave, a tendency not only to stretch punk to its extremes, but to combine it with previously foreign avant-garde traditions. The Contortions, in particular, were treated as the ultimate art/pop combinatorial band, having fused the edginess of punk with the "screaming eruptions" of free jazz.[30] Chance's version of the free jazz saxophone was inspired not by Ornette Coleman's free melodic improvisations operating over freely improvised bass and rhythmic lines—which his elementary skills could not have approximated anyway—but from the free timbral improvisations of the "frantic Albert Ayler" style, the screeches, scratches, squawks, and growls of the saxophone.[31]

The fusion discourses concerning the Contortions soon got out of hand, no doubt aided and abetted by shifts in the music. The Contortions went from being perceived simply as a free jazz/punk merger to a jazz/punk/funk/disco potpourri, Chance now a punk James Brown, George Clinton, and Chic, as well as a punk Ayler.[32] Other listeners claimed to discover elements of Duke Ellington, Iggy Pop, Nico, Kool and the Gang, Julius Hemphill, and Fred Frith in Contortion music and performances, or even the dissonance, atonality, and polytonality of modernist art music.[33] By the time that media coverage had peaked, the Contortions had been transformed into an almost indecipherable mishmash of influences from high and low.

No Wave: What Commercial Potential?

Between 1978 and 1980 no wave bands were the beneficiaries of considerable press attention, with *New York Rocker* at the forefront. It might have seemed odd that this starry-eyed fanzine of the CBGB pop scene should suddenly become a promoter of music on the edge of the art world. It would have made more sense for a magazine like the *SoHo Weekly News,* ensconced in the downtown art scene, to have been the vanguard standard bearer for the no wave. But with the apparent waning of the first wave, *Rocker* was in a crisis of survival. Anything brazen enough to appear like the next wave was eagerly seized upon. There was also the accident that Roy Trakin, the major journalistic promoter of the no wave (and the one who apparently gave it its name), left the artier *SoHo Weekly News* for *Rocker* at the time that the no wave bands were emerging as a perceived alliance.

But if the much more accessible bands of the first wave had not broken through into the commercial mainstream, why would anyone think that bands considerably artier, noisier, more dissonant, less melodic, more cerebral, and more confrontative have a better chance? Trakin's defiant response was that despite no wave's immediate lack of commercial potential, it represented the long-term future of popular music, when people would no longer want "to be soothed by old-fashioned love songs." No wave "is the music we will, in all likelihood, be listening to for stimulation and escape in the possible boredom and excitement of the '80s and '90s. Modern romance will have to be carried on in an atmosphere of dissonance and stridency; you may as well get used to it."[34]

Thus, the optimism about no wave's commercial potential was based primarily on a belief in a future mass reversal of popular taste, from saccharine, simplistic, comforting, and rhythmically basic musical formulas to atonal, disorienting, disturbing, confrontative, and experimental musical devices. In the short run, Trakin allowed, it would "only be through some incredibly fluky circumstances that we will ever hear Lydia Lunch intoning" on commercial radio. But, in the long run, no wave would leave "its indelible mark on the world of culture. All future rock 'n' roll music will be forced to at least nod in [its] direction," as it enters into a "post-revolutionary society."[35] "Lydia Lunch is no overnight sensation, no Wild Man Fischer, but a genuine underground prophetess, whose time will assuredly come. Just remember where you heard it first," Trakin predicted confidently.[36]

It is difficult to believe that such wishful thinking about the future commerciability of a music praised for its inaccessibility and audience-unfriendliness, however kindled by desperation and a sense of crisis, could account for the journalistic embrace of no wave as the sound of the future. No avant-garde musical genre had ever crossed successfully into the commercial arena, even when incorporating pop elements, as is attested by the history of modern jazz. Why would a borderline music, though closer to the pop sphere, be expected to enjoy a radically different fate? As it turns out, other considerations played an important part to fuel this optimism, not the least of which was James Chance's turn toward African American pop music.

White into Black

Among the no wave bands, Chance's Contortions were widely perceived as having the best chance for commercial success, a hope stemming from their successful blending of punk with black popular music, the funk of James Brown and George Clinton and later disco.[37] Chance's adoption of black musical forms represented a dramatic shift in the history of New York new wave, which beforehand had presented itself as a decidedly white music with decidedly white roots. This is especially true of the discourses of rock criticism that surrounded the new wave and sought to define it.

Of course, the institution of rock criticism, made up almost exclusively of white males, had from the beginning concentrated its accreditory attention on white music. Any cursory survey of the early *Crawdaddy!, Rolling Stone,* and *Creem* issues makes that palpably clear. In their attempt to establish the cultural credentials of rock—its seriousness, meaningfulness, subversiveness, experimentalism—the early critics invariably turned to Dylan, the Stones, the Beatles, the Beach Boys, and so on. But they did create a minor pantheon for African American rock musicians either as the venerable grandfathers, pioneers, the providers of roots (Robert Johnson, Chuck Berry, Little Richard), or as the contemporary sources of fun and escape (James Brown, Wilson Pickett). One *listened* to white rock for significance and one *danced* to black music for fun.

But even this marginalized dual role of black music within the rock critic canon was gradually undermined with the development of the punk/new wave aesthetic in the early to mid-1970s. The emergence of punk discourse in the early 1970s did much to shape a rock aesthetic defined almost exclusively in terms of white male music and the needs of white male teenagers. The new "roots" pantheon was now altogether white—rockabilly and garage rock. (Probably not known at the time and certainly not emphasized was the fact that a large number of garage band members were Hispanic.) Punk/new wave may well be the first significant rock music movement not to display an explicitly blues or soul foundation.

Further, punk/new wave is the first of the seventies rock genres to assume an explicitly hostile posture toward disco, the most popular black music of the time. By devoting the editorial of its inaugural issue to an attack on that "disco shit"—"the epitome of all that's wrong with Western Culture"—*Punk* magazine was effectively from the beginning defining "punk" as the opposite of disco.[38] Lester Bangs, in a later article on punk/new wave racism (in which he confessed his own faults on the matter), recounts a party he gave attended by the staff of *Punk.* "When I did what we always used to do at parties in Detroit—put on soul records so everybody could dance—I began to hear this:

'What're you playing all that nigger disco shit for, Lester?' 'That's not nigger disco shit,' I snarled, 'that's Otis Redding, you assholes.'"[39] So the second pillar of the early rock critic canon for black music, namely music for dancing and fun, also disappeared from the punk canon. Legs McNeil of *Punk* explained it this way:

> We [punks] had all the same reference points: White Castle Hamburgers, muzak, malls. . . . There were no black people involved with this. In the sixties hippies wanted to be black. We were going: "Fuck the blues; fuck the black experience." . . . It was funny: you'd see guys going into a Punk club, passing black people going into a disco, and they'd be looking at each other, not with disgust, but "Isn't it weird that they want to go there."[40]

Bangs was not altogether uncomplicit with this attitude. He may have liked to dance to soul music, but he spent little time writing about it or any other black music. He may have taken private pleasure in black music, but he constructed his public aesthetic almost completely out of white music. And note that he did not offer to put a disco recording on the turntable.

Thus, when in 1978 the Contortions introduced a black vernacular into the new wave musical language, they broke dramatically with an already entrenched discursive and musical legacy. Not coincidentally, this redirection of new wave aesthetics occurred when African American music was undergoing a powerful commercial and critical resurgence. Disco was enjoying a spectacular year (*Saturday Night Fever,* etc.), while funk, under George Clinton's leadership, was finally crossing over into the white consumer base. Reggae, in large part due to an alliance with British punk, was making headway in New York new wave circles. Rap appeared for the first time on the charts in 1979, with the Sugar Hill Gang's "Rapper's Delight," itself loaded with samples from Chic's disco classic "Good Times."

In this context, it is no surprise that promoters of no wave could view the Contortions' original fusion of funk rhythms with free jazz atonalities and punk noises as the perfect formula for that commercial breakthrough that had all along eluded the first wave. With this "sinister murky brew" of "jazz, R&B, and soul," the Contortions were anointed the no wave band with the "most potential for commercial success."[41] And, indeed, by 1979 the Contortions were acknowledged as one of the "top-drawing [bands] on the New York circuit," getting requests for interviews "at almost every gig."[42]

All Chance needed to add to his punk-funk mix, it was averred, was "the right disco-slick production" in order to "fulfill his ambitions—Mr. Soul 1984."[43] With this idea in mind, he formed the spin-off "disco" band James White and the Blacks in 1979. Chance declared hotly that he was not, however, selling out to disco—"I mean, disco is *disgusting*"—but appropriating and transforming it. "There's something in it that's always interested me—*monot-ony*. It's sort of jungle music, but whitened and perverted. On this album I'm trying to restore it to what it *could* be. Really primitive."[44] As others saw it, disco was Chance's "latest weapon in his personal baby-bites-mother crusade against the new wave," in his ongoing role of enfant terrible of the new wave. Sporting a new persona, he now emerged onstage "in a white tuxedo and butch-waxed pompadour," playing "the suave rat, the aloof cad instead of the bare-fanged rodent of previous Contortions gigs where everyone within spitting distance went home with a neck wound." He was perceived as simultaneously adopting and critiquing his black musical sources, coming up "with arrange-ments which you *could* call Disco, and you *could* call Funk, but which manage to sound like comic insults aimed at the previous rigidity of the forms he is ex-ploring. He strips down the elements and reconstitutes them into the bizarre style of the Contortions without ever losing the boogie."[45] That is, he purport-edly remained true to the avant-garde while indulging in the pop musical genre at the time deemed most "disgusting." In an odd and arrogant promotional stunt, *Rocker* published a dialogue between Chance and George Clinton as if they were equally godfathers of funk, each in their own domains.[46]

As it turns out, first wave bands like the Talking Heads and Blondie belat-edly achieved commercial success only after following Chance's lead in appro-priating black music within the new wave framework. The Talking Heads scored a modest hit (number 26) in late 1978 with their cover of Al Green's "Take Me to the River." A few months later, Blondie's discolike "Heart of Glass" became the first number one new wave hit, which the group achieved again a year later with a cover of the classic reggae recording by the Paragons, "The Tide Is High." In England the Clash and the Police independently were exploiting the punk-reggae musical connections with encouraging returns. In 1980 the Talking Heads ensemble was enlarged to include a number of African American musicians (notably Bernie Worrell of Parliament/Funkadelic) for a tour to promote their Africanesque fourth album, *Remain in Light,* their most successful commercial venture yet.

The new wave press were even slower than the musicians in acknowledging the importance of contemporary black music. Only in late 1978 did an article appear in *New York Rocker* defending disco against the hackneyed complaints of the "well-stocked New Wave mind" (e.g., disco as "a soulless, mechanical plot to hurl all rock's passion and inspiration down to defeat"). The author commended disco producers for not being afraid "to explore modern studio and instrumental technology," "unlike many terminal New Wave nostalgia cases." Readers predictably responded in outraged fashion against this music "played too loud in bars where total jerks meet total jerks."[47] *Rocker* did not publish an article on black performers until its twenty-third issue, in October 1979, with a spread on the reggae artist Linton Kwesi Johnson. American black artists were not featured in an article until the thirty-fourth issue (Chic in December 1980) and not in a cover story until the fortieth issue (Prince in June 1981). True to its principles, *Punk* pursued its anti-disco campaign until the end and never covered any black artists.

Decline of No Wave

But this outreach to black musical culture, which the Contortions initiated within no wave, did the latter little good commercially. Like the other no wave bands, they failed to cross over into a wider market after the initial flurry of attention. *No New York,* the inaugural no wave LP starring Teenage Jesus, the Contortions, D.N.A., and Mars and produced by Brian Eno, was "launched into the record world with all the fanfare of a stillbirth."[48] "While the Talking Heads skillfully manage to integrate the new African sensibility to widespread praise and boffo sales on their new album," complained no wave prophet Trakin, "Chance (and most of his cohorts) continues to struggle, as far from commercial success as he's ever been."[49] In light of this, Chance's invention of James White and the Blacks, rather than a bold deconstructive move on disco, may have been nothing more than a last-ditch effort to escape oblivion by cashing in on disco's success. Trakin finally had to admit that the "fantasy," engendered by Chance, "of the commercial triumph of an avant-garde derived rock/jazz fusion" now appeared as "the pipe dream it always was." This article proved to be Trakin's valediction to Chance, who then disappeared from the media screen.

In disbanding Teenage Jesus and replacing it with 8-Eyed Spy, Lydia Lunch was also moving decidedly toward the mainstream. In response to the consternation of her avant-garde fans, she declared somewhat disingenuously that for her to turn mainstream is an avant-garde act. "I've already played the art-fart route. I've already gone so extremely overboard" that "the only way to be completely out is to be completely in at this point, is to be completely mainstream." Actually, she admitted, in the midst of this rather creative rationalization, that she just wanted "to reach more people," having so far reached only "the *least* amount that would listen." But 8-Eyed Spy and a successor band, 13.13, survived only a few months, after which Lunch retreated into a moderately successful poetry career. Ultimately her music never appealed beyond a "rabid" but "tiny cult."[50]

It did not augur well for the original no wave bands when in October 1980 *Rocker* devoted a special issue to the birth of the "Sons and Daughters of No

New York"—the Raybeats, the Bush Tetras—thus intimating that the parents, having lived only two years, were already facing decline if not death. By 1982 D.N.A, the only remaining no wave band, was facing "steadily diminishing returns," averaging "one New York gig every four months."[51] Critic-admirers resignedly referred to D.N.A. as "the most consistently exciting and innovative band currently starving in the Big Apple" and "the Great Rock and Roll Band No One Remembers," or even worse, "the Greatest Rock and Roll Band No One Ever Heard of in the First Place."[52] By 1982 no wave had effectively come to an end.

Pastiche

But, as it turns out, there was more to the second wave than the no wave movement. What might be called the "pastiche" or "irony" bands—the B-52s, Devo, and the Lounge Lizards—received as much media attention in New York and had much more commercial success nationally. Unlike the no wavers, this second wave clearly situated itself on the pop side of the cultural fault line, while pursuing the art/pop dialectic initiated by the first wave.

The original new wave pastiche group, Blondie, though born of the first wave, just as rightly belong to the second wave. They were the last of the original CBGB groups to receive any recognition from the rock press and achieved popularity beyond their narrow constituency only during the years of the second wave. Though not thought to be a great band and hardly sounding punk, they exemplified, like no other first wave band, the bivalent aesthetic posture of their New York bohemian audiences: on the one hand, cool, blasé, and utterly jaded, on the other, nostalgic for an age of innocence, desirous for a return to roots, and sporting an affection for the degraded objects of lowbrow mass culture. The solution to this aesthetic tension was ironic distance, a nonidentification through distance that disguises a certain identification.

Blondie evoked the sweet sounds of the early 1960s girl groups—the pretty melodies, the vulnerable sexuality, framed by Deborah Harry's play at mild lowbrow "cheesecake." But everything was in bolded quotes. Blondie's persona was too much beyond innocence, too schooled in the ways of the grimy and sophisticated New York bohemia simply to be resurrecting the teen symphonies of the Shangri-Las and the Crystals, whose sound Harry had "down to a perfect snotty whine." In the first serious article on Blondie, Bangs commended the band for treating these sixties sounds like "ready-mades" sufficiently recontextualized "so they don't sound like nostalgia or some horrible 'tribute.'" Bangs was quick to tie this new "pastiche" rock to the sixties punk (i.e., garage band) tradition. "Punk was kind of a joke in the first place" "and given the campily ironic distance" that Blondie and other CBGB groups brought to it, it became "a joke once removed."[53]

Blondie were easily the most successful band to come out of the New York new wave, entering the top ten album charts twice, a feat not achieved even once by any other such band, not even the Talking Heads. By the end of the decade, pastiche bands—like the B-52s, Devo, the Lounge Lizards, and the Feelies—were increasingly gaining favor in the New York scene. If no wave had galvanized critics in the alternative press, the pastiche bands were thrilling New York audiences and delighting the mainstream press critics.

Whereas Blondie confined much of their retro imagery to pop music history, the B-52s, in their lyrics and performative presentations, went beyond musical imagery to a broad retro-trash aesthetic, evoking the worlds of fifties/ sixties horror and beach-party movies, of polyester clothing and beehive hairdos. "Decked out in dime-store wigs and suburban-housewife garb," the two women performers looked "for all the world as if they were on their way to the supermarket."[54] Fronted by Fred Schneider "in his Hawaiian shirt and dapper slacks," the B-52s were the pioneers of a "thrift store rock," which "lovingly reconstruct[ed] the sounds and attitudes of post-Sputnik, pre-Vietnam pop America within a new wave context." Their most popular song, "Rock Lobster," conjured up "a surrealistic '60s beach party where bikini-clad mermen frug with warbling manta-rays and narwhals."[55]

Though the B-52s were clearly on the pop side of the art/pop borderline, their adoption of a trash aesthetic connected them just as surely to the art world as to the pop world. Trash aesthetics had its provenance in the art world camp of the 1960s and was being revived by a new generation of artists just as the B-52s were entering the scene. Some of these artists had apprenticed in the School of Visual Arts, whose teachings strongly informed the practices of *Punk* magazine, itself a major purveyor of trash aesthetics. Hadn't Legs McNeil, the resident magazine philosopher, celebrated the essence of punk as television reruns, cheeseburgers, comics, B movies, and the Three Stooges? But the B-52s were the first new wave group consciously to exploit this new sensibility in a thoroughgoing manner. "Urbane, funny and sharp, they use *American Graffiti*–era trash with the precision and purpose of 'serious artists,'" noted one critic.[56] Though inhabiting "the same world of big cars, make-out parties, and mass-consumer pleasure that Jan and Dean celebrated," the B-52s were "just intellectual enough to be self-conscious about how surreal it is."[57] In this surreal world, trash was transformed into something quite different. "Try imagining a beach party surfing band put through the Sun Ra school of interplanetary inspiration. Beach blanket bingo on the lunar surface."[58]

But if the B-52s satisfied the art predilections of their bohemian New York audiences, they also provided them with the occasion, and the excuse, to have fun. Indeed, how are self-described jaded and hip sophisticates to have "fun" (and not merely pleasure) while maintaining that posture? The B-52s brought levity to such a desultory scene in the form of "great, bouncy dance music, as seductive as the Beach Boys, and just as much fun."[59] Beforehand, dancing, because "uncool," was virtually absent from the New York new wave scene, at a time when it seemed to be the craze everywhere else, at the disco and funk venues, of course, but also emphatically in the high-energy punk clubs of London and Manchester, where the "pogo" ruled the floor.

Meanwhile, nothing could be "more depressing," noted one observer, than "drag[ging] your tattered ass to Max's or CBGB, or any of the 'in' toilets on the downtown kick-and-vomit circuit," where "nobody would be moving. Under-nourished hyperthyroids, pressed up against the graffiti, would be listening to some funereal jackboot aria by The Punctured Scumbags." "Five minutes there could provide you with hard proof that most punk rock caused consti-pation" and "varicose veins." Then, exuded this observer, along came the B-52s "like a CARE package from Mars," to release these overwrought sophis-ticates from their self-imposed inhibitions. The B-52s "didn't know, for in-stance, that it wasn't cool to play dance music anymore" or "to have a sense of humor." Initially, they got "a lot of blank looks from stunned punks," but "by the end of those first gigs everybody was dancing."[60]

Soon the media was raving about the "driving danceability of the music." "With half the CBGB's crowd dancing away in response, the innocent fun of rock-and-roll seemed happily returned."[61] Indeed, the normally demure Rockwell (at least in his writerly style) was observed at a B-52s gig "lurching around in a black leather jacket with day-glo racing stripes on the sleeve, clutching a broken bottle of Lowenbrau and bellowing, 'Fan-fucking-tastic! I'll fight anybody in the house who says no!'"[62] All this enthusiasm was the expression of a widespread belief that finally in the B-52s and other pastiche bands, the new wave had found a musical style and posture that would secure a large national audience.

Some pastiche bands turned the retro-trash aesthetic on its head, by trans-forming legitimate art forms into trash, rather than the other way around, or by exploiting the clichés that inevitably attach themselves to such forms. Such were the Lounge Lizards, those purveyors of a "fake jazz" aesthetic, led by John Lurie. Critics delighted in their "affectionate recreation" of the "clichés of 1950's jazz" and their "humorously dextrous" "simulations" of "low-brow B-movie soundtracks." They were, in effect, "conceptual artists who enjoy toying with the form and content of musical idioms and sometimes satirizing the asso-ciated behavioral stances." Indeed, they dressed the part and looked the part, in the sleek suits and slicked-back hair recalling the 1950s lounge jazz scene. "The Lounge Lizards don't just sound like a 1950's jazz band gone berserk, for example; they even look like one."[63] Performatively, they were the new wave's "Ghouls of Cool (for whom cool is the rule)," about whom New York's "smart set" was "all abuzz." "At any Manhattan nighterie, a Lizards gig is jammed with hepcats and schlepcats alike digging the newest in spazz jazz."[64]

The pastiche bands stand at the divide of an important historical shift in the history of the recording industry, the dramatic expansion of the retro market, which beforehand had existed on the periphery catering to collectors and nostalgics. The causes are perhaps more economical than aesthetic. At a moment when the recording industry was experiencing its first major recession since the rise of rock 'n' roll, the companies had a strong incentive in opening up their vaults to rerelease material lying dormant for years. This cheap mode of production was certainly especially welcome at a time when studio recording costs were rising precipitously. This turn to retro was abetted by the market of aging baby boomers now as interested in recollection as in experiencing the new. From the late seventies onward, the pop field would be subject to constant recyclings or revivals of old styles. Some no doubt were a return to a perceived past authenticity: the 1980s blues revival, the 1990s singer-songwriter revival, perhaps the two ska revivals (1980s and 1990s). But others were clearly ironic reappropriations, in the manner of the New York pastiche bands: the neo-psychedelic and rockabilly revivals of the 1980s, and certainly the surf and neo-swing movements of the 1990s. The New York pastiche bands were in the vanguard of the retro-pop aesthetics that is a persistent feature of our musical culture.

Downtown!

Borderline aesthetics did not disappear with the demise of no wave. Taken up immediately by other musicians with a different penchant, the borderline legacy has since become an enduring trademark of the New York music scene. From the beginning, the music of the post–no wave borderliners (Glenn Branca, Rhys Chatham, Laurie Anderson, Peter Gordon, and so on) was simply dubbed "the downtown sound." Strictly speaking, these musicians really represented a second-generation "downtown," supplanting the fading 1970s downtown scene of Glass, Reich, Riley, Meridith Monk, and Robert Ashley. In effect, the new downtown presented itself in a triangular opposition both to the old downtown and to no wave. Against the first-generation downtown but on the side of no wave, the new downtown altogether committed itself to a borderline aesthetic. But with its downtown foreparents and in contrast with no wave, the new downtown stressed pure musicality and experimentalism at the expense of extra-musical aggressions and antics.

Rhys Chatham and Glenn Branca, the first of the downtown borderliners, had previously operated on the no wave periphery or, more accurately, had been occasionally dubbed by the media as "no wave." Both appeared at the original Artists Space festival, Branca with Theoretical Girls and Chatham with the Gynecologists. But from its first days, no wave proved to be volatile in its designations and divisions. It did not take long for a split to appear between the East Village groups closer to the pop scene at CBGB's—Teenage Jesus, the Contortions, among others—and the SoHo "art fags," such as Branca and Chatham.[65] The East Village groups soon were perceived as central to the no wave movement and the SoHo groups only as marginal to it. This separation was permanently fixed in 1979 with the release of the *No New York* album, that canonical no wave compilation, which included only the East Village bands. This did not stop SoHo art rock from flourishing, if only within its own antiseptic domain, increasingly alienated from no wave and poised to fill the void in borderline music, under the guise of the new downtown, when the no wave boomlet fizzled.

This geographical and brand-name split was reflective of important aesthetic differences between East Village no wave and the new SoHo downtown sound and correspondingly of important differences in the media constituencies that promoted them. The punk component of no wave survived only as a pale residue in the new downtown music. The shock aesthetic, now rid of its confrontative aspects, was reduced to formal experiments with jarring and loud timbres outside the conventional range of musicality. Minimalism played only a subsidiary role and was bereft of any references to creative amateurism and autodidactism. The new downtown sound did continue to operate within the vague ambience of the by now generic new wave scene. Indeed, in the early 1980s, it constituted the third and last wave of the new wave.

With the emergence of downtown, promotional leadership passed from the *New York Rocker* to the *Village Voice* and, within the latter, from the Riffs section to the Music section. It is interesting that in this period of intense high/low crossover, both the *Voice* and the *New York Times,* despite their supposed cultural hipness, continued to segregate coverage of "high" music from "low" music (including jazz) in their cultural pages, reserving the Music section for "art" music. The *Times* relegated popular music to its Pop section and the *Voice* to its Riffs section. But here the similarities ended. While the *Times,* in its Music section, was mainly preoccupied with the mainstream uptown scene (e.g., at Lincoln Center), the *Voice* from the early 1970s had been aggressively promoting the (first-generation) downtown scene in its own neighborhood (Glass, Reich, and the Kitchen events). So it was natural in the early 1980s for the highbrow critics of the *Voice*'s Music section to transfer their allegiance to the second-generation of downtown musicians and hence to the cause of borderline music, even though the rock critics of the Riffs section previously had the responsibility for covering borderline music in its no wave manifestations.[66] For the next few years, as rock critics receded to the background, the highbrow perspectives of the *Voice*'s Music section would weigh in heavily in shaping the public discourses on borderline aesthetics and the new meaning of downtown.

In the now decades-old tradition of downtown borderline music, there really are no cumulative commonalities in the way in which the various bands have hoed a middle line between art and pop. But in the first incarnation in the late 1970s, in the music of Rhys Chatham and Glenn Branca, the art-rock border was easily decipherable and highly stable. Borderline here meant "classical music for loud guitars."[67] "The idea is to make experimental music in a rock context and get back to the most basic rock unit," argued one journalistic promoter of the downtown sound. And, rock is less "about the beat," less about "bass and drums," than it is "about guitars"—"The electric guitar, after all, is *the* rock metaphor."[68] Branca and Chatham focused narrowly on that instrument's timbres, on distortion, feedback, various "noises"—in their view what is rock's distinctive contribution to the guitar—rather than on its melodic or chordal capacities, which, though indispensable, were not thought to be unique to rock. In effect, they sought to expand the guitar's timbral possibilities, which they thought had only partially been developed in rock because of the encumbrances of melody and harmony.

Chatham's new approach to the guitar, announced in 1979, was to use "overtones as the primary musical material." The idea was to work with unusual tunings, exploiting the variety of harmonics produced as the strings are being made to vibrate constantly "through almost brutal downstrokes and double strumming."[69] Branca soon went beyond Chatham by massing many guitars in one band, all given nonstandard tunings, thus creating dense multilayers of overtones. The intended result was to produce incredibly loud but grand sonic structures of constantly shifting overtones. This was a "minimalism" in the restricted sense of being a "tunnel-visioned" music, focusing on only a few parameters, mainly timbral, while producing no melodies to speak of and avoiding anything but the most rudimentary chord changes (insofar as one could call these sonic conglomerations chords).

It was a matter of considerable interest, on the part of both musicians and media, of highbrow and middlebrow enthusiasts alike, to perceive a thoroughgoing rock sensibility at work in this programmatically high-art music, in this "classical music for loud guitars." To the question "is this music rock or classical," Gregory Sandow, the highbrow "new music" critic for the *Village*

Voice, answered: "I'll come down on both sides: I'd like to see these people get the grants classical composers get, but their music *sounds* like rock, and the sound of the music is aesthetically decisive."[70] Indeed, there was an almost purposeful ambivalence about how to classify the new music: not the unqualified assertions that it is both rock and fine art, but the happy admission that one couldn't decide what it was of the two, so closely were they intertwined.

"Although this music can certainly be seen as innovative or modern," said Branca of Chatham, "the final effect is still that of vicious, uncompromising hard rock. *This* is what [Lou Reed's] *Metal Machine Music* should have sounded like."[71] This was a striking compliment for someone with impeccable credentials in purist avant-garde music. Trained in classical music, a student of Morton Subotnick, and inspired by Cage and Riley, Chatham became the first music director of the Kitchen in 1971 when only in his teens. He left just two years later, confused about his musical "voice." The moment of epiphany occurred in the mid-1970s when he was taken by a musician friend to a Ramones concert. "I had never been to a rock concert in my life, and I loved what they were doing. There seemed to me real connections between the minimalism I had been involved with and that kind of rock." Thus, he made "a conscious effort to become a rocker" and admitted to being "intrigued by the sex and violence of the rock milieu." But, of course, his music was too "austere" and "concerned with the working out of specific musical ideas" to function as pure rock.[72] By his own admission, he was more of a "not-not-rocker."[73]

Like Chatham, Branca was rooted in high culture, having studied theater and written and directed some plays. Unlike his colleague, he had not acquired any reputation in his art field, since he turned to rock as soon as he arrived in New York in the mid-1970s and had no credentials in art music. In his first musical ventures, Branca (with his band Theoretical Girls) had enthusiastically taken no wave's punk posture. One of his early nightclub numbers was described as "a pseudo-anthem for the no wave: a long, atonal deafening song based entirely on the lyrics 'Fuck yourself! Fuck yourself!'"[74] But as Branca developed beyond the no wave aesthetic, the "fuck yourselves" disappeared from his act and "the atonal deafening" sounds took on a certain detached conceptuality.

Nonetheless, even as he moved toward formal experimentalism, Branca and his promoters consistently emphasized his rock 'n' roll moorings. His massive guitar bands reportedly exhibited "the power of rock and roll in such a primal, intimidating way that one [could not] help getting goose flesh at the sight."[75] "'Experimental' is [one] popular way to describe my music, but I guess I think of it as rock 'n' roll," said Branca, who made no bones about his music being "vicious and violent." Yet since "none of [rock has] been particularly original," he needed to transcend it. "I don't want to mislead people into thinking I play pogo music because it's certainly not that."[76] This qualification did not prevent Branca onstage from "contort[ing] himself like a rock star in the last throes of divine ecstasy."[77] And in interviews he did speak "fluent rock 'n' roll." There were plenty of "likes," "you knows," and "I means."[78]

What more than anything confirmed the rock credentials of the new downtown was its somewhat warm reception in the rock clubs, such as Hurrah's, Tier 3, and even CBGB's. The *Voice* Music section critic was "surprised to see people dancing to Rhys Chatham's new piece" at one such club.[79] Branca insisted that "the ideal environment" for his music "is a small, sleazy club at about three in the morning."[80] There was no need for him to cater to the "stereotype of the 'modern music concert'"—the "small, polite group of people assembled in some dingy hall for a program of academically uninteresting, knottily dissonant music."[81] His concerts attracted "hundreds of people," "eager crowds, packed so tightly into the performance space that they can't move," cheering "after every movement, like an ill-bred classical audience."[82]

Even while doling out praise to them for their experimentations with rock, critics were constantly reminding readers that Chatham's and Branca's aesthetic was, for all that, ultimately a high-culture aesthetic—not merely art rock in the manner of new wave, but high art with a rock foundation. Sandow of the *Voice* zealously sought to establish the artistic credentials of the new downtown music in the face of resistance from his uptown highbrow colleagues. Chatham's and Branca's work, he insisted, "should be heard not just in clubs and in art spaces, but on new music series of all kinds, even at the Group for Contemporary Music, where it would probably cause riots." "I want to hear [them] blasting away from an orthodox contemporary music stage" (e.g., the Brooklyn Academy of Music, the Whitney Museum, or Alice Tully Hall at Lincoln Center). "The minority who don't flee in outraged shock may never think of music in the same way again."[83]

Sandow accentuated to his readers that Chatham's and Branca's music is not merely rock music that uses classical techniques. For the "classical structures come right to the surface of the music; in fact they *become* the music—there are no tunes, no words, nothing but patterns." In fact, by dominating the rock material, the "classical" structures and components, strangely enough, release what is "pure" to rock, thus generating a music that is "more basic than almost any rock you'll hear." The result, it appears, is a seamless synthesis of classical and rock, a borderline music that erases the borderline. "Chatham's fusion of rock and new music" is "elegant" and "uncompromising," both "brash and punky" and "severe and classical."[84]

"For a long time," said Branca, "I wanted to call my music rock." But as he moved toward "large, full-length, full-evening, ensemble pieces," he thought it appropriate to refer to his work as "symphonies" and to perceive himself as a "composer."[85] Sandow avidly took up this line, avowing that though he "used to think that [Branca's] work was powerful but compositionally rough," he now viewed him as "frighteningly good, one of the best composers alive."[86] There was some worry that Branca's development as a composer might be "impeded by his inability to read music with any fluency." His symphonies were notated, "but in a kind of shorthand that does not correspond to conventional notation." Rockwell turned this apparent deficiency to advantage by casting Branca as an exemplar "of the post-literate avant-gardism that has sprung up in the electronic era—an era in which the recording studio and electronics provide the 'permanent' documentation that written notation used to provide."[87]

Aftermath (1982 and Onward)

By 1982 there was a flourishing downtown music scene, altogether committed to a borderline aesthetic but moving in various directions, no longer reducible simply to "classical music for loud guitars." *New York Rocker* published a special issue, "That Downtown Sound . . . from A to Z," with thumbnail sketches of musicians and venues.[88] The list of over thirty musicians, in addition to Branca and Chatham, included Laurie Anderson, Robert Ashley, the Avant Squares, Barbara Ess, the Golden Palominos (Arto Lindsay, David Van Tieghem, and John Zorn, among others), the Love of Life Orchestra (led by Peter Gordon), Mofungo, and Sonic Youth.

In the lead article, Tim Carr, the special projects director at the Kitchen, asserted that downtown was now the leading edge in the New York music scene, whether pop or art—the proper successor to the new wave that otherwise was degenerating into self-nostalgia. The generic label "downtown" referred no longer merely to SoHo, that "primordial" site of "incubation" turned "into an affluent Disneyland," but to a "wide swatch of lower Manhattan, from Alphabet City to the Fulton Fish Market, NoHo to TriBeCa," to which artists escaping gentrification had fled. Appearing typically alongside "performance art," "poetry marathons, experimental theater," and "video screenings," these "rockers turned artists" and "artists turned rockers," driven by "high-minded art ideas," were "mellow[ing] the wacky drive of rock 'n' roll," thereby coming up with a "glorious sound" for a fresh "new rock." They disproved the old adage that "the butt can move the brain, but the brain can't move the butt" by encouraging audiences "to do less sitting on their brains and more dancing in their heads." Art is not a "tarnish" on rock coming from alien sources, since it is "through its natural evolution that rock has come to share a turf with art." Despite "having lost a little innocence in the process," this "art rock" provided enough "goofy good times, cheap thrills," and "out-jokes-for-the-in-crowd" and "in-jokes-for-the-out-crowd" for it not to matter. Such, in a nutshell, was the emerging conception of borderline aesthetics, as the "downtown sound" spread beyond the work of Branca and Chatham.[89]

In 1982 Laurie Anderson was emerging as the new star of the downtown sound, with promises of national crossover success. Armed with the surprise 1981 British top ten single hit "O Superman (For Massenet)," she signed a recording contract with Warner and peaked in the *Billboard* top 200 at number 124 with her first album, *Big Science,* a minor commercial achievement not even closely approximated by any downtown sound performer since. By the late 1970s, Anderson had established herself as a leader in the burgeoning multimedia performance art scene in the New York alternative spaces. From the beginning, reviewers were noting the pop components in Anderson's otherwise rarefiedly conceptual performances.[90] Thus, there was no surprise when Anderson crossed over to the pop field with an album of songs from *United States,* her massive, highly technologized performance cycle. Anderson ironically exploited the "rigid" conventions of the pop song by encasing them in wry, slightly disturbing thematic material that ran counter to the implied innocence and frivolousness of these forms. She was praised for her "cryptic yet somehow warmly accessible texts" that "partake of popular song and street poetry" and "yet aspire beyond that" and that embody "the coolly minimalist drama" of New York underground music. Writers also noted her ironic use of technologies (e.g., the vocoder) not as mere "tricks," but to amplify the mood of "mock seriousness" that pervades her work.[91] Anderson's successful crossover seemed to open the door for a nationwide commercial acceptance of the New York downtown sound. Such did not happen, but downtown has since continued to thrive in its own bailiwick. Today the downtown sound is celebrated at the Knitting Factory, where John Zorn is the major domo.

The no wavers and downtown musicians, the initiators of a borderline aesthetics tethered to the new wave rock scene, soon found themselves dwarfed by the viruslike spread of borderline aesthetics through the downtown art world, particularly in painting and underground film. Here again, even in nonmusical fields, the ambience of punk and new wave provided the point of reference. This burgeoning vogue naturally led to the emergence of borderline institutions, nightclubs that were also art galleries and galleries that played at being nightclubs. The Mudd Club has acquired the status of legend as the pioneering and emblematic borderline institution, the embodiment of the combined cultures of SoHo, the East Village, and TriBeCa in the early 1980s. The next chapter continues the narrative of borderline aesthetics in these other media and new institutions.

FIGURE 12

Poster advertising a multimedia and performance art show at the Mudd Club. "The imagery," said one critic, "was both fire and ice, exciting, but unsetting." Courtesy of Lynne Augeri.

CHAPTER 13
AT THE MUDD CLUB

"Art after Midnight"

It did not take long for borderline aesthetics, as it spread in performance practices, to take on an institutional form. The Mudd Club, opening in October 1978, was the first of these borderline institutions, a rock nightclub that was also performance space and art gallery, a site for "art after midnight."[1] It did not start full-blown as an art/pop borderline institution, but stumbled onto the concept after various fits and starts. Operating behind "the unmarked doors of a factory building in Tribeca," the Mudd Club was first conceived by its owner, Steve Mass, as a "disco for punks," modeled on Chicago's Mère Vipère.[2] Once, thanks to the B-52s, it had become "hip" to dance to live punk/new wave bands, the next logical step was for a club to emerge that would provide CBGB scenesters with the recorded dance music suited to their singular tastes, in effect appropriating disco for a punk format. The Mudd Club was the first New York club to fulfill that function. In addition to punk, reggae, and the new power pop, Mudd Club DJs played "oldies" dance tunes or anything that appealed to the reigning retro-trash aesthetic. "One minute you can't resist shaking to Blondie's disco-oriented 'Heart of Glass,' the next it's Carl Perkins' rockabilly 'Blue Suede Shoes,'" but the "cut that got Talking Heads reluctant dancer David Byrne to move his feet the fastest was James Brown's 'Hot Pants.'"[3]

Initially, the Mudd Club positioned itself as the "downtown" dance alternative to the slick disco scene at the "uptown" Studio 54. Perversely mirroring the "chi chi pretensions" of Studio 54 at the same time that it opposed them, the Mudd Club had its own restrictive door policy (where "poor chic" was ranked above "rich chic") and its own set of celebrities (David Bowie, Lou Reed, the Clash, as well as the peripatetic Warhol, who frequented both places).[4] Gaining entry were a mix of "local loft-dwelling artists and new wave glitterati," "fashion plates" sporting the latest punk clothing from Fiorucci's East Village boutique, "*Interview* editors and record company ex-

ecs," and the "funkily chic of almost every occupation, taste and persua-
sion."[5] In the words of a Studio 54 habitué, "Studio was disco, coke, glam,
multicolored and polymorphous sexuality," whereas "Mudd was punk, heroin,
glum, black leather," and "straight."[6]

Under the pressures of its multifarious art/pop clientele, the Mudd Club
soon began to vary its entertainment fare, first showcasing live bands in compensation for the decline of CBGB's, Max's Kansas City, and the rest of the
downtown nightclub scene. The B-52s soon became the unofficial "house"
band, performatively alternating with the DJ-driven musical stream. The
downtown and no wave bands, already equally at home at clubs and the alternative art spaces, quite naturally gravitated toward the Mudd Club. Composer
Jeffrey Lohn, formerly in Branca's Theoretical Girls, recorded his "Music for
Small Chamber Orchestra, Female Chorus and Percussion" at the Mudd Club,
but not without disenchantment. "We were given no rehearsal time, half the
crowd just wanted to party, and the sound system was terrible."[7]

The artists soon joined in with their own spectacles. As the increasingly
successful alternative spaces, like the Kitchen and the Artists Space, were becoming less "alternative" and accessible to untested art, the new wave of
young artists turned increasingly to the accommodating Mudd Club as the
site where, in Warhol's words, "mistakes" could be called "experiments."[8] The
adventurous new arts, such as video and performance, were the first to exploit
the new spaces created by the club's expansion to the upper floors. Eclecticism prevailed: trash culture and avant-garde productions coexisted comfortably, Nam June Paik videos followed by episodes from the *Gong Show*.

Seizing on the idea of doing performance art as retro trash, the B-52s' Fred
Schneider organized a "theme party" with sixties beach movies in mind. "I
went out and bought all those tacky Polynesian records and Hawaiian party
store decorations."[9] Would-be performance artists eagerly picked up on this
cue and produced theme parties on a regular basis, following in the highly
conceptualized tradition of sixties be-ins and happenings. There were blond
nights, monster parties, sixties revival parties, pajama parties, cha-cha parties, and a Joan Crawford Mother's Day celebration.[10]

With the later inclusion of the traditional visual arts, the Mudd Club completed its conversion into an aesthetically borderline institution. The neo-
pop artist Keith Haring, paid by Mass simply to "hang out," decided to turn
an empty room on the fourth floor into a "late night gallery."[11] He curated a
show involving a hundred artists, mostly friends still on the outskirts of the
art world, which he followed with shows on photography and graffiti art. So,
in a short time the Mudd Club had transformed itself from a "one-floor out of
the way bar to a multileveled talk-of-the-town art-and-performance club."

"At Max's and other early art bars, it was all art babble," noted one observer, whereas "the Mudd Club hit on the idea of art in action rather than just art talk."[12] The more adventurous gallery owners (e.g., Mary Boone) were scouting the Mudd Club scene regularly, as were other visual artists on the rise, such as Julian Schnabel, later dubbed by Boone "Mudd Club grads," all "interested in the music scene."[13] While the rock press was reviewing the music scene at the Mudd Club, some major national art magazines took note of special performance events, such as *Cold War Zeitgeist,* a "lively" and "somewhat frightening evening of music, multimedia performance, live transcontinental communications, and 'military briefings.'" The reviewer, lured to the "ultra-hip downtown Manhattan discotheque" by an "unsettling poster . . . rich in Nazified imagery," was moved by a performance that was "both fire and ice, exciting, but unsettling." "*Cold War* demonstrated that advanced art can both edify and entertain."[14]

Punk Art Emerges

The institutionalization of a borderline aesthetic at the Mudd Club, anchored in popular music and cutting across all the art media, could hardly have succeeded without highly propitious changes in the art world, where indeed borderline aesthetics was running rampant. A new generation of artists in the late seventies and eighties banded together around new styles, practices, cross-media alliances, and aesthetic ideologies. The resulting mix was called "punk art" (or alternatively "new wave art"). The Mudd Club provided at the opportune time a facilitating setting for the coalescence of those previously disparate components that together were to constitute this "punk art."

The generation of artists who came to New York in the mid-1970s was strikingly more steeped in mass culture, particularly pop music and television, than had been their predecessors. It was, in the words of Glenn Branca, the first generation "to grow up and spend its entire life with rock and roll as a sort of collective background music."[15] However "high" they may have conceived their own art, when turning to music, this generation identified more readily with the punk/new wave music at CBGB's than with the austere avant-garde music being showcased at the Kitchen or even the more accessible minimalism of Philip Glass and Steve Reich.

This cross-medium, cross-hierarchy identification was further reinforced by the grim conditions of the art world in the 1970s—economic recession, inaccessibility of the gallery system to young artists, and the oft-repeated declaration that painting is dead. Young painters and filmmakers moved away from the inhospitable confines of SoHo to the East Village, many settling in tenements on Third Street, in close proximity to CBGB's, where they whiled their time away. "We consciously stood against what was happening in SoHo," said one. "I abandoned ship," recalled another. "I gave up ten years of art training and my whole career in the art business and started hanging out at CBGB's."[16]

Many of the artists discouraged by the art market sought a second career in rock bands. Such was the animus behind the no wave movement, which was dominated by unemployed artists. But others, while remaining totally committed to their original arts of choice, nonetheless took up rock instruments as a hobby and performed in public when they could. Robert Longo, successful at the outset of his arrival in New York with the landmark *Pictures* show at the Artists Space (1977), played in various rock bands, including Rhys Chatham's, in which he was seen "thrashing" his guitar "wildly," while his "handsome slides" were displayed in accompaniment.[17] "All my visual art is completely inspired by music, specifically by the punk and new wave music that's been happening in New York over the past few years," said Longo later, when riding the first wave of the 1980s art boom. "I wanted to be sure of my visual art before I went into music. Now I'm forming a rock band of my own. I find working with music incredibly therapeutic."[18]

Another artist altogether committed to success as a painter, Jean-Michel Basquiat, spent his early years of obscurity at the Mudd Club, moonlighting with his "noise" rock band, Gray. He was the consummate bohemian regular at the club, "extremely gorgeous, extremely stylish, and danc[ing] fantastically" when not making music.[19] His "burned-out robotic dances" seemed a good fit with Gray's raw industrial aesthetic, to which he contributed by raking combs and files across his guitar, in addition to playing bells, synthesizer, and clarinet.[20] "I was inspired by John Cage at the time—music that isn't really music. We were trying to be incomplete, abrasive, oddly beautiful."[21] It was supposedly a matter of "controlled naiveté," "ignorance as an aesthetic" —concepts by then altogether familiar in punk/new wave music but just seeping into the art world.[22]

The East Village filmmakers of the late 1970s, now recognized as the progenitors of what we call "independent cinema," were especially complicit in their work with punk/new wave music. Amos Poe, who got the movement rolling, authored two films on the early CBGB scene, *Night Lunch* and *Blank Generation*, the latter now a cult classic, named after the well-known Richard Hell song. Poe was instrumental in the formation of the Mudd Club, which evolved out of the idea to form a film company called "Mud Films," so named according to Poe because "a critic had written that my films looked like mud."[23] Rock musicians were often hired as "star" actors in these East Village films or collaborated on the film soundtracks as composers and performers. Deborah Harry, who first appeared in *Blank Generation,* was consistently in demand for acting roles, as were Lydia Lunch, Anya Phillips, James Chance, and John Lurie.[24] Lurie also directed films and provided music scores for Jim Jarmusch's early work (and later for the well-known *Stranger than Paradise* and *Down by Law*), as well as for Eric Mitchell's classic *Underground U.S.A.* (1980), filmed on location at the Mudd Club. Filmmakers also moonlighted as rock musicians: Jim Nares on guitar with the Contortions and Jarmusch on keyboards with the obscure Del Byzantine.[25] In filmmaking circles, recalled art impresario Edit DeAk, "music was the mercury that floated everything. Jamming became an almost obligatory social ritual, an indispensable social skill." Said Nares: "We all began jamming together, playing music and working on each other's Super-8 films."[26] Conversely, freshly minted Super-8s were screened at clubs as opening acts for no wave performances.[27] Among the painters drawn into this web, Basquiat starred in *New York Beat* (1980), acting out a day in the life of an unrecognized artist (which he was at the time) to the music of Kid Creole, the Contortions, and Gray, with supporting roles by Deborah Harry and Amos Poe.[28]

In this incestuous, cross-media art world, the suspicion was growing that a "punk" aesthetic was seeping into painting and underground film production. The connection between these arts and popular music was, it appeared, no mere extrinsic alliance, but the expression of a shared aesthetic comportment. It was as if the borderline aesthetic initiated by no wave, with punk/new wave as its fulcrum, had traversed to the visual and cinematic arts. By 1978 the expression "punk art" began to circulate on the margins of the art world, though its designation was by no means clear. At the Deauville Film Festival in France, where his *Blank Generation* was very well received, Poe was celebrated by critics as the first "punk" director. The first punk art exhibit, sponsored by the Washington Project for the Arts (1978), had at first been conceived merely as a collaboration with *Punk* magazine, the main exhibit being photographs taken at CBGB's. But as a consequence of the spiraling advance publicity, a number of artists from the CBGB scene insisted on being included, forcing a broadening of the scope of the exhibit to include the question "Does Punk Art exist, and if so, how serious is it?" Even Warhol got involved and when told he invented punk, he answered: "No, we just knew a few drag queens."[29]

"New wave" was also gaining currency as an art world designator, making its first appearance at the *New Wave Vaudeville* (late 1978), an avant-garde variety show, mixing dada with gay cabaret and trash aesthetics. Directed by Ann Magnuson, later to gain fame as a new wave performance artist, the show included Beanie the talking dog, a stripper performing with a dancing bird, someone harmonizing with his voice on tape while playing "air guitar," and someone smashing a guitar and playing the amplifier—hardly anyone played real guitar. There was a raffle for a mystery date with James Chance, who apparently bit the winner.[30] "One of the nice things about new wave [art]," noted a reviewer, is that "you don't have to be a pro to have a gig." Of course, she admitted, this is also true of conceptual art, where "you can sling rubber chickens around your head, masturbate, drool, repeat three words over and over again and call it a performance." But unlike conceptual art, which is "sanctified by artistic pretensions," new wave art is "self-parodying: the tattered costumes, sleazy atmosphere and pure unprofessionalism of it all remind you that it's just a stance, a hype, a pose. Pretense is all there is and no one's pretending it's otherwise."[31]

Times Square Show (1980): Punk Art Erupts

With the hype and controversy generated by the *Times Square Show* (1980), the concepts of punk art and new wave art finally entered into the art world mainstream, that is, into the discourses of major art magazines and institutions. A new "hot" art movement seemed afoot and thus a definition was in order, for which the by then interchangeable terms "punk" and "new wave" seemed to provide the right cues. The *Times Square Show* was curated by a renegade group of artists, the Colab group, in a former massage parlor/bus depot, purposely far from the chic gallery districts, with art to match the tenderloin district that surrounded it.[32] After being greeted by hawkers and carnival music, those who entered the door of the exhibit were first confronted by a motorized James Brown cutout that "danced and jerked to one of his records spinning on a plastic phonograph."[33] One encountered "plaster rats scuffling among real garbage around a sewer-pipe fountain," "whiskey bottles swallowing photos of burned-out Bronx streets like notes from a shipwreck," "spike heeled shoes on hubcap platters," a "broomhandle spiked with broken glass," and pornographic fans.[34]

How did art critics conceptualize this punk/new wave art? How was it supposedly connected to the music? Was it a matter of shared formal devices or commitments? Or more a matter of contexts, comportments, alliances, markets? It was all of the above, depending on who was speaking. The art was, of course, "raw, raucous, trashy," "rebellious," and "messy."[35] "Like the new wave music" in which many of the artists were involved, "the art celebrated American cultural quirks," such as "media-hyped, sex-starved mass murderers, idiotic television plots, and useless plastic consumer goods."[36] The art "merged with its surroundings, melting into its sleazy Times Square context like camouflage." The show "subverted" the gallery system by "play[ing] dumb," producing art that "couldn't be defaced because it embodied deface-ment."[37] "Their colors are loud, their textures are cheap and fake, everything we've been taught to despise."[38] The art exuded a "makeshift, casual, carefree air of an amateur endeavor, as if nothing were at stake"—"three-chord art anyone can play."[39] The paint was "indelicately and hastily applied," and people did not even bother "to stretch a proper canvas."[40] The critics con-nected punk art with a larger art "phenomenon abroad in the land," desig-nated also as "bad painting," "new image" painting, and "stupid" art. The "trademarks" of this broad movement were "inept drawing," "unschooled color," "tasteless" imagery, "odd and impractical assemblage," "disinterested paint application," and "a general preference for squalor over reason," all of which was seen as a "simple spillover from the loudest rock music played at the grungiest clubs."[41]

This fashion for "bad art" added further momentum to the "postmodern" return to figurative painting, where the intended look of "badness" or inepti-tude is more graphically conveyed. But the "overwhelmingly figurative" char-acter of the works represented only one aspect of their "breakthrough" to a "truly post-modernist art." The exhibition was also, it appeared, an exercise in "postmodern salvage art," which "exults not in progress but in its littered aftermath, and thus relegates the Modernist dreams of a utopian future to the past."[42] There was also the rampant "blurring" of all the boundaries so en-demic to the borderline aesthetic, "between high and low," of course, but also between the different media (e.g., "between visual art, performance art and rock concerts") and "between who is 'qualified' to be an artist, a musician, or both."[43] What could be more "postmodern" than a borderline aesthetic that operated on all borders? This was the historical moment when the somewhat inchoate discourses of aesthetic postmodernism crossed into the marketplace as tokens of the latest intellectual fashion. The critical reception to punk art seems to have galvanized and brought into the fray that confusing mix of concepts associated with aesthetic postmodernism: the return to represen-tation, trash aesthetics, retro aesthetics, eclecticism, irony and pastiche, quirky playfulness, and high/low crossovers.

There was also in punk art, it appears, a certain postmodern predilection toward art-historical quotation. In spite of its "appearance of artlessness and its anti-intellectual stance" and however much the artists "boasted about their ignorance of even rudimentary art history," the critics insisted that "most of the work exuded knowing references to art history and recent art," "that there were plenty of art-historical models mixed in with the popular culture inspirations." To critics and dealers, it was obvious that "Dada and Pop were the grandaddies of Punk," or even that dada and pop were being merged in punk.[44] Such art-historical consciousness, it was assumed, was already at work in punk/new wave music itself, as evidenced by bands "appearing with names like Pere Ubu and Cabaret Voltaire" and the "constructivist overtones" of record sleeves and album covers.[45]

But the formalist approach to punk art could only be pushed so far, given the heterogeneity of the work of the over 150 artists represented at the *Times Square Show,* not to speak of the heterogeneity of the punk/new wave music to which these works were being compared. So there was an equal tendency to explain punk art by its shared contexts with the music or by its causal inter-actions with it. Punk art, it was said, embodies "a whole lifestyle," a prevailing "zeitgeist . . . that started with punk rock and now runs through just about all the contemporary artistic modes." Most agreed that punk/new wave music functioned as much as an energizer or a stimulant for the new art as a formal model. Given the "dullness" of the art scene in the late 1970s, the young artists, as "naturally" they are "always wont to do, gravitated towards the newest, hottest energy around, which happened to be coming out of music." For Glenn Branca, alienated when arriving in New York by a "closed-off, insular scene—I mean, going to the Kitchen was like going to church!"—the "really exciting thing" was to "go into a rock club and just do my thing. . . . I think the best art has the same kind of energy and intensity as the music I was so attracted to."[46] "Punk art" turns out to have been a multiple-use label, designating certain art scenes energized by the punk/new wave music scene, a vaguely designated zeitgeist, a rough array of attitudes and comportments, certain formal traits and subject matters, and a dense historical backdrop.

New York/New Wave (1981): Art as Pop Culture

Ultimately, what gave punk art its unique character as borderline aesthetic was neither the formal appropriation of punk/new wave devices nor the receptivity to its stimulations. Since the heyday of modernism, high art has periodically borrowed from mass culture or been energized by it while remaining, for all that, high art pure and simple. Such was the case of sixties pop art, which, despite its ready appropriation of garish pop-cultural imagery, was altogether ensconced within the high-art institutional framework. Pop art was hardly pop culture.[47]

On the other hand, the leading punk artists were clearly attempting to work as mass artists while continuing to benefit from the perquisites of high art. Such was the most striking and innovative aspect of their borderline aesthetic. As one art dealer put it, most of the artists "want two audiences: the academic intellectuals and the masses. Music, especially a form as popular and accessible as rock music, is an obvious avenue to do that." "Music's a great way to get out of the art ghetto," one artist enthused. "I just got bored with all the insularity in the art scene," concurred another. "Just contrast the atmosphere at your typical performing space with a rock club: one is quiet, sterile, reverential; the other is noisy, crowded assaultive. . . . It just seems a lot closer to real, street-level life at a rock club." One performance artist found "greater mobility" in rock clubs, where his noise act evoked "applause" and "shouts." "I was stunned."[48]

It was at the *New York/New Wave* show (1981) that the movement of high art toward pop spectacle, implicit at first, first assumed a palpable form. Curated by Diego Cortez, the lead organizer for the *Times Square Show,* this show was clearly intended to follow upon and exploit the momentum generated by the latter.[49] Far away from the ramshackle confines of Times Square, *New York/New Wave* was exhibited at P.S. 1, a former high school in Long Island City, a "safer" nontraditional site, the alternative space occupied by the well-established Institute for Art and Urban Resources. The art was correspondingly safer. If punk/new wave art burst shockingly into the art world at the *Times Square Show,* it was smoothly assimilated into its well-entrenched alternative confines at P.S. 1. Appropriately, the sleeker and more sanitized expression "new wave" replaced the grungier "punk" as the label of preference, as it had three years earlier in pop music for the same reasons.

Having had the "punk/new wave" label imposed on them from the outside in the *Times Square Show,* Cortez and associates seized upon it to thematize the P.S. 1 show, which turned out to be less an exhibition of new wave art than a display of works about *new waveness.* It was more a "social documentary on the new wave scene," the "walk-in documentation of a social set." "Sex, drugs, rock 'n' roll, death, violence, fashion, science fiction, cult and T.V.," which form "the common repertoire of club initiates," were proclaimed in artworks sporting "the artificial colors of the stage, city lights and video screen."[50]

The big draws were the celebrity artists, mainly rock musicians, who had works on display or were displayed in works. There was a "shrinelike homage to John Lennon and Yoko Ono," a whole wall with "photographic documentation of their New York residency." David Byrne's large color photographs were the "most aloof," displaying a "cool disengagement," which, according to a frustrated critic, hardly fit the style and comportment of new wave art. "So, why is Byrne in the show? Well, if you haven't guessed by now, he's there because *he is New Wave*." It seemed that "Byrne's participation, not his photographs," were "the issue."[51] Patti Smith and Deborah Harry were each represented in a series of photographs, the former by the equally famous Robert Mapplethorpe. Harry's expression "never changed," seemingly "stuck in neutral," with that aura of having been "kissed . . . by 'fame/remember my name.'" She was, for the reviewer, the perfect muse for the *New York/New Wave* show, the complete "New York creation."[52]

This "fevered exhibition," with its celebration of rock stars and hip venues, looked less like an aesthetic "explanation" of punk/new wave art than "an advertisement for a Club Med–Mudd Club Party." It was, more than anything, "a celebration of celebrity, about pose and about clothes."[53] The show was not easily distinguishable from comparable mass-culture spectacles or exhibits, such as sports halls of fame, fashion shows, or programs on the lifestyles of the rich and famous. "The sixties brought pop into art; the eighties are taking art to pop," announced Nicolas Moufarrege, the critic-muse of this new art scene.[54] All the new styles and movements—"the 'with a vengeance' return of the figurative mode, the 'Bad Painting,' the emerging nightclub art," as well as the "hyper-glittering Mary Boonism" of the gallery scene—were, in his eyes, clear signs that "art is approaching show-biz as it strives for greater mass appeal in the eyes of a rapidly growing mass public."[55] The new art scene has become a center for "entertainment and spectacle."[56]

This extension of art into show biz implied the transformation of the artists into "pop stars," which complemented rather than supplanted their status as cultural "celebrities." Moufarrege proclaimed "the role of the artist in these green '80s" to be similar "to that of the rock musician of the '60s." Indulging in Baudelairian imagery, he continued: "It is the crowd that is the artist's audience and not merely the gallery-frequenting public." But what "move[s] this crowd" has little do with "knowledge of art history" or "academic training," and everything to do with "intuition and instinct."[57] This is why art must "hitch" itself "onto entertainment." "To move the crowd, the artist impersonates himself, translates himself into what is obvious and presents the whole person and cause in a simplified version." To become pop stars, artists must create images of themselves, or better still become these images. Through "repetitive drumming of the sign," the "artist and persona" become "the same person."[58] This Baudelairian rhetoric was, however, hardly Baudelairian in content. For Baudelaire, the artist only confronts the crowd in his leisurely moments, when playing the role of *flâneur*. The crowd is a stimulant for the artist's future creativity, not the audience for his product. For the "painter of postmodern life," on the other hand, the crowd is intimately there at every point of production.

The labels "punk" and "new wave" faded out within a year, to be replaced by "neo-expressionism," "neo-pop," "East Village," "graffiti," and so on. But the tendency to create art that could be promoted both in the traditional art market and the mass market continued unabated. Such an agenda would have been impossible without the spectacular art market boom that set the tone for the 1980s, initiated by Schnabel's highly successful show at the Mary Boone Gallery in 1979 and followed by equally successful ones for David Salle, Robert Longo, Francesco Clemente, Sandro Chia, and a host of others. Reporters and critics were dazzled by "earnings [that] easily run into six figures" for artists who were virtual unknowns a few years previously and the phenomenal growth in the number of galleries.[59] It would, of course, have been odd to talk about "art stars" unaccompanied by a discourse of corporate interests, astronomical incomes, and rags-to-riches stories. "It's not chic to be a starving artist any more." "It's more chic to be making millions." "Some of us have finally gotten to the point where we don't feel we have to suffer . . . 'the Van Gogh syndrome,' where, if you're an artist, people don't like you to make money until you're dead," concurred Keith Haring.[60] "They want us to cut our ears off," said the by then rich Robert Longo, who obviously resisted the suggestion.[61]

The leading new wave/punk artists—Basquiat, Keith Haring, and Kenny Scharf—rode the crest of the second wave of this boom. They were also at the forefront of the cultivation of the artist as pop star, a trend duly explored in a *New York Times Magazine* article dealing with the marketing of all three. In separate photographs, each comported himself in a rock star pose, albeit of the new wave kind, in the manner of David Byrne or Deborah Harry: distant, sexy, vacant yet intellectual, self-knowingly hip, and utterly exuding glamour and "aura." "As a result of the current frenzied activity, which produces an unquenchable demand for something new, artists such as Basquiat, Haring or the graffitist Kenny Scharf, once seized upon, become overnight sensations." Basquiat, asserted one critic, "is hardly a primitive," despite the primitive look of his paintings. "He's more like a rock star. . . . [He] reminds me of Lou Reed singing brilliantly about heroin to nice college boys."[62]

This turn to art stardom coincided with a second career for Andy Warhol, who contributed some of his celebrity photographs to the P.S. 1 show and who was omnipresent in the "art after midnight" scene. Haring, Scharf, and Basquiat pursued and extended the concept of artist as star pioneered by Warhol in his scenester appearances at Max's Kansas City and other venues of the night. But for Warhol, stardom was always a matter of ironic play, a detached appropriation of pop-cultural motifs. He toyed with the idea, denoting it in his practices rather than embodying it. His practices were *about* pop stardom rather than being directed to it as a goal. In contrast, Haring, Scharf, and Basquiat were literally dead serious about becoming pop stars and were so marketed at that moment when it first seemed possible.

After the Mudd Club

Clearly the Mudd Club, as *institutionalized* borderline aesthetics, was an accident waiting to happen, given the proliferation of the *practices* of borderline aesthetics in the art, film, and music worlds. In this capacity, the club was not bringing together high and low, since all performances and objects that entered into its confines had already negotiated that opposition, either as themselves borderline (e.g., no wave music, punk art) or as art or pop already riddled by the art/pop oppositions (e.g., new wave rock). Rather, the Mudd Club was borderline in the sense that it mediated between different media that themselves had already mediated between high and low.

It was also no accident that institutionalized borderline aesthetics should take the form of the nightclub, given the particular borderline agenda of punk art to develop a mass-market apparatus alongside the already existing art market apparatus. The "art after midnight" nightclub functioned as the symbolic mass-cultural outlet for punk art. The Mudd Club was a "star-making" machinery for artists like Basquiat, to complement the celebrity-making machinery of the traditional gallery. It was art as entertainment, art as hip, art in the streets, art as grit, art as B movie, and so on. Glimmers of this had existed before, in the Montmartre cabarets or among the beat poets (who were mythological precursors of the Mudd Club crowd), but never before had it seemed so possible or desirable for art to cross the line into pop while remaining art, for the art world to merge with the pop world without losing its specificity and in particular its traditional markets.

When the Mudd Club closed in spring of 1983, other clubs stood in line to carry on its borderline functions, but with even more panache. Indeed, an early competitor, Club 57, on St. Mark's Place in the East Village, appeared on the scene only a few months after the birth of the Mudd Club. Managed by performance artist Ann Magnuson, Club 57 followed in the silly pastiche tradition of the *New Wave Vaudeville* show. There were cheesy horror flicks every Monday night (*Invasion of the B-Girls, She Demons*, and *Hercules in the Haunted World*) evoking audience repartees, fifties kitsch performance parties (pajama parties, majorette baton twirling, Elvis Presley memorial), and various one-night art exhibits (e.g., of Kenny Scharf's space age Jetsons paintings and toy dinosaurs glued to objects).[63] Club 57 positioned itself as the "other" to the Mudd Club, "a sort of frat house gone wild, a playpen of fanciful make believe" with its "sweet and silly conceits," over against "Mudd's post-punk aloofness and ultracool severity."[64] As Scharf, an habitué of Club 57, put it, "It was like two camps. We called ourselves the Groovy camp, and they were the Cool. We were more like up. They were more cold. Heroin! It was basically heroin versus psychedelics." Basquiat said: "Aesthetically I really hated the Club 57. I thought it was silly."[65]

Basquiat was more pleased with the resplendent and slick "art after midnight" clubs that followed after the demise of the Mudd Club, such as Danceteria, Area, and the Palladium. Danceteria was the first club carefully conceived from the beginning as a borderline-aesthetic institution. "Where else could you go at 5 o'clock in the morning to have a drink, buy, sell, or take drugs, run into the Rolling Stones, watch X-rated Keith Haring videos, see murals by Kenny Scharf, and dance?" Operating without a license, Danceteria was closed down after a few months, but the flame quickly passed to Area in the fall of 1983, which took the art-curatorial approach to the club scene a step further.[66] Expanding on the concept of theme party, the club was completely rebuilt every six weeks along an altogether enigmatic motif, such as "Indeterminate," "Faith," "Gnarly," and "Body Oddities."[67] Area paid artists for materials and provided them with carpenters to create large-scale installations or sculptures along these themes. The result was "a museum room gone wild, a gallery where you can drink, dance, and let go."[68] The roster of contributing "art stars" included Sol Lewitt, Sandro Chia, Clemente; the threesome of Basquiat, Haring, and Scharf; and, of course, Warhol, whose installation was himself as a statue standing in an alcove.[69] In the midst of all of this, patrons danced to live and recorded music.

In 1985 Steve Rubell, former owner of Studio 54 and just out of jail, proclaimed that "artists are the rock stars of the eighties," simply echoing what critics had been saying for a few years. So, quite naturally, he opened the most ostentatious of the "art after midnight" clubs, the Palladium, a high-tech synthesis of Studio 54 and Area, where, he said, "uptown meets downtown."[70] It seemed as if anyone who mattered in the hot new art world was co-opted into the Palladium agenda. Henry Geldzahler, former curator for the Metropolitan Museum and presently New York's art commissioner, was hired to curate the club's permanent exhibit. Haring painted the backdrop for the dance floor; Clemente, the murals for ceilings and walls; Basquiat provided large canvases for the bar area; Scharf "customized" the bathrooms and telephone booths with lurid fake fur and kitsch statuettes; and Fischl, Anderson, and Salle composed videos for the massive banks of monitors.[71] "The truth is that in this environment, the art looks sensationally good," said the *New*

Yorker art critic. Basquiat's and Haring's paintings "set a standard for disco art, a new form whose time has clearly come."[72]

Gallery "Clubism"

As nightclubs became quasi-galleries, galleries became quasi-nightclubs. Such was especially the case in the East Village in the early eighties, where the new gallery scene positioned itself against SoHo's sleek austerity as the arena of clutter and fun. Indeed, the East Village's "hottest" gallery was the Fun Gallery, headed not by a traditional art world habitué, but by an underground film star and retro-fifties "blond bombshell," Patti Astor, who had never beforehand sold a painting. The Fun began with an exhibit of the work of the Contortions' keyboard player and soon achieved celebrity status with major shows of Scharf's and Basquiat's work just when they were becoming the rage of the alternative art scene.[73] By 1984 the East Village art scene had spawned sixty new galleries.[74]

In a breathless panegyric on the East Village galleries, Moufarrege described the typical East Village opening as "high festival: the art all-exuberant, floating, dancing, mocking, childish and blissful, summoning freedom above all things, affirming joy and planetary awareness." "The galleries aren't heated but the crowds are coming—because the art is hot." "High and low art intermingle, causing a headiness in the streets and in the arteries and veins." The art is "personal, funny, provocative, reckless, and ambitious." It is "rife with vitalism, it gushes forth wildly with a kind of no-holds-barred intoxication." This was exactly the kind of art that Moufarrege had been calling for, the kind that "moved the mob" by "providing entertainment and spectacle."[75] Indeed, others noted that the art "imagery" in these galleries was definitely "easier for the average person to understand—paintings of Fred Flintstone, silk-screens of Kraft grape-jelly jars, poems about Ozzie Nelson," and "performance art featuring live versions of 'The Dating Game.'" How could the crowd not be drawn to paintings that looked like fun, produced by artists who seemed to be having fun? Said painter Kenny Scharf: "O.K., it's like I want to have fun when I'm painting. And I want people to have fun looking at the paintings. When I think, what should I do next? I think: more, newer, better, nower, funner."[76]

Moufarrege's "crowd" was by no means the "riffraff," the lowbrow element, or the amorphous mass that this word might evoke. Nor was it the ragtag bohemia of old. This was a high-middlebrow mass culture at work with aspirations toward high-middle-class income or better. The "crowd" at the "fun" galleries was "a blue-chip bohemia where artists talk tax shelters more than politics, and where American Express Gold Cards are more emblematic than garrets." The "crowd," it seemed, simply shared the same values as the "art stars" it was adulating, which were no different than those of the "yuppies uptown." This was apparently a trend-setting bohemia that "titillated" rather than "shocked": people were more often "desperately seeking its style." "Just as bohemians have grown more like yuppies, so a credit-card culture dizzy with consumption has grown instantly eager for the product of bohemia." Designers in gritty Avenue A shops barely had time to hand up their creations before "buyers from Macy's [were] down here scrounging for it."[77]

Critics and the new breed of cultural theorists bemoaned this new avant-garde culture that so obviously embraced capitalism, in contrast with bohemias of yore that supposedly resisted its incursions. This raised "the question of whether a bohemia that is instantly co-opted and exploited for commercial purposes, both by the artists themselves and by others, has lost its function in society."[78] For critic-theorist Craig Owens, the East Village was merely "a *simulacrum* of the [bohemian] social formation from which the modernist avant-garde first emerged."[79] It had all the external trappings, but ultimately was only mass (middlebrow) culture masquerading as bohemia. This new "bohemia" was being widely critiqued for its role in the gentrification of the East Village, one of the last Manhattan vestiges of immigrant culture. It was the first wave (the avant-garde) of gentrification, to be succeeded by doctors and other professionals. "If the old image of bohemia was falling off the edge of the earth, now it's building a condo on the edge of the earth."[80]

In their attempts at entertainment for this "fun" crowd, the East Village galleries seemed increasingly to be converging with the nightclub scene. "Openings and clubs are becoming hard to distinguish," observed one art critic. "One picks up where the other leaves off. . . . Art spaces see their own likeness mirrored in the exclusivity and resulting tension of club life."[81] The term "clubism" was introduced to denote globally the aesthetic of the new emerging gallery scene as it was spreading beyond the narrow confines of the East Village to engulf the whole downtown world. The Fun Gallery is the "apotheosis" of "clubism," exclaimed Rene Ricard, prognosticator extraordinaire of the 1980s art world. According to him, the art gallery had supplanted the pure rock club and the underground-film screening room as the hottest and trendiest site for nightlife exploits. Art, now also a form of pop culture, was outpacing its pop-cultural competitors in the fast-changing nightlife of downtown New York. The "underground movie scene" has "played itself out," Ricard argued, and the "rock scene," that "sperm of the great club period in the second half of the seventies," has "run to water, losing the music war, and now, except for a few skinhead arsenals, barely exists." Painting was now the "big news." When graffiti artists, showcasing at the Fun Gallery, "walk into a club, it sparks the same sparks usually reserved for rock or movie stars." Economics reflected this "power shift." "New bands don't make the kind of money that very young painters do."[82]

The Fun and like-minded galleries, far away from the "cold, quiet . . . white walls" of SoHo, provided artists with a "place to show and see our friends, and to play music and dance."[83] Rock bands soon became a necessary accoutrement at stylish gallery openings and dancing a de rigueur ritual. A typical night on the town for the downtown crowd would begin with gallery hopping for art and dancing followed seamlessly by club hopping for art and dancing. Such practices quickly spread beyond the hermetic confines of New York downtown even to provincial outposts in mid-America. Each city soon had its own Village-style bohemian art/rock scene, its "funky" galleries sporting the aggressive "on-the-edge" work of recent art school graduates, fronted by the more experimental local rock bands, themselves oftentimes products of art schools.

The art establishment quickly jumped on this bandwagon. There were the monthly "gallery nights," smoothly coordinated to allow for easy gallery hopping by nighttime revelers, drawn by the predictable appetizers and cheap wine, and the prospect for schmoozing, people watching, and not infrequently for partying and dancing. Even the stodgy local museums began to lace their openings and events with the sounds and sights of club life. In Milwaukee the art museum presented a lecture by Talking Head Jerry Harrison, on the "Art of the Talking Heads," to a standing-room crowd where black leather and retro-chic clothing held sway. There was also the opening night for the psychedelic-era performance artists Gilbert and George, set to the dance music of an underground neo-psychedelic band bathing in a neo-psychedelic light show. Such was the advent of the "museum as mass culture."[84]

The end of the art boom in the later 1980s arrested the crossover tendencies of art into pop. Certainly, art has not been the "rock music" of the 1990s and current artists no longer are included in the pantheon of stars—Basquiat was perhaps the last. Borderline aesthetics is confined mainly to "downtown" New York and the imitation "downtowns" in other cities. For its part, rock and the related pop musics have severed their connections with the art world, or more accurately, simply conduct themselves obliviously of it. But the trappings of mass culture remain in museum and gallery practice. There are still recurrent "gallery nights," though with considerably less fanfare and glitz. The museums have turned to the "blockbuster" show, with the accompanying marketing apparatuses, to lure unprecedented crowds (in Moufarrege's sense), such as the *Van Gogh's Van Goghs* show at the Los Angeles County Museum of Art, which in 1999 drew over 800,000 customers.[85] Certainly such exhibitions are more like pop extravaganzas than the churchlike ceremonies characteristic of past museum practice.

Nonetheless, the collapse of the art boom in the late 1980s brought to a close the last of the great engagements between popular music and the avant-garde. We may wonder whether this is the last chapter in what has turned out to be a long and convoluted history. Did the New York new wave go as far as was possible in bridging the barriers between art and pop, outstripping all its predecessors? We may question also whether the intense, but short-lived, art/pop crossover activity in New York has left more than a local legacy in the discourses and practices of popular music. Or has it simply disappeared with hardly a trace, like so many cultural vogues and styles, only to be occasionally resuscitated for the retro market? I take up these questions in the coda.

CODA

AS A MEANS OF CLOSURE, I will entertain certain observations about the New York new wave and its legacy that seem to run counter to the themes of this book. There is some truth to these perceptions, but in the larger frame they turn out to be misleading or false.

First, it might be claimed that the glossy sheen of newness in New York's art/pop engagements merely disguised a repetition of the same old rituals of modernist bohemias dating back to nineteenth-century Montmartre. The Mudd Club, it might appear, was simply a replay of the Chat Noir in contemporary garb, the last evocation of the tired old mantras of bohemia. And, like in Montmartre, the initiative seems mainly to have come from the avant-garde. Does this mean that, in the past century, there have been no irreversible transformations in the relations between popular music and avant-garde high culture, that the different historical moments that this book has studied collectively amount to no more than a return of the same? Were there no irreversible shifts from Montmartre to the Parisian Jazz Age to bebop, the Beatles, and finally the Mudd Club?

Meanwhile, the great alliance between pop and art, acted out during the period of the new wave, seems since then to have fizzled to no effect. In the various "indie rock" centers that followed upon the demise of New York's new wave—Washington, D.C., Austin, Minneapolis, and Seattle—the local punk bands avoided the art world and in some instances defined themselves against it. New York new wave seems to have been a historical dead end. Finally, must we not conclude that there is no longer any distinction between high culture and pop culture? What remains is a heterogeneous and nonhierarchical mix of niche markets—classical music, jazz, electronica, dance, and so on—all jostling against each other on a flattened cultural plane. In the words of a recent book, "nobrow" is the prevailing physiognomy of cultural space.[1]

I   I have no difficulty with the idea that the Mudd Club represented a kind of return to Montmartre, since it did bring to completion a tradition that started with Montmartre. There is no question that New York, since World War II, has been a site for the continual replaying of the bohemian rituals of modernist European provenance. The 1980s "art after midnight" venues of New York, in bringing art and pop together "on the same stage," were roughly following the same performance format as the artistic cabarets that effectively were their ancestors. The fact that the transactions between New York art and pop took place at a relatively "low-tech" level—the privileging of live over recorded performance, the plastic over the video-electronic arts—makes the assimilation to dowdy old Montmartre even more plausible.

But this is only one side of the story and the less interesting. The New York art/pop world operated in an altogether different universe than that of nineteenth-century Paris, reflecting the latter only along its shimmering surfaces. This is by all accounts what postmodernism does, which is to remix the familiar materials of modernism in an altogether unfamiliar way. So while the cabaret spectacles of Montmartre were situated outside the Parisian art institutions—at some *cultural* distance from the galleries of the rue Lafitte, the salons at the Palais d'Industrie, and even the riotous poetic *cénacles* of the Latin Quarter—the Mudd Club, the Palladium, the *Times Square Show* and the Fun Gallery operated quite centrally in the downtown New York art world. No longer a fringe activity, nightlife altogether permeated the New York art institutions, where "clubism" was the ruling fashion for exhibiting paintings and underground film. Montmartre's engagements of high and low were firmly consigned to the arena of secondary aesthetic practices, crucial but only ancillary to the primary aesthetic practices of postimpressionist painting and symbolist poetry, whereas in New York's "art after midnight," the formerly primary and secondary practices coalesced into one.

Nor did Montmartre approach anything like a "borderline" aesthetic. In the artistic cabarets, it was the asymmetrical logic of appropriation that ruled the agenda and high culture that set the terms. Borderline aesthetics, on the other hand, is a symmetrical practice of merger and synthesis, in which it is not clear where the "popular" ends and the "avant-garde" begins nor who has the upper hand. In Montmartre the "popular," however aestheticized, was always distinguishable from the "artistic," however popularized. The Montmartrian cabarets did produce artists of some repute (Satie, Steinlen) and popular songsters with some fame (Bruant, Gilbert), but it did not produce major artists who were also pop icons or sought to be so (like Basquiat).

The most glaring contrast between Montmartre and New York pertains less to the nature of the partnership between art and pop than to the resources that popular music brought to this partnership. In the late nineteenth century, *la chanson* was the most successful, resplendent, and, at the same time, delightfully tawdry medium of the youthful mass-culture industry. It thus brought an enormous amount of entertainment capital to the alliance—which modernists could then exploit to break out of their isolation—but little or no cultural capital. Punk/new wave rock had comparatively less entertainment capital to offer, having by the early 1980s only sporadically made the charts, but brought a considerable amount of cultural capital. Riddled by the tensions of an inner art/pop dialectic, it could simultaneously satisfy the increasingly populist proclivities of young highbrows while providing them with the thrills of cutting-edge aesthetic pleasure. Meanwhile, some of the traditional arts, particularly painting, were finding themselves in dire cultural (and, of course, economic) straits. By the mid-1970s, the proclamation that "painting is dead" had become a commonplace. Thus painting, whose cultural capital was declining, could clearly benefit from an alliance with the new wave, whose cultural capital was increasing and which in addition had sufficient local entertainment value to draw in sizable crowds. Furthermore, the look and rituals of the New York bohemia was wholly defined by the new wave rock scenes—black leather, sharp red lipstick à la Blondie, torn shirts, disheveled short hair, the vacant bored look, heroin, and the appropriate argot. In New York, pop had taken over bohemia and the art world only imitated, whereas in Montmartre, bohemia was altogether an artifact of the art world.

Thus there occurred, in the historical interval bounded by Montmartre and the Mudd Club, a massive change in the cultural positioning of popular music that requires a decidedly different account of even the superficial similarities between these two worlds. In Montmartre the fact that the avant-garde were the primary initiators in art/pop engagements was a mark of their overwhelming advantage in cultural capital over the popular. In New York that same fact was more an indicator of cultural weakness on the part of the avant-garde, which turned to the new wave not only to accrue some of its hip cultural capital by association, but also to draw upon its energy, scavenge its formal devices, and assume its postures. Finally, it must be emphasized that new wave was itself by no means passive in the engagements between high and low. If the avant-garde took the leadership in *explicit* engagements between art and pop (where also a number of pop musicians were clearly active, e.g., David Byrne), the new wave had from the beginning engaged in an *implicit* art/pop dialectic that made possible and helped define the later explicit exchanges between New York art and pop worlds.

Thus, in tracing the narrative of high/low engagements from Montmartre to the Mudd Club, this book does not come "full circle," but at best "full spiral." The Mudd Club was a symptom of the cultural triumph of the "popular," whereas Montmartre only signaled its rise as a stimulant and ally for modernist practice.

II   This stark contrast between the Mudd Club and the Montmartrian cabarets is by no means due only to the innovations wrought by the New York new wave but, as this book has amply shown, is the cumulative result of much cultural work done in the century-long interval between Montmartre and the Mudd Club, to which the new wave only added the final twist. Each of the cultural moments I have analyzed went significantly beyond the previous ones, while building on them, in breaking barriers between high and low and empowering popular music. There were also periods of retrenchment between these moments, intervals in which the barriers were partially restored and popular music partially decertified, but these did not sustain themselves in the long run. From the Jazz Age to the bebop revolution to the accreditation of rock in the 1960s and ultimately to the Mudd Club, not only were the cultural gains made by the "popular" in the earlier moments superseded in the later, but a qualitative change was effected at each stage in the relation between high and low.

Clearly, such qualitative transformations were at work in the Jazz Age and during the bebop revolution. French popular song of the nineteenth century never achieved the status accorded to jazz in the 1920s by Parisian high culture—that of being a truly avant-garde popular music, a popular music construed as both utterly modern and utterly primitive. French popular song had to be upgraded to share the same stage in the cabarets with the modernist arts. Milhaud appropriated jazz in an "authenticist" manner; he did not upgrade it. And bebop, by actively engaging with avant-garde practice, reversed a century-old condition of disempowerment for popular music affecting even 1920s jazz, which, whatever its intimate connections with the European avant-garde, remained for all that a passive beneficiary. But what are we to say of the cultural accreditation of rock music in the mid-1960s? Did rock's transition from entertainment to art at that time really represent a qualitative advance in cultural empowerment over the similar transition effected by jazz in the 1940s? Did it further transform the terms of engagement between high and low? Or did rock simply follow in the footsteps of jazz, accumulating the same kinds of cultural benefits in the same manner?

In point of fact, there are glaring contrasts between rock's transition to art in the 1960s and that of modern jazz two decades before. In the 1940s jazz critics and musicians had been almost alone in proclaiming the music's modernist and avant-garde trajectories. In effect, they brought about the entertainment-to-art transition almost single-handedly, with no help from high culture, which barely took notice, and with only mixed and sporadic support from the middlebrow press. This may partially explain why jazz, though by now internationally recognized as one of the major art forms of the last century, continues to operate from a relatively segregated niche in the cultural field. On the other hand, all sectors of the cultural hierarchy, some with breathless encomiums, partook in the cultural accreditation of rock music in the mid-1960s. Rock was perceived by many cultural authorities, including some in the jazz field, to be the pathbreaking music of its time, the augur of the future, a stimulant but also a cultural threat to more prestigious musical fields (such as experimental art music).

Jazz was especially vulnerable to the threat of rock's cultural accreditation, which meant a precipitous loss of its college-age audience to rock. Overwhelming jazz economically (as it always had), rock was competing for cultural capital with jazz and winning. Young consumers with adventurous taste, among them future artists and literary figures, were drawn increasingly to rock, despite the bracing experimentalism of the new jazz avant-gardes, which, however, was not cutting a wide swath of interest within and outside the jazz worlds. Jazz was in a crisis for survival from which it has never fully recovered. This was so, despite the fact that by the 1960s jazz had acquired international prestige that the rock family of musics has still not matched, a prestige that would grow in the ensuing decades with jazz's anointment as "America's classical music" and its accordance of a permanent institutional presence at Lincoln Center for the Performing Arts. But this growing international prestige did not provide a successful counter to the loss of young "elite" audiences to rock. Academicized prestige is only one component of cultural capital and not always the most effective, a point I will take up again toward the end of this chapter.

Rock music's cultural advantage stemmed from the way it and its discourses negotiated the transition from entertainment to art, which was to move toward art while always asserting the music's pop foundations. That is, the cultural accreditation of rock was driven by the binary of art/pop, in which each term is held in dynamic tension with the other rather than absorbing the other. The tendency has been to opt for art that is also pop, to combine art with pop and to disdain any "pretentious" rock music that borrows indiscriminately from art (e.g., from classical music) while losing its pop edge. For jazz, the pop side of the binary simply got overwhelmed by the art side. As the minuscule audiences for free jazz made clear, jazz did not generate a form of modernist experimentalism or avant-garde confrontativeness deemed "accessible" or meaningful for the public at large—in particular the rapidly growing college population—whereas the electronic musique con- crète of the Beatles and the Beach Boys, the surrealist lyrics of Dylan, the ironic detachment of Zappa, the sonic breakthroughs of Hendrix, bridged the gap between modernist/avant-garde art and a large-scale popular base.

Racial matters should not be discounted here. The leading free jazz musi- cians of the mid-1960s (e.g., Archie Shepp, Cecil Taylor) were black and as- sertive on issues of racial politics, whereas most "art" rockers, as was the great majority of new college students, were white. By the mid-sixties the rock 'n' roll market was divided racially between white rock—the art compo- nent—designed for listening, and black soul and funk—the entertainment component—for dancing and fun. Having increasingly lost black audiences to the various forms of rhythm and blues, jazz found itself increasingly de- pendent on a white middle-class college-educated audience that now increas- ingly was turning to white "art" rock.[2]

Rock gained surplus cultural capital from the mere fact of successfully combining pop and art. First, because it could offer substantial audiences for any high art form that might seek an alliance with it. Secondly, and more im- portantly, in the increasingly populist climate of the postmodern high-art world, there was more cultural capital to be gained for a popular music that re- mained popular while becoming "art." The decreasing popularity of jazz thus turned out to be a cultural and aesthetic liability rather than a badge of honor. Clearly jazz seemed more in need of fusion with rock than rock was with jazz, both for the economic and cultural capital that would ensue. But through fusion, jazz made its own contribution to the cultural accreditation of rock, without, it seems, having gained much cultural capital—indeed, it may have lost—and with only short-term economic gains.

Thus, it was rock and not jazz that was prepared in the early 1980s to suc- cessfully form institutional connections with the art world, which, increas- ingly peopled by young practitioners nurtured on the vernacular of rock, was revitalizing and transforming the aesthetics of Warholian "popism." To enter this new partnership, rock of course, had to purge itself of kitsch ornamenta- tion and arena exorbitance and to situate itself more explicitly and dynami- cally on the boundaries of art and pop. In contrast, the jazz-loft movement of the 1970s, far-reaching in its innovations, only played a marginal role in New York's downtown art world. Unlike rock, jazz never entered into a second stage in its alliances with the high-cultural avant-garde—a stage beyond dis- course into institutional connections and aesthetic mergers in which it would be the dominant force. In the fifties the reigning avant-garde, the beat poets, did enthusiastically appropriate jazz aesthetics, discourses, and bohemian practices (the "hipster" lifestyle), but this was a one-sided affair, due to the initiatives of the poets themselves and their critical entourage, toward which jazz musicians and critics took on a rather diffident or contemptuous attitude, if they seemed aware at all. Jazz's climb up the respectability ladder took place more through academicization and secure placement in such traditional art venues as the Lincoln Center for the Performing Arts.

I am by no means denying that jazz has continued to develop in highly original and stimulating ways since 1970, nor that it has continued to push in avant-garde fashion against its own limits. Nor am I praising rock for having, on its own terms, achieved certain institutional alliances with the avant-garde world. In the larger picture, this may ultimately be seen as a mistake or a corruption or an aberration. My remarks only relate the diverse ways in which both jazz and the rock family (which includes anything from punk to hip-hop) have acquired their cultural credentials and capitals, and how rock has won that competition. But to say that it won that cultural competition is not any reason to prefer rock over jazz. As this book has shown, the distinctions between the aesthetics of jazz and rock are complex and always shifting, not easily reducible to oppositions between simple properties (swing vs. a strong back beat, improvisatory vs. riff-based). They are better described in terms of the differences between complex and changing aesthetic discursive formations in which even the shared binaries (art/commerce, black/white, authenticity/artifice) operate in complexly diverse ways.

III   One might still question the long-term significance of New York new wave's admittedly radical departure in high/low engagements. These grand displays of "art meets pop" came to an early end in New York and did not spread and take root in any other center of pop music innovation. In particular, the history of pop music since the early 1980s does not reveal any significant growth in borderline aesthetics nor any extensive border crossings with the art world. There are, of course, modest but lively remnants of this phenomenon, for example, New York's downtown music scene at the Knitting Factory. Could it be that the New York new wave was simply a historical aberration, reflecting the unique conditions of a pop music scene altogether overwhelmed by its contiguity with the Western world's major art center? If we combine this fact with the claim that pop music no longer needs the art world for its cultural capital—or even that the high/low cultural distinction is no longer of significance—then the New York new wave may well have been a dead end.

I am sympathetic with some of the concerns that motivate these observations. But, so baldly stated, they elide too many important factors to give anything but a highly distorted view of the art/pop engagements of the past two decades. First, they are blind to what is New York new wave's most important legacy, which is not borderline aesthetics or explicit institutionalized engagements between the art and pop worlds. Rather, new wave laid the groundwork for what would become institutionally and aesthetically a separate avant-garde sector within the pop music field itself—a sector identified as "indie rock" in the 1980s and mainstreamed as "alternative rock" in the 1990s. "Indie rock" is identified less by stylistic commonalities than by certain "alternative" institutional indicators, such as independent record companies, college radio, fanzines, and mutually networked local scenes. Though commonly associated mostly with (white) "rockist" formations (e.g., hardcore punk), the avant-garde sector includes certain strains of hip-hop and funk, as well as that variety of musical practices that the music industry has seen fit to label "electronica."

In effect, the pop field has not abandoned any engagements with the avant-garde, but rather has internalized it, and this in two ways. First, there is the fieldwide opposition between an avant-garde and a mainstream within the pop field, the former an alliance of niche markets rather than one uniform market. Second, the pop avant-garde is itself consistently riddled by the dialectic of art and pop, sometimes expressed as blatant anti-art (e.g., in punk), sometimes as the combination of electronic experimentation and dance (e.g., in drum and bass), in the refusal of high-powered electronics (e.g., in lo-fi), or in "postmodern" eclectic samplings of even the detritus of pop history (e.g., Beck). Such a duality is expressed in the oft-quoted description of Detroit techno as "George Clinton and Kraftwerk stuck in an elevator with only a sequencer to keep them company."[3] One often finds a resolute assertion of the music's pop credentials—the look, the posture, the discourse—accompanied by an ironic detachment from the popular, or even resistance (expressed, say, as opposition to "corporate rock"). This incessant tension between art and pop is one of the features that most distinguishes the rock/funk/electronic, and so on, avant-gardes from their jazz counterparts, where the relation to pop is much more ambiguous if not oppositional.

There is no better expression of this bifurcation of the pop field into mainstream and avant-garde sectors than the striking and ever-widening split between economic and critical success, which began with the emergence of punk/new wave in the mid-1970s. Before then, since the inception of rock criticism in the late 1960s, there had been a remarkable overlap between what the critics liked and what sold on the market. But today, even after the decline of "alternative" as a promotional category, the rift continues unabated. For example, there was only the slightest overlap between *Billboard*'s top 100 albums and the *Village Voice*'s "Pazz and Jop Poll" of critics for the best albums of 1999. Only five of the forty top recordings in the critic's poll, and none from their top twenty, made the *Billboard* top 100 (e.g., Mary J. Blige, TLC). In effect, the separation of an avant-garde sector from a mainstream sector in the pop field simply reflects the stark tension between the accumulation of cultural capital and economic capital within that field.

In sum, the new wave's primary legacy is not borderline aesthetics or even the most egalitarian exchanges between the art and pop worlds ever achieved historically. The latter practices, appearing in the waning years of the new wave's career, were not needed for pop's by now assured climb toward cultural accreditation and respectability. Rather, what the new wave left behind was the institutionalization within the pop world itself of the dichotomies of art and pop, of critical and economic success, and of cultural and economic capital. These latter structures were built into the new wave practice from the very beginning and may be said to constitute its legacy.

IV   It is now possible provisionally to deal with the question of whether the distinction between high and low culture, insofar as it relates to music, is no longer relevant. Actually, this is not one, but a series of questions, the first of which asks: Has classical music (including all contemporary "art" music) been reduced to a small niche market with no appreciable advantage in cultural prestige over some other niches, such as modern jazz, indie pop, and so on? There has no doubt been a flattening of the hierarchical musical pyramid that has classical music at the top and pop music at the bottom. Classical music continues to benefit from its prestigious concert hall venues and its dominance over conservatory education. But its hegemony is being contested in musicology and ethnomusicology, and in cultural studies literature it is totally marginalized. Classical music's decreasing cultural advantage is also evidenced by the merger of the formerly separate music and pop departments of such important middlebrow publications as the *New York Times* and *Village Voice*. However, given the educational requirements for a full "appreciation" of classical music and the financial requirements for full consumer enjoyment, we can assume that classical music, insofar as it survives, will continue to have constituencies with high cultural capital.

But if the hegemony of classical music does indeed come to an end, would this mean the end of cultural hierarchy in music, of the art/pop distinction, or of cultural highbrowism? Would the ultimate cultural triumph of popular music bring about the democratization of culture? The answer to all these questions is negative. First, as I have already argued, the art/pop and art/entertainment distinctions are alive and well within the pop music sphere itself and will continue to be so long as there is no full overlap between the accumulation of cultural capital and economic capital within the music industry. And as long as there is a struggle for cultural capital within the pop field, with winners and losers, there will be an institutionalized hierarchy of "higher" and "lower" types of pop musical products.

Furthermore, there is no reason to believe that the distinction of highbrow, middlebrow, and lowbrow will thereby disappear with the withering away of classical music's hegemony, though we can assume that highbrow likings will shift dramatically. For there is no reason for highbrows to be wedded exclusively to classical music or to be irretrievably hostile to pop music. The hierarchy of highbrow to lowbrow is not based on a hierarchy of cultural products but reflects, rather, a hierarchy of cultural consumer stances and discourses of authority. That is, so long as cultural capital is distributed unequally among consumers and putative critics, with the highest prestige accorded to the academic sector and the next highest imputed to sophisticated urbane journalistic criticism, the hierarchy of highbrow, middlebrow, and lowbrow will remain in place.

John Seabrook, a *New Yorker* writer, disagrees with this assessment. He has proclaimed the emergence of "nobrow," "neither high nor low," but that exists "outside the old taste hierarchy altogether."[4] He experiences such "nobrow-ism" while listening to hip-hop on his Discman in the subways, attending a Chemical Brothers concert, or meandering through the various CD bins at the Virgin Megastore. But Seabrook writes of his "nobrow" musical experiences very much in the high-middlebrow tradition of the *New Yorker*. He has a distinctive high-middlebrow take on types of music that all "brows" seem to like. For what Seabrook's narrative effectively establishes is not that the highbrow-to-lowbrow hierarchy no longer exists, but that the aesthetics of each class of that hierarchy has undergone a major transformation.

Thirty years ago it was quite possible to distinguish the different cultural classes in terms of the types of music they would consume—highbrows the more demanding types of classical music, middlebrows jazz and the more accessible classical music, and lowbrows rock 'n' roll or country and western. Highbrows were gatekeepers, highly restrictive in their musical taste. Today the highbrow-taste public has bifurcated into two groups (at least), the traditional highbrow beholden to high culture and the emerging "hip" highbrow with much more eclectic and voracious taste—liking anything from Stockhausen to Kraftwerk to George Clinton and Sleater-Kinney, and even the Spice

Girls. "Hip" highbrows are simultaneously populist and elitist, populist in the music they choose to like but elitist in the somewhat inaccessible theoretical discourse through which they express these likings. Their musical tastes are not altogether indeterminate. We can expect "hip" highbrows to be more drawn to experimental art music and to the more arcane indie pop when consuming seriously and, at the same time, to take a camp delight in anything from lounge music to "kiddie pop" (e.g., Hanson). In fact, the art/pop dialectic of indie pop exemplifies well the populist elitism now so much in fashion among "hip" highbrows and middlebrows. There is, in fact, considerable overlap between the likings of "hip" highbrows and middlebrows, the major difference being in the discursive takes and aesthetic dispositions each group brings to bear on the same musical items—the difference, say, between the discourses of academic cultural studies and those of the *Village Voice*. These are the similarities that Seabrook has captured with the concept of nobrow.

The point ultimately is that popular music's triumph over classical music—if that indeed has occurred—has not required the end of cultural hierarchy and the art/pop difference. There is nothing inevitably democratic about the pop music field. Indeed, the creation of new hierarchies and new art/pop dynamics were indispensable factors in the empowerment of popular music, to which the rise of the "hip" highbrows and middlebrows have also made a significant contribution. In this century-long process through which pop has steadily encroached on classical music's erstwhile monopoly over cultural capital, it has continually been involved with modernist ideas of art and the avant-garde and caught up with the tensions of high and low. That it no longer needs *explicitly* to be allied institutionally with the art world, or otherwise to merge with it, takes nothing away from this overwhelming historical fact.

NOTES

Chapter 1

1.   Fiedler 1977, 270–94.
2.   See, for example, Blake 1999; Clark 1985; Crow 1985; Frey 1994; Huyssen 1986; Jelavich 1985; Seigel 1985.
3.   Lyotard 1984; Rorty 1989; Nicholson 1990; Jameson 1991.
4.   Geyh, Leebron, and Levy 1998, 193–95.
5.   There have been a few attempts to provide such an alternative account, but, though useful in many ways, they remain too sketchy or too preoccupied with high culture to provide the needed comprehensive theory. I want especially to acknowledge Andreas Huyssen's (1986) pathbreaking work on the "great divide" to which my work is substantially beholden. He was perhaps the first to clearly enunciate the view that in breaching the divide between high and mass culture, postmodernism was revolting not against modernism per se, but against the high modernism of the 1930s and 1940s, which, both in theory and practice, was unrelentingly hostile to mass culture. Huyssen maintains that modernism has been involved in a complicated dance with mass culture since its inception in the mid-nineteenth century, involving recurrent acts of distancing and rapprochement. I have appropriated this very important contribution into my own work.

But Huyssen's account of the differences between modernist and postmodernist breachings of the "great divide" strike me as somewhat incomplete. The rapprochement between high and low in postmodernism, according to him, was effected mainly by a reappropriation of the practices of the historical avant-garde (e.g., dada) in the 1960s and the emergence of feminism and other previously precluded "others" in the 1970s. Since the historical avant-gardes, as he has shown, were especially conciliatory with mass culture, it is no surprise that the reintroduction of their practices in the 1960s would stimulate a return toward the popular in avant-garde circles. Huyssen has also shown how in the patriarchal discourses of modernism, mass culture was treated as the feminized component of the high/low tandem, avant-garde culture being the masculinized component. So again, it stands to reason that the decline of patriarchal aesthetics within the postmodern condition resulting from feminist politics would facilitate further breachings of the high/low divide.

Though these are helpful and insightful suggestions, they do not go far enough in explaining the plethora of ways in which modernist and postmodernist high cultures have breached the barrier between themselves and mass culture. But ultimately what most skews Huyssen's account of the great divide is the fact that he approaches it almost exclusively from the point of view of high culture and its practices. Such a neglect of mass culture's own contributions to high/low dialogues might not undermine Huyssen's account of modernism, when mass culture played a rather passive role. But it creates serious distortions in his account of the postmodernist breachings of the divide, which, as I shall argue, are especially distinguished by mass culture's aggressive breachings of these boundaries.
6.   See, for example, Cate and Shaw 1996; Perloff 1991; Rose 1989; and Watkins 1994.
7.   Bourdieu 1984.

8. This is something not sufficiently recognized by Bourdieu (1971), who tends to relegate the market for "symbolic goods" to high culture and that for economic goods to popular culture—which explains his tendency to overestimate the historical separation and hostility between high culture and low culture. Though in this respect very much like Adorno, Bourdieu, as a "populist," delights in elaborating on the (rightful) hostility of mass culture toward high culture.

9. See the coda for a further explication of this point.

10. See, for example, Foucault 1980, 78–92.

11. The quoted expression is taken from the title of Hager 1986.

12. The one exception was Jon Landau, who purposely countered the almost "whites only" predilection of both journals in a series of articles on black music. See chapter 8, pp. 219–22.

13. Huyssen 1986, 188–95; Hassan 1987, 29.

14. See the work of Peterson and Kern 1996 and Zill and Robinson 1994.

15. "What Songs the Beatles Sang" 1963.

16. Bourdieu 1971.

17. See Baudelaire 1972, 390–93, 402–6.

18. See, for example, de Man 1996; Bennett 1990; Eagleton 1990; and Foster 1983.

19. See, for example, Bourdieu 1984, 18–62; Hebdige 1979, 128–33.

20. For example, George Levine, ed., *Aesthetics and Ideology* (New Brunswick, N.J.: Rutgers University Press, 1994); Elaine Scarry, *On Beauty and Being Just* (Princeton: Princeton University Press, 1999); James Soderholm, ed., *Beauty and the Critic: Aesthetics in an Age of Cultural Studies* (Tuscaloosa: University of Alabama Press, 1997).

Chapter 2

1. Bourdieu has argued forcefully for this thesis. On Kant, see his "Postscript: Toward a Vulgar Critique of 'Pure' Critiques," in Bourdieu 1984, 485–500.

2. Motherwell 1989, xxv.

3. I discuss below (pp. 32–33) some recent literature that looks at cabaret through aesthetic lenses. Seigel (1985), from whose work I have benefited, assumes an approach to the artistic cabarets that comes closest to mine. But he stresses the sociological role of cabarets as apparatuses of publicity for modernism at the expense of their aesthetic role, whereas I suture these two roles together.

4. I have in mind particularly Cate and Shaw 1996 and Segel 1987.

5. Among other things, Salis had formed the Iriso-Subversive School of Chicago, whose stated purpose was to do battle against a supposed intrusion by Germans into the American art market, but which in point of fact devoted itself to the assembly-line production of religious paintings depicting the various stations of the cross. One artist painted only hands, a second heads, a third clothing and draperies, while Salis specialized in backgrounds and landscapes (M. Herbert 1967, 58–59).

6. On the *petit cénacle* and the Jeunes-France, see Richardson 1969, 27–55; Easton 1964; Labracherie 1967, 18–37.

7. Gautier 1874, 64–65.

8. Cited in Richardson 1969, 30–34.

9. Ibid., 30–34, 49–52.

10. Gautier 1946, 42–43.

11. Huyssen 1986, 57.

12. This all-purpose term included not only businesspeople from shopkeepers to industrial capitalists, but anyone with financial means (including the modernized aristocracy), as well as professionals, academicians, and people with mainstream cultural status.

13. On the bohemian cafés in that period, see Richardson 1969, 98–106; Bradshaw 1978, 35–48.

14. For an excellent account of impressionist representations of the bohemian café, see R. Herbert 1988, 65–76.

15. Oberthür 1984, 49.

16. Today it can be seen at the Musée de Montmartre. M. Herbert 1967, 61–62; Oberthür 1992, 37–39.

17. Goudeau 1888, 51–52.

18. In the words of one young poet, quoted approvingly by Goudeau (1888), modern poetry had become "an immense, forsaken temple," emitting "a stale odor" of "biblical candles and old [monks'] frocks," where "the remaining faithful speak in low voices" (35–37). All translations in chapters 2–5 are mine unless indicated otherwise.

19. Goudeau 1888, 35–37; quote on p. 33.

20. Ibid., 62–65; M. Herbert 1967, 38; also Pakenham 1992, 35.

21. Goudeau 1888, 95, 100.

22. Ibid., 77; Vinchon 1921, 52–53.

23. Citations in Vinchon 1921, 52–53, 78; Bersaucourt 1921, 92.

24. Vinchon 1921, 80; Bersaucourt 1921, 91.

25. Vinchon 1921, 52–53, 72, 80–82; Goudeau 1888, 78.

26. Bersaucourt 1921, 92.

27. For an insightful reading of the spastic gesticulations of nineteenth-century Parisian popular singers, see Gordon 1989.

28. Goudeau 1888, 129–30, 150–52.

29. Ibid., 152–54, 206.

30. Ibid., 155–57.

31. M. Herbert 1967, 32, 34; Goudeau 1888, 157, 161.

32. Goudeau 1888, 159.

33. Ibid., 160–61, 157.

34. Ibid., 39.

35. Ibid., 220–21.

36. Ibid., 157.

37. Richard 1961, 35.

38. M. Herbert 1967, 65.

39. Oberthür 1992, 29.

40. Ibid., 26, 33; Rovetch 1985, 8; M. Herbert 1967, 69.

41. M. Herbert 1967, 64–65, 70, 73.

42. Ibid., 73–74, 79–81.

43. Ibid., 67–68, 77; Richard 1961, 41.

44. M. Herbert 1967, 85–115; Segel 1987, 35–48.

45. M. Herbert 1967, 115–20; Segel 1987, 54–66.

46. Clark 1985.

47. Therien 1985, 149.

48. Condemi 1992, 15–17, 21, 35.

49. Ibid., 15–24, 29, 34–35.

50. Erismann 1967, 78–87; Touchard 1968, 1:115–17.

51. Therien 1985, 37–38, 42, 71, 73–74.

52. Ibid., 69, 92, 126.

53. Condemi 1992, 32–33.

54. Klein 1991, 21–22, 27; Therien 1985, 161–62. Only with the advent of the Third Republic in the 1870s did the *café-concert* song begin to transgress against the constraints of censorship, and then only in matters of sex and scatology rather than politics. The most frequent performative device was to mispronounce, or accent in an eccentric manner, the innocent lyrics of an approved song to produce a bawdy or off-color effect. For example, the line "Viens te rouler dans la mer, Dominique" (Come frolic in the ocean, Dominique) could be reaccented to read, "Viens te rouler dans la mer D . . . ominique" (Come and frolic in shit, Ominique) (Cadarec and Weill 1980, 63–69).

55. Klein 1991, 15; Therien 1985, 152, 155, 157.

56. Condemi 1992, 68, 72–75.

57. Klein 1991, 13, 16–17; also Cadarec and Weill 1980, 45–53.

58. Condemi 1992, 35; Cadarec and Weill 1980, 23–24, 37–42.

59. Clark 1984, 207–10.

60. R. Herbert 1988, 78–86; Clark 1984, 205–58.

61. M. Herbert 1967, 86–87, 115, 253.

62. Condemi 1992, 46; M. Herbert 1967, 85–88.

63. Oberthür 1992, 17–18; Condemi 1992, 40; Rovetch 1985, 20.

Chapter 3

1. On 12 rue de Laval, today the rue Victor-Massé. For a description, see M. Herbert 1967, 150–51; Oberthür 1992, 11–12.

2. Oberthür 1992, 40–51; M. Herbert 1967, 159–64.

3. M. Herbert 1967, 164; Segel 1987, 20.

4. Lemaître 1888, 319–20. Unless otherwise indicated, all translations in this chapter are mine.

5. M. Herbert 1967, 164.

6. Oberthür 1992, 40–42; M. Herbert 1967, 169.

7. *Erik Satie à Montmartre* 1982, 10–14; Perloff 1991, 65–85.

8. Oberthür 1992, 13–16.

9. Ibid., 81–82; M. Herbert 1967, 249–53.

10. Oberthür 1992, 77, 66, 85, 73–76, 73; M. Herbert 1967, 260, 294, 267–68, 257–58, 394–95.

11. Pessis and Crépineau 1990, 11–14; Klein 1991, 37.

12. Pessis and Crépineau 1990, 48–50; Rearick 1985, 42–48.

13. Pessis and Crépineau 1990, 56, 58; Klein 1991, 40–41.

14. Feschotte 1965, 76–77; Klein 1991, 41–45.

15. Cited in Pessis and Crépineau 1990, 60–61.

16. Richard 1961, 36–39; M. Herbert 1967, 50–51.

17. *Lutèce* (May 4, 1883): 3. The series on the Hirsutes ran from June 1, 1883, to August 3, 1883.

18. *Chat Noir,* August 18, 1883.

19. Richard 1961, 45–55.

20. *Lutèce* (December 12, 1883): 3.

21. Richard 1961, 56–58. *Lutèce* (January 5, 1884): 3; (January 12, 1884): 3; (January 19, 1884): 3; (January 26, 1884): 3; (February 9, 1884): 3; (February 16, 1884): 3.

22. Goudeau resigned from the Chat Noir on March 1, 1884. The *Lutèce* announced the "resurrection" of the Hydropathes on its front page on February 23, 1884.

23. *Lutèce* (March 22, 1889): 3. The *Lutèce* articles on the new Hydropathes appeared under the titles of "Zigs-Zags" or "Les Hydropathes" on the following dates: (February 23, 1884): 2; (March 1, 1884): 2; (March 8, 1884): 3; (March 15, 1884): 3; (March 22, 1884): 3; (March 29, 1884): 3.

24. Richard 1961, 56–58.

25. "Le Manifeste symboliste de Jean Moréas," in Mitchell 1966, 21–32; Michaud 1947, 340; Butler 1967, 35–62.

26. Mitchell 1966; see Cornell 1951, 201–6; Butler 1967, 37–38; Michaud 1947, 2:343–68, 3:483.

27. Michaud 1947, 2:363–68, 377–85; Raynaud 1903, 425–30.

28. Raynaud 1903, 432–40.

29. Crespelle 1978, 151, 156–62, 164.

30. Ibid., 163; Klüver and Martin 1989, 24, 36, 48.

31. Klüver and Martin 1989, 18, 29, 31.

32. Segel 1987, 90–107.

33. For helpful accounts on the Elf Scharfrichter, see Appignanesi 1984, 35–47; Jelavich 1985, 139–85; and Segel 1987, 143–82.

34. Marc Henri. See Segel 1987, 143–46; Appignanesi 1984, 41; Jelavich 1985, 179.

35. Jelavich 1985, 163–64; Appignanesi 1984, 31–32.

36. Segel 1987, 145; Jelavich 1985, 161.

37. Segel 1987, 160–74, Jelavich 1985, 164–67, 171–79.
38. Cited in Segel 1987, 151; see also Appignanesi 1984, 42–43.
39. Cited in Jelavich 1985, 182, 165.
40. Ball 1974, 4–5; Steinke 1967, 56–68; Melzer 1980, 14–16.
41. Melzer 1980, 26, 28.
42. Cited in Melzer 1980, 28–29.
43. Ball 1974, 40–41.
44. Ibid., 50.
45. Richter 1978, 12; Melzer 1980, 12; Ball 1974, 50.
46. Huelsenbeck 1974, 9.
47. Ball 1974, 50–51.
48. Motherwell 1989, xxv.
49. Ball 1974, 51–56, 60; Huelsenbeck 1974, 9.
50. The word "dada" first appeared in print on May 15, 1916, three months into the Cabaret Voltaire era, though there is considerable debate over when and by whom it was first coined. The Tzara-Arp version places it origin sometime between February 8–28, and the Ball-Huelsenbeck version between April 11–17. See Elderfield 1974.
51. Ball 1974, 57–58, 63–64, 70.
52. Huelsenbeck 1974, 8–9; Melzer 1980, 42–43.
53. Huelsenbeck 1974, 16.
54. Ball 1974, 63.
55. Ball referred to the "five of us"—that is, Arp, Ball, Huelsenbeck, Janco, and Tzara—thus excluding both Hennings and Sauphie Taeuber (later Arp's wife), who were the only other resident participants at the Cabaret Voltaire (Ball 1974, 63; see Melzer 1980, 218 n. 52). Ball, in his memoirs, never discussed Hennings's performances.
56. Huelsenbeck 1974, 10, 16.
57. Ibid., 5.
58. Ball 1974, 67.
59. Filippo Tommaso Marinetti, "The Variety Theatre," in Kirby and Kirby 1986, 179–83.
60. Ball 1974, 100, 101.
61. Cited in Melzer 1980, 77.
62. Ball 1974, 100–16; Melzer 1980, 75–85; Greer 1969, 306–10.
63. Richter 1978, 77–79.
64. Citations in Melzer 1980, 140–41; Sanouillet 1993, 182–83.
65. Cited in Melzer 1980, 143–44, 148. The classic account of the Parisian dada manifestations is in Sanouillet 1993, 159–81; see also Erickson 1984, 52–64.
66. Jelavich 1993, 145, 153.
67. Ibid., 1–2; Appignanesi 1984, 94–95.

Chapter 4

1. Sachs 1939, 136. Except where otherwise indicated, the translations in this chapter are mine.
2. Ibid., 131.
3. Huyssen 1986, vii–xii, 3–15, 179–221.
4. David Chinitz persuasively contests this too tidy view of Eliot as a high modernist altogether hostile to mass culture. See Chinitz 1995.
5. Personal communication.
6. For an excellent account of the engagement of postimpressionist painters with mass culture, see Crow 1985, 233–66.
7. Huyssen (1986, 189) has emphasized the key role of "high modernist" critics and theorists in promoting a relation of hostility toward mass culture.
8. For recent work on the cultural context of Milhaud's *Creation,* see Perloff 1991 and G. Watkins 1994.
9. Milhaud 1953, 118. This is Milhaud's autobiography, not to be confused with *Notes sur la musique,* which is a collection of his essays.

10. Cocteau 1921, 14. For a brief description of the Deslys-Pilcer act, see chapter 5, p. 109.
11. Milhaud 1953, 119.
12. Ibid.; Milhaud 1982, 99–100 (my translation).
13. Milhaud 1953, 135; Milhaud 1982, 102.
14. Milhaud 1982, 101–2.
15. Milhaud 1953, 136–37.
16. Ibid., 137.
17. Milhaud 1982, 103–5.
18. Ibid., 104; Milhaud 1953, 136.
19. Milhaud 1982, 104–5.
20. Milhaud 1953, 137.
21. Hodeir 1956, 252–54. See also Collaer 1982, 116–22.
22. Walsh 1988, 87–88; Jameson 1971, 33–34.
23. Walsh 1988, 88–89.
24. Hodeir 1956, 246, 251.
25. Ibid., 258, 261.
26. See Sales 1984.
27. For an exemplary account and critique of the formation of the jazz canon, see DeVeaux 1991.
28. Baudelaire 1972, 397, 399, 400.
29. Ibid., 400, 402.
30. Milhaud 1953, 73–74, 88, 74–75.
31. Baudelaire 1972, 390, 399, 402, 403.
32. Milhaud 1982, 99.
33. Milhaud, 1924, n.p.
34. Milhaud 1927, 22; cited in Hodeir 1956, 249.
35. Milhaud 1953, 192–93.
36. Cocteau, quoted in Francis Steegmuller 1970, 138–39.
37. Cocteau 1946–51, 316–19.
38. Cocteau 1921, 22–23; Steegmuller 1970, 207.
39. Cocteau 1921, 23.
40. Ibid., 14, 23; Cocteau 1948, 140, 141, 138.
41. Cocteau 1948, 141, 139, 141.
42. Ibid., 141; Cocteau 1921, 23; 1948, 139.
43. Steegmuller 1970, 87; Cocteau 1946–51, 316–19.
44. Sachs 1932, 21.
45. Cocteau, quoted in Steegmuller 1970, 138–39, 163.
46. Sachs 1932; *Au temps du Boeuf sur le Toit* 1981, 10. The latter is the catalog for an art show (May–July 1981) at the Centre d'Art Plastique Contemporain in Paris and not to be confused with Maurice Sachs's book with the same title, cited below.
47. Sachs 1939, 134; Sachs 1932, 23.
48. Cocteau 1946–51, 330; Jean Wiener 1978, 43–45.
49. Personal communication from Martine Meyer.
50. Milhaud 1953, 152–53.

Chapter 5

1. Cocteau 1935, 72–73. Except where otherwise indicated, the translations of French texts are mine.
2. Ibid., 73–74; cited in Ries 1986, 3.
3. For example: "The word 'modern' always strikes me as a bit naive. One thinks of a negro prostrate before a telephone" (Cocteau 1948, 138).
4. Prasteau 1975, 88; Collier 1978, 314.
5. Cocteau 1935, 70–73.
6. Rubin 1984, 254.
7. Paudrat 1984, 141–42; Rubin 1984, 255.

8.   Paudrat 1984, 138–41.

9.   Ibid., 151–54, 158–59 (the first two quotes); the third is cited in P. Rose 1989, 45.

10. Clifford 1989, 901.

11. Laude 1968, 527–28, 11.

12. Ibid., 528.

13. Morand 1928, 118; see Clifford 1989, 903.

14. Steins 1977, 8.

15. P. Rose 1989, 67.

16. Morand 1928, 118.

17. Noble Sissle, cited in C. Goddard 1978, 12–15.

18. Sachs 1946, 103.

19. Prasteau 1975, 86–89.

20. Cocteau 1921, 14.

21. Wiener 1978, 48.

22. See chapter 4, p. 88.

23. Cocteau 1948, 140.

24. Ansermet 1962, 121–22.

25. Haggerty 1984, 30–31.

26. Paudrat 1984, 155; Harding 1972, 58–60.

27. Harding 1972, 60–62.

28. Steegmuller 1970, 210.

29. Milhaud 1953, 120; Harding 1972, 97–98.

30. Paudrat 1984, 157–58.

31. Cited in Grender 1986, 123.

32. Cited in Willett 1978, 59.

33. Cocteau 1921, 23; 1948, 140. See chapter 4, pp. 96–97.

34. Cited in Steins 1977, 83 n. 66.

35. Steegmuller 1970, 239; Milhaud 1953, 101.

36. Steegmuller 1970, 241.

37. Cocteau 1946–51, 330; Wiener 1978, 43–45. See chapter 4, pp. 97–100.

38. Steegmuller 1970, 260.

39. "Opinions sur l'art nègre" 1920, 24.

40. Steegmuller 1970, 259.

41. Blachère 1981, 85.

42. Cocteau 1948, 137.

43. Steins 1977, 17, 10, 5; Collaer 1982, 118.

44. Rosenstock 1984, 480.

45. de Maré 1931, 20.

46. Ibid., 67; see also Grender (1986) for a helpful account of the involvement of the Ballets Suèdois in *La Création du monde*.

47. Milhaud 1982, 103, 105; 1953, 136–37.

48. Collaer 1982, 118.

49. P. Rose 1989, 8, 17–18; de Maré 1931, 27; Willett 1978, 60–61.

50. For a fine history of African Americans in Paris, see Stovall 1996.

51. P. Rose 1989, 5–6, 20–21, 24–25; Clifford 1988, 197–99; Prasteau 1975, 199–218.

52. Milhaud 1927, 22.

53. Willett 1978, 169.

Chapter 6

1.   I want to thank the staff of the Institute of Jazz Studies, Rutgers University at Newark, and particularly Dan Morgenstern, for their invaluable research assistance without which this and the next chapter would not have been possible.

2.   See chapter 1, pp. 10–12.

3.   *Johnny Strikes Up the Band*. See "From Minuet to Swing," in Krenek 1939, 242–61.

4.   I have already argued for this point (chapter 1, pp. 10–12), but it bears restatement at this juncture.

5.   DeVeaux 1997.

6.   I have located ten revivalist journals operating in this country alone, but there are others also in Europe. The American journals were *H.R.S. Society Rag* (New York, 1938–41), *Jazz Information* (New York, 1939–41), *Jazz* (Forest Hills, New York, 1942–43), *Recordiana* (Norwich, Connecticut, 1943–44), *Jazz Magazine* (New York, 1944–45), *Record Changer* (New York, 1942–55), *Jazz Quarterly* (Kingsville, Texas, 1942–43), *The Jazz Record* (New York, 1943–47), *Jazz Session* (Chicago, 1944–46), *Jazette* (Boston, 1944–45), *Needle* (Jackson Heights, New York, 1944–45), *Jazz Finder* (New Orleans, 1948+), and *Playback* (New Orleans, 1949–52).

7.   Ulanov 1942. This date and metaphor were suggested to me by Dan Morgenstern.

8.   See, for example, Stearns 1956, 153–54; Collier 1978, 280–92; Sales 1984, 158–63.

9.   Huyssen 1986.

10. Foucault 1972.

11. Borneman 1944a, 38. See also, Borneman 1945b, 8; Blesh 1945; Berton 1945; and Borneman 1945a. "Head" arrangements were developed usually in jam sessions and communicated to other musicians through performance and example rather than by written score. The Count Basie Band was noted for its head arrangements.

12. The Two Deuces 1944, 22; Feather 1944b.

13. Feather 1945b, 26–27.

14. For two excellent accounts of the history of swing music and culture, see Stowe 1994 and Ehrenberg 1998.

15. "Is Dixieland Stuff Coming Back?" 1935, 25.

16. "Swing, Swing, Oh Beautiful Swing" and "Fats Waller Demonstrates Swing" 1936, 19.

17. The Two Deuces 1944, 33. In 1936 Marshall Stearns initiated a yearlong series of articles on the "History of 'Swing' Music" for *Down Beat,* which covered what today we would call the "history of jazz." See especially *Down Beat* (June 1936): 4. The translation (1936) of Hughes Panassié's *Le Jazz hot* was subtitled *The Guide to Swing Music,* even though the book dealt only with jazz that came before swing and the author was to become one of the more hostile critics of swing.

18. For example, in 1940 Glenn Miller had ten top ten hits, and Tommy Dorsey, seven. Swing bands in particular got 65 percent of all top ten hits that year, while all bands together—"sweet" as well as "hot"(= "swing")—were responsible for 80 percent; based on Whitburn 1986.

19. Blesh 1945, 12; "Jazz of Yesteryear" 1944, 8; Borneman 1956, 47.

20. "Jazz of Yesteryear" 1944, 8; Ulanov 1944, 31.

21. Ulanov 1944, 19.

22. Feather 1944b, 35.

23. By 1943 the percentage of top ten hits by swing bands had declined to 29 percent (from 65 percent in 1940), and in 1946 it would be 19 percent; based on Whitburn 1986.

24. Stepanek 1944, 5; "What Is This Thing Called Jazz?" 1944, 2; Borneman 1944b, 6–7.

25. Borneman 1944a, 5, 36–39.

26. Borneman 1944c, 18, 64–65.

27. For a revivalist response to these "symphonic" tendencies in Ellington, see Hammond 1945.

28. Borneman 1956, 46.

29. Borneman 1944a, 37–38.

30. Feather 1944b, 129.

31. "Jazz Looks Ahead" 1945, 10.

32. "The Jazz of Yesteryear" 1944, 8.

33. Feather 1944b, 129.

34. "So You Want to Read about Jazz" 1944c, 25.

35. Blesh 1958, 190.

36. Borneman 1946, 12.

37. Gleason 1944, 54–55.

38. Borneman 1944b, 9.

39. Ertegun 1947, 7; Borneman 1944b, 10.

40. Ulanov 1944, 31; "The Jazz of Yesteryear" 1944, 8.

41. "The Jazz of Yesteryear" 1944; Ulanov 1943, 14; Blesh 1958, 289.

42. "The Jazz of Yesteryear" 1944; "So You Want to Read about Jazz" 1944c, 28; Feather 1944d, 26–27.

43. Feather 1944d, 27; McAuliffe 1945, 21; see also, Feather 1945c, 16; 1944c, 14.

44. Hubner 1944, 8–9.

45. Borneman 1944a, 37.

46. Ibid.; Blesh 1958, 289; "The Word 'Jazz' Kicked Around Too Freely" 1945, 10; Hubner 1944, 9; Modlin 1944, 21.

47. Hubner 1944, 8; Blesh 1945, 5.

48. Modlin 1944, 21; Hubner 1944, 9; "From One Poll to Another" 1945, 27; Moynahan 1944, 7.

49. "Everything must be organized. 'Attention! . . . Present Riffs! Forward Riffs! Riffs Right! . . . Sax Section Riff!—brass riff—piano riff . . . Scream, louder, scream, higher, riff-scream, LOUDER, HIGHER!" (Hodes 1945, 16).

50. Ulanov 1943, 21; Modlin 1944, 21; Moynahan 1944, 7.

51. Broome 1945, 5.

52. Hubner 1944, 9; Ulanov 1947d, 50; Crawley 1944, 38; Modlin 1944, 21; see also, Echeverria 1944, 9.

53. Broome 1945, 4; Glotzer 1944, 7; Ulanov 1947d, 50.

54. Harvey 1937, 100; "The Jargon of Jazz" 1936, x.

55. Modlin 1944, 21; Blesh 1958, 290.

56. Borneman 1956, 46.

57. Blesh 1958, 291, 290.

58. Feather 1945c, 16; Ulanov 1943, 14; "So You Want to Read about Jazz" 1944b, 28.

59. "The Moldy Fig in Reverse" 1945, 20; Editorial 1945, 16. Not everyone took this latest skirmish very seriously. A pseudo-right-wing article in *Record Changer* inveighed against the "new leftist rabble rousers," Barry U. Leninov and William Z. Feather—the latter named after William Z. Foster, a founder of the American Communist Party—who were "injecting" modernist musical "poison into our country's veins." It also gave a right-wing inflection to the names of leading revivalists, e.g., "Westbrook Blesh," from "Rudi Blesh" plus "Westbrook Pegler" (B. Brown 1945, 34).

60. "Ist Das nicht . . . " 1944, 2.

61. "Delauney on . . . " 1946, 1.

62. "Because!" 1943, 4; see also, "Music Can Destroy Our Racial Bigotry" 1945, 10.

63. "Duke, Cole Win Band Contests" 1945, 9.

64. Trussell 1944b, 4–5.

65. Blesh 1958, 262.

66. "So You Want to Read about Jazz" 1943, 21; Editorial 1944, 4.

67. Hammond 1944, 7 ff.; Eckles 1944, 9.

68. *Down Beat* (August 1, 1944): 1; (July 29, 1946): 1; (August 15, 1944): 12; (August 26, 1946): 12.

69. "Jazz Looks Ahead" 1945, 10; "The Cover of Metronome" 1945, 17.

70. Feather 1944b.

71. In two recent important books on swing, Ehrenberg (1998, 210–18) and Stowe (1994, 223–36, 230–32) devote brief sections to the revivalist movement, though the latter discusses it mainly in its later opposition to bebop or its entry into the discourses of politics.

72. See Gennari 1991, a very informative and useful account of the history of jazz criticism, but that virtually leaps over the 1940s. For a critique of the jazz canon, especially as it was articulated in the 1940s, see DeVeaux 1991.

Chapter 7

1.   By far the most comprehensive account of the origins of bebop has been given by De-Veaux in his magisterial *The Birth of Bebop: A Social and Musical History* (1997), a richly detailed study that takes as its point of departure Coleman Hawkins's innovations within the swing big band system and concludes its narrative in 1945 when, in his view, the major musical innovations of bebop had been achieved. DeVeaux's superb analyses of music and style are complemented by extensive archival work on the economics of 1940s jazz, the conditions of record production, the emergence of small clubs, jam sessions, and so on. He traces the origins of bebop through the career struggles of young musicians and their entanglements with the demands of record companies, tour packages, and various jazz venues. For other accounts of the origins of bebop, see Gillespie 1979, 134–51; Russell 1973, 130–44; and Gitler 1985, 75–117.

2.   I have found only one, very perfunctory, reference to these jam sessions by the jazz press at the time: Feather 1943, 18.

3.   For accounts of bebop on Fifty-second Street, see DeVeaux 1997, 284–94; A. Shaw 1971, 264–311; Gitler 1985, 118–159; Russell 1973, 162–77; and Gillespie 1979, 202–21, 231–41.

4.   "Chords and Discords: Case against Dizzy" 1946, 12; "Influence of the Year: Dizzy Gillespie" 1946, 24.

5.   Feather 1944a, 16, 31; 1945a, 11.

6.   "Dizzy Gillespie's Style, Its Meaning Analyzed" 1946, 14; Feather 1945a, 11.

7.   "Dizzy Gillespie's Style, Its Meaning Analyzed" 1946, 14; "Influence of the Year: Dizzy Gillespie" 1946, 24.

8.   "Influence of the Year: Dizzy Gillespie" 1946, 24; Feather 1945a, 11.

9.   For Gillespie's early bebop recordings (1945) as a small combo leader, see DeVeaux 1997, 411–36.

10.   For converging, though different accounts, see McRae 1988, 36; Gillespie 1979, 208; and A. Shaw 1971, 270–71.

11.   Gillespie 1979, 208, 506–7; Review of "Bebop," *Down Beat* (August 1, 1948): 8. This recording was associated with a current fad for songs with scat titles, such as Louis Jordan's "Mop-Mop" and Helen Humes's "Be-Baba-Leba," which had little to do with jazz schools and ideologies. The Humes piece was sanitized and transformed by Lionel Hampton into "Hey! Ba-Ba-Re-Bop," a major early 1946 hit that slyly incorporated the term "rebop"—a then widespread, though less "hip," alternative to "bebop" (Dawson and Propes 1992, 9–13; Hampton 1989, 203–4).

12.   As Max Roach put it, "Nobody considered the music as 'bop' until it moved downtown. So to derogate the music and make it look like it was one of them things, they started hanging labels on the music. For example, don't give me all that 'jazz,' or that's 'bop' talk, this thing or the other. We argue these points because words mean quite a bit to all of us. What we name our things and what we call our contributions should be up to us so that we can control our own destiny" (Gillespie 1979, 209).

13.   See B. Brown 1945, 34; C. Brown 1946, 12, 20; "Chords and Discords," *Down Beat* (April 22, 1946): 10; "Chords and Discords," *Down Beat* (October 21, 1946): 10.

14.   "Ted Steele Jab at Hot Jive Smells" 1946, 10; F. Ticks 1946, 44–45.

15.   "Be-bop Be-bopped" 1946, 52.

16.   "Be-Bop Invades the West!" 1945, 1. See also, "Dial Builds Be-Bop Backlog" 1946.

17.   Gaillard also recorded with the Gillespie band during their stay in Hollywood.

18.   A. Ticks 1946, 26.

19.   "Ted Steele Jab at Hot Jive Smells" 1946, 10.

20.   "Steele Bans 'Be-Bop' at L.A. Station; but What He Means by 'Be-Bop' Ain't" 1946, 15.

21.   "Feud for Thought" 1946, 10; "Steele Bans 'Be-Bop' at L.A. Station; but What He Means by 'Be-Bop' Ain't" 1946, 15. See also F. Ticks 1946, 44–45.

22.   "New Orleans can't be reproduced out of its environment and . . . bebop is often a poor translation of 1900 classical" (M. Levin 1947, 16). That is, Levin asserts that neither New Orleans jazz, which is rooted in a different era and locale, nor bebop, whose supposed novelties

are merely derivative of harmonic innovations of early-twentieth-century classical music, can be construed as authentic contemporary successors to swing.

23. See the following articles, all in *Down Beat*: "Zu-Bop Now" (October 21, 1946): 15; "Jack Goes from Bach to Bebop" (September 10, 1947): 3; "Czechs Check Bop" (December 17, 1947): 1; Bill Gottlieb, "Posin" (June 3, 1946): 3; also, "Kern Music Takes a Beating from Diz" (August 9, 1946): 15; "Bop: The End!" (February 11, 1948): 7.

24. See the following articles, all in *Down Beat*: "So, Re-bop, etc." (April 22, 1946): 13—a report on the evacuation of the Russian army from Iran to the tune of a thirty-seven-piece band; "Scotch Re-bop" (May 20, 1946): 2—on three drunken musicians playing Scottish folk songs on instruments they stole in a break-in; "Symphony Man Seeks Bebop—Bopped" (April 9, 1947): 1—on the mugging of a famous symphony conductor on his way to hear jazz in the black ghetto of Los Angeles; and "Hears Bop, Blows Top" (February 12, 1948).

25. M. Levin 1946, 21–22.

26. B. Gottlieb, "Fouls on Every Line in Collier's Article on Slim Gaillard," *Down Beat* (October 21, 1946): 4 ff.—in response to T. Shane, "Song of the Cuckoo," *Colliers* (October 5, 1946): 21 ff.; "Champion of Be-Bop Assails Dexter," *Down Beat* (March 26, 1947): 5—in response to D. Dexter, "The End of an Era; Be-Bop Is Dead in Southern California," *Capitol News* (March 1947): 6; on the latter diatribe, see also, B. Ulanov, "Who's Dead, Bebop or Its Detractors?" *Metronome* (June 1947): 50.

27. "Band of the Year: Dizzy Gillespie" 1948, 17–18; "Influence of the Year: Charlie Parker" 1948, 19.

28. Ulanov 1947b, 2; Ulanov 1947c, 50.

29. Ulanov 1947a, 15, 44.

30. "Musician of the Year—Lennie Tristano" 1948, 19; Ulanov 1949a, 14–15, 32–33; Ulanov 1949b, 14, 26.

31. Tristano 1947b, 16; Tristano 1947a, 14, 31.

32. M. Levin 1948, 1.

33. Gillespie 1979, 337.

34. "Zombies Put Kiss of Death on 52nd St. Jazz" 1946, 3; "Worrisome Days along the Street; Biz Is Bad" 1946, 1. See also, Feather 1948b, 16.

35. Between 1946 and 1947, a number of scare headlines were emblazoned in large print on the pages of *Down Beat*: "Big Payrolls, Loud Brass Must Go" (August 12, 1946): 1; "Music Biz Just Ain't Nowhere" (November 18, 1946): 1; "Job Panic Hits Hollywood Ranks" (May 21, 1947); "Things Are Getting Tough Everywhere" (May 5, 1947): 8.

36. Ulanov 1947a, 15.

37. "Whose Goose Is Golden, Or the Egg and They" 1947, 10.

38. During the 1946–48 interlude, *Jazz Record* actually produced two sympathetic accounts, as against one fiercely anti-bebop diatribe: Heard 1947, 10; M. L. Williams 1947, 23; Winter, October 1946, 12, 18; and November 1946, 12–13. The *Record Changer*, for its part, indulged in a few scattered negative reviews of bebop records, for example, a reviewer described Charlie Parker's "Ornithology" and "A Night in Tunisia" as "incredibly dull music," "phoney," with "superficial" effects and an "awful" rhythm section (September 1946).

39. Borneman 1947a, 11; Borneman 1947b, 16.

40. All in *Down Beat*: "Police Avert . . ." (July 1, 1947): 3; "A Jazz Purist . . . " (June 17, 1946): 16; "Bop Gets . . . " (November 11, 1948): 4; "Dixieland Nowhere . . . " (September 23, 1946): 4; "Condon Raps . . . " (October 7, 1946): 4, 17.

41. Ulanov 1947e, 15, 23; "How Deaf Can You Get?" 1948, 76–77.

42. Simon 1946, 18. For a contemporaneous "modernist" critique of Goodman, see Connell 1946, 14.

43. Simon 1948a, 12. Goodman later shed crocodile tears over the apparent demise of bebop: Simon 1949, 15, 35.

44. Dorsey was upbraided for this breach of peer etiquette in a lead *Down Beat* article: Gleason 1949, 1, 12.

45. "Satchmo Comes Back" 1947, 32.

46. "'Bop Will Kill Business Unless It Kills Itself First'—Louis Armstrong" 1948, 2.

47. "Satchmo Comes Back" 1947, 32; Simon 1948b, 14–15.

48. "'Bop Will Kill Business Unless It Kills Itself First'—Louis Armstrong" 1948, 2–3. The issue continued to plague Armstrong, even years later. See, for example, J. Wilson 1949, 3, when Armstrong jibes the boppers for walking "around with them little hot water bottles on their heads; don't even shave." For a more recent assessment of this controversy, see Gillespie 1979, 295–96.

49. "Band of the Year: Dizzy Gillespie" 1948, 17–18.

50. M. Levin 1947a, 1, 3; Ulanov 1947c; Feather 1948a, 19, 35.

51. "How Deaf Can You Get?" 1948, 77.

52. "Nightly Bop Bashes" 1948, 2.

53. "Customers Outbop the Boppers" 1948, 3.

54. See the following articles in *Down Beat*: "Roost, Clique Bopping Mad" (January 28, 1949): 1; "Roost Will Switch Bop to New Shop" (April 11, 1949): 1; "City Halts Birdland Debut" (July 21, 1949): 3.

55. "Huh? Bop in the Village?" *Down Beat* (September 23, 1949): 2.

56. See the following articles in *Down Beat*: "Bop-Styled BG Septet Stars All but Goodman" (July 14, 1948): 6; M. Levin, "Barnet Kentonized Crew Bops, Swings at the Same Time" (April 11, 1949): 1; J. S. Wilson, "Nat Nominates Himself Advance Man for Bop" (March 25, 1949): 2; J. S. Wilson, "Chubby Aglow with Truth and Love" (April 8, 1949): 3; "Charlie Tells Them What's with Bop" (April 22, 1949): 7.

57. See the following articles in *Down Beat*: "Georgia Hip-Dogs Build Prestige with Bop Touch" (April 22, 1949): 5; "Exciting Bop Group Found in Pittsburgh" (May 20, 1949): 15; "U. of Washington Crew Bop Pioneers" (July 15, 1949): 6; "Marshall College Crew Bops Sweet" (May 20, 1949): 5; "South America Takes Bop Away" (October 6, 1948): 3; "Bop Cooling Off Tennessee Town" (February 25, 1949): 12.

58. See the following articles in *Down Beat*: "'Be or Bop' Is a Fine Catalogue" (September 8, 1948): 20; "New Book on Bop Styles an Aid to Progressives" (May 20, 1949): 11; "Moldy or Modern, Folks Should Read 'Inside Bop'" (July 15, 1949): 11; G. Fuller, "The Bop Beat" (January 14, 1949): 22; T. Hallock, "Bop Jargon Indicative of Intellectual Thought" (July 28, 1948): 4.

59. Banks 1948, 16; Lee 1949, 2.

60. "Seems We Heard that Song Before" 1949, 10.

61. Gillespie 1979, 342–43; "Improved Dizzy Band Cuts Old to Shreds" 1948, 3.

62. "Bebop" 1948, 138–42; "Bopera on Broadway" 1948, 63–64.

63. Editorial 1948, 4.

64. Some of these essays are collected in M. Williams 1959, 187–214.

65. Ulanov 1949d, 2.

66. See the following articles in *Down Beat*: "Clique Bop Folds; Gals Take Over" (April 8, 1949): 1; "Empire, Berg's, Bebop's Hollywood Homes, Close" (May 6, 1949): 9; "Royal Roost Pulls a Fast Fold" (June 17, 1949): 3; "With Bop City Kaput, Birdland Only Broadway Bop Joint Left" (December 1, 1950): 5.

67. See the following articles in *Down Beat*: "Biz May Be Off but Not This Much" (December 1, 1948): 10; "'48 Should Teach a Lesson for '49" (December 29, 1948): 10; "Worst Business in Years, Say Owners, Local Cats" (June 3, 1949): 4.

68. See the following articles in *Down Beat*: "Hillbilly Boom . . . " (May 6, 1949): 1; "Music, Where Is Thy Swing? Cowboys, Barn Dancers Romping and Stomping" (July 15, 1949): 3; "That Hillbilly Threat Is Real" (June 3, 1949): 10.

69. See *Down Beat*: advertisement (July 15, 1949): 5; "New Word for Jazz Worth $1,000" (June 15, 1949): 10; "Crewcut Contest's $" (November 4, 1949): 1; "Jazz Still 'Jazz' after a Struggle" (November 4, 1949): 10.

70. See *Down Beat*: "Why Barnet Had to Break Up" (December 2, 1949): 1; "Woody Herman Tosses in Towel" (December 16, 1949): 1.

71. "Why the Slump in the Dance Biz? 'Beat' Plans to Find Out" 1949, 1, 10.

72. See the following articles in *Down Beat*: J. Tracy, "Jazz Being Plagued by a Cult—Jackson" (October 20, 1950): 1; "Buddy Gives Boot to His Boppers" (January 14, 1949): 1;

"Where Are Cats of Tomorrow?" (August 12, 1949): 11; "Let's Dance, I'm Sick of Bop, Is Dee-jay's Plea" (May 19, 1950): 23.

73. "Bop Dead, Ventura Agrees" 1949, 12.

74. Ulanov 1949c, 12, 36.

75. Ulanov 1950, 17, 32.

76. See *Down Beat*: "Diz to Put Bop Touch to More Standard Tunes" 1949, 3; "Bird Wrong; Bop Must Get a Beat" 1949, 1.

77. See *Down Beat*: Harris 1950, 8; Levin and Wilson 1949, 1.

78. See *Down Beat*: Tracy 1950, 1; J. S. Wilson 1950, 1; Gleason 1950, 14.

79. See Ulanov 1952; Stearns 1958; Hodeir 1956; L. Jones 1963; and M. Williams 1970.

80. Two fine attempts in this direction are Gennari, "Jazz Criticism: Its Development and Ideologies," and DeVeaux, "Constructing the Jazz Tradition: Jazz Historiography," both in *Black American Literature Forum* (fall 1991): 449–523, 525–60.

Chapter 8

1. I will consistently be using the term "rock" to stand more generically for the large family of related musics that include rhythm and blues, rock 'n' roll, soul music, the guitar bands of the British Invasion, heavy metal, punk, reggae, hip-hop, and so on.

2. For example, see Lynes 1949.

3. Norman 1981, 187–88.

4. "Beatlemania" 1963; Lewis 1963, 126.

5. "The New Madness" 1963; "George, Paul, Ringo, and John" 1964, 54.

6. "Beatlemania" 1963.

7. For example, the pop art movement in England, initiated in the mid-fifties, was significantly more "populist" than the American counterpart, initiated somewhat later. See Alloway 1988; Lippard 1985.

8. "What Songs the Beatles Sang . . . " 1963. See also the following entries in Wiener 1994, 31: "Dec. 27 [1963]: John Lennon and Paul McCartney were named 'Outstanding Composers of 1963' by the music critics of the *London Times*. Dec. 29: *Sunday Times* music critic Richard Buckle called Lennon and McCartney the 'greatest composers since Beethoven.'"

9. Thanks to David Brackett for help with this concept. The original definition, given by Nicholas Slonimsky, goes as follows: "Pandiatonicism is the technique of free use of all degrees of the diatonic scale, melodically, harmonically, and contrapuntally. Wide intervallic skips are employed, and component voices enjoy complete independence, while the sense of tonality is very strong due to the absence of chromatics" (cited in Denis Arnold, *The New Oxford Companion to Music* [Oxford: Oxford University Press, 1983], 1387). Here is a somewhat clearer explication: "Pandiatonic writing is a specific kind of static harmony in which an entire scale is used to form the members of an implied secundal, static chord. The vertical structures are combinations of any number of tones from the prevailing scale, placed in variable spacings. The horizontal chord succession has no tonal direction; scale tones are manipulated as basic chordal material without creating harmonic motion outside the underlying static and unaltered scale. The harmony has no characteristic functions, the counterpoint is rhythmically active, and the chord spacing erratic" (Vincent Persichetti, *Twentieth Century Harmony* [New York: Norton, 1961], 223).

10. Though Mann's examples don't serve their purpose very well, it has been noted that the early Beatles' music makes use of modes outside the dominant modern Western diatonic major and minor scales. For example, in a number of pieces ("I Saw Her Standing There," "A Hard Day's Night"), they tend to flatten the seventh note of the scale, thus alternating between the major scale and the Mixolydian mode and creating uncertainty about when resolution takes place. Many of the early Beatles' songs were structurally quite complex, given the rock 'n' roll standards of the time, and displayed inventive harmonies. "She Loves You," for example, doesn't reveal its tonal center (and hence its key) till the end of the opening chorus (on the final "Yeah!") and that on a vocal harmony with only a whole tone separation. "She Loves You," going beyond the conventional AABA and AAB formats, is structured fairly complexly along the lines: ABCBCD (= A/C)BCD.

11. Strongin 1964.

12. See, for example, Hertsgaard 1995; Kozinn 1995; Mellers 1973.

13. "The Unbarbershopped Quartet" 1964, 46.

14. "George, Paul, Ringo, and John" 1964, 54.

15. Gould 1964.

16. Lewis 1963, 126; "Beatlemania" 1963.

17. John S. Wilson (1964), music critic of the *New York Times,* gave an aesthetic twist to this view in a snide review of the Beatles' concert at Carnegie Hall that treated the teen fans as the central performers at this event. "Twenty-nine hundred ecstatic Beatlemaniacs gave a concert . . . accompanied by the thumping twanging rhythms of the Beatles. The Beatles enthusiasts . . . paid $3 to $3.50 for outshrieking their idols. . . . The audience participation lasted for 34 minutes, from the moment the first B mophead could be discerned. . . . Through the first two selections, the audience maintained a sustained falsetto baying. . . ."

18. Dempsey 1964, 15, 69–71.

19. Letters to the Editor 1964.

20. "George, Paul, Ringo, and John" 1964, 54.

21. Gould 1964; "George, Paul, Ringo, and John" 1964, 54.

22. "The Unbarbershopped Quartet" 1964, 46.

23. "Amerry Timble" 1964, 109.

24. "All My Own Work" 1964, E7; "Amerry Timble" 1964, 109.

25. "Amerry Timble" 1964, 109.

26. "All My Own Work" 1964, E7.

27. "Amerry Timble" 1964, 109.

28. "Adult Okay Endangers Beatles?" 1964.

29. Crowther 1964.

30. Knight 1964.

31. "Yeah Indeed" 1964.

32. Crowther 1964.

33. Knight 1964.

34. "Yeah Indeed" 1964.

35. Crowther 1964.

36. Ibid.; Sarris 1964.

37. Sarris 1964.

38. Knight 1964; "Yeah Indeed" 1964.

39. Knight 1964.

40. Crowther 1964.

41. David Brackett, however, maintains that the Beatles' music "had shifted from 'Please, Please Me' through 'Help,' but that these shifts were more subtle than what happened with *Rubber Soul* and its successors" (personal communication).

42. Freed 1965c; Freed 1965a.

43. Orff is an interesting and not entirely flattering choice, since he is often described in mass-cultural terms for the glaring showmanship of his works and the harmonic simplicity. It is said, for example, that "his intention is to create a spectacle" and to produce "direct physical excitement." "Polyphony, extended melodic writing and thematic development are rarely found; instead the most basic means are pressed into service to generate effects of wild abandon. . . . There is, for example, no problem in understanding his harmonic thinking since it is so simple." Inspired by Stravinsky's work, he is sometimes accused of having "coarsened and vulgarized his model" (*Grove Dictionary of Music,* vol. 13, 707–8).

44. Even some young Beatlemaniacs, benefiting admittedly from elite musical training, subscribed to the "musicological" line. To two musically well-pedigreed fourteen-year-old girls, the *Saturday Review* asked the "burning question" why should "this bundle of metallic guitar strings and ragmop hair," producing "loud, screechy, and cacophonous" music with "thumpingly insipid" lyrics, "command such fevered passion?" The young women replied calmly to this somewhat overwrought query that the Beatles can be "more accurately" described as "driving" than "loud," and that "by making full use of their instruments and

voices," they succeed in "creat[ing] a great deal of depth." In consonance with their adult musicological colleagues, the two refined Beatlemaniacs stressed the innovative "beautiful harmonics" that set the Beatles off from the rest of the rock 'n' roll crowd. "In none of their songs do they move up in parallel triads for the whole bridge," but rather "get their voices moving in opposite directions" (Fuller 1965).

45. Freed 1965a.

46. Bernstein 1992, 230–32, 264–65. The composer Abram Chasins, in his *McCall's* article "High-Brows vs. No-Brows," had argued that one value of the Beatles' music was to get young people to like music, so that they could take the next step into classical music, on the principle that "the more you love music, the more music you love. . . . The Beatles seem to have succeeded precisely where [parents and music educators] failed—in making music a rich and joyful part of [their children's] life" (Chasins 1965, 46). Chasins was especially critical of that "whole senseless paraphernalia of making music in a vacuum, the isolated drudgery of practicing an instrument not of [their] own choosing and before [they] had any desire for music." As proof, Chasins reported that a number of "children" who started first with the Beatles now had their Beatles' records "alphabetically stored between Bach and Beethoven." In the next few years, a number of highbrow critics would continue to pursue the line of valuing the Beatles primarily as an antidote against the educational and performative deadening of art music in the twentieth century.

47. Gardner 1966, IV, 1; IV, 3.

48. Gardner 1966, IV, 3. Though the Gardner article appeared in 1966, it was reporting on views that Bernstein was known to hold at least by early 1965. See also Cook (1965) for another article on Bernstein at home with another brief mention of the Beatles.

49. Freed 1965a, 61; Freed 1965c.

50. Freed 1965b.

51. "P.D.Q. Bach (1807–1742)? and the Baroque Beatles Book" 1965, 510.

52. Jacobson 1966.

53. Freed 1965b, 57; Jacobson 1966; "P.D.Q. Bach" 1965, 510.

54. Jacobson 1966; Freed 1965b.

55. Jacobson 1966.

56. Even *Life* chimed in on this theme, noting that the Beatles' "added interesting embellishments" to the rock 'n' roll sound, such as "counterpoint, madrigal effects [and] tonal progressions," are "so adroitly done that musicologists openly wonder if the British lads know what on earth they are doing" ("Hear That Big Sound" 1965, 94).

57. Fuller 1965.

58. See Dowlding 1989, 105–7, 122–24, 142, 147–49, 149–51, 179–84.

59. A number of groups followed in the use of baroque or classical instruments, thus giving some apparent substance to a "baroque rock" movement. The Rolling Stones, at this time following one step behind the Beatles, were almost as productive in the classical baroque genre as the Beatles themselves: for example, a string quartet in "As Tears Go By"; harpsichord and dulcimer in "Lady Jane"; and recorder, piano, and cello in "Ruby Tuesday." Other well-known examples are Left Banke, "Walk Away Renée" (harpsichord and string quartet); the Lovin' Spoonful, "Rain on the Roof" (harpsichord-sounding guitars); Spanky and Our Gang, "Sunday Will Never Be the Same" (strings and harpsichord); and the Stone Poneys, "Different Drum" (harpsichord and string quartet). See further, Duxbury 1985, 115–43.

60. Freed 1965c.

61. Shelton 1965a.

62. "Hear That Big Sound" 1965, 83.

63. Ibid.

64. Robinson 1965, 52.

65. "Hear That Big Sound" 1965, 94.

66. M. Williams 1965a, 26.

67. "Hear That Big Sound" 1965, 85.

68. Ibid., 83, 85.

69. B. Friedman 1965, 45, 98.

70. "Hear That Big Sound" 1965, 93.

71. Shelton 1965a.

72. Freed 1965c.

73. Shelton 1965a.

74. Bart 1965b; 1965a, 140.

75. Friedman 1965, 45, 98.

76. In fact, between November 1963 and February 1965, *Billboard* discontinued its separate rhythm and blues charts, because of their large overlap with the pop charts. For a nuanced account and explanation of this development, see Brackett 1994.

77. Robinson 1965, 55, 52. Bogaloosa, Louisiana, at the time was a major site for civil rights strife and racist violence.

78. M. Williams 1965a, 27.

79. Thomson 1965, 93.

80. Shelton 1986, 308–9.

81. The label seems to have appeared in August and was introduced officially by *Billboard* to baptize the new musical movement (Sternfield 1965).

82. Shelton 1965a.

83. "The Folk and the Rock" 1965; "Message Time" 1965.

84. For example, during his folk protest period, Dylan was described by lower-middlebrow publications as a "dime-store philosopher" and "men's room conversationalist" with "deliberately atrocious grammar" and a voice that "sounds as if it were drifting over the walls of a tuberculosis sanatorium" ("Let Us Now . . . " 1963; "I Am My Words" 1963).

85. "The Folk and the Rock" 1965, 88, 90.

86. "Message Time" 1965, 102.

87. Newfield 1965a, 4; Silber 1964, 67; Shelton 1986, 259.

88. Silber 1966, 102.

89. Turner 1962, 24; Shelton 1961, 17; Meehan 1965, 133.

90. Irwin Silber, editor of the leftist folk music magazine *Sing Out!* and previously an enthusiastic supporter of Dylan, was the major spokesperson for the old guard opposing Dylan's entry into rock 'n' roll. Robert Shelton, folk music critic for the *New York Times* and the first to write favorably about Dylan, and Paul Nelson, a writer for *Sing Out!*, were the leading young supporters of Dylan's innovations.

91. P. Nelson 1966, 104; Ochs 1965.

92. Kretchmer 1965; Shelton 1963, 29.

93. Shelton 1963, 28; Ochs 1965; P. Nelson 1965, 75; P. Nelson 1966, 106–7.

94. Letters to *Sing Out!* 1966, 118; Shelton 1965b.

95. Shelton 1966b; "A Symposium: Is Folk Real?" 1966.

96. "A Symposium: Is Folk Real?" 1966.

97. Shelton 1986, 288, 292, 294. In February 1965 the Beatles recorded Lennon's folkish tribute to Dylan, "You've Got to Hide Your Love Away."

98. *Life*, at that time in decline, may have been trying to shore up its readership by going against the journalistic grain. *Ebony* had obvious interests in the cultural recognition of rock 'n' roll, since it meant more recognition of African American artists.

99. Robert Shelton, folk music critic for the *New York Times* and writerly "discoverer" of Bob Dylan, was an important exception to this rule. One of its most vociferous defenders, he effectively joined the folk rock movement and initiated the practice of reviewing rock music, occasionally even going beyond the "folk" pale.

100. Robinson 1965, 52; Friedman 1965, 98.

101. The twist craze was, in part, an adult craze, generated when "relentless midtown night club goers—a bizarre amalgam of press agents, actors' managers, and what are usually called, probably by default, 'socialites' and 'celebrities'—took their jaded tastes to a West Side bar called the Peppermint Lounge. . . . Very soon adults everywhere began to get into the act" (M. Williams 1965a, 39). For an account of the twist, see Dawson 1995. Early rock critics give testimonial to the importance of the Beatles in drawing them back to rock 'n' roll

after having abandoned it in their early college years. See Marcus 1991, 212–14; Winner 1969, 38–44.

Chapter 9

1. There was a small flurry of not terribly sympathetic attention given to the raga rock movement, which, initiated by the Beatles' "Norwegian Wood," was nothing other than the use of the Indian sitar in rock music (e.g., in the Rolling Stones' "Paint It Black"). The *New York Times* gleefully reported on Ravi Shankar's disdain for the unskilled playing of rock sitarists and his prediction that the fad would soon fade: "Next year it might well be the Japanese koto" (Lelyveld 1966). According to a wry report in the *Village Voice,* the label "raga rock" was the brainchild of the Columbia Records publicity department, who unveiled it at a press conference to promote the latest album by the Byrds, the alleged "invent[ors]" of this "new form" (Kempton 1966). However, the "Byrds' innovation burst upon the world with something less than the force which Columbia intended," since the attending audience "consisted mostly of girl reporters from teen magazines and business music types in white on white ties." "Several reporters eyed the offending instrument [the sitar] as though it were an untrustworthy animal."
2. "Is Beatlemania Dead?" 1966, 389–91.
3. "Blues for the Beatles" 1966, 94; "Is Beatlemania Dead?" 1966, 389–91.
4. "Blues for the Beatles" 1966, 94.
5. Shelton 1965a, 40.
6. Shelton 1965b, 17.
7. Shelton 1966b, 21.
8. P. Williams 1966a, 1.
9. Goldstein 1989, xvii.
10. Ibid., xvi.
11. Goldstein 1966c, 16, 33.
12. Goldstein 1966a, 6, 8.
13. Shelton's earlier review, as indicated above, dealt with ten albums in a somewhat superficial manner.
14. Goldstein 1966b, 23.
15. "Pops and Boppers" 1966, 66; *"Crawdaddy!"* 1967, 114.
16. "Explicit aesthetic choices are in fact often constituted in opposition to the choices of groups closest in social space, with whom the competition is most direct and most immediate, and more precisely, no doubt, in relation to those choices most clearly marked by the intention . . . of marking distinction vis-à-vis lower groups . . . " (Bourdieu 1984, 60).
17. "Bards of Pop" 1966; "Other Noises, Other Notes" 1967.
18. "The Messengers" 1967, 60.
19. "It's Getting Better . . . " 1967.
20. "Other Noises, Other Notes" 1967.
21. "The Messengers" 1967, 68, 60, 68.
22. "Bards of Pop" 1966.
23. "The Messengers" 1967, 68.
24. Ibid., 62.
25. "Bards of Pop" 1966; "The Messengers" 1967, 61; "It's Getting Better . . . " 1967.
26. "Other Noises, Other Notes" 1967; "The Messengers" 1967, 61.
27. "It's Getting Better . . . " 1967.
28. "The Messengers" 1967, 60.
29. Ibid.; "Other Noises, Other Notes" 1967.
30. "The Messengers" 1967, 61.
31. Rifkin 1987, 114, 114–15, 124, 126.
32. Rorem 1968a, 23.
33. Rorem 1968b, 162.
34. Goldstein 1967d.
35. Christgau 1967d, 283, 284.
36. Rorem 1968b, 19.

37. Goldstein 1967a, 14.
38. Rorem 1968a, 26.
39. Poirier 1967, 530.
40. Rorem 1968b, 18.
41. Poirier 1967, 529–30.
42. Rorem 1968a, 24.
43. Ibid., 26.
44. Mellers 1969, 181; Peyser 1967, 129.
45. Mellers 1969, 183.
46. Rorem 1968a, 25.
47. Peyser 1967, 126–27, 135.
48. Sontag 1965; Fiedler 1977, 189–210.
49. Rorem 1968a, 25, 27.
50. Poirier 1967, 528, 529.
51. Sontag 1965, 302; Rorem 1968a, 25.
52. Rorem 1968a, 26.
53. Rorem 1969; Rorem 1968b, 20.
54. Rorem 1969.
55. "The Nitty-Gritty Sound" 1966, 102.
56. Ibid., 102; "Open Up, Tune In, Turn On" 1967.
57. "Forget the Message; Just Play" 1967.
58. "This Way to the Egress" 1967.
59. Shelton 1966c, 11.
60. Kempton 1968.
61. Conferences organized around the topic of "the future of jazz" were asking whether jazz is "on the rocks?" (R. Wilson 1967). A *New York Times* article, with the headline "3-Day Jazz Talks Strike Grim Note," reported that a conference on "The Many Positive Faces of Jazz" had "difficulty in finding anything positive" and was reduced to whining about the "dwindling number of outlets for live performances, inadequate promotion of recordings, bickering among factions of fans and musicians, and the popularity of rock 'n' roll among teen-agers" (J. S. Wilson 1967).
62. Goldstein 1967c, 13, 16.
63. Ibid., 13.
64. Gabree 1967a, 20.
65. Morgenstern 1967, 13.
66. Editorial 1966, 5.
67. Editorial 1967, 5, 17, 5, 17.
68. Gabree 1967a, 20, 22.
69. Burks 1968.
70. Christgau 1968b, 26.
71. Ibid.
72. Winner 1969, 53.
73. Simon Frith, theorist and critic, has done the most to lay the foundation for the analysis of rock criticism; see Frith 1981, 48–57, 165–77; 1996, 64–71.
74. Marcus 1969, 24.
75. Winner 1969, 53.
76. Landau 1968b, 18.
77. Marcus 1969, 8–9.
78. Ibid., 8–17.
79. Landau 1968b, 18.
80. Christgau 1967b, 16.
81. On his lack of technical knowledge of music and its relevance or irrelevance to being a rock critic, Christgau had this to say: "I don't know anything about music, which ought to be a damaging admission but isn't, or I wouldn't be making it. The fact is that pop writers in general shy away from such arcana as key signature and beats to the measure. . . . I used to

confide my worries about this to friends in the record industry, who reassured me. They didn't know anything about music either. The technical stuff didn't matter, I was told. You just gotta dig it" (Christgau 1968b, 26).

82. Christgau 1968b, 26. The reference to "middlebrow subterfuge" was added to a later version of the same text (Christgau 1973, 61).

83. Willis 1968d, 56–57.

84. Willis 1968b, 176–77.

85. Christgau 1967a, 233–34.

86. Willis 1968e, 87.

87. Ibid., Landau 1968b, 19.

88. Willis 1968e, 87; Christgau 1968a, 20.

89. Christgau 1968a, 20, 22, 24.

90. "Tapping the Roots" 1968.

91. Landau 1968b, 18.

92. Ibid. See also: "Berry has lasted best. Many of his songs . . . now have the feel of folk poetry in a previously unexplored idiom. . . . The driving facility of Berry's guitar is still unduplicated, the clever clarity of his voice still a wonder. He is a classic" (Christgau 1967b, 18). For a critique of rock as folk, see Frith 1981, 48–52.

93. Christgau 1967a, 232.

94. Christgau 1967b, 16; Landau 1968b, 18.

95. Landau 1968b, 18. For one rock critic, however, the reissued fifties rhythm and blues— "especially the more popular Atlantic stuff"—"does not hold up well," when subject to the "stricter standard" of "earlier blues." The lyrics "are sexually and poetically anemic. The music is less basic than the old blues, more ephemeral, more *Pop*. It is meant for the radio, not the archives, and, more significantly, it is meant for the marketplace" (Willis 1968c, 149). Such a conclusion did not bode well for a rock aesthetic if indeed early rock 'n' roll were to set the standard against which all future rock would be measured.

96. Willis 1968d, 56.

97. Christgau 1967b, 18.

98. Goldstein 1969.

99. Winner 1969, 44.

100. Willis 1968e, 87.

101. "The Messengers" 1967, 62.

102. "It's Getting Better . . . " 1967.

103. Poirier 1967, 540, 542.

104. Anson 1981, 26.

105. Ibid., 51–52, 90; Draper 1990, 57.

106. Winner 1969, 52, 53.

107. Wenner 1968, 22.

108. Denson 1966.

109. Cited in Peck 1985, 172.

110. Cited in J. Wiener 1984, 60.

111. Christgau 1973, 100.

112. Marcus 1969, 91, 95, 93, 96, 93.

113. Ibid., 96, 97, 103–4.

114. J. Wiener 1984, 65, 53–57, 64–69.

115. Gleason 1967, 72–73.

116. Cited in J. Wiener 1984, 66.

117. Landau 1969, 99, 100, 101, 100.

118. Cited in Peck 1985, 173.

119. To confirm this, one would need to compare the proportionate amount of print devoted to white male rock musicians in the major accreditory journals in a given year with the proportion of top hits on the *Billboard* charts (say, the top ten) credited to white males.

120. Draper 1990, 66, 20.

121. "*Crawdaddy!*" 1967; Draper 1990, 20.

122. P. Williams 1966b, 29.
123. Gleason 1967, 67, 68.
124. Christgau 1967c, 56.
125. See, for example, Marcus's outstanding essay "Sly Stone: The Myth of Staggerlee," which originally appeared in 1975 (1990, 65–95) and Miller 1980. On the other hand, see Marcus's edited work *Stranded* (1980), in which leading rock critics picked their favorite "desert island" recordings. Out of the nineteen first choices, only five were black, and all came from the pre-Beatles era. None of the selecting writers were African American.
126. In Marcus's *Stranded* (see n. 125), of the nineteen "desert island" selections in which only four women critics participated, only two albums by women artists were picked.
127. "Music Educators Urge 'Rock' Garden in Capital" 1969.
128. "Music Teachers Listen to Youth at Symposium in Tanglewood" 1967.
129. Anderson 1968, 87.
130. Hughes 1969, 12.
131. "Fab? Chaos" 1968.
132. "Mannerist Phase" 1968.
133. Christgau 1976b.

Chapter 10
1. Shaw 1970, 4.
2. Cited in R. S. Friedman 1997, 11–12.
3. Shaw 1970.
4. Bangs 1971b.
5. Marsh 1971a, 63.
6. Shaw 1971c; Bangs 1987, 61, 34.
7. Marsh 1971a, 63.
8. Shaw 1971d, 9; 1971f, 4.
9. Shaw 1971d, 9.
10. Shaw 1972b, 62; See also Shaw 1973d, 68.
11. Bangs 1987, 36, 37.
12. Shaw 1971d, 9.
13. Shaw 1971b, 73. "Right now we're doing research on a number of fronts that should result in a number of special issues next year, and we need your help. . . . Secondly, if you have any similar info on what I have chosen to call 'punk rock' bands—white teenage hard rock of '64–66 (Standells, Kingsmen, Shadows of Knight, etc.), get it to me as soon as possible" (1971g, 7).
14. Shaw 1973d, 68.
15. Bangs 1970a, 36.
16. Marsh 1971b, 43.
17. Bangs 1970a, 1970b, 1971b; anthologized in Bangs 1987.
18. Bangs 1987, 55, 56. For a biography of Bangs, se DeRogatis 2000.
19. Meltzer 1975, 128.
20. Bangs 1987, 32, 38. Bangs wrote in a style that, it can be surmised, works as this kind of electroshock therapy.
21. Ibid., 56.
22. Ibid., 39, 40.
23. Ibid., 10, 17. It should be clear that minimalism and rank amateurishness, though they may sometimes coincide in practice, are quite distinct aesthetic concepts. Amateurish work oftentimes aims at complexity, and the pursuit of a minimalist aesthetic can require the highest professional competence.
24. Ibid., 40, 44, 45–46, 32. Nonetheless, for Bangs, the Stooges and their neo-punk compatriots, the MC5, had strayed off the true road of punk laid down by the mid-sixties bands (the Troggs, Count Five, etc.), and thus were not the answer to the decadence of the 1970s. Though they could "do things that the Troggs would never have dreamed of," the Troggs had "a consistency and a sure sense of direction that the other two, the best bands of this sort

surviving today, lacked or lost sight of" (56). What they created, even when it approached the power of "Wild Thing," emanated too much from "a standpoint of intellectualized awareness and consequent calculation" (64).

25.   Doo-wop was for the most part amateurish and "stripped down," but not of aspiration. There was an attempt to cultivate beautiful voices and complex vocal harmonies (the "blow" harmony), and the groups were trained to develop professional-appearing choreography.

26.   Cited in Bangs 1987, 18–19.

27.   Ibid., 101.

28.   Shaw 1974.

29.   Marsh 1971c, 25.

30.   Shaw 1974.

31.   Bangs 1987, 32, 65, 66, 67.

32.   See, for example, Hebdige 1979; Marcus 1989.

33.   See Strickland 1993, 1–14, 241–53.

34.   Shaw 1974.

35.   Shaw 1973d, 68.

36.   Bangs 1987, 43, 41.

37.   Ibid., 43, 44, 41, 48, 42.

38.   It compares somewhat with the way in which the modernist revivalist debates of the 1940s jazz world set the conditions for the reception of bebop. See chapter 6.

39.   Bangs 1971a, 46, 49.

40.   Bangs 1987, 42, 48.

41.   Bangs 1971a, 46.

42.   Ibid., 66.

43.   Willis 1979, 72.

44.   "*Creem* Delivers" 1972.

45.   Kaye 1972.

46.   Edmonds 1972, 54.

47.   Shaw 1973d.

48.   "The 1972 *Creem* Rock 'n' Roll Readers' Poll Results" 1973, 47.

49.   Shaw 1971a, 47.

50.   Shaw 1972a, 52, 46; 1974.

51.   Shaw 1972b, 62; 1971b, 72; 1972b, 62.

52.   Shaw 1973a, 78; 1973b, 74.

53.   Shaw 1974, 4; Shaw 1975, 4.

54.   Smucker 1972.

55.   P. Carr 1972, 42; Moore 1972, 46.

56.   P. Carr 1972, 44.

57.   Swenson 1973.

58.   O'Grady 1973.

59.   P. Nelson 1974.

60.   M. Phillips 1971.

61.   "Scenes" 1972.

62.   P. Nelson 1974.

Chapter 11

1.   The B-52s and Devo migrated from Georgia and Ohio, respectively, to become part of the New York new wave.

2.   McCarthy 1974b.

3.   In performance style, Smith was also tethered by the musical press more to the past than the future. Male writers reveled in portraying Smith as a "macho woman" rocker, "a female version of Keith Richard"—perhaps "the most macho performer in the macho-obsessed rock scene," who sings "male-supremacist rock songs" with "a swaggering conviction" (McCarthy 1974b; Wolcott 1975b, 120, 121). Keith Richard—style "swagger" was not to be a hallmark of the early CBGB underground, except when accompanied by irony.

4. Heylin 1993, 186, 133.
5. Feigenbaum 1974.
6. Betrock 1975c.
7. Cited in Heylin 1993, 95.
8. Cited in Ibid., 121, 96, 99, 124.
9. Cited in Ibid., 124–25, 134, 135, 137, 200.
10. Cited in Ibid., 204.
11. Mortifoglio 1975.
12. Ibid.
13. Christgau 1976a.
14. Betrock 1975c.
15. Wolcott 1975c, 94; Rockwell 1975b; Wolcott 1975d.
16. Wolcott 1975c.
17. Cited in Bessman 1993, 34.
18. Lisa Robinson 1975, 22; Persky 1976, 28.
19. Hickey 1977.
20. Cited in Bessman 1993, 31–32, 34.
21. Betrock 1975b; Altane 1976; Hickey 1977.
22. Rockwell 1975b; Wolcott 1975c; cited in Bessman 1993, 34.
23. Cited in Bessman 1993, 31–32.
24. Hickey 1977.
25. Cited in Bessman 1993, 34.
26. Palmer 1978.
27. Cited in Heylin 1993, 213.
28. Rockwell 1976d; Rockwell 1978c. Rockwell's colleague Robert Palmer had little patience for the Ramones' "aggressively inane lyrics, and their insistence on the most banal instrumental patterns" (1978). He found it "difficult to believe that people have formed serious intellectual attachments" to them or consider them "even good rock-and-roll." "They are the kind of joke one tires of very rapidly."
29. Rockwell 1976a; Rockwell 1975c; see also, Rockwell 1976c.
30. Rockwell 1977a. The Talking Heads' quickly found status as an art-rock unit was confirmed by an early invitation (March 1976) to appear at the Kitchen, the premier venue for avant-garde music, performance, and electronic media art. "Over two hundred [were] thronged inside, cross-legged and side-saddled on the floor." The Kitchen program soberly introduced the Talking Heads as "a group of performing artists whose medium is rock and roll music" with "the pursuant 'band' organization," which expresses "their anti-individualist stance as a group concept" (Balm 1976; Hager 1986, 13).
31. F. Rose 1977, 53.
32. Goldstein 1976.
33. Ibid.; F. Rose 1977.
34. Cited in Davis 1986, 71, 69, 70.
35. Cited in Heylin 1993, 210.
36. Bosco 1975. See also, Rockwell 1976c: "The abrupt layerings of their music recalls planes of color in minimalist art"—not surprising, given the Talking Heads' "background at the Rhode Island School of Design."
37. Wolcott 1975d.
38. Cited in Heylin 1993, 211, 213–14, 215.
39. Wolcott 1975a.
40. Shelton 1966c, 11.
41. "The Nitty-Gritty Sound" 1966; "Open Up, Tune In, Turn On" 1967.
42. Shaw 1971e, 22; 1972b, 62; 1973c, 66.
43. Wolcott 1975a.
44. Betrock 1975c.
45. McCormack 1975; Wolcott 1975a.
46. Rockwell 1975c; 1976d; 1976b; 1975b; Christgau 1975.

47. Holmstrom 1996, 9–12.
48. Cited in Savage 1991, 131.
49. Cited in Bessman 1993, 31.
50. Nooger 1974.
51. McNeil 1996, 203, 204.
52. Cited in Heylin 1993, 242.
53. Holmstrom 1996, 18.
54. McNeil 1996, 204.
55. Cited in Heylin 1993, 241.
56. Wolcott 1976, 88.
57. Altane 1976.
58. Cited in Bessman 1993, 57–59, 52.
59. Rockwell 1977b.
60. Cited in Gimarc 1994, 24, 26.
61. Issue #1, anthologized in Perry 2000.
62. Coon 1977, 19.
63. Coon 1976.
64. In the trade press, R. Watkins 1976; in a fanzine, Needs 1976.
65. "Fashion's Outrageous Punks" 1977; "Anthems of the Blank Generation" 1977.
66. In *Rolling Stone,* Young 1977; Waters 1977. Two earlier reports, more factual than eval-
uative, had been provided by *Rolling Stone*'s British correspondent. In the *Voice*, Christgau
1977; Goldstein 1977.
67. Holmstrom 1996, 18.
68. Cited in Heylin 1993, 242.
69. Cited in Gimarc 1994, 29.
70. Persky 1976, 28.
71. Rockwell 1976c; Palmer 1977b.
72. Emerson 1977.
73. Marsh 1977b; see also 1977a.
74. Shaw 1976, 40, 41.
75. Bangs 1980, 20.
76. Kozak 1976, 86. For a good account of new wave music and culture, see Cateforis 2000.
77. Donald Clarke, ed., *The Penguin Encyclopedia of Popular Music* (New York: Viking,
1989), 855.
78. Eric Weisbard, *Spin Alternative Record Guide* (New York: Vintage, 1995), 204, viii.
79. Savage 1991, 159.
80. September 28, 1976, issue; anthologized in Perry 2000.
81. Coon 1976; 1977, 73, 80; my italics.
82. Cited in Gimarc 1994, 48, 52, 56.
83. Lyrics from "I'm So Bored with the U.S.A." (Strummer/Jones, 1977).
84. July 9, 1977: 26 ff.
85. "Anthems of the Blank Generation" 1977, 47.
86. Needs 1976, 17.
87. Needs 1977.
88. Betrock 1977b; my italics.
89. Betrock 1977a.
90. Carson 1977, 20–21.
91. "Anthems of the Blank Generation" 1977, 46.
92. Goldstein 1977; Christgau 1977.
93. Trakin 1978a, 31.

Chapter 12
1. Schwartz 1978, 4.
2. Ibid.
3. Greg Shaw, the original prophet of punk/new wave, initiated the jeremiad. In "a sum-

mer so boring even the punks couldn't stand it," there was a "disturbing suspicion" in the air that something was "going wrong with the whole new wave 'movement,'" which in "nearly three years" hadn't "really gone anywhere" (1978, 34).

4. Betrock and Schwartz 1978, 30, 32.
5. Barnes 1978a.
6. Shaw 1978, 34.
7. Cited in Betrock and Schwartz 1978, 31.
8. Rockwell 1978d.
9. Trakin 1979b.
10. Rockwell 1978d.
11. See Sandler 1996, 218.
12. D. Phillips 1981, 93.
13. Trakin 1979a; Piccarella 1979; Trakin 1978a, 31, 37.
14. Carson 1978b, 11; Rockwell 1978d.
15. Piccarella 1979; Trakin 1980, 30.
16. Trakin 1980; Carson 1978b, 10.
17. Rockwell 1979a.
18. Piccarella 1979.
19. Trakin 1979a; 1978b.
20. R. Brown 1979.
21. Trakin 1979b, 14.
22. Piccarella 1979; Rockwell 1978d; Farber 1982; Trakin 1979a.
23. R. Brown 1979, 36.
24. Piccarella 1979.
25. Farber 1982.
26. Trakin 1978b.
27. Rockwell 1978b.
28. Trakin 1978b.
29. Platt 1979c, 25.
30. Rockwell 1978b; Trakin 1979b, 14.
31. Piccarella 1979.
32. Nooger 1979, 7; Trakin 1979b; Platt 1979b, 26.
33. Trakin 1979b; Jasper 1979.
34. Trakin 1978a, 37.
35. Trakin 1978b, 18, 69.
36. Trakin 1978c, 19.
37. Carson 1979b, 42–43; Trakin 1978a, 31.
38. Holmstrom 1996, 8.
39. Bangs 1979; see Bangs 1987, 277–78.
40. Savage 1991, 138.
41. Trakin 1979a.
42. Page 1979a, 12.
43. Trakin 1979a.
44. Platt 1979c, 39.
45. Platt 1979b, 41.
46. Nooger 1979.
47. Barnes 1978b, 36; Linna 1979.
48. Trakin 1979a.
49. Trakin 1981.
50. C. Nelson 1980, 20; Trakin 1978c, 19.
51. Carr 1982, 30.
52. "30 New York Bands" 1980, 27; Carr 1982, 30.
53. Bangs 1977, 63.
54. Rockwell 1978a.

55. Rockwell 1978a; Carson 1978a; Holden 1979.

56. Holden 1979.

57. Carson 1978a.

58. Shore 1978.

59. Carson 1978a.

60. Platt 1979a.

61. Rockwell 1978a.

62. Carson 1979a.

63. Palmer 1981, III, 4; "30 New York Bands" 1980, 27.

64. Wheeler 1981. The Lounge Lizards soon tired of the "fake jazz" tag so gleefully applied by the media (and originally suggested by Lurie). For if "their intent [was] partly satirical," they were still "searching for fresh sounds and novel juxtapositions, using an existing body of American popular music as their raw materials." And it was allowed that when playing "jazz tunes from the 1950's," the Lounge Lizards "executed the written music crisply and accurately." Perhaps, but when it came to improvisation and other criteria for "real jazz," Lurie had to admit that his group was wanting. "Steve Piccolo [one of the Lounge Lizards] is sort of a jazz player, but the rest of us . . . well, I can't run through complex chord changes the way jazz musicians are supposed to be able to do" (Palmer 1981, III, 5).

But the Lounge Lizards did not need to be stuck with the "fake jazz" label, since alternative classifications and demarcations were readily available in the fluid second wave scene. There were the designations "punk-jazz" or "funk-jazz," which grouped the Lounge Lizards with the Contortions, James Blood Ulmer, and Defunkt, and took them out of the pastiche camp. So viewed, the Lounge Lizards were miraculously turned into a no wave band—indeed "the most amusing and effective representatives of the burgeoning 'no wave' rock movement"—with no change in performance style, just different perceptions (Rockwell 1979b).

65. Foege 1994, 30.

66. Even in rock magazines like *New York Rocker,* coverage of the new borderline downtown scene was more often not taken up by associates of SoHo's alternative art spaces (e.g., Tim Carr) than habitués of rock clubs.

67. Sandow 1980a.

68. Bither 1980, 45.

69. Cited in Branca 1979.

70. Sandow 1980a.

71. Branca 1979.

72. Recoil 1981.

73. Sandow 1980b.

74. Page 1979c, 23.

75. Bither 1980, 45.

76. McKenna 1981, 25; Sandow 1980a.

77. Rockwell 1982.

78. McKenna 1981, 24.

79. Sandow 1980b.

80. McKenna 1981, 25.

81. Rockwell 1982.

82. Rockwell 1982; Sandow 1981a.

83. Sandow 1981c; 1981a, 112.

84. Sandow 1980a, 62; 1981c. If there was any doubt about the high-culture side to Chatham's music, one needed only consult his program notes for a concert at the Kitchen that were "as full of composer's shop talk as anything I've seen uptown at the Group for Contemporary Music, which comes from a no-bones-about-it cerebral academic tradition" (Sandow 1981c).

85. Rockwell 1982.

86. Sandow 1980b.

87. Rockwell 1982.

88. Carr 1982.

89. Ibid., 27.

90. At the Holly Solomon Gallery (1977), the "performance" was nothing but a jukebox with twenty-four recordings by Anderson surrounded by her wall hangings. The recordings were all "artsy sort of semi-popular vein"—"largely vocals, about three or four minutes long"—which at the same time "broke" if not completely "ignored" some of the other "conventions of pop music" (Johnson 1977). "Speaking voices expressed insincere concern for one another, made casual unspecified lunch dates, and generally carried on in a cool, frivolous way, against a background of unpleasant, raspy string sounds produced on a tamboura." Anderson, the former art history teacher, was clearly viewed as "part of the SoHo gestalt" usually at work "at the Kitchen or similar avant-garde media," and thus not "overtly" a pop performer. But from the very beginning, it was asserted that "ultimately, the pop aspects of her [performance] work dominate" (Palmer 1977a).

91. Rockwell 1980b; Sandow 1980c.

Chapter 13

1. Frank and McKenzie 1987, 63; Hager 1986.

2. Wadsley 1979, 53; Farber 1979.

3. Wadsley 1979, 53.

4. Farber 1979.

5. Wadsley 1979, 53.

6. Haden-Guest 1997, 101.

7. Page 1979c, 21.

8. Frank and McKenzie 1987, 63.

9. Hager 1986, 60.

10. Ibid., 62, 64; Frank and McKenzie 1987, 65.

11. Hager 1986, 106.

12. Frank and McKenzie 1987, 65, 63.

13. Hager 1986, 56; Shore 1980, 84.

14. Deitch 1980a, 134–35.

15. Shore 1980, 83.

16. Cited in Hager 1986, 15.

17. Sandow 1980a; Rockwell 1979a.

18. Shore 1980, 78.

19. Edit DeAk, cited in Hager 1986, 55.

20. Hoban 1999, 47.

21. Haber 1986, 49.

22. Hoban 1999, 49.

23. Hager 1986, 11, 49.

24. Sui 1979.

25. Buckley 1981.

26. Hager 1986, 95–96, 53, 17.

27. Rockwell 1979a.

28. Hager 1986, 96.

29. Ibid., 46, 19.

30. Ibid., 29–30; Black 1978.

31. Black 1978.

32. The organizing group Colab—or more formally Collaborative Projects, Inc.—in this case was under the leadership of Diego Cortez.

33. Deitch 1980b, 59.

34. K. Levin 1980, 89.

35. Deitch 1980b, 60; K. Levin 1980, 87.

36. Deitch 1980b.

37. K. Levin 1980, 88.
38. Shore 1980, 85.
39. K. Levin 1980, 87, 88.
40. Deitch 1980b, 61.
41. Plagens 1981, 11.
42. Deitch 1980b, 61, 63; K. Levin 1980, 89, 90.
43. Shore 1980, 79.
44. Deitch 1980b, 61; K. Levin 1980, 88, 89.
45. Shore 1980, 80.
46. Cited in ibid., 85, 79, 81. Robert Longo: "The music's been a real resource and energizer for artists. It's helped promote and reinforce a concern with the primary levels of experience . . . " (cited in Shore 1980, 83).
47. Warhol, in some of his practices, was somewhat an exception, a point to which I will return later.
48. Shore 1980, 82, 83.
49. Cortez was the curator, but on his own, without Colab.
50. Perreault 1981; V. Smith 1981, 56.
51. Flood 1981, 86. The same critique was directed at Chris Stein of Blondie concerning his photographs.
52. Ibid., 87.
53. Kay Larson, cited by Hoban 1999, 66; Perreault 1981.
54. Moufarrege 1983, 36.
55. Moufarrege 1982, 69.
56. Moufarrege 1983, 36.
57. Moufarrege 1982, 69; 1983, 36.
58. Moufarrege 1982, 69.
59. McGuigan 1985, 23, 24.
60. Cited in Dowd 1985, 28, 38.
61. Brenson 1982.
62. McGuigan 1985, 23, 32. This was a sly allusion to the well-known fact that Basquiat, in rock star fashion, consumed heavy amounts of drugs while producing paintings at a frenzied pace in the basement of galleries.
63. Hager 1986, 66, 70, 72, 79; Frank and McKenzie 1987, 68.
64. Frank and McKenzie 1987, 66.
65. Haden-Guest 1997, 106.
66. Ibid., 73.
67. Frank and McKenzie 1987, 73; Hoban 1999, 253.
68. Frank and McKenzie 1987.
69. Haden-Guest 1997, 266–67.
70. Hoban 1999, 252.
71. Haden-Guest 1997, 269.
72. Calvin Tomkins, cited by Hoban 1999, 252.
73. Hager 1986, 110; Hoban 1999, 153.
74. Hager 1986, 124.
75. Moufarrege 1983, 36.
76. Dowd 1985, 33, 40.
77. Ibid., 28, 33.
78. Ibid., 100.
79. Owens 1984, 162; my italics.
80. Cited in Dowd 1985, 87.
81. V. Smith 1981, 56.
82. Ricard 1982, 43.
83. Cited in Hoban 1999, 153.
84. Huyssen 1995.
85. Dobrzynski 2000.

Coda

1. Seabrook 2000.
2. For an extended study of these issues, see my "Before Fusion: Jazz in Crisis (1965–67)," forthcoming in a special jazz issue in *Current Musicology*.
3. This quote, which has circulated for some time, is rather more contorted than it looks. Globally, Clinton stands for the pop and African American side, Kraftwerk for the art and white European side, but the discourses on each, and the practice of each, are riddled with the art/pop dialectic.
4. Seabrook 2000, 12.

BIBLIOGRAPHY

"According to John." 1966. *Time* (August 12): 38.

Adorno, Theodor. 1989–90. "On Jazz," trans. by Jamie Owen Daniel. *Discourse* (fall—winter): 45–69.

"Adult Okay Endangers Beatles?" 1964. *Variety* (August 19): 3.

"All My Own Work." 1964. *Time* (May 1): E7-100.

Allais, Alphonse. 1880. "L'Hydropathe 'Illustre Sapeck,'" *L'Hydropathe* (March 15): 2.

Alloway, Lawrence, et al. 1988. *Modern Dreams: The Rise and Fall and Rise of Pop*. Cambridge: MIT Press.

Altane, Brock. 1976. "The Ramones." *New York Rocker* (February): 4.

"Amerry Timble." 1964. *Newsweek* (April 27): 108–9.

"Amps in the Pants." 1965. *Newsweek* (September 6): 67–68.

Anderson, Simon. 1968. "The Role of Rock." *Music Educators Journal* (January): 37 ff.

Ansermet, Ernst-Alexandre. 1962. "Bechet and Jazz Visit Europe, 1919." In *Frontiers of Jazz,* edited by Ralph de Toledano. New York: Frederick Unga.

Anson, Robert Sam. 1981. *Gone Crazy and Back Again: The Rise and Fall of the "Rolling Stone" Generation*. New York: Doubleday.

"Anthems of the Blank Generation." 1977. *Time* (July 11): 46.

Appignanesi, Lisa. 1984. *Cabaret*. London: Methuen.

"Apples for the Beatles." 1968. *Time* (September 6): 59–60.

Arthur, Bob. 1944. "The Great Enlightenment." *Jazz Record* (February): 4–5.

"Attack Hamid Pier 'Jim Crow' Policy." 1944. *Down Beat* (September 1): 1.

Au Temps du Boeuf sur le Toit. 1981. Paris: Artcurial.

Baillet, Eugène. 1885. "Fragments de l'histoire de la goguette." In *Chansons et petits poèmes*. Paris: L. Labbé.

Ball, Hugo. 1974. *Flight Out of Time: A Dada Diary*. New York: Viking.

Balm, Trixie A. 1976. "Talking Heads Speak Out." *Hit Parader* (September): 16–17.

"Band of the Year: Dizzy Gillespie." 1948. *Metronome* (January): 17–18.

Bangs, Lester. 1970a. "Of Pop and Pies and Fun: A Program of Mass Liberation in the Form of a Stooges Review, Or, Who's the Fool?" Part I. *Creem* (November): 34–37. Also in Bangs 1987, 31–44.

———. 1970b. "Of Pop and Pies and Fun: A Program of Mass Liberation in the Form of a Stooges Review, Or, Who's the Fool?" Part II. *Creem* (December): 36–39. Also in Bangs 1987, 44–52.

———. 1971a. "Dead Lie the Velvets Underground." *Creem* (May): 44 ff.

———. 1971b. "James Taylor Marked for Death, or What We Need Is a Lot Less Jesus and a Whole Lot More Troggs." *Who Put the Bomp* (fall–winter): 59–84. Also in Bangs 1987, 53–81.

———. 1971c. "Psychotic Reactions and Carburetor Dung: A Tale of These Times." *Creem* (June): 56–63. Also in Bangs 1987, 31–52.

———. 1972. "White Witch." *Creem* (October): 65. Also in Bangs 1987, 101–2.

———. 1977. "Blondie Is More Fun." *Village Voice* (January 10): 63–65.

———. 1979. "The White Noise Supremacists." *Village Voice* (March 30): 45.

———. 1980. *Blondie*. New York: Delilah.

———. 1987. *Psychotic Reactions and Carburetor Dung*. New York: Vintage.

Banks, Dave. 1948. "Be-Bop Called Merely the Beginning of a New Creative Music Form." *Down Beat* (February 11): 16.

"Bards of Pop." 1966. *Newsweek* (March 21): 102.

Barnes, Ken. 1978a. "Stranger in Town." *New York Rocker* (July–August): 26.

———. 1978b. "Stranger in Town." *New York Rocker* (November): 36, 47.

Bart, Peter. 1965a. "The California Sound." *Atlantic* (May): 140, 142.

———. 1965b. "Macabre Songs Come from Coast." *New York Times* (December 22): 21.

Baudelaire, Charles. 1972. "The Painter of Modern Life." In *Baudelaire: Selected Writings on Art and Artists,* translated by P. E. Charvet. New York: Cambridge University Press.

"Beatle Man." 1963. *New Yorker* (December 28): 23–24.

"A Beatle Metaphysic." 1967. *Commonwealth* (May 12): 234–36.

"Beatlemania." 1963. *Newsweek* (November 18): 104.

"Beatles Are 'Helpful,' Prince Philip Thinks." 1964. *New York Times* (February 26): 18.

"The Beatles Is Coming." 1964. *Newsweek* (February 3): 77.

"Beatles vs. Stones." 1968. *Newsweek* (January 1): 162–63.

"Be-bop Be-bopped." 1946. *Time* (March 25): 52.

"Be-Bop Invades the West!" 1945. *Jazz Tempo* (December): 1.

"Bebop." 1948. *Life* (October 11): 138–42.

"Because!" 1943. *Metronome* (April): 4.

Bennett, Tony. 1990. *Outside Literature*. London: Routledge.

Bernier, Georges. 1985. *Paris Cafés: Their Role in the Birth of Modern Art*. New York: Wildenstein.

Bernstein, Leonard. 1992. *Young People's Concerts*. New York: Doubleday.

Bersaucourt, A. de. 1921. *Au Temps des Parnassiens: Nina de Villard et ses amis*. Paris: La Renaissance du Livre.

Berton, Ralph. 1945. "Blesh, Jazz, and Metronome." *Jazz Record* (August): 6 ff.

Bessman, Jim. 1993. *Ramones: An American Band*. New York: St. Martin's Press.

Betrock, Alan. 1975a. "Know Your New York Bands: The Dictators." *SoHo Weekly News* (March 27): 24, 30.

———. 1975b. "Know Your New York Bands: The Ramones." *SoHo Weekly News* (May 1): 28.

———. 1975c. "Know Your New York Bands: Television." *SoHo Weekly News* (April 3).

———. 1975d. "Television at CBGB." *SoHo Weekly News* (January 23): 26.

———. 1977a. "New Wave Hangs Ten." *New York Rocker* (July–August): 43.

———. 1977b. "12 Topics." *New York Rocker* (March): 29.

Betrock, Alan, and Andy Schwartz. 1978. "The Future's Gleam." *New York Rocker* (September): 30–33.

"Bird Wrong; Bop Must Get a Beat." 1949. *Down Beat* (October 10): 1.

Bither, David. 1980. "Glenn Branca/Notekillers/Hurrah." *New York Rocker* (November): 45, 47, 63.

Blachère, Jean-Claude. 1981. *Le Modèle nègre*. Paris: Nouvelles Éditions Africaines.

Black, Pam. 1978. "Say Yes-Yes to the No-No New Wave." *SoHo Weekly News* (November 16): 82.

Blake, Jody. 1999. *Le Tumulte noir: Modernist Art and Popular Entertainment in Jazz-Age Paris, 1900–1930*. University Park: Pennsylvania State University Press.

Blesh, Rudi. 1945. "Louis Armstrong and *Metronome*." *Jazz Record* (July): 4 ff.

———. 1958. *Shining Trumpets*. New York: Da Capo.

"Blues for the Beatles." 1966. *Newsweek* (August 22): 94.

"Bop Dead, Ventura Agrees." 1949. *Down Beat* (December 16): 12.

"Bop Gets Monday Night Home in Dixie Hangout." 1948. *Down Beat* (November 11): 4.

"'Bop Will Kill Business Unless It Kills Itself First'—Louis Armstrong." 1948. *Down Beat* (April 7): 2.

"Bopera on Broadway." 1948. *Time* (December 20): 63–64.

Borneman, Ernest. 1944a. "The Anthropologist Looks at Jazz," *Record Changer* (May): 5 ff.

———. 1944b. "From Jazz to Swing." *Record Changer* (December): 6–10.

———. 1944c. "Questions and Answers." *Record Changer* (October): 18 ff.

———. 1944d. "Responses to Letters." *Record Changer* (July): 41.

———. 1945a. "The Musician and the Critic." *Jazz Record* (September): 9 ff.

———. 1945b. "Questions and Answers." *Record Changer* (June): 38.

———. 1946. "Questions and Answers." *Record Changer* (February): 11–12.

———. 1947a. "Both Schools of Critics Wrong." *Down Beat* (July 30): 11.

———. 1947b. "Both Schools of Critics Wrong." *Down Beat* (August 13): 16.

———. 1956. "The Jazz Cult." In *Eddie Condon's Treasury of Jazz,* edited by Eddie Condon and Richard Gehman, 33–67. New York: Dial Press.

Bosco, Freddy. 1975. "Hold the Pickles, Hold the Garnish." *SoHo Weekly News* (December 11): 41.

"Bouquets . . . Brickbats . . . with Due Humility." 1943. *Metronome* (July): 5.

Bourdieu, Pierre. 1971. "Le Marché des biens symboliques." *L'Année Sociologique* 22: 49–126.

———. 1984. *Distinction: A Social Critique of the Judgement of Taste.* Translated by Richard Nice. Cambridge: Harvard University Press.

Brackett, David. 1994. "The Politics and Practice of 'Crossover' in American Popular Music, 1963–65." *Musical Quarterly* 78 (no. 4, winter): 774–97.

Bradshaw, Steve. 1978. *Café Society.* London: Weidenfeld and Nicholson.

Branca, Glenn. 1979. "Rhys Chatham." *New York Rocker* (November): 16.

Brenson, Michael. 1982. "Artists Grapple with the New Realities." *New York Times* (May 15): II, 1, 30.

Broome, John. 1945. "On the Feather in *Esquire*'s Bonnet." *Jazz Record* (August): 4–5.

Brown, Bilbo [pseud.]. 1945. "Rebop and Mop Mop." *Record Changer* (October): 34.

Brown, Carlton. 1946. "Hey! Ba-Ba-Revolt!" *Record Changer* (May): 12, 20.

Brown, Rick. 1979. "DNA." *New York Rocker* (August): 36.

Buckley, John. 1981. "Leapin' Lizards." *SoHo Weekly News* (August 4): 56.

Burks, John. 1968. "Monterey Jazz Festival." *Rolling Stone* (November 9): 14.

Burton, Humphrey. 1994. *Leonard Bernstein.* New York: Doubleday.

Butler, John Davis. 1967. *Jean Moréas.* The Hague: Mouton.

Cadarec, François, and Alain Weill. 1980. *Le Café-concert.* Paris: Hachette.

Callahan, Ellen. 1977. "Manic Panic." *New York Rocker* (September–October): 39.

Carr, Patrick. 1972. "Cheap Thrills: The Essential Stuff of Growing Up Wild." *Village Voice* (October 10): 42, 44.

———. 1973. "Cheap Thrills: Making Ripples of a New Wave." *Village Voice* (April 12): 54.

Carr, Tim, et al. 1982. "Downtown Sound." *New York Rocker* (June): 27–38.

Carson, Tom. 1977. "Talking Heads." *New York Rocker* (September–October): 20–21.

———. 1978a. "B-52s Take Off." *Village Voice* (June 12): 44.

———. 1978b. "Brian Eno." *New York Rocker* (July–August): 10–11.

———. 1978c. "Saturday Night Stalemate at CBGB." *Village Voice* (April 10): 57.

———. 1979a. "B-52s." *New York Rocker* (July): 4–6.

———. 1979b. "You Burn Some, You Rust Some." *Village Voice* (October 22): 41 ff.

Cassagne, Albert. 1906. *La Théorie de l'art pour l'art en France.* Paris: Lucien Dorbon.

Cate, Phillip Dennis, and Mary Shaw, eds. 1996. *The Spirit of Montmartre: Cabarets, Humor, and the Avant-Garde, 1875–1905.* New Brunswick, N.J.: Rutgers University Press.

Cateforis, Theodore Philip. 2000. *Are We Not New Wave? Nostalgia, Technology and Exoticism in Popular Music at the Turn of the 1980s.* Ph.D. diss. Stonybrook, SUNY.

Cesana, Otto. 1936. "Swing Is—Well, It's Here." *Metronome* (June): 14.

Chasins, Abram. 1965. "High-Brows vs. No-Brows." *McCall's* (September): 42, 46.

Chinitz, David. 1995. "T. S. Eliot and the Cultural Divide." *PMLA* 110 (March): 236–47.

"Chords and Discords: Case against Dizzy." 1946. *Down Beat* (March 25): 12.

Christgau, Robert. 1967a. "Rock Lyrics Are Poetry (Maybe)." In Eisen 1969, 230–39.

————. 1967b. "Secular Music." *Esquire* (June): 16 ff.

————. 1967c. "Secular Music." *Esquire* (October): 54 ff.

————. 1967d. "Secular Music." *Esquire* (December): 283 ff.

————. 1968a. "Secular Music." *Esquire* (May). Also in Christgau 1973, 51–61.

————. 1968b. "Secular Music." *Esquire* (June): 26 ff.

————. 1973. *Any Old Way You Choose It: Rock and Other Pop Music.* Baltimore: Penguin.

————. 1975. "Voice Choices." *Village Voice* (April 7): 108.

————. 1976a. "Television Don't Play by Numbers." *Village Voice* (March 22): 83 ff.

————. 1976b. "Yes, There Is a Rock-Critic Establishment (but Is That Bad for Rock?)." *Village Voice* (January 26): 83 ff.

————. 1977. "A Cult Explodes—and a Movement Is Born." *Village Voice* (October 24): 57 ff.

Clark, T. J. 1984. "A Bar at the Folies-Bergère." In *The Painting of Modern Life.* Princeton: Princeton University Press.

Clayton, Peter. 1966. "Revolver." *Gramophone* (October): 233.

"Clayton's Choice." 1966. *Gramophone* (February): 414.

Clifford, James. 1988. *The Predicament of Culture.* Cambridge: Harvard University Press.

————. 1989. "1933, February: Negrophilia." In *A New History of French Literature,* edited by Denis Hollier. Cambridge: Harvard University Press.

Cocteau, Jean. 1921. *The Cock and the Harlequin.* London: Egoist Press.

————. 1935. *Portraits-souvenir (1900–1914).* Paris: Éditions Bernard Grasset.

————. 1946–51. "La Jeunesse et le scandale." In *Oeuvres Completes,* vol. IX. Lausanne: Marguerat.

————. 1948. "Jazz-Band." In *Le Rappel a l'ordre,* 137–41. Paris: Delamain et Boutelleau.

Coley, Byron. 1981. "Lydia Lunch & 13.13 o.n.klub l.a." *New York Rocker* (September): 18–19.

Collaer, Paul. 1982. *Darius Milhaud.* Paris: Éditions Slatkine.

Collier, James Lincoln. 1978. *The Making of Jazz.* New York: Dell.

Condemi, Concetta. 1992. *Les Cafés-concerts.* Paris: Quai Voltaire.

Connell, Tom. 1946. "The King of Swing Abdicates." *Metronome* (August): 14.

Cook, Joan. 1965. "Bernstein at Home: Relaxed." *New York Times* (November 22).

Coon, Carolyn. 1976. "Punk Alphabet." *Melody Maker* (November 27): 33.

————. 1977. *1988: The New Wave Punk Rock Explosion.* London: Omnibus Press.

Cornell, Kenneth. 1951. *The Symbolist Movement.* New Haven: Yale University Press.

"The Cover of Metronome." 1945. *Metronome* (October): 17.

"*Crawdaddy!*" 1967. *Newsweek* (December 11): 114.

Crawley, Robert. 1944. Letter to the Editor. *Metronome* (March): 7 ff.

"*Creem* Delivers: Mardi Gras & Punkitude [advertisement]." 1972. *Creem* (July): inside back page.

Crespelle, Jean-Paul. 1976. *La Vie quotidienne à Montparnasse à la grande epoque (1905–1930).* Paris: Hachette.

————. 1978. *La Vie quotidienne à Montmartre au temps de Picasso (1900–1910).* Paris: Hachette.

Crow, Thomas. 1985. "Modernism and Mass Culture in the Visual Arts." In *Pollock and After,* edited by Francis Frascina. New York: Harper.

Crowther, Bosley. 1964. "Screen: The Four Beatles in 'A Hard Day's Night.'" *New York Times* (August 12): 41.

"Customers Outbop the Boppers." 1948. *Down Beat* (August 25): 3.

Damase, Jacques. 1960. *Les Folies du music-hall.* Paris: Spectacles.

Davis, Jerome. 1986. *Talking Heads.* New York: Vintage Books.

Dawson, Jim, and Steve Propes. 1992. *What Was the First Rock n' Roll Record?* Boston: Faber and Faber.

Dawson, Jim. 1995. *The Twist: The Story of the Song and Dance that Changed the World.* Boston: Faber and Faber.

Deitch, Jeffrey. 1980a. "'Cold War Zeitgeist' at the Mudd Club." *Art in America* (May): 134–35.

————. 1980b. "Report from Times Square." *Art in America* (September): 59–63.

"Delauney on First Visit to America." 1946. *Down Beat* (August 26): 1.

de Man, Paul. 1996. *Aesthetic Ideology.* Minneapolis: University of Minnesota Press.

de Maré, Rolf. 1931. "Naissance et evolution des Ballets Suédois." In *Les Ballets Suédois dans l'art contemporain.* Paris: Éditions du Trianon.

Dempsey, David. 1964. "Why the Girls Scream, Weep, Flip." *New York Times Magazine* (February 23): 15 ff.

Denson, Ed. 1966. "Rock 'n' Roll Is Dead." *Berkeley Barb* (March 11): 5.

DeRogatis, Jim. 2000. *Let It Blurt: The Life and Times of Lester Bangs.* New York: Broadway.

Deutsche, Rosalyn, and Cara Gendel Ryan. 1984. "The Fine Art of Gentrification." *October* (winter): 91–111.

DeVeaux, Scott. 1991. "Constructing the Jazz Tradition: Jazz Historiography." *Black American Literature Forum* XXV (no. 3, fall): 525–60.

————. 1997. *The Birth of Bebop: A Social and Musical History.* Berkeley: University of California Press.

"Dial Builds Be-Bop Backlog." 1946. *Jazz Tempo* (April).

"Diz to Put Bop Touch to More Standard Tunes." 1949. *Down Beat* (March 11): 3.

"Dizzy Gillespie's Style, Its Meaning Analyzed." 1946. *Down Beat* (February 11): 14.

Dobrzynski, Judith. 2000. "Blockbuster Shows Lure Big Crowds into U.S. Museums." *New York Times* (February 3).

Dowd, Maureen. 1985. "Youth-Art-Hype. A Different Bohemia." *New York Times Magazine* (November 17): 26 ff.

Dowlding, William. 1989. *Beatlesongs.* New York: Simon and Schuster.

Draper, Robert. 1990. *Rolling Stone Magazine: The Uncensored History.* New York: Doubleday.

"Duke, Cole Win Band Contests; Seven New All-Stars Elected." 1945. *Metronome* (January): 9 ff.

Duxbury, Janell. 1985. *Rockin' the Classics and Classicizin' the Rock.* Westport, Conn.: Greenwood Press.

Eagleton, Terry. 1990. *The Ideology of the Aesthetic.* Cambridge, Mass.: Basil Blackwell.

Easton, Malcolm. 1964. *Artists and Writers in Paris: The Bohemian Idea (1803–1867).* New York: St. Martin's Press.

Echeverria, Tom. 1944. Letter to the Editor. *Metronome* (May): 9 ff.

Eckles, Mick. 1944. "Too Much Music." *Metronome* (March): 9.

Editorial. 1943. *Music Dial* (July): 3.

Editorial. 1944. "Our Contemporaries." *Metronome* (February): 4.

Editorial. 1945. *Jazz* (October): 16.

Editorial. 1948. *Record Changer* (February): 4.

Editorial. 1966. *Jazz* (April): 5.

Editorial. 1967. *Jazz* (August): 5, 17.

Editorial. 1976. *Punk* (April). Also in Holmstrom 1996, 18.

Edmonds, Ben. 1972. "Psychedelic Punkitude Lives!!" [Review of *Nuggets.*] *Creem* (December): 54–56.

"Educators Urged to Heed Beatles." 1967. *New York Times* (July 25): 29.

Eger, Joseph. 1968. "Ives and Beatles!" *Music Journal* (September): 46, 70–71.

Ehrenberg, Lewis A. 1998. *Swingin' the Dream: Big Band Jazz and the Rebirth of American Culture.* Chicago: University of Chicago Press.

Eisen, Jonathan, ed. 1969. *The Age of Rock: Sights and Sounds of the American Cultural Revolution.* New York: Vintage Books.

————. 1970. *The Age of Rock 2: Sights and Sounds of the American Cultural Revolution.* New York: Vintage Books.

Elderfield, John. 1974. "Dada: A Code Word of Saints?" *Artforum* (February): 42–47.

Ellison, Ralph. 1953. *Shadow and Act.* New York: Random House.

Emerson, Ken. 1977. "Television Takes to the Air." *Village Voice* (March 14): 81.

Erickson, John. 1984. *Dada: Performance, Poetry, and Art.* Boston: Twayne.

Erik Satie à Montmartre. 1982. Paris: Musée de Montmartre.

Erismann, Guy. 1967. *Histoire de la chanson.* Paris: Éditions Hermes.

Ertegun, Nesuhi. 1945. "Esquire 1945." *Record Changer* (February): 3–5.

———. 1947. "A Style and a Memory." *Record Changer* (July): 7; reprinted from *Record Changer* (April 1943).

"Fab? Chaos." 1968. *Time* (January 5): 60–61.

"Face to Face with the Editor of a Rock and Roll Magazine." 1967. *Seventeen* (April): 59.

Farber, Jim. 1979. "The Mudd Club: Disco for Punks." *Rolling Stone* (July 12): 18.

———. 1982. "8 Eyed Spy's Desperate Living." *Village Voice* (January 13): 92–93.

"Fashion's Outrageous Punks." 1977. *Newsweek* (June 20): 80b.

"Fats Waller Demonstrates Swing." 1936. *Metronome* (February): 19 ff.

Feather, Leonard. 1943. "Pettiford-of-the-Month." *Metronome* (November): 18.

———. 1944a. "Dizzy Is Crazy Like a Fox." *Metronome* (July): 15 ff.

———. 1944b. "Jazz Is Where You Find It." *Esquire* (February): 35 ff.

———. 1944c. "Maxie Speaks Up." *Metronome* (September): 14.

———. 1944d. "What Makes a Good Jazz Critic?" *Metronome* (May): 26–27.

———. 1945a. "Dizzy—21st Century Gabriel." 1945. *Esquire* (October): 11.

———. 1945b. "Louis on Jazz and Swing." *Metronome* (June): 26–27.

———. 1945c. "On Musical Fascism." *Metronome* (September): 16 ff.

———. 1948a. "Europe Does Dizzy." *Metronome* (May): 19, 35.

———. 1948b. "The Street Is Dead." *Metronome* (April): 16.

Feigenbaum, Josh. 1974. Review of Television performance at CBGB. *SoHo Weekly News* (April 25).

Feschotte, Jacques. 1965. *Histoire du music-hall.* Paris: Presses Universitaires.

"Feud for Thought." 1946. *Metronome* (April): 10.

Fiedler, Leslie. 1977. *A Fiedler Reader.* New York: Stein and Day.

Flood, Richard. 1981. "Skied and Grounded in Queens 'New York/New Wave' at P.S. 1." *Art Forum* 19 (summer): 84–87.

Foege, Alec. 1994. *Confusion Is Next: The Sonic Youth Story.* New York: St. Martin's Press.

"The Folk and the Rock." 1965. *Newsweek* (September 20): 88–89.

"Forget the Message; Just Play." 1967. *Time* (October 27): 53.

Foster, Hal ed. 1983. *The Anti-Aesthetic: Essays on Postmodern Culture.* Port Townsend, Wash.: Bay Press.

Foucault, Michel. 1972. *The Archaeology of Knowledge.* New York: Pantheon.

———. 1980. *Power/Knowledge: Selected Interviews and Other Writings, 1972–1977.* Edited by Colin Gordon. Translated by Colin Gordon et al. New York: Pantheon.

"Four Beatles and How They Grew: Publicitywise, Moneywise, Peoplewise." 1964. *New York Times* (February 17): 1, 20.

Fragerolle, George. 1880. "Le Fumisme." *L'Hydropathe* (May 12): 2–3.

"Framing The Beatles." 1968. *Newsweek* (August 19): 89.

Frank, Peter, and Michael McKenzie. 1987. *New, Used and Improved: Art for the 80's.* New York: Abbeville.

Freed, Richard D. 1965a. "B Is for Beatles (and Baroque)." *Saturday Review* (December 25): 57, 61.

———. 1965b. "Beatle Tunes Become Baroque 'n' Roll." *New York Times* (November 9): 50.

———. 1965c. "Beatles Stump Music Experts Looking for Key to Beatlemania." *New York Times* (August 13): 17.

Frey, Julia. 1994. *Toulouse-Lautrec: A Life.* New York: Viking.

Friedman, Bruce. 1965. "The New Sounds of Rock 'n' Roll." *Holiday* (August): 44–45, 98, 102.

Friedman, R. Seth, ed. 1997. *The Factsheet Five Zine Reader.* New York: Three Rivers Press.

Frith, Simon. 1981. *Sound Effects.* New York: Pantheon.

———. 1996. *Performing Rites: On the Value of Popular Music.* Cambridge: Harvard University Press.

Frith, Simon, and Howard Horne. 1987. *Art into Pop.* New York: Methuen.

"From One Poll to Another." 1945. *Jazz Session* (May–June): 26–27.

Fuller, John G. 1965. "Trade Winds." *Saturday Review* (September 18): 14.

Gabree, John. 1967a. "The Beatles in Perspective." *Down Beat* (November 16): 20 ff.

———. 1967b. "The World of Rock." *Down Beat* (July 13): 18.

Gardner, Marilyn. 1966. "At Home in Connecticut." *Milwaukee Journal* (June 22): IV, 1–3.

Gautier, Théophile. 1873. *Les Jeunes France.* Paris: Charpentier.

———. 1874. *Histoire du romantisme.* Paris: Charpentier.

———. 1946. *La Préface de "Mademoiselle de Maupin."* Paris: Librairie Droz.

Gennari, John. 1991. "Jazz Criticism: Its Development and Ideologies." *Black American Literature Forum* (fall): 449–523.

"George, Paul, Ringo, and John." 1964. *Newsweek* (February 24): 54–57.

Geyh, Paula, Fred G. Leebron, and Andrew Levy, eds. 1998. *Postmodern American Fiction: A Norton Anthology.* New York: W. W. Norton.

Gillespie, Dizzy. 1979. *To Be or Not . . . to Bop.* New York: Doubleday.

Gimarc, George. 1994. *Punk Diary: 1970–1979.* New York: St. Martin's Press.

Gitler, Ira. 1985. *Swing to Bop.* New York: Oxford University Press.

Gitlin, Todd. 1987. *The Sixties: Years of Hope, Days of Rage.* New York: Bantam.

Gleason, Ralph. 1944. "Featherbed Ball." *Record Changer* (September): 48 ff.

———. 1949. "TD Told to Open Ears to Bop." *Down Beat* (September 23): 1, 12.

———. 1950. "Dizzy Getting a Bad Deal from Music Biz." *Down Beat** (November 17): 14.

———. 1967. "Like a Rolling Stone." *American Scholar.* Also in Eisen 1969, 61–76.

Glotzer, Fred E. 1944. Letter to the Editor. *Metronome* (July): 7.

Goddard, Chris. 1978. *Jazz Away from Home.* London: Da Capo.

Goddard, J. R. 1965a. "Dylan Meets the Press." *Village Voice* (March 25): 24.

———. 1965b. "Plugged in, Turned on: Thwump, Rackety-Whoomp." *Village Voice* (October 21): 7.

Goffin, Robert. 1946. "From the Blues to Swing." *Jazz Record* (January): 12–13.

Goldstein, Richard. 1966a. "Evaluating Media." *Village Voice* (July 14): 6.

———. 1966b. "On 'Revolver.'" *Village Voice* (August 25): 26.

———. 1966c. "Soundblast '66." *Village Voice* (June 16): 33.

———. 1967a. "I Blew My Cool through the *New York Times.*" *Village Voice* (July 20): 14.

———. 1967b. "The New Jazz." *Village Voice* (June 22): 12 ff.

———. 1967c. "Real Jazz Should Blow the Mind." *New York Times* (August 20): 13 ff.

———. 1967d. "We Still Need the Beatles, but . . . " *New York Times* (June 18): II, 24.

———. 1969. "Listen, Ned Rorem, for the Bang." *New York Times* (November 2): 19.

———. 1976. "Talking Heads Hyperventilate Some Clichés." *Village Voice* (February 2): 84.

———. 1977. "The Possibilities of Punk." *Village Voice* (October 10): 44.

———. 1989. *Reporting the Counterculture.* Boston: Unwin Hyman.

Gordon, Rae Beth. 1989. "Le Caf'conc'et l'hystérie." *Romantisme* 64: 54–66.

Goudeau, Émile. 1888. *Dix ans de bohème.* Paris: Librairie Illustrée.

Gould, Jack. 1964. "TV: The Beatles and Their Audience." *New York Times* (February 10): 53.

Gracyk, Theodore. 1996. *Rhythm and Noise: An Aesthetic of Rock.* Durham, N.C.: Duke University Press.

Greenberg, Clement. 1939. "Avant-Garde and Kitsch." *Partisan Review* (fall): 34–49.

Greer, Thomas Henry. 1969. "Music and Its Relation to Futurism, Cubism, Dadaism, and Surrealism, 1905–1950." Ph.D. diss. Denton, North Texas State University.

Grender, R. 1986. "Reinventing Africa in Their Own Image: The Ballets Suédois' 'Ballet Nègre,' *La Création du monde.*" *Dance Chronicle* IX (no. 7): 123.

Grojnowski, Daniel, and Bernard Sarrazin. 1990. *L'Esprit fumiste et les rires fin de siècles.* Paris: José Corti.

Haden-Guest, Anthony. 1997. *The Last Party: Studio 54, Disco, and the Culture of the Night.* New York: William Morrow.

Hager, Steven. 1984. *Hip Hop.* New York: St. Martin's Press.

———. 1986. *Art after Midnight: The East Village Scene.* New York: St. Martin's Press.

Haggerty, Michael. 1984. "Transes Atlantiques." *Jazz* (special issue on "La France découvre le jazz") (January): 30–31.

Hammond, John. 1944. Letter to the Editor. *Metronome* (February): 7 ff.

———. 1945. "Is the Duke Deserting Jazz?" *Jazz Record* (February): 2–3.

Hampton, Lionel, with James Haskins. 1989. *Hamp: An Autobiography.* New York: Warner Books.

Harding, James. 1972. *The Ox on the Roof.* London: Macdonald.

Harris, Pat. 1950. "Diz Sacrifices Spark to Get His 'Bop with a Beat.'" *Down Beat* (January 13): 8.

Harrison, Richard G. 1946. "Room for Two Schools of Jazz Thought Today." *Down Beat* (January 4): 10 ff.

Harvey, Holman. 1937. "It's Swing." *Readers Digest* (January): 99–102.

Hassan, Ihab. 1987. *The Postmodern Turn: Essays in Postmodern Theory and Culture.* Columbus: Ohio State University Press.

"Hear That Big Sound." 1965. *Life* (May 21): 83–98.

Heard, J. C. 1947. "Rebop Is Not Jazz." *Jazz Record* (March): 10.

Hebdige, Dick. 1979. *Subculture: The Meaning of Style.* London: Methuen.

Herbert, Michel. 1967. *La Chanson à Montmartre.* Paris: La Table Ronde.

Herbert, Robert L. 1988. *Impressionism: Art, Leisure, and Parisian Society.* New Haven: Yale.

Hertsgaard, Mark. 1995. *A Day in the Life. The Music and Artistry of the Beatles.* New York: Delta.

Heylin, Clinton. 1993. *From the Velvets to the Voidoids: A Pre-History for a Post-Punk World.* New York: Penguin.

Hickey, Dave. 1977. "Martin on Ramones: Now That's Freedom." *Village Voice* (February 21): 79.

Hoban, Phoebe. 1999. *Basquiat.* New York: Penguin.

Hodeir, André. 1956. *Jazz: Its Evolution and Essence.* New York: Grove.

Hodes, Art. 1945. Editorial. *Jazz Record* (December): 16.

———. N.d. *Oral History File,* vol. II. Newark: Institute of Jazz Studies (Rutgers University).

Holden, Stephen. 1979. "The B-52s' American Graffiti." *Village Voice* (August 13): 50.

Holmstrom, John, ed. 1996. *Punk: The Original.* New York: Original Trans-High Publishing.

"How Deaf Can You Get?" 1948. *Time* (May 17): 76–77.

Hubner, Alma. 1944. "Must Jazz Be Progressive?" *Jazz Record* (April): 8–9.

Huelsenbeck, Richard. 1974. *Memoirs of a Dada Drummer.* New York: Viking.

Hughes, Allen. 1969. "The Kids Want Rock; Why Won't Teachers Teach It?" *New York Times* (August 17): 11, 12.

Hunt, David. 1968. "Rock Changes for the Better!" *Music Journal* (September): 42 ff.

Huyssen, Andreas. 1986. *After the Great Divide: Modernism, Mass Culture, and Postmodernism.* Bloomington: Indiana University Press.

———. 1995. "Escape from Amnesia: The Museum as Mass Medium." In *Twilight Memories: Marking Time in a Culture of Amnesia.* New York: Routledge.

"I Am My Words." 1963. *Newsweek* (November 4): 94–95.

"Improved Dizzy Band Cuts Old to Shreds." 1948. *Down Beat* (October 20): 3.

"Influence of the Year: Charlie Parker." 1948. *Metronome* (January): 19.

"Influence of the Year: Dizzy Gillespie." 1946. *Metronome* (January): 24.

"Is Beatlemania Dead?" 1966. *Time* (September 2): 389–91.

"Is Dixieland Stuff Coming Back?" 1935. *Metronome* (September): 25.

"Ist Das nicht Eine Sad Riff, Himmler?" 1944. *Down Beat* (May 1): 2.

"It's Getting Better . . . " 1967. *Newsweek* (June 26): 78.

Jacobson, Bernard. 1966. "By an Unknown Master—The Baroque Beatles Book." *High Fidelity Musical America* (February): 67.

Jameson, Fredric. 1971. *Marxism and Form.* Princeton: Princeton University Press.

———. 1991. *Postmodernism, or, The Cultural Logic of Late Capitalism.* Durham, N.C.: Duke University Press.

"The Jargon of Jazz." 1936. *American Mercury* (May): x.

Jasper, Leon. 1979. "The Contortions: Vandal's Delight." *Village Voice* (November 12): 85.

"Jazz Looks Ahead." 1945. *Metronome* (October): 10.

"The Jazz of Yesteryear." 1944. *Metronome* (April): 8.

Jelavich, Peter. 1985. "Cabaret Modernism: Between Political Aggression and Aesthetic Intimacy." In *Munich and Theatrical Modernism: Politics, Playwriting, and Performance, 1890–1914.* Cambridge. Harvard University Press.

———. 1993. *Berlin Cabaret.* Cambridge: Harvard University Press.

"Jim Crow Stuff Still Spreading!: Girl Trumpeter Tastes Southern Chivalry and Color Ousts Mab's Men." 1946. *Down Beat* (July 29): 1.

Johnson, Tom. 1972. "Someone's in the Kitchen—with Music." *New York Times* (October 8): 21.

———. 1977. "Artsy Pop on a Gallery Jukebox." *Village Voice* (February 28): 56.

Jones, Leroi. 1963. *Blues People.* New York: Morrow Quill.

"Kansas City Court Makes Just Ruling." 1946. *Down Beat* (January 14): 10.

Kaye, Lenny. 1972. Liner Notes to *Nuggets.* Elektra.

Kempton, Sally. 1966. "Raga Rock: It's Not Moonlight on the Ganges." *Village Voice* (March 31): 23.

———. 1968. "Zappa & the Mothers: Ugly Can Be Beautiful." *Village Voice* (January 11): 1.

Kirby, Michael, and Victoria Nes Kirby. 1986. *Futurist Performance.* New York: PAJ Publications.

Klein, Jean-Claude. 1991. *La Chanson à l'affiche.* Paris: Éditions du May.

Klüver, Billy, and Julie Martin. 1989. *Kiki's Paris.* New York: Harry N. Abrams.

Knight, Arthur. 1964. "Beatles Anyone?" *Saturday Review* (September 19): 30.

Kozak, Roman. 1976. "Punk Grows in N.Y." *Billboard* (November 20): 1, 66, 86.

Kozinn, Allan. 1995. *The Beatles.* London: Phaidon.

Krenek, Ernst. 1939. *Music Here and Now.* Translated by Barthold Fles. New York: W. W. Norton.

Kretchmer, Arthur. 1965. "Newport: It's All Right, Ma, I'm Only Playin' R & R." *Village Voice* (August 5): 6.

Labracherie, Pierre. 1967. *La Vie quotidienne de la bohème littéraire au XIXième siècle.* Paris: Hachette.

Landau, Jon. 1968a. "Bob Dylan: John Wesley Harding." *Crawdaddy!* (May): 11–17.

———. 1968b. "Rock and Art." *Rolling Stone* (July 20): 18–19.

———. 1969. Review of *Beggar's Banquet.* In *The Rolling Stone Record Review* 1971, 96–103.

———. 1972. *It's Too Late to Stop Now.* San Francisco: Straight Arrow Books.

Laude, Jean. 1968. *La Peinture française (1905–1914) et l'art nègre.* Paris: Éditions Klincksieck.

Lee, Amy. 1949. "Figs Might Do Well to Take a Hint from Bop." *Down Beat* (May 6): 2.

Lees, Gene. 1967. "Beatles, Op. 15." *High Fidelity Magazine* (August): 94.

Lelyveld, Joseph. 1966. "Ravi Shankar Gives West a New Sound That's Old in East." *New York Times* (June 20): 22.

Lemaître, Jules. 1888. *Impressions de théâtre.* Deuxieme série. Paris: Lecène et Oudin.

———. 1894. *Les Gaîtés du Chat Noir.* Paris: Paul Ollendorff.

"Let Us Now Praise Little Men." 1963. *Time* (May 31): 40.

Letters. 1966. *Sing Out!* (January). Also in McGregor 1972, 117–20.

Letters to the Editor. 1964. *New York Times* (April 19): VI, 46, 48.

Levin, Kim. 1980. "The Times Square Show." *Arts* (September): 87–89.

Levin, Michael. 1946. "Diggin' the Discs with Mix." *Down Beat* (October 21): 21–22.

———. 1947a. "Dizzy, Bird, Ella, Pack Carnegie." *Down Beat* (October 22): 1, 3.

———. 1947b. *Down Beat* (August 13): 16.

———. 1948. "Jazz Is Neurotic—Kenton." *Down Beat* (January 14): 1.

Levin, Michael, and John S. Wilson. 1949. "No Bop Roots in Jazz: Parker." *Down Beat* (September 9): 1.

Levine, George ed. 1994. *Aesthetics and Ideology*. New Brunswick, N.J.: Rutgers University Press.

Levy, Jules. 1928. *Les Hydropathes*. Paris: Andre Delpeuch.

Lewis, Fredrick. 1963. "Britons Succumb to Beatlemania." *New York Times* (December 1): 124–26.

Linna, Miriam. 1979. "Next Big Thing." *New York Rocker* (July): 27.

Lippard, Lucy R., et al. 1985. *Pop Art*. New York: Thames and Hudson, 1985.

Lucas, John. 1944. "More on Semantics." *Jazz Record* (December): 5 ff.

———. 1945. "Gettin' the *Esquire* Bounce." *Jazz Session* (November–December): 16 ff.

Lynes, Russell. 1949. "Highbrow, Middlebrow, Lowbrow." *Harper's* (February): 19–28.

Lyotard, Jean-Francois. 1984. *The Postmodern Condition: A Report on Knowledge*. Minneapolis: University of Minnesota Press.

MacDonald, Ian. 1994. *Revolution in the Head: The Beatles' Records and the Sixties*. New York: Henry Holt.

"Mannerist Phase." 1968. *Time* (December 6): 53.

Marcus, Greil. 1975a. *Mystery Train: Images of America in Rock 'n' Roll Music*. New York: Plume Books.

———. 1975b. "Patti Smith Exposes Herself." *Village Voice* (November 24): 97–98.

———. 1977. "Ramones Loosen Up." *Village Voice* (December 12): 57.

———. 1980. *Stranded*. New York: Alfred A. Knopf.

———. 1989. *Lipstick Traces: A Secret History of the 20th Century*. Cambridge: Harvard University Press.

———. 1991. "The Beatles." In *The Rolling Stone Illustrated History of Rock & Roll*, edited by Anthony DeCurtis et al., 209–22. New York: Random House.

Marcus, Greil, ed. 1969. *Rock and Roll Will Stand*. Boston: Beacon Press.

Marsh, Dave. 1971a. "Looney Toons." *Creem* (March): 63.

———. 1971b. "Looney Toons." *Creem* (May): 42–43.

———. 1971c. "Looney Toons." *Creem* (October): 24–25.

———. 1977a. "Hey Rocky, What's a Punk?" *Rolling Stone* (March 10): 29.

———. 1977b. "Punk, Inc." *Rolling Stone* (December 29): 33.

McAuliffe, Arthur. 1945. "On Moldy Figs." *Metronome* (August): 13 ff.

McCarthy, Tom. 1974a. "Looking Back at the Prophets." *Village Voice* (May 2): 73.

———. 1974b. "Patti: Poet as Macho Woman." *Village Voice* (February 7): 42.

McCormack, Ed. 1975. "N.Y. Club's Talent Search: Anybody Listening?" *Rolling Stone* (September 23): 26.

McGregor, Craig. 1972. *Bob Dylan: A Retrospective*. New York: Morrow Quill.

McGuigan, Cathleen. 1985. "New Art, New Money: The Marketing of an American Artist." *New York Times Magazine* (February 10): 20 ff.

McKenna, Kristine. 1981. "Glenn Branca's Heavy Metal." *New York Rocker* (November): 24–25.

McLean, Greg. 1979. "Static." *New York Rocker* (November): 16.

———. 1980. "Dark Day." *New York Rocker* (October): 30.

McNeil, Legs, and Gillian McCain, eds. 1996. *Please Kill Me: The Uncensored Oral History of Punk*. New York: Grove Press.

McNeill, Don. 1967. "Report on the State of the Beatles." *Crawdaddy!* (September): 6.

McRae, Barry. 1988. *Dizzy Gillespie*. New York: Universe Books.

Meehan, Thomas. 1965. "Public Writer No. 1?" *New York Times* (December 13): VI, 44.

Mellers, Wilfrid. 1968. *Caliban Reborn: Renewal in Twentieth-Century Music*. London: Gollancz.

———. 1969. "New Music in a New World." In Eisen 1969, 180–88.

———. 1973. *Twilight of the Gods: The Beatles in Retrospect*. London: Faber.

Meltzer, Richard. 1975. "The Dictators' Bad Guys *Per Se*" [mistakenly entitled "Transcribing Bessie Smith"]. *Village Voice* (May 5): 124, 128.

Melzer, Annabelle. 1980. *Latest Rage the Big Drum*. Ann Arbor, Mich.: UMI Research Press.

"Message Time." 1965. *Time* (September 17): 102 ff.

"The Messengers." 1967. *Time* (September 22): 60–62 ff.

Miannay, Régis. 1981. *Maurice Rollinat: Poète et musicien du fantastique*. Paris: Éditions Minard.

Michaud, Guy. 1947. *Message poetique du symbolisme*. 3 vols. Paris: Librairie Nizet.

Michener, James A. 1965. "One Near-Square Who Doesn't Knock the Rock." *New York Times* (October 31): 56–57, 96.

Milhaud, Darius. 1924. "Les Resources nouvelles de la musique." *L'Esprit nouveau* (no. 25).

———. 1927. *Études*. Paris: Claude Aveline.

———. 1953. *Notes without Music*. Translated by Donald Evans. New York: Alfred A. Knopf.

———. 1982. *Notes sur la musique*. Edited by Jeremy Drake. Paris: Flammarion.

Miller, Jim ed. 1980. *The Rolling Stone History of Rock and Roll,* 2nd ed. New York: Random House.

Mitchell, Bonner. 1966. *Les Manifestes littéraires de la Belle Epoque*. Paris: Seghers.

"Mix-Master to the Beatles." 1967. *Time* (June 16): 67.

Modlin, Jules. 1944. "Notes toward a Definition of Jazz." *Needle* (June): 20–21.

"The Moldy Fig in Reverse." 1945. *Jazz Session* (September–October): 20–21.

Moore, Carmen. 1972. "New Time: Shaking Music out of the Boas." *Village Voice* (December 21): 45–46.

Morand, Paul. 1928. *A.O.F. Paris-Tombouctou*. Paris: Flammarion.

Morgenstern, Dan. 1967. "A Message to Our Readers." *Down Beat* (June 29): 13.

Mortifoglio, Richard. 1975. "Watch Television." *Village Voice* (July 7): 95.

———. 1977. "Richard Hell Jangles the Void." *Village Voice* (September 26): 62.

———. 1978. "Devo's Entropy Party: Bring Your Own Soul." *Village Voice* (October 30): 79.

Motherwell, Robert, ed. 1989. *The Dada Painters and Poets*. Cambridge, Mass.: Belknap Press.

Moufarrege, Nicolas A. 1982. "Another Wave, Still More Savagely Than the First: Lower East Side, 1982." *Arts* (September): 69–73.

———. 1983. "East Village." *Flash Art* (March): 36–41.

"Movies Fix Merit by Color of Skin." 1946. *Down Beat* (July 29): 10.

Moynahan, Jim. 1944. "Jazz—A Vanishing Art." *Jazz Record* (July): 6–8.

"Music Can Destroy Our Racial Bigotry." 1945. *Down Beat* (September 15): 10.

"Music Educators Urge 'Rock' Garden in Capital." 1969. *New York Times* (November 1): 39.

"Music Teachers Listen to Youth at Symposium in Tanglewood." 1967. *New York Times* (July 28): 21.

"Musician of the Year—Lennie Tristano." 1948. *Metronome* (January): 19.

Needs, Kris. 1976. "London/The Clash." *New York Rocker* (December): 17, 30.

———. 1977. "New Wave Records." *New York Rocker* (March): 10.

"Negro Bands Lose 'Busses.'" 1943. *Metronome* (February): 5.

Nelson, Chris. 1980. "A Brief Debriefing of 8-Eyed Spy." *New York Rocker* (May 28): 20, 39.

Nelson, Paul. 1965. "Newport Folk Festival, 1965." *Sing Out!* (November). Also in McGregor 1972, 73–76.

———. 1966. "Bob Dylan: Another View." *Sing Out!* (February–March). Also in McGregor 1972, 104–7.

———. 1974. "Moonstruck over the Miamis." *Village Voice* (December 16): 132.

"The New Madness." 1963. *Time* (November 15): 64.

"The New Troubadours." 1966. *Time* (October 28): 92 ff.

Newfield, Jack. 1965a. "Blowin' in the Wind: A Folk-Music Revolt." *Village Voice* (January 14): 4.

———. 1965b. "Mods, Rockers Fight over New Thing Called 'Dylan.'" *Village Voice* (September 2): 1.

Nicholson, Linda J., ed. 1990. *Feminism/Postmodernism*. New York: Routledge.

"Nightly Bop Bashes. 1948. *Down Beat* (May 9): 2.

"The 1972 *Creem* Rock 'n' Roll Reader's Poll Results." 1973. *Creem* (June): 44–49.

"The Nitty-Gritty Sound." 1966. *Newsweek* (December 19): 102 ff.

Nooger, Dan. 1974. "Punkoid Pleasure." *Village Voice* (May 2): 68.

————. 1979. "The Rap: Clinton/Chance on Records, Reactions, and Rip Offs." *New York Rocker* (November): 7–10.

Norman, Philip. 1981. *Shout!: The Beatles in Their Generation.* New York: Simon and Schuster.

Nussner, Richard. 1972. "Velvet Underground." *Village Voice* (November 9): 61.

Oberthür, Mariel. 1984. *Cafés and Cabarets of Montmartre.* Salt Lake City: Peregrine Smith.

————. 1992. *Le Chat Noir (1881–1897).* Paris: Réunion des Musées Nationaux.

Ochs, Phil. 1965. "It Ain't Me, Babe." *Village Voice* (August 12): 4.

O'Grady, Lorraine. 1973. "Dealing with the Dolls Mystique." *Village Voice* (October 4): 52.

"An Open Letter to Fred Robbins." 1946. *Jazz Record* (October): 12, 18.

"Open Up, Tune In, Turn On." 1967. *Time* (June 23): 53.

"Opinions sur l'art nègre." 1920. *Action* (April 3): 24.

"Other Noises, Other Notes." 1967. *Time* (March 3): 63.

Owens, Craig. 1984. "Commentary: The Problem with Puerilism." *Art in America* (summer): 162–63.

Page, Tim. 1979a. "Contortions Crack Up." *New York Rocker* (August): 12–13, 43.

————. 1979b. "Contortions: James White & the Blacks: Club 57." *New York Rocker* (April–May): 47.

————. 1979c. "Jeffrey Lohn: Thoughts of a Theoretical Girl." *New York Rocker* (July): 21, 23.

Pakenham, Michael. 1992. "L'Illustre Sapeck." *Romantisme* (no. 75): 37–44.

Palmer, Robert. 1977a. "Laurie Anderson: Mostly Pop." *New York Times* (August 29): 34.

————. 1977b. "A New Life for the Bowery." *New York Times* (March 15): C1.

————. 1977c. "Rock: New Theater Opens with Punk." *New York Times* (December 29): III, 14.

————. 1978. "Rock: The Ramones." *New York Times* (January 9): III, 27.

————. 1981. "Esthetic of the Fake Stirs Rock World." *New York Times* (February 13): III, C1, C25.

Panassié, Hughes. 1934. *Le Jazz hot.* Paris: Correa.

————. 1942. *The Real Jazz.* New York: Smith and Durrell.

Paudrat, Jean-Louis. 1984. "From Africa." In *"Primitivism" in 20th Century Art,* edited by William Rubin, vol. 1, 125–78. New York: Museum of Modern Art.

"P.D.Q. Bach (1807–1742)? and the Baroque Beatles Book." 1965. *American Record Guide* (February): 508–10.

Peck, Abe. 1985. *Uncovering the Sixties: The Life and Times of the Underground Press.* New York: Pantheon Books.

Perloff, Nancy. 1991. *Art and the Everyday: Popular Entertainment and the Circle of Erik Satie.* New York: Oxford University Press.

Perreault, John. 1981. "Low Tide." *SoHo Weekly News* (February 25): 49.

Perry, Mark. 2000. *Sniffin' Glue: The Essential Punk Accessory.* Edited by Terry Rawlins. London: Sanctuary Publishing.

Persky, Lisa. 1976. "Are the Ramones or Is the Ramone?" *New York Rocker* (September): 28–29.

————. 1977. "Pimp-Rock?" *New York Rocker* (July–August): 43.

Pessis, Jacques, and Jacques Crépineau. 1990. *The Moulin Rouge.* New York: St. Martin's Press.

Peterson, Richard A., and Roger M. Kern. 1996. "Changing Highbrow Taste: From Snob to Omnivore." *American Sociological Review* 61 (October): 900–7.

Peyser, Joan. 1967. "The Music of Sound or, The Beatles and the Beatless." In Eisen 1969, 126–37.

Phillips, Deborah C. 1981. "New Faces in Alternate Spaces." *Art News* 80 (November): 90–100.

Phillips, McLandish. 1971. "Mercer Stages Are a Supermarket." *New York Times* (November 2): 44.

Phillips, Tom. 1967. "Beatles' 'Sgt. Pepper': The Album as Art Form." *Village Voice* (June 22): 15.

Piccarella, John. 1978. "Blondie Enters Rock and Roll Heaven." *Village Voice* (November 27): 83.

———. 1979. "Anarchy in No New York." *Village Voice* (January 1): 55.

Plagens, Peter. 1981. "The Academy of the Bad." *Art in America* 69 (November): 11–13.

Platt, Alan. 1979a. "Hairdos by Laverne." *SoHo Weekly News* (August 9): 17.

———. 1979b. "James Chance Passes for White." *SoHo Weekly News* (February 8): 41, 42.

———. 1979c. "No Chance." *SoHo Weekly News* (January 4): 25, 26, 39.

Poirier, Richard. 1967. "Learning from the Beatles." *Partisan Review* (fall): 526–46.

"Pops and Boppers." 1966. *Newsweek* (December 19): 66.

Prasteau, Jean. 1975. *La Merveilleuse aventure du Casino de Paris.* Paris: Denoel.

"Racial Hatred Rears Ugly Mug in Music." 1944. *Down Beat* (August 1): 1.

"Racial Prejudice Crops Out Again." 1945. *Down Beat* (December 1): 10.

Raynaud, Ernest. 1903. "Les Samedis de *La Plume.*" *La Plume* (April 15): 425–40.

———. 1918, 1920, 1922. *La Mêlée symboliste.* 3 vols. Paris: La Renaissance du Livre.

Rearick, Charles. 1985. *Pleasures of the Belle Epoque: Entertainment and Festivity in Turn-of-the-Century France.* New Haven: Yale University Press.

Recoil, John. 1981. "Rhys Chatham: Classical Road to Rock." *New York Times* (April 17): III, 15.

Ricard, Rene. 1982. "The Pledge of Allegiance." *Artforum International* (November): 42–49.

Richard, Noel. 1961. *A l'Aube du symbolisme.* Paris: Nizet.

Richardson, Joanna. 1969. *The Bohemians: La Vie de bohème in Paris 1830–1914.* New York: A. S. Barnes.

Richter, Hans. 1978. *Dada: Art and Anti-Art.* New York: Oxford University Press.

Ries, Frank W. D. 1986. *The Dance Theatre of Jean Cocteau.* Ann Arbor, Mich.: UMI Research Press.

Rifkin, Joshua. 1987. "On the Music of the Beatles." In Thomson and Guitman 1987, 113–25.

Robinson, Lisa. 1975. "The New York Bands." *Hit Parader* (October): 20 ff.

Robinson, Louie. 1965. "Rock 'n' Roll Becomes Respectable." *Ebony* (November): 48–56.

Rockwell, John. 1975a. "Bowery Is 'Home' to Young Bands." *New York Times* (July 23): 22.

———. 1975b. "Speculations about Rock Spectacles." *New York Times* (May 16): 24.

———. 1975c. "A Trio that Shows Art's Effect on Rock." *New York Times* (September 16): 52.

———. 1976a. "Orchestra Luna Plays Club Date." *New York Times* (July 2): 14.

———. 1976b. "The Pop Life." *New York Times* (May 5): III, 10.

———. 1976c. "Talking Heads: Cool in the Glare of Hot Rock." *New York Times* (March 24): 25.

———. 1976d. "Two Rock Groups at Bottom Line." *New York Times* (May 12): 35.

———. 1977a. "The Artistic Success of the Talking Heads." *New York Times* (September 11): 14.

———. 1977b. "A Guide to the City-Suburb Rock and Pop Scene." *New York Times* (October 28): C10–11.

———. 1977c. "Rock: Blondie." *New York Times* (January 24): 17.

———. 1978a. "B-52's, Rock Band from Georgia." *New York Times* (June 3): II, 1.

———. 1978b. "Punk Rock: Contortions, a Quintet." *New York Times* (December 12): C17.

———. 1978c. "Ramones, Doyens of Punk Rock in the Big Time." *New York Times* (January 6): III, 11.

———. 1978d. "Rock: Underground." *New York Times* (May 8): III, 14.

———. 1979a. "Rock: 2 of the No-Wave." *New York Times* (June 28): III, 17.

———. 1979b. "Rock: 'No Wave' Lounge Lizards." *New York Times* (July 8): 28.

———. 1980a. "The Connections of 'Punk-Jazz.'" *New York Times* (January 20): 22D.

———. 1980b. "Laurie Anderson Grows as a Performance Artist." *New York Times* (October 27): III, 4.

———. 1982. "His Forte Is Massive Sonic Grandeur." *New York Times* (May 2): II, 23.

"Rod McKuen Says Beatles Saved Folk Music." 1964. *Variety* (April 25): 12.

The Rolling Stone Record Review. 1971. New York: Pocket Books.

Rorem, Ned. 1967. "Some Last Thoughts on the Beatles." *Village Voice* (December 21): 26 ff.

———. 1968a. "The Music of the Beatles." *New York Review of Books* (January 18): 23–27.

———. 1968b. *Music and People.* New York: George Braziller.

———. 1969. "Oh, Richard Goldstein, Don't You Groove for Me." *New York Times* (October 28): 19.

Rorty, Richard. 1989. *Contingency, Irony, and Solidarity.* Cambridge: Cambridge University Press.

Rose, Frank. 1977. "Babytalking Heads." *Village Voice* (November 11): 53–54.

Rose, Phyllis. 1989. *Jazz Cleopatra: Josephine Baker in Her Time.* New York: Doubleday.

Rosenstock, Laura. 1984. "Léger: *The Creation of the World.*" In Rubin 1984, vol. 2, 475–86.

Rovetch, Emily. 1985. "The Chat Noir and the Mirliton: Creating the Myth of Montmartre." Senior thesis, Harvard University, n.d.

Rubin, William. 1984. "Picasso." In *"Primitivism" in 20th Century Art,* edited by William Rubin, vol. 1, 241–343. New York: Museum of Modern Art.

Russell, Ross. 1973. *Bird Lives!* London: Quartet Books.

Sachs, Maurice. 1932. *La Décade de l'illusion.* Paris: Gallimard.

———. 1939. *Au Temps du Boeuf sur le Toit.* Paris: Éditions de la Nouvelle Revue Critique.

———. 1946. *Le Sabbat, souvenirs d'une jeunesse orageuse.* Paris: Correa.

Sales, Grover. 1984. *Jazz: America's Classical Music.* Englewood Cliffs, N.J.: Prentice-Hall.

Sander, Ellen. 1968. "The Beatles: Plain White Wrapper." *Saturday Review* (December 28): 58.

———. 1969. "The Rolling Stones: Beggars' Triumph." *Saturday Review* (January 25): 48.

Sandler, Irving. 1996. *Art of the Postmodern Era.* New York: HarperCollins.

Sandow, Gregory. 1980a. "Classical Music for Loud Guitars." *Village Voice* (February 25): 62.

———. 1980b. "From Rags to Rockers." *Village Voice* (October 15): 94.

———. 1980c. "Laurie Anderson: American on the Move: Touching, Funny, Vivid, Assured." *Village Voice* (November 5): 78.

———. 1981a. "Branca's Progress." *Village Voice* (August 14): 92, 112.

———. 1981b. "But Is It Art?" *Village Voice* (March 4): 63.

———. 1981c. "The New Music." *Village Voice* (May 13): 92.

Sanouillet, Michel. 1993. *Dada à Paris.* Paris: Flammarion.

"Sarah Vaughan Beaten Up by Gang." 1946. *Down Beat* (August 26): 2.

Sargeant, Winthrop. 1969. "Working on the Rockpile." *New Yorker* (November 11): 211–13.

Sarris, Andrew. 1964. "A Hard Day's Night." *Village Voice* (August 27): 13.

"Satchmo Comes Back." 1947. *Time* (September 1): 32.

Savage, Jon. 1991. *England's Dreaming: Anarchy, Sex Pistols, Punk Rock and Beyond.* New York: St. Martin's Press.

Scarry, Elaine. 1999. *On Beauty and Being Just.* Princeton: Princeton University Press.

"Scenes." 1972. *Village Voice* (November 16): 54.

Schwartz, Andy. 1978. "To Our Readers." *New York Rocker* (April–May): 4.

Seabrook, John. 2000. *Nobrow.* New York: Knopf.

"Seems We Heard that Song Before." 1949. *Down Beat* (January 14): 10.

Segel, Harold B. 1987. *Turn-of-the-Century Cabaret.* New York: Columbia University Press.

Seigel, Jerrold. 1985. *Bohemian Paris.* New York: Viking.

"Sgt. Pepper." 1967. *New Yorker* (June 24): 22–23.

Shaw, Arnold. 1971. *The Street that Never Slept.* New York: Coward, McGann, and Geoghegan.

Shaw, Greg. 1970. "R.I.A.W.O.L." *Who Put the Bomp* (July–August): 4.

———. 1971a. "Feedback." *Who Put the Bomp* (fall–winter): 45–58.

———. 1971b. "Juke Box Jury." *Creem* (March): 72–73.

———. 1971c. "Juke Box Jury." *Creem* (May): 94.

———. 1971d. "Prelude to the Morning of an Inventory of the 60's." *Who Put the Bomp* (spring): 9–10.

———. 1971e. "The Real Rock 'n' Roll Underground—Fanzines." *Creem* (June): 22–27.

———. 1971f. "R.I.A.W.O.L." *Who Put the Bomp* (spring): 4–6.

———. 1971g. "R.I.A.W.O.L" *Who Put the Bomp* (fall–winter): 4–8.

———. 1972a. "Feedback." *Who Put the Bomp* (spring): 40–53.

———. 1972b. "Juke Box Jury." *Creem* (December): 62–63.

———. 1973a. "Juke Box Jury." *Creem* (January): 78, 80.

———. 1973b. "Juke Box Jury." *Creem* (February): 74–75.

———. 1973c. "Juke Box Jury." *Creem* (April): 66–67.

———. 1973d. "Punk Rock: The Arrogant Underbelly of Sixties Pop." *Rolling Stone* (January 4): 68, 70.

———. 1974. "The Beat." *Who Put the Bomp* (summer): 4 ff.

———. 1975. "The Beat." *Who Put the Bomp* (spring): 4 ff.

———. 1976. "The *WBTB* Punk Gallery." *Who Put the Bomp* (October): 40–41.

———. 1978. "New Wave Goodbye?" *New York Rocker* (September): 34–35.

Shelton, Robert. 1961. "Bob Dylan: A Distinctive Folk-Song Stylist." *New York Times* (September 29).Also in McGregor 1972, 17–18.

———. 1963. "Bob Dylan Sings His Compositions." *New York Times* (April 13). Also in McGregor 1972, 28–29.

———. 1965a. "The Beatles Will Make the Scene Here Again, but the Scene Has Changed." *New York Times* (August 11): 40.

———. 1965b. "Pop Singers and Song Writers Racing Down Bob Dylan's Road." *New York Times* (August 27): 17.

———. 1966a. "A Law Firm They're Not." *New York Times* (August 28): 15 ff.

———. 1966b. "On Records: The Folk-Rock Rage." *New York Times* (January 30): II, 21.

———. 1966c. "Son of Suzy Creamcheese." *New York Times* (December 25): 11–12.

———. 1986. *No Direction Home: The Life and Music of Bob Dylan*. New York: William Morrow.

Shore, Michael. 1978. "Hullabaloo in the Twilight Zone." *SoHo Weekly News* (July 28): 10.

———. 1980. "How Does It Look? How Does It Sound?" *Art News* (November): 78–85.

Silber, Irwin. 1964. "An Open Letter to Bob Dylan." *Sing Out!* (November). Also in McGregor 1972, 66–68.

———. 1965. "Newport Folk Festival, 1965." *Sing Out!* (November). Also in McGregor 1972, 71–72.

———. 1966. "Topical Song: Polarization Sets In." *Sing Out!* (March). Also in McGregor 1972, 102–3.

Simon, George T. 1946. "B. G. Explains." *Metronome* (October): 18.

———. 1948a. "Benny Blows Bop." *Metronome* (August): 12.

———. 1948b. "Bop's the Easy Way Out, Claims Louis." *Metronome* (March): 14–15.

———. 1949. "Bop Confuses Benny." *Metronome* (October): 15, 35.

Smith, Charles Edward. 1942. *The Jazz Record Book*. New York: Smith and Durrell.

———. 1944. "The Jazz of Yesteryear." *Metronome* (May): 18–19.

Smith, Valerie D. 1981. "New Waive New Wane No Wonder." *Flash Art* 103 (summer): 56–58.

Smucker, Tom. 1972. "When Punk Rock Met the Vietcong." *Village Voice* (June 1): 45.

"So You Want to Read about Jazz." 1943. *Metronome* (December): 21.

"So You Want to Read about Jazz." 1944a. *Metronome* (February): 28.

"So You Want to Read about Jazz." 1944b. *Metronome* (March): 28.

"So You Want to Read about Jazz." 1944c. *Metronome* (June): 25.

Soderholm, James ed. 1997. *Beauty and the Critic: Aesthetics in an Age of Cultural Studies*. Tuscaloosa: University of Alabama Press.

Sontag, Susan. 1965. "One Culture and the New Sensibility." In *Against Interpretation and Other Essays,* 293–304. New York: Dell, 1967.

"Sop-Pop Celebrity." 1991. *Economist* (September 14): 75.

Stearns, Marshall. 1956. *The Story of Jazz*. London: Oxford University Press.

Steegmuller, Francis. 1970. *Cocteau*. Boston: David R. Godine.

"Steele Bans 'Be-Bop' at L.A. Station; but What He Means by 'Be-Bop' Ain't." 1946. *Metronome* (April): 15.

Steinke, Gerhardt Edward. 1967. *The Life and Work of Hugo Ball.* The Hague: Mouton.

Steins, Martin. 1977. *Blaise Cendrars: Bilans nègres,* No. 169 of *Archives des lettres modernes.* Paris: Minard.

Stepanek, Anton. 1944. "Jazz and Semantics." *Jazz Record* (November): 5 ff.

Sternfield, Aaron. 1965. "Rock + Folk + Protest = An Erupting New Sound." *Billboard* (August 21): 1, 14.

"Stompin' at the Savoy." 1943. *Metronome* (June): 5.

Stovall, Tyler. 1996. *Paris Noir: African Americans in the City of Light.* New York: Houghton Mifflin.

Stowe, David W. 1994. *Swing Changes: Big Band Jazz in New Deal America.* Cambridge: Harvard University Press.

Strickland, Edward. 1993. *Minimalism: Origins.* Bloomington: Indiana University Press.

Strongin, Theodore. 1964. "Musicologically . . . " *New York Times* (February 10): 53.

Sui, Anna. 1979. "Directory." *New York Rocker* (February–March): 44–45.

Sukey, Pett. 1977. "New Wave Air Waves." *New York Rocker* (September–October): 23.

Swenson, John. 1973. Riffs. *Village Voice* (July 26): 53.

"Swing, Swing, Oh Beautiful Swing." 1936. *Metronome* (February): 19 ff.

"A Symposium: Is Folk Real?" 1966. *New York Times* (February 20): II, 22.

"Tapping the Roots: Upsurge of Interest in Old-Fashioned Rock 'n' Roll." 1968. *Time* (March 22): 46.

"Ted Steele Jab at Hot Jive Smells." 1946. *Down Beat* (April 8): 10.

Therien, Nathan Ashline. 1985. *Popular Song as Social Experience in 19th Century France: From National Culture to Commodity.* Ph.D. diss., Harvard University.

"They Battle for Their Beatles." 1967. *New York Times* (July 2): II, 4D.

"30 New York Bands." 1980. *New York Rocker* (December): 26–27.

"This Way to the Egress." 1967. *Newsweek* (November 6): 101.

Thomson, Elizabeth, and David Guitman. 1987. *The Lennon Companion.* New York: Shirmer Books.

Thomson, Thomas. 1965. "Music Streams." *Life* (May 21): 93.

Ticks, Ana. 1946. "Jazz à la Billy Berg." *Metronome* (February): 26.

Ticks, Fran. 1946. "The Be-bop Feud." *Metronome* (April): 44–45.

Touchard, Jean. 1968. *La Gloire de Béranger.* 2 vols. Paris: Armand Colin.

Tracy, Jack. 1950. "Gillespie's Crew Great Again, but May Break Up." *Down Beat* (June 16): 1.

Trakin, Roy. 1978a. "Avant Kindergarten (Sturm und Drone)." *SoHo Weekly News* (January 26): 31, 37.

———. 1978b. "Nobody Waved Goodbye: Bands at Artists Space." *New York Rocker* (July–August): 18, 69.

———. 1978c. "Out to Lunch." *New York Rocker* (July–August): 19–20, 60.

———. 1979a. "Getting to No You." *New York Rocker* (January): 13.

———. 1979b. "Q. Why Interview James Chance?" *New York Rocker* (January): 14–15.

———. 1980. "D.N.A." *New York Rocker* (October): 29, 30, 31, 33.

———. 1981. "James White and the Blacks—The 80's." *New York Rocker* (January): 41.

Tristano, Lennie 1947a. "What's Right with the Beboppers." *Metronome* (July): 14, 31.

———. 1947b. "What's Wrong with the Beboppers." *Metronome* (June): 16.

Trussell, Jake, Jr.1944a. "The Jazz of Yesteryear." *Metronome* (May): 18.

———. 1944b. "Jim Crow—Upside Down." *Jazz Record* (April): 4.

Tucker, Kenneth. 1975. "CBGB Rock Festival: Bowery Woodstock." *SoHo Weekly News* (July 24): 30.

Turner, Gil. 1962. "Bob Dylan—A New Voice Singing New Songs." *Sing Out!* (October–November). Also in McGregor 1972, 22–27.

The Two Deuces. 1944. "Jazz vs. Swing, Which Is Which? Are They Both the Same?" *Metronome* (April): 22–23.

"An Ugly Story." 1943. *Metronome* (November): 4.

Ulanov, Barry. 1942. "It's Not the Book, It's the Attitude." *Metronome* (March): 11

———. 1943. "Panassié Book Draws Reverse Rave." *Metronome* (February): 14, 21.

———. 1944. "Jazz of Yesteryear." *Metronome* (May): 19 ff.

———. 1947a. "A Call to Arms—and Horns." *Metronome* (April): 15, 44.

———. 1947b. "Dizzy Gillespie." *Metronome* (September): 2.

———. 1947c. "Dizzy Heights." *Metronome* (November): 50.

———. 1947d. "The Heartless Modernists?!" *Metronome* (July): 50.

———. 1947e. "Moldy Figs vs. Moderns." *Metronome* (January): 15, 23.

———. 1947f. "Moldy Figs vs. Moderns." *Metronome* (November): 15, 23.

———. 1949a. "Master in the Making." *Metronome* (August): 14–15, 32–33.

———. 1949b. "The Means of Mastery." *Metronome* (September): 14, 26.

———. 1949c. "Skip Bop and Jump." *Metronome* (December): 12, 36.

———. 1949d. "Wha' Hoppen?" *Metronome* (February): 2.

———. 1950. "After Bop, What?" *Metronome* (April): 17, 32.

———. 1952. *A History of Jazz in America*. New York: Viking.

"The Unbarbershopped Quartet." 1964. *Time* (February 21): 46–47.

Unger, Irwin. 1974. *The Movement: A History of the American New Left 1959–1972*. New York: Harper and Row.

"Vagrant Chicks Blamed in Part for Racial Row." 1944. *Down Beat* (August 15): 12.

Vinchon, Émile. 1921. *Maurice Rollinat*. Paris: Jouve & Cie.

"The Voice of Experience." 1967. *Newsweek* (October 9): 90, 92.

Wadsley, Pat. 1979. "The Mudd Below." *SoHo Weekly News* (February 1): 53, 58.

Walsh, Stephen. 1988. *The Music of Stravinsky*. London: Routledge.

Ward, Ed. 1976. "The Kids Are All Right." *Village Voice* (November 21): 79.

Waters, Charlie. 1977. "Punk: Pretty Vacant Music." *Rolling Stone* (October 6): 103.

Watkins, Glenn. 1994. *Pyramids at the Louvre: Music, Culture, and Collage from Stravinsky to the Postmodernists*. Cambridge: Harvard University Press.

Watkins, R. 1976. "British Punk Rock Assault on Morality Only Beefs up Sales." *Variety* (December 12): 1 ff.

Watts, Michael. 1976. "So Shock Me, Punks." *Melody Maker* (September 11): 37.

Welding, Pete. 1968. "I'm Looking through You." *Down Beat* (January 11): 18–19.

Welles, Chris. 1964. "The Angry Young Folk Singer." *Life* (April 10): 109 ff.

Wenner, Jann. 1968. "Musicians Reject New Political Exploiters: Groups Drop Out from Chicago Yip-In." *Rolling Stone* (May 11): 1 ff.

"What Is This Thing Called Jazz?" 1944. *Downbeat* (April 15): 2.

"What Songs the Beatles Sang . . . " 1963. *London Times* (December 27): 4.

Wheeler, Drew. 1981. "Snakes Crawl . . . Lizards Lounge." *New York Rocker* (May): 38.

Whitburn, Joel. 1986. *Pop Memories 1890–1954*. Menomonee Falls, Wis.: Record Research.

"Whose Goose Is Golden, Or the Egg and They." 1947. *Down Beat* (January 29): 10.

"Why?" 1943. *Metronome* (March): 34.

"Why the Slump in the Dance Biz? 'Beat' Plans to Find Out." *Down Beat* (December 12): 1, 10.

Wiener, Allen J. 1994. *The Beatles: The Ultimate Recording Guide*. Holbrook, Mass.: Bob Adams.

Wiener, Jean. 1978. *Allegro appassionato*. Paris: Pierre Belfond.

Wiener, Jon. 1984. *Come Together: John Lennon in His Time*. New York: Random House.

Willett, John. 1978. *Art and Politics in the Weimar Period*. New York: Pantheon.

Williams, Martin, ed. 1959. *The Art of Jazz*. New York: Oxford University Press.

———. 1965a. "One Cheer for Rock and Roll!: Part I—There Are Some Compensations." *Down Beat* (October 7): 26–27, 39.

———. 1965b. "One Cheer for Rock and Roll!: Part II—The Razing of Vienna." *Down Beat* (October 21): 20–21.

———. 1970. *The Jazz Tradition*. New York: Oxford University Press.

Williams, Mary Lou. 1947. "Music and Progress." *Jazz Record* (November): 23.

Williams, Paul. 1966a. "Get off My Cloud." *Crawdaddy!* (February 7): 1

———. 1966b. "Gettin' Ready: The Temptations." *Crawdaddy!* (September): 29.

———. 1966c. "Revolver: The Beatles Capitol 2576." *Crawdaddy!* (September): 3–5.

———. 1967. "Sergeant Pepper as Noise." *Crawdaddy!* (September): 14.

Willis, Ellen. 1968a. "Electronic Rock." *New Yorker* (March 30): 29 ff.

———. 1968b. "Pop Ecumenicism." *New Yorker* (May 4): 175 ff.

———. 1968c. "Records: Rock, Etc." *New Yorker* (April 6): 148–49.

———. 1968d. "Records: Rock, Etc." *New Yorker* (July 6): 56 ff.

———. 1968e. "Records: Rock, Etc." *New Yorker* (August 10): 87 ff.

———. 1969. "Records: Rock, Etc.: The Big Ones." *New Yorker* (February 1): 55 ff.

———. 1979. "Velvet Underground." In *Stranded,* edited by Greil Marcus, 71–83. New York: Knopf.

Wilson, John S. 1949. "Armstrong Explains Stand against Bop." *Down Beat* (December 30): 3.

———. 1950. "Bop at End of Road, Says Dizzy." *Down Beat* (September 8): 1.

———. 1964. "2,900-Voice Chorus Joins the Beatles." *New York Times* (February 13): 26.

———. 1967. "3-Day Jazz Talks Strike Grim Note, Field Is Said to Be suffering from Dwindling Outlets." *New York Times* (October 1): 83.

Wilson, Russ. 1967. "The Future of Jazz: On the Rocks?" *Down Beat* (June 15): 67.

Winner, Langdon. 1969. "The Strange Death of Rock and Roll." In Marcus 1969, 38–55.

Winter, Carter. 1946. "An Open Letter to Fred Robbins." *Jazz Record* (October): 12, 18 and (November): 12–13.

Wolcott, James. 1975a. "A Conservative Impulse in the New Rock Underground." *Village Voice* (August 18): 6–7.

———. 1975b. "Patti Smith: Mustang Rising." *Village Voice* (March 14): 120 ff.

———. 1975c. "The Ramones: Chord Killers." *Village Voice* (July 21): 94 ff.

———. 1975d. "Voice Choices." *Village Voice* (June 23): 114.

———. 1975e. "Voice Choices." *Village Voice* (July 21): 97.

———. 1976. "The Rise of Punk Rock." *Village Voice* (March 1): 87–88.

"The Word 'Jazz' Kicked Around Too Freely." 1945. *Down Beat* (June 15): 10.

"Worrisome Days along the Street; Biz Is Bad." 1946. *Down Beat* (November 11): 1.

Yaw, Ralph. 1936. "What Is Swing?" *Metronome* (May): 22 ff.

"Yeah Indeed." 1964. *Newsweek* (August 24): 79.

"Yeah, Yeah, Yeah." 1964. *Newsweek* (February 17): 88.

"Yeah? Yeah. Yeah!" 1964. *Time* (August 14): 67.

Young, Charles M. 1977. "Rock Is Sick and Living in London." *Rolling Stone* (October 20): 68–75.

"Youth Music—A Special Report." 1969. *Music Educators Journal* (November): 43–74.

Zill, Nicholas, and John Robinson. 1994. "Name that Tune." *American Demographics* (August): 22–27.

"Zombies Put Kiss of Death on 52nd St. Jazz." 1946. *Down Beat* (February 25): 3.

INDEX

Abbaye de Thélème, 60, 61

Adorno, Theodor, 121

aesthetic appropriation: of black music by no wave, 285–86; of Brazilian music by Milhaud, 93; in high/low alliances, 16–17, 19; of jazz by Milhaud, 88–89, 100–1, 114–15; of jazz by rock, 206–7; of Negro culture, 110–12; of popular music by Stravinsky, 89–90, 91

aesthetic development of punk. *See* punk aesthetic

aesthetic discourses on jazz: artistic progress disagreements, 131–32; bebop arrival, 139; binary oppositions, 139–40; commercial success vs. artistic merit, 128–29; Dixieland war role, 124–26; emotion's place in music, 134–35; folk vs. European music role, 129–30; "jazz" vs. "swing," 126–28, 336 nn. 11, 17; political discourse interjection, 135–36, 337 n. 59; racial conflicts in jazz press, 137–38; standards debate, 132–34; written arrangements implications, 130–31

aesthetic discourses on no wave: attention given by press, 282–83; dominance by white males, 284–87; incorporation of violence in acts, 281–82; punk's relation to no wave, 279–80; rank amateurism requirement, 281. *See also* punk aesthetic

aesthetic discourses on rock, 21–23; aesthetic alternatives to Beatles, 204–5; aesthetic attitude reversal by critics, 175–76; assertions of autonomy of rock, 208–9; authenticism concept, 213; beginnings of rock as art-music, 192–93; critiques of Beatles' techniques, 165, 341 n. 10; cultural capital emphasis, 347 n. 95; early failure to achieve full ac-

creditation, 183–84, 185; first rock journals, 191–92; focus on sounds, 177–79; folk rock impact, 183; highbrow accreditation of the Beatles, 197–98; legitimacy of rock due to independence, 216; need for professional rock critics, 190; popism and inauthenticist movements, 213–15; reception of Beatles' movie, 168–70; reception of Lennon's poetry, 167–68; shifts in adult attitudes, 167; turn away from Beatles, 205

African American culture: appropriation in negrophilia, 110–12; consolidation into negrophilia, 106–7

African American music: accreditation for early rock 'n' roll, 179–80, 344 n. 76; bebop's adoption by whites, 156; commercial and critical resurgence (1978), 285; description by Cocteau, 104–5; jazz and, 9, 88; post-WWI influx into France, 108–9; rock critics' neglect of black musicians, 220–21, 284–85

African culture: appropriation in negrophilia, 110–12; artifacts' influence on French artists, 105–6; consolidation into negrophilia, 106–7

alternative rock, 324

amateurism requirement in new wave: of no wave, 281; of punk, 234–36, 245–46, 348 n. 23, 349 n. 25

Amazing Stories, 230

American Sherbo Sextette, 109

Anderson, Laurie, 297, 354 n. 90

Ansermet, Ernst-Alexandre, 110

Anthologie nègre (Cendrars), 113

Apollinaire, Guillaume, 68, 106

appropriation of aesthetics. *See* aesthetic appropriation

Aragon, Louis, 77

Area (club), 311

missing highbrow certification, 171–72; music reappraisal impetus (1965), 174–75; reception by rock press, 209; *Sergeant Pepper* review, 199–200

cultural accreditation of rock 'n' roll: critical rock press beginnings, 190–93; due to Beatles, 174–77; jazz compared to, 161–62; low-middlebrow press's turnaround, 194–96, 345 n. 16; middlebrow culture's role, 162. *See also* critical discourses on rock

cultural capital, 5–7, 12, 330 n. 8; competition between jazz and rock, 320–23; dominance of white males in rock, 221, 348 n. 125; dual market theory and, 15; vs. economic capital in rock, 324–25; emphasis in rock, 347 n. 95; highbrow attention to Beatles, 197–98, 203; new hierarchies creation, 326–27; New York vs. Montmartre, 319–20; postmodernism and, 12; rock's claim on youth, 209

cultural recognition, 5

D.N.A., 277, 288

dada movement, 30; beginnings, 74–75; coining of term, 333 n. 50; emergence of dadaists, 74; entry into avant-garde vaudeville, 77–78; post-artistic café program, 76–77; punk's connection to, 237–38

dance music: cancan, 62; at music halls, 63; no wave and, 290; punk vs. disco, 284–87

Danceteria, 311

DeAk, Edit, 303

Deauville Film Festival, 303

Debussy, Claude, 87

deca-rock, 244

Degas, Edgar, 36

Delauney, Charles, 136

Delvard, Marya, 56, 71

de Maré, Rolf, 113, 114, 115, 116

Deslys, Gaby, 109

Detroit sound, 178

deutsches Chansons in Germany, 70

Devo, 7

Dictators, 262

Dietrich, Marlene, 71

Dîners du Caveau (Dinners of the Vault), 50

disco vs. punk, 284–87

Divan Japonais, 60, 61

Dixieland revival: bebop movement vs., 150–51; Dixieland vs. swing war role, 124–26; place in jazz history, 123, 124

Dôme, 69

Doors, 205

doo-wop, 349 n. 25

Dorsey, Tommy, 151

Down Beat: decision to cover rock, 206; defense of bebop, 145, 146, 154; early accreditation for rock, 179–80; political interjections, 136; reception of the Beatles, 207; reports on Dixieland vs. bebop war, 150–51; response to bebop, 147–48, 149–50; swing endorsement, 123, 128

Down by Law, 303

downtown sound: as a borderline aesthetic, 291–93; downtown crossover success, 297; label connotations, 296–97; promotional leadership of, 292–93, 353 n. 66; rock credentials confirmation, 295. *See also* new wave movement

dual market theory, 14–16. *See also* cultural capital; economic capital

Dufy, Raoul, 68

Dylan, Bob, 162–63; art-rock elements of songs, 211; critical discourses on, 181, 344 nn. 84, 90, 99; folk music and, 180; migration into rock 'n' roll, 181–82, 190; rock aesthetics and, 211

East Village: gallery scene, 312–13; new bohemia, 313; vs. SoHo aesthetic, 292

East Village Other, 217

Ebony, 179, 344 n. 98

economic capital: Beatles' success, 174–75; bebop's commercial success, 152–53; *cafés-concerts'* commercial success, 53–54; commercial success vs. artistic merit, 128–29; vs. cultural capital in rock, 324–25; dual market theory and, 15; mass culture and, 330 n. 8; middlebrow press's awareness of market factor, 186; post-teen migration into rock, 185–86, 344–45 n. 101; rock 'n' roll's attainment of, 175–76; sought by La Chanson performers, 47–48

8-Eyed Spy, 287

electronica, 324

Elektra, 268

Elf Scharfrichter (Eleven Executioners), 70, 71

elite culture. *See* high culture

Elks, Mr. and Mrs., 104, 105

Ellington, Duke, 131

England. *See* Britain

Esquire, 137, 193, 207

Europe, James Reese, 108

discourses on punk); first wave (*see* first wave of punk); relation to no wave, 279–80; search for bands, 232, 348 n. 13; second wave (*see* no wave); third wave (*see* downtown sound). *See also* new wave movement

punk aesthetic: art/pop binary, 238–39, 242, 245; disco vs., 284–85; fanzines start, 229–31; minimalism theme, 234, 238, 258; movement into art world, 303–4; music/discourse relation, 246–47; popist avant-garde position, 237–38; punk/art dichotomy from new groups, 244–45; punk spread through critical discourse, 242–44; rank amateurism requirement, 234–36, 245–46, 348 n. 23, 349 n. 25; rock counteraesthetic development, 228; rock revival model search, 231–33; shock and assault theme, 233–34; teen appeal acknowledgment, 236

punk art: artist as star, 309–10; art/music crossover, 301–4; characteristics of, 304–6; extension of art into showbiz, 307–8; gallery scene, 312–13; new bohemia, 313; new "punk/new wave" label, 307

Punk magazine, 248; initiation of punk label, 262–64; punk art and, 303; revivalist component, 264

Quatre Gats (Four Cats), 70
Question Mark and the Mysterians, 232–33, 234
Quicksilver Messenger Service, 204
Quine, Robert, 253

racial matters: bebop movement affected by, 156; in jazz press, 137–38; jazz and rock and, 9; rock's dominance by white males, 219–21, 284–87, 330 n. 12, 347 n. 119, 348 n. 125. *See also* negrophilia

radio and new wave, 276
raga rock, 345 n. 1
ragtime appropriation by Stravinsky, 89–90
Ramone, Joey, 248
Ramones, 7, 227; art/pop contrast with Talking Heads, 256–59; assaultiveness and minimalism, 254–56; commercial success, 276; critical discourses on, 350 n. 28; punk label attached to, 264; start at CBGB's, 250; underground label attached to, 261

rank amateurism requirement. *See* amateurism requirement in new wave

rap, 285
Rapsodie nègre (Poulenc), 111
Raybeats, 288
Raynaud, Ernest, 66
r&b charts, 221, 344 n. 76
rebop, 338 n. 11
Record Changer, 150, 153, 339 n. 38
Reed, Lou: on changes to his music, 241; endorsement by Bangs, 239–40, 242; in *Punk* magazine, 262, 264
reggae, 285
Reich, Steve, 238, 301
Renoir, Jean, 36
restricted markets, 15
revivalists in jazz: basis of dislike for swing, 128, 130–31; emotion's place in music, 134–35; fight against bebop, 150; "moldy figs" label creation, 123; standards debate, 133–34; view that jazz was in decline, 131–32. *See also* modernists vs. revivalists in jazz
revivalists in rock: industry hit reissues, 211–12; praise for early rock, 212–13; punk as revival movement (*see* punk aesthetic)
"Revolution" (Beatles), 218
Revolver (Beatles), 189, 192
Revue nègre, 115–16
rhythm and blues charts, 221, 344 n. 76
Ricard, Rene, 313
Rich, Buddy, 154
Richard, Keith, 349 n. 3
Richard Hell and the Voidoids, 227, 253
Richman, Jonathan, 242
riffs, 134, 337 n. 49
Rifkin, Joshua, 172, 173
Riley, Terry, 238
Rimbaud, Arthur, 65
Rivière, Henri, 57
Roach, Max, 143, 338 n. 12
Robinson, Lisa, 255
rock 'n' roll: accreditation link to Beatles, 175; aesthetic discourses on (*see* aesthetic discourses on rock); apparent appropriation of jazz, 206; Beatles' placement above, 197; completion of highbrow accreditation, 222–23; counteraesthetic from punk (*see* punk aesthetic); critical discourses on (*see* critical discourses on rock); cultural capital competition with jazz, 320–23; dominance by white males, 219–21, 330 n. 12, 347 n. 119; drug culture treatment by rock press, 215–16; folk rock movement (*see* folk rock movement); high culture and, 1–2; message lyrics

Stravinsky, 87, 89–90, 91
Studio 54, 299–300
Suicide, 245
Supremes, 178, 220
swing music: artistic progress views, 132; brand-name connotations, 127–28; commercial success vs. artistic merit, 128–29, 336 nn. 18, 23; Dixieland vs. swing war, 124–26; "jazz" vs. "swing" terms, 126–28, 336 n. 11; revivalists' dislike of emotional element, 135; riff use and criticisms, 134, 337 n. 49; standards debate, 133–34
Symbolist Manifesto, 65

Talking Heads, 7, 8, 227; art/pop contrast with Ramones, 256–59; at CBGB's, 250, 251; commercial success, 276, 286; Kitchen debut, 350 n. 30; minimalism theme, 350 n. 36; new wave connection, 272; punk label inappropriateness, 267
Taverne du Bagne (the Penal Colony Tavern), 60, 61
Taylor, James, 231
Teenage Jesus and the Jerks, 277, 280, 287
Teenage Lust, 245
Television, 7, 227; art/pop dichotomy, 252–54; at CBGB's, 250, 251; punk label inappropriateness, 267; underground label attached to, 261
Theoretical Girls, 277
Thérèsa, 52
third wave of punk. See downtown sound
13.13 (band), 287
Thunders, Johnny, 253
timbres, 177–78
Time magazine, 153; accolades for the Beatles, 194–97; bebop beginnings and, 145; comments on folk rock, 181; Dixieland vs. bebop war comment, 151; drug culture in rock treatment, 215; early disparagement of rock, 185; on new wave music, 272; punk coverage, 266; revivalist surge comments, 212
Times Literary Supplement, 168
Times Square Show, 304–7
Tone Deaf, 277
Tough, Dave, 150
Toulouse-Lautrec, 47, 62
Trakin, Roy, 273, 283, 287
transvestite rock, 244
trash aesthetics, 289
TriBeCa, 278
Tristano, Lennie, 149
Troggs, 233, 348 n. 24

Trussell, Jake, 137
Tzara, Tristan, 73, 77, 78

Ulanov, Barry: bebop demise notice, 154–55; on bebop term, 150–51; on desirability of commercial success, 128–29; on "jazz" vs. "swing," 126; response to bebop, 148, 153
underground label for punk, 259–61
Underground U.S.A., 303
United States: critical reception of the Beatles, 163; high/low divide in, 12–13; new wave vs. punk label, 271–73
Utrillo, 68

van Dongen, Kees, 68
vaudeville. See music halls
Vega, Alan, 256
Velvet Underground: cultural accreditation, 240–42; endorsement by Bangs, 239–40; status in punk, 260, 261
The Velvet Underground, 241
Velvet Underground and Nico, 240
Ventura, Charlie, 152, 154
Verlaine, Paul, 65
Verlaine, Tom, 251, 252
Village Voice: critical appraisals of rock, 191–92; critique of Beatles' movie, 170; promotional leadership of downtown scene, 292–93; punk coverage, 266
Voidoids, 227, 253

Warhol, Andy, 303, 309–10
Washington Project for the Arts, 303
Wedekind, Frank, 71
Wenner, Jann, 216
Weymouth, Tina, 261
Whistler, 36
White Light/White Heat, 241
Who, 207, 232
Who Put the Bomp, 243; coalition with Creem, 230–31; start of, 229
Wiener, Jean, 99, 109
Willette, Adolphe Leon, 37, 45, 62
Williams, Martin, 179
Williams, Paul, 191, 193, 220, 222–23
Willis, Ellen, 193, 210, 220, 242
Winner, Langdon, 208, 209
Wolcott, John, 259, 264
women and the music movements: Baker at Revue nègre, 115–16; blues singers, 88; in German cabarets, 71; Deborah Harry, 288, 303, 308; Lydia Lunch, 277, 280, 281, 283, 287, 303; Patti Smith, 251–52, 308, 349 n. 3; white male dominance in rock, 220, 221–22, 348 n. 125